Allotment Gardening FOR DUMMIES®

Allotment Gardening FOR DUMMIES®

by Sven Wombwell

WILEY

A John Wiley and Sons, Ltd, Publication

Allotment Gardening For Dummies®

Published by
John Wiley & Sons, Ltd
The Atrium
Southern Gate
Chichester
West Sussex
PO19 8SQ
England

E-mail (for orders and customer service enquires): cs-books@wiley.co.uk

Visit our Home Page on www.wiley.com

Published by John Wiley & Sons, Ltd, Chichester, West Sussex

For general information on our other products and services, please contact our Customer Care Department within the U.S. at 877-762-2974, outside the U.S. at 317-572-3993, or fax 317-572-4002.

For technical support, please visit www.wiley.com/techsupport.

Wiley also publishes its books in a variety of electronic formats. Some content that appears in print may not be available in electronic books.

British Library Cataloguing in Publication Data: A catalogue record for this book is available from the British Library

ISBN-13: 978-0-470-68641-6

Printed and bound by CPI Group (UK) Ltd, Croydon, CR0 4YY

C9780470686416_181223

WILEY

About the Author

Sven Wombwell had his own vegetable patch, as part of his grandfather's garden, from the age of five. This early exposure to gardening left a lasting impression that proved vital in his career. Sven trained in garden design at Capel Manor College in North London, and then gained indispensable hands-on building experience working for a large company specialising in adventure playgrounds and public spaces in London. A surprise opportunity led to a break on television, where his design talents were immediately noticed. This proved to be the first of well over 150 television appearances over the next six years.

In 2004 Sven published his first book, *Lifescapes: Garden designs for your life-style,* and has contributed regularly to magazines and newspapers. He has lectured at the Chelsea Flower Show, the Gardeners World Exhibition, and the Urban Gardens exhibition.

Sven is currently one of the garden experts on ITV's *This Morning* and runs his own garden design company, with projects spanning the UK, Portugal, Spain, Italy and the USA. He shares an allotment with his father and his three children and is currently number 86 on the waiting list to get his own, after moving to a new area.

Dedication

This book is dedicated to Kate, whom I am lucky enough to be able to call my best friend and the mother of our three beautiful children, Ashley, Freddie and Amalea. It is also dedicated to the memory of my grandfather, George, who started off my passion for gardening.

Author's Acknowledgements

I would personally like to thank Nicole Hermitage from Wiley for commissioning me to write this book on such a fascinating and topical subject. I would also like to thank the whole production team at Wiley, including Simon Bell (a plot holder himself) for his patience and guidance, and Sue Fisher, the technical editor, whose keen eye was invaluable. Also I would like to thank Kate O'Leary, Anne O'Rorke and Mary White for all their work on this project.

Special thanks go to my better half Kate, who was a *For Dummies* widow for 5 months: thank you for keeping the kids entertained while I spent days on end with my eyes glued to the screen, and thank you for putting up with me. Thanks also go to my dad, Rob, who as a plot holder himself helped me no end with the creation of this book, by checking and reading every word.

I'd especially like to thank my Grandfather George, who without even knowing it influenced me greatly at such a young age, leaving a lasting impression and great memories.

Publisher's Acknowledgements

We're proud of this book; please send us your comments through our Dummies online registration form located at www.dummies.com/register/.

Some of the people who helped bring this book to market include the following:

Commissioning, Editorial, and Media Development

Project Editor: Simon Bell

Commissioning Editor: Nicole Hermitage

Assistant Editor: Jennifer Prytherch

Copy Editor: Anne O'Rorke

Technical Editor: Sue Fisher

Publisher: David Palmer

Production Manager: Daniel Mersey

Cover Photos: ©Mike Harrington/GettyImages

Cartoons: Ed McLachlan

Composition Services

Project Coordinator: Lynsey Stanford

Layout and Graphics: Samantha K. Cherolis

Proofreaders: Jessica Kramer, Dwight Ramsey

Indexer: Claudia Bourbeau

Special Help

Brand Reviewer: Carrie Burchfield

Contents at a Glance

Table of Contents

Part IV: Extending Your Allotment Repertoire 307

Chapter 17: Growing Fruitful Fruit 309

Chapter 18: Nurturing Flowers on an Allotment 339

Introduction

So, you want to be an allotmenteer. At least, I'm guessing so, since you're reading this. You have decided to join the fabulous world of allotment gardening, growing your own fruit, vegetables, herbs and flowers. Once you pick up your spade for the first time on your own plot of land, you'll be hooked for life. And when you serve your first home-grown, freshly picked vegetables you'll never want to buy supermarket imports again. You'll be one of the lucky ones – able to eat seasonal fresh produce all year round, and to know exactly how your food has been produced. You, your family and friends are going to reap the rewards year upon year as you develop into an allotmenteer.

Allotments are hard work, but that's all to the good: You keep fit and get the buzz of eating food you've really put something into. Your family benefits from healthy food and exercise too. I'm not going to gloss over the hours you have to put in, but those hours will reap rewards far greater than just raising your own crops (great though that is). You get to master a whole range of new skills (outlined in this book), you get closer to the land and back into harmony with the seasons, and you can honestly say you've made a personal impact in terms of living sustainably.

About This Book

Allotment Gardening For Dummies provides you with the know-how you need to run a viable allotment. Each chapter is rammed with information on every aspect of cultivating your own plot, from analysing your soil to dealing with codling moth. I've written the book so that a complete novice can equip himself or herself with the basic skills to be a success, but also so that gardeners who know some of the basics already can learn a few new tricks. Throughout, I've focused on tried and tested methods: there simply isn't room for all the weird and wonderful wrinkles perfected by allotmenteers down the decades, or for the avalanche of folklore associated with raising crops. I've stuck to what I know works.

Conventions Used in This Book

To help you get the most from this book, I follow a few conventions:

- *Italic* emphasises and highlights new words or terms that I define.
- **Boldfaced** text indicates the action part of numbered steps.
- `Monofont` text displays web addresses.
- I give all measurements in metric (so that's centimetres and metres rather than inches and feet).

What You're Not to Read

You don't have to read everything in this book. From time to time you'll see grey boxes – sidebars – which contain interesting bits of info which may amuse or inform, but which aren't crucial to your understanding of the nitty-gritty. Read them or ignore them with impunity.

You'll also see a couple of icons above text which you can take or leave: I hope you'll pay attention to the 'Organic Way' icon, and your tastebuds will certainly benefit from my 'Cooking Tips' but I won't be offended if you choose to skip them.

Foolish Assumptions

In writing this book, I made a few assumptions about who you are:

- You're keen to grow your own produce, even though you may not be 100 per cent sure how to go about it.
- You have rented, or are seeking to rent, an allotment plot, probably from your local council.
- You're interested in hearing about organic methods of producing crops.
- You're not afraid of a bit of hard graft.

Beyond those, I've not assumed too much, I hope. This book is for you whether you're male or female, eighteen or eighty.

How This Book Is Organised

I've organised *Allotment Gardening For Dummies* into six parts. Each part covers a range of subjects to help get you growing on your own patch, and is further divided into chapters containing all the information you need.

Part I: Getting to Grips with Allotment Gardening

Before you can pick up a spade in anger, you need to know certain basic information. After all, I'm mindful that you may not even have an allotment plot yet. This part tells you, amongst other things, how to go about getting one, and what other options may be available if the waiting lists are chock-a-block. I then go on to discuss the rules and regulations you're likely to come across, and the basic tools and equipment you need to get you started.

Part II: Preparing for Allotment Success

This part covers everything you need to do to prepare your allotment for a successful growing season. First, I address what to grow, what to grow it from, and when to get started. I then move on to the serious business of preparing your plot, from the initial tidy up, through developing beds and coming up with planting plans through to assessing the soil. This part also covers keeping that crucial soil in good nick, and how to look after the plants you'll be growing in it, from sorting out rotations to dealing with common pests. I finish by offering some tips to the would-be organic gardener.

Part III: Growing Your Favourite Vegetables

This part is the meat and veg of the book. Well the veg, anyway. In these eight chapters I introduce all the main vegetables you're likely to want to grow on your allotment, covering everything you need to need to do to establish and maintain all you vegetable crops, from roots to cucumbers. Along the way I talk about all the staples, as well as some of the more exotic crops you might not have considered turning your hand to.

Part IV: Extending Your Allotment Repertoire

This part covers everything you might want to know should you want to branch out (literally, in the case of growing fruit trees). The main business of allotment gardening is usually held to be producing vegetables, but there's no good reason why you shouldn't give over at least part of your allotment to growing tasty, sweet, nutritious fruit. I also cover a bit of food for the soul, by suggesting that you can use allotment land to grow things of beauty: there's a chapter on growing flowers here, too.

Part V: Getting the Most Out of Your Allotment

Working an allotment is about so much more than just turning over soil and digging in manure. This part covers the ways in which your allotment can work for you beyond simply generating a cornucopia of good food. Here you'll find suggestions on how to become part of the allotment community, whether through learning or passing on skills, or sharing in the work of your Allotment Society. The allotment is a place for all the family, and I cover the ways in which you can involve and engage children with the idea of an growing their own plants and running their own projects. I finish up with weightier matters: what to do if you want to grow real, show-stopping champion veg.

Part VI: The Part of Tens

Every *For Dummies* book has one. The Part of Tens offers two fun-sized chapters covering some dos and don'ts of allotment gardening, and some fresh ideas on how to revitalise a tired patch.

Icons Used in This Book

Sprinkled through the book you'll see various icons to guide you on your way. Icons are a *For Dummies* way of drawing your attention to important stuff, interesting stuff, and stuff you really need to know not to do.

Handy tips and tidbits to help you get the best from your plot.

This is stuff you need to know: whatever else you carry away from this book, note these bits with care.

Take careful note of the advice under this icon, and you'll avoid allotment calamities – ignore at your peril.

The whole point of growing most of what you grow is to eat it. These tips help you make the most of your allotment flavours and goodness.

If you're interested in gardening organically, keep your eyes peeled for this icon, which introduces my pearls of organic wisdom.

Where to Go from Here

I've organised this book so that you can just dip in and out of it as you like. It isn't specifically written to be read from start to finish, although you can do that if you want. In general, though, you'll probably find that you look up what you want to read about in the Table of Contents – or the index – and dive straight in at that section. It's entirely your choice. If you're not sure where to start, Part I gives you the basics on getting started from scratch, and signposts places later in the book where you can go for more detailed information on topics in which you're interested.

Best of luck, and happy growing!

Part I
Getting to Grips with Allotment Gardening

'Go ahead — make my day.'

In this part . . .

Don't know where to start? Don't fret. Allotment gardening is all about finding out what you can do and what you can't. You need to start with the basics, and they're what this part is all about.

Here I lead you through the business of getting yourself an allotment, letting you in on what you can do to beat the waiting lists as well as giving you some handy hints about what to look for in a plot.

I also tell you all you need to know to get set up to tackle your own plot, whether it's in outlining which rules you have to abide by, or explaining how to tell one end of a fork from the other.

Chapter 1

Discovering What Allotments Are All About

In This Chapter

- Dipping into the history of allotments
- Considering the advantages and disadvantages of working an allotment
- Preparing for some hard graft
- Being connected to the land, nature and the seasons

I want to be perfectly clear right from the start – working an allotment takes dedication and involves a lot of hard graft. You'll have your successes and experience plenty of disappointments, but few more wholesome pursuits allow you to reap so many rewards. You become part of an exclusive club, with access to a pool of knowledge passed from generation to generation. My grandfather was my gardening guru, and some of my fondest memories involve working the soil with him as a child. Once you start, be prepared for a life-changing experience.

To start you off on the road to perfect produce I want you to take a look at the roots of allotment gardening; why we feel the need to grow our own food and why sustainability has countless benefits for both individuals and the rest of society. Let's get growing.

How It All Began

According to archaeologists, the first evidence of humans cultivating the soil to produce food comes from Syria, about 13,000 years ago, when drought forced people to grow wheat and rye as a means of survival. This small moment in history may have been the catalyst that began the demise of the hunter gatherer, and ushered in the era of people cultivating the land to produce food. These pioneers of grow-your-own are the initial source of the seeds and plants we use today. As a result of centuries of human development and plant selection, we now have a vast range of food crops available to grow on the allotment. Our reasons for growing our own food obviously differ, though; nowadays a parcel of land offers a means of saving money, eating healthily, being more environmentally aware, and exercising.

Looking at today

Nowadays, allotments are no longer necessary for survival but provide a valuable pastime for hundreds of thousands of people, offering a way to feel closer to the land and become more self-sufficient . Growing your own has seen a massive growth in popularity in recent years because:

- The rise in demand for organic food and the backlash against genetically modified crops has shown that people do care where their food comes from. Intensive farming methods and reliance on chemicals are potentially detrimental to people's health.
- Financial recession has reduced many people's income and made sources of cheap fruit and vegetables more attractive.
- TV chefs and gardeners have become champions of home-grown food. As a result, people are much more interested in sourcing fresh ingredients for cooking.
- People are concerned about the effects on the planet of transporting food round the world, using finite oil reserves and causing pollution.

Unfortunately, not enough allotments now exist to meet demand. Local councils are inundated with applications for plots way beyond the number they can provide. Thankfully, all across the country schemes are being launched in which councils and landowners join forces to create new plots to provide for the demand. In pretty much every county throughout the UK you find projects and schemes where people are campaigning and working tirelessly to have their allotment demands met. In fact, I'd go so far as to say that a national movement is now under way that's a force to be reckoned with. Hopefully it'll get what it wants – an allotment for each and every person who wants one. Chapter 2 covers the business of getting hold of an allotment.

Weighing up the Pros and Cons of Working an Allotment

Allotments are ultimately satisfying things to work and extremely beneficial to many areas of life, but plusses and minuses exist, and you should be aware of both, so there are no surprises. In this section I weigh up the pros and cons.

Feasting on fresh food

The benefits of eating fresh food can't be disputed. As soon as an item of fruit or veg is picked it starts to deteriorate in some way. For example, green beans can lose up to 40 per cent of their folic acid, zinc and vitamin C within two days of being picked and I bet that not many large supermarkets can get produce from grower in to store in less than a day. In contrast, from an allotment you can have fresh produce from garden to plate within hours, (minutes, sometimes) giving you all the goodness, just as nature intended. It's not just the nutrient content that suffers with time but the flavour too – by picking produce at the peak of ripeness, you get it at its absolute best and bursting with flavour.

Seasonality is a word that holds less and less meaning to our diets these days as convenience foods have become the norm. Seasonality basically means eating foods grown during that season. We're so used to having strawberries and Egyptian green beans in the depths of winter that we forget how fresh ones actually taste. It seems absurd to import produce halfway around the world when you can grow it yourself or simply buy it locally, and usually a lot cheaper than imported varieties. As soon as you become an allotment holder and you become in tune with the seasons, your days of buying Egyptian green beans will be over, I assure you.

With financial and flavour issues put aside, think about the cost to the environment. What's the sense in wasting precious energy and adding to an already polluted planet simply so we can have food out of season? The beauty of an allotment garden is that as one season ends another comes sprinting along offering alternative treats to tempt you. By embracing what your allotment offers seasonally you end up having a much more varied, fresh and exciting diet whilst also cutting out your contribution to CO_2 emissions through 'food miles'.

Keeping fit

I know many people that spend hundreds of pounds (and shed far fewer!) slaving away in overcrowded, overpriced gyms, whereas working over an allotment can offer a great way to help you keep fit and healthy. An allotment needs at least ten hours a week of digging, planting, mulching (laying well rotted organic matter around plants), weeding and sowing to keep it relatively productive and weed free. You can turn most activities on the allotment into a workout. Even a vigorous session with the hoe can do you the world of good – letting your frustrations out and breathing in the fresh air gives you a new lease of life.

An amazing fact is that during the Second World War people in the UK were generally healthier; not only because they had more home-grown fresh vegetables to eat but because of the hard physical work involved in maintaining their vegetable plots.

Now I wouldn't ever suggest that your allotment routine should replace your other exercise programmes, but it can help greatly. Research has shown that simply digging a bed for half an hour can burn off up to 250 calories. A proven fact is that regular gardening can improve muscle tone, flexibility, reduce the risk of stroke and osteoporosis in the middle-aged and even help lower blood pressure and improve heart function. Now add that to the fact that the fruit and veg you'll be eating will be the most nutritious you can ever find and you'll be superhuman within a year! (No guarantees though!)

On the allotment you have to engage in many physical activities that, if done right, can benefit your general health and well-being. Such activities include digging holes, raking, hoeing, lifting, and sweeping, but you do need to ensure that you do them safely and with care. An amazing amount of gardening-related injuries occur every year so I'm going to give you a slightly obvious, yet important, list of tips on how to avoid injury.

- Be sure to stretch properly before engaging in any physical activity.
- Don't overdo it, if you feel any twinges, aches or pains, take a break.
- Watch out on hot days, wear sun screen, a hat (an allotment must-have accessory) and protect yourself from the sun.
- Drink plenty of fluids (I don't mean your secret stash of brandy in the shed).
- Take care when lifting – bend your knees and keep your back straight.
- Take time to warm down if you've had a physical allotment session (now is the time for the secret brandy!).

WARNING!

The main injuries allotment gardening can cause are lower-back strain (which I suffer from constantly), ligament and joint strain, general aches and pains and the odd lost toe or finger. All these injuries can be easily avoided with a bit of care, proper use of tools, and the right warming-up and warming-down techniques.

Getting connected

Being an allotment holder gives you access to a secret and exclusive club, and as soon as you get the keys to your new world you're usually met with open arms by an enthusiastic group of new friends. The best way to get in with the crowd is to ask questions, most people's favourite topic of conversation is their veggies so ask questions and they'll be answered. You'll find a wealth of knowledge as every allotment holder has pearls of wisdom that you should listen to with glee!

One thing I would wholeheartedly suggest is not to go in with all guns blazing, chemical weed spray in hand, to blitz your new space with gusto. Many allotments have a non official 'organic' code of practice that's worth adhering to if you want to get connected and keep your new friends happy. Many sneak the odd slug pellet down but just speak to people first to see what the consensus is.

Being sustainable

Sustainability is the latest buzz word in the gardening world and is one of those terms that can apply not only to gardening but to all facets of life, from gardening to business development and building. Being *sustainable* refers to those biological systems that have an ever-repeating circle of renewing themselves. The problem with modern-day life is that most of what we do isn't sustainable, for example, the use of fossil fuels.

Now I am going to get on my sustainability high horse for a minute so please bear with me! Although we're all responsible for readjusting the way in which we live in an effort to return the planet's natural resources to being sustainable, it requires a group effort by every individual, government and company on the planet to ensure that the resources we use are replaceable in some way. Before we humans came along, the earth was ticking along nicely, but now, natural resources are in decline, which is having a dramatic impact on ourselves and other living things around us.

In terms of allotment gardening it simply means leaving as small a *carbon footprint* (total amount of waste carbon produced by a person) on the planet as possible, and here are a few suggested ways in which to achieve that:

- Conserve rain water.
- Limit chemical fertiliser use.
- Limit chemical pesticide use.
- Use physical and biological pest control.
- Don't use peat.
- Compost, compost and compost.
- Recycle everything possible.

Chapter 8 covers greener, organic gardening.

Working hard (but not all the time!)

I think it's really important for people to realise that owning an allotment does mean you have to put in some serious graft to prepare, maintain and benefit properly from it. When you inherit your plot you may well get a piece of land that has been lovingly tended for the past 50 years by an allotment guru, a plot that's a joy to dig and pretty much ready to go. But you're more likely to find yourself faced with a rock-hard, weed-ridden patch of scrub that has been chemical sprayed and holds very few nutrients in the soil. This is a typical starting point for a new allotment holder, and I cover ways in which to deal with it in Chapter 5.

Preparing the soil

The hardest work involved on an allotment is the preparation of the soil. Vegetables and fruiting plants are extremely demanding on your soil because as they grow they suck the goodness from it. This goodness needs replacing from time to time. There are a few ways in which this can be done and this is covered in Chapter 6.

Defeating the weeds

Weeding is one of those things that just won't ever go away, especially if your neighbours aren't religious weed pullers! Initially you need to rid your new plot of weeds, which can involve some serious digging and using methods that I go into in Chapters 5 and 6. Weeding is a perennial problem (they just keep coming back) that you simply must keep on top of. Weeds spread in various ways: they spread from your neighbours' plots via their seeds being dispersed by the wind. Others spread by adventurous roots underground and if you miss a small piece of that root when you dig them out, they simply grow back. Weed seeds can also remain dormant in the soil for years and years so by digging the soil you expose the buried seeds, which then spring quickly into life. Maintaining an allotment really is a constant battle! Chapter 7 covers what you need to do to keep your plants healthy.

Sowing the seeds

Seed sowing is by no means hard work but it does involve dedication and attention to detail. You need to adhere to a planting calendar as potting on and planting out all takes time. Also you have to prepare yourself for failures. You may find that you've lost a tray of courgette seedlings because you forgot to water them or they've simply given up on you, so you have to start again.

Each of the chapters from 9 to 16 gives you the low-down on sowing seeds and planting seedlings for the various types of vegetables you might want to grow.

Working with the weather

The weather, too, can wreak havoc on your plot with hail storms or really heavy rain, which are often the culprits for damaging many an allotment. However, these things are all part of the learning experience and it takes tenacity to overcome them.

All plants need water to survive, and vegetables are thirsty things, needing at least an inch (25 millimetres) of water a week to prosper, so if it doesn't rain it's totally down to you to ensure that they get a drink. During really hot periods this can mean daily visits to keep on top of things. And you often find that allotments have only one water butt and a hose ban, so it's a case of buckets and watering cans I'm afraid!

TIP

If you're canny you'll install a means of rain water collection from your shed roof so you don't have so far to walk.

Making time

Making time to own an allotment is a lifestyle decision and involves a shift in priorities and a realisation that allotment gardening can be fun, immensely rewarding and should not be seen as chore. It involves a shift in emphasis in your weekly life – instead of thinking, 'I need some peas . . . I'm going to drive to the shop and buy some', you should to be thinking, 'I'll pop up to the allotment and plant some ready to pick in summer'. This involves planning an allotment calendar (Chapter 4 has more on this), so that you can harvest seasonal vegetables all year round and it involves making time in your weekly schedule to fit in the allotment jobs. Admittedly most of us lead incredibly busy lives and struggle to fit in our basic daily needs but you can always make room for a hobby and now you have made the decision to run an allotment that needs to be your new hobby.

Now it's not all doom and gloom so please don't be put off! There are periods when you're really busy prepping and planting your plot, but you also have periods when you simply do some light weeding, a bit of watering and a lot of harvesting. The positives far outweigh the negatives and once your fingers become green those apparent negatives quite frankly stop being negatives and become a part of life that you can never live without.

In a way, I feel calling this section 'making time' a misrepresentation of the reality of having an allotment. I don't make time to do the gardening, it's a part of life that I enjoy enormously, my family enjoy it and it's a passion that never goes away. It becomes an addiction that needs an almost daily fix; you become desperate to check how your sprouting broccoli is getting on. Nothing beats the excitement and anticipation of the simple act of pulling up a carrot or digging up some spuds that have been hidden for months underground, and are as precious as buried treasure.

The truth is that many people, once they've started with the joy of allotment gardening, find it hard to make time for anything else!

Saving precious pennies

I can't tell you that growing your own saves you barrow loads of cash as, if you factor in the time involved, it probably costs more initially than locally grown market vegetables. But you probably end up with more fruit and vegetables than you can possibly eat, so your friends and family can all benefit and save a few pennies as well.

Certain areas can save you money. Take cut-and-come-again salad leaves. In the shops they cost at least a pound a bag, whereas one packet of seed provides you with many bags more over a period of time at a far reduced cost. When you become more experienced you'll find other ways of greatly reducing costs, such as by collecting seed, growing from seed, taking cuttings and sharing with other allotment holders, to name just a few. You can find out all about these techniques later on in this book.

Over a long period of time an allotment can become almost totally self-sustainable. My grandfather only bought seed potatoes, a few packets of seed and some string and our vegetable garden was always overflowing with home-grown produce grown at very little cost. Although initial set-up costs may seem a little steep, with the right skills – the ones I outline in this book – your allotment will eventually pay for itself.

Chapter 2

Getting Hold of an Allotment

In This Chapter

- Understanding the application process
- Working out what to do if you can't get an allotment
- Exploring alternatives
- Dealing with the waiting game

You've made the decision to get yourself an allotment, and now you have the task of actually finding an available plot. This can be a waiting game in some areas, but in others you may find it a bit easier. Applications for allotments have really taken off in recent years, and long waiting lists aren't unusual – 40 years in some London boroughs! The Allotments Act states that there should be 20 allotment sites per 1,000 residents, which should in theory be plenty to meet demand. But the simple fact is that there aren't that many!

Don't despair though. The national average time on a waiting list is around three years and, as I mentioned before, far less in some areas. Local councils are trying to find new sites, and many are looking to private landowners to work together in offering new sites to meet demand. If you look at the bigger picture, this is a fantastic problem to have and is a sign that there's a massive shift in society towards living a healthier, more sustainable lifestyle.

Getting the Low-Down on Leasing or Owning an Allotment

Leasing an allotment is a really simple process. The first port of call is always your local council, which will more than likely be the one dealing with your application. Councils sometimes hand the application process over to the local allotment society. Allotment societies are usually charities set up to look after your rights as an allotment holder, and quite often they handle the application process for you when you want an allotment. You will usually have to become a paying member of the society, and this cost is minimal:

usually around £4 per year. To find your local allotment society, either contact your local authority or do a quick internet search and you will easily find it.

If you find yourself in the unusual position that you are offered allotment space to buy, it will usually be from an individual in a group of people who have bought their own piece of land to use as allotments. This is rare, but there are a few other options you can look into. You can consider finding a group of people and buying your own area of land to divide up into smaller plots, but I would definitely get a good solicitor to protect your interests, and check with the local planning office about what rules would apply. Cases where groups of people have set up allotment association charities that fund the purchase of the land and then run the site are on the increase. This is no small undertaking, but if you are determined, it would be a great thing to do for your community and may be a way of getting a plot.

The Allotments Act

The right to allotment spaces has evolved through various acts of parliament. Most important was the Small Holdings and Allotments Act 1908, which states that local authorities have a duty to provide sufficient allotments to meet demand. This act also makes provision for the compulsory purchase of land to provide allotment space. In a nutshell: if you want an allotment, you should be provided with one. Unfortunately, for the Government to actually provide all of us with one is almost impossible.

Local authorities have a duty to provide plots, where there is a perceived demand for them. If an allotment authority believes that there is a demand for allotments in its area, section 23 of the Small Holdings and Allotments Act 1908 puts the authority under a duty to provide a sufficient number of allotments and to let them to people who want them.

The Allotments Act of 1950 was a result of the reforming of the Allotments Advisory Body which, among other things, recommended at least 4 acres of land dedicated to allotments per 1,000 of the population. This was in response to the huge demand for land on which to build new housing. In reality, this ratio of land to people is rarely met these days because of the loss of so many sites to development.

Legislation does not lay down minimum standards or say what the land should be like. Allotment authorities have room to exercise discretion about the level of provision of allotment gardens and facilities on site.

On top of this legislation, local planning policy number 17 encourages local authorities to make adequate provision for all types of open space that may be of public value. In setting standards, local authorities would be expected to allow for the demand for allotments alongside other forms of open space.

These regulations seem pretty ambiguous, and a clause usually exists to give a local authority the ability to exercise discretion when it comes to providing enough plots to go around. Nevertheless, these laws exist, and we do have rights!

Addressing your right to an allotment

If you find that there aren't enough allotments to go around, you can then formally request that provision be made by your local council to supply them. You need to find six like-minded individuals who are registered on the electoral roll, and you can then put your case to the local council. All you need to do is write to the local authority with a list of names and addresses of interested people and it should legally find you all space for an allotment. This is all well and good, but in their defence there is no time limit to when they have to provide you with the spaces. But it's worth a shot.

Applying for an allotment

The first place to go when you want to apply for an allotment is your local council. Most council websites have a section on applying for an allotment, which guides you through the application process.

Approaching the council

Allotments are usually really cheap, with rents varying from £16 to £30 a year and many sites offering half plots, which usually cost half as much.

The process itself is pretty straightforward. Write a letter to the relevant local authority department with your name, address and which allotment site you want to be considered for, and that's it: you are on the waiting list. And when the time comes to actually get your plot, you'll need to fill in some forms and complete a tenancy agreement.

The main problem is that with so many people now applying, huge waiting lists have formed. While researching for this book, I called a few local councils to see whether they had any available plots. I found a huge variation in waiting times. In one town with two different sites, one site had two people on the waiting list, whereas the other site 3 miles away had 67 waiting – a difference that you'll probably find all over the country.

If your local council doesn't have any allotments or free plots available, it may be able to put you in touch with private or alternative schemes in your area.

Getting a wait off your mind

Waiting lists for allotments are a sad fact of life for most applicants, with waiting lists in some areas being totally closed to new applications due to over-demand. You may get lucky and find that you move along the list fairly swiftly, or you may be faced with waiting for years. If you simply have to satisfy your urge to grow your own, I would whole-heartedly suggest looking for a temporary alternative until your plot becomes available. This may mean turning some of your own garden over to fruit and veg production or asking friends and family with spare land whether you can cultivate a small corner in return for some produce throughout the year. Many local farmers or landowners have uncultivated land that's ideal for allotment gardening, and we will look at this a little more closely later in this chapter.

It's always worth checking from time to time where you stand on the waiting list, by calling whoever runs it. You may suddenly find yourself jumping to the front and being unexpectedly lumbered with a plot you're not ready to take on. When you know you're nearing the point of getting the keys to your new plot, you can then start planning your attack and preparing.

The time of year when you get your plot will greatly affect your strategy, so monitor your wait carefully.

Going private

Private allotments are usually run by local landowners who have spare land and want to give something back to their communities (or in some cases make a few bob). But if you search on the Internet or ask your local authority, you may well be able to find a suitable scheme near you. You often find these are more expensive than local-authority-run allotments, with rents ranging from £75 a year to some really expensive ones which may top £300 a year. You will usually be given an annual lease and will have to pay in advance or monthly.

The only drawback with these sites is that you have no guarantee that the landowner won't sell or decide to put the land to another use in the future. Even so, if this is your only alternative, it is still a good one!

Looking at alternative schemes

Because allotment gardening has become so popular in recent years, hundreds of schemes and projects have started up where people can get involved in growing their own food in some way. For example, the 2012 scheme in London was set up with the mission of creating 2,012 new grow-your-own sites by the time the Olympic games comes to the capital. Now of course, many of these sites won't be true allotments and aren't available to everyone, but they offer communities space to grow their own food, and raise awareness of a fast-expanding grow-your-own movement.

Other schemes are those run by charities, where you may be able to get a share of a plot's produce if you're willing to help the elderly. Age Concern (www.ageconcern.org.uk) runs a scheme in Wandsworth in London that does exactly that. Not only do you get some great produce, but you are enabling others to continue with their love of gardening, when otherwise they would have to stop. Doing this can also really work to your advantage, because an older gardener probably has a lifetime's worth of knowledge that he or she would love to pass on to the next generation.

Many places run community gardens and allotments where people can volunteer their time in return for a share of the produce. This is obviously nowhere near as good as having your own plot but is a great way of dipping your toe in the water to see whether you're cut out to grow your own food, without having to stay for ages on waiting lists or spend money getting your own plot up and running. Most community gardens and allotments are shared enterprises open to anyone from the local community. Often a small membership fee is payable, but the community shares the labour along with the produce. The best way to find such a scheme is to ask your local authority. If you trawl the Internet, you can find countless schemes, community projects, community centres and council-run initiatives offering people the opportunity to grow their own, so if you're faced with years on a waiting list, check out these alternatives.

For me, the beauty of allotment gardening is that you get away from people and get some head space while tending your own plot. With community schemes, the getting-away-from-it element will have to remain a dream until you can get your hands on your own plot. But community schemes are a great way to meet like-minded people and gain vital knowledge that you can use later on.

You can also look into other initiatives such as Channel 4's Landshare website. The initiative aims to give people new opportunities to grow their own produce, through a matchmaking service where both landowners and would-be growers can register via a postcode-driven mapping system. For more information, visit landshare.channel4.com.

Knowing Which Patch to Pick

If waiting lists are a problem in your area, choosing your plot on the allotment site may not be possible, but it's worth knowing what to look for in the perfect plot. A pecking order usually exists on allotments, so when a plot becomes vacant an existing plot, holders may be waiting to move onto it if it's a better plot than the ones they currently hold. This usually means you get the pick of a bad bunch, but at least you'll be on a site.

If you're given the option of choosing a plot, you need to look out for certain factors, which I cover in the following sections.

Getting the size right

The average plot is around 250 square metres, but plots vary greatly from area to area. Plots are usually measured in *poles*. A pole is roughly 5½ yards (just over 5 metres) in length, and the average plot is 10 poles long. (A pole was historically the length from the back of a plough to the tip of an oxen's nose, since you ask.) A plot this size should be plenty big enough to produce enough fruit and vegetables to keep your family supplied all year round. If this seems too large an area for you to handle alone, then why not share it with a friend or someone else on the waiting list? Many allotment sites now offer half plots for those who can't handle a full one, and now some even offer quarter plots. Although you can grow vegetables in a pot on a tiny balcony, in reality anything smaller than a half plot is not large enough to be of much use unless you just want to grow a few staples. However, smaller plots do offer more people the chance to make a start and get growing.

If you do find yourself with a huge plot that you can't handle, you may like to consider leaving some of it covered with black plastic, or even turfing it, in readiness to be cultivated later on. In the rotation system (have a look at Chapter 7), it's advisable to let an area recover for a few years after a spell of cultivation, by leaving it uncultivated. This allows the delicate balance of micro-organisms in the soil to return to their natural state and refresh the soil ready for cultivation later. Alternatively, you can simply plant a large area and dedicate it to permanent plants that need little attention; try fruit trees, fruiting shrubs and permanent herbs such as rosemary and bay.

Choosing your plot

You need to consider the location within the wider site of the plot you've been offered, as well as the state it's in and its potential for success. A few pointers so you know what to aim for include:

- **Choose a plot that's near a tap.** This will make your life much easier, especially during the height of summer.
- **Try to get a plot near the entrance.** At least get one that's reachable from the main track. If you can get your car near the plot, then even better because this saves a lot of back-breaking lugging of compost, manure and equipment.
- **Avoid a plot near the part-timers.** Try to steer clear of untidy plots that are covered in weeds, because the weeds are likely to spread onto your plot! Especially avoid plots near those with perennial weeds on them, because these weeds are the hardest to eliminate. (You can find out more about weeds in Chapter 5.)

- **Avoid plots that are shaded.** Look out for overhanging trees, buildings and high hedges. Your crops need as much light as possible.
- **Check the state of the soil.** Dig down and check what the soil is like. Is it stony or hard clay, or has it been recently cultivated? If the soil is bad, you'll need to put in some hard groundwork to get it ready for planting. Also watch out for a waterlogged plot, because this makes cultivation really difficult. The plot may have some serious drainage issues that you'll need to fix.
- **Try to avoid a plot that's over-exposed to strong winds.** This causes problems with growing some crops, especially climbing beans like runners. However, some plants that are susceptible to aphid and fly attack, such as potatoes and carrots, can benefit from a windy site where greenfly and other aphids can't establish themselves.
- **Choose a level plot.** If your plot slopes, water washes downhill and plants suffer. If you're faced with a sloping site, you need to create terraces or install raised beds that improve how the soil takes up water. (Chapter 5 covers how to do this.)
- **Be wary of plots that have existing plants on them.** This may sound a bit silly, and you may be grateful for some freebies, but you never know what pests and diseases may be lurking on existing plants. Always err on the side of caution and keep a close eye on plants you inherit, for the first year, to monitor their health. Many fruit bushes and plants only last for a few years before they should be replaced, so you'd be better to start afresh.
- **Look for a shed.** A plot with an existing shed or greenhouse is a real bonus and saves you the hassle of erecting one. Make sure that the shed is waterproof and in good condition, otherwise you'll have to replace it with a new one at your own expense.
- **Try and choose a site that's secure and safe.** Nothing is worse than all your hard work being ruined by some mindless act of vandalism. Most sites now have fencing around them and lockable gates.

Part II
Preparing for Allotment Success

'This was his last wish–and it would be ironic if this made everything grow, because he couldn't grow a thing while he was alive.'

In this part . . .

It's all in the soil, they say. In this part I certainly address everything you need to know about assessing, improving and troubleshooting your soil, but there's more to it than that.

I talk you through the basic jobs you need to get done when you first take over an allotment, from tidying up to preparing proper beds for your plants and developing a rotation system that works for what you want to grow.

I also cover how to decide what to grow, when to grow it and how to prevent it being eaten by anything you don't want to eat it. I finish up the part by discussing the pros and cons (OK, mostly the pros) of the organic allotment.

Chapter 3

Getting Started

In This Chapter

- Discovering the rules and regulations
- Being safe on your plot
- Keeping livestock
- Getting tooled up
- Finding shelter for your plants

You have your plot and you want to get going as quickly as possible. Steady on: you need to know a few things before you go in all guns blazing. All allotments have strict rules that you need to follow. You should receive a copy of your site's regulations with your tenancy agreement. Most allotments have standard rules that need to be enforced to keep things in order, but some regulations are a little more obscure and I look at these more closely in this chapter. Health and safety can also be an issue on your allotment, so I provide some tips for making your gardening as safe as possible. I also cover the tools, essential equipment and other bits and bobs you need to make your life easier and your garden more successful.

Getting to Grips with the Rules and Regulations

Every new plot holder receives a welcome pack in the post containing the rules and regulations of the site plus a tenancy agreement. Whether it relates to a private or council-owned site, the tenancy agreement is a legally binding contract similar to the ones you sign when you rent a house. The agreement has your name and address at the top and an area for you and the landlord to sign the agreement at the bottom. The agreement usually states at the top how much rent you have to pay and when it's due, whether it's monthly or annual. Because the amounts are usually minimal (varying from £8 per year to over £100 depending on the location), the money is usually paid annually. The agreement also shows the date from which you can occupy the plot and the plot number. You need to sign the agreement and return it, keeping a copy.

Adhering to general rules

In the past, allotments were usually controlled by the local parish and with them came strict rules as to how tenants were to behave. The extract below is from the Kyddington Garden Allotments' rules and regulations, as printed in *The Times*, 23 November 1872:

> All tenants shall maintain a character for morality and sobriety, and shall not frequent a public house on the Sabbath-day. All the tenants are earnestly requested to attend regularly at the House of God during times of Divine service, with their families, to the best of their abilities.

Thankfully, the rules aren't quite so tough these days, but are still there to protect the rights of tenants, local residents and councils or landowners.

Specific rules and regulations vary slightly from site to site, but some core rules apply nationwide. For example, some sites don't allow sheds (ridiculous, but there you go), and some sites allow livestock whereas others don't. Most of these rules are common sense, but some are a little more specific, so be sure to read your tenancy agreement closely.

A few of the most common rules and regulations concerning allotments are:

- You must keep the plot clean and in a productive state. Most allotments are regulated and checked regularly to ensure that the plots are being used and well cared for. If you're not tending your plot, you're sent a warning and eventually turned out of your plot.
- You must keep the plot free from weeds and well manured to maintain soil fertility.
- You must keep paths and access points clear from obstruction at all times.
- You must not sub-let plots to other people.
- You may not remove sand, gravel or clay from the site without permission.
- You may not cut or remove trees or shrubs that are not within an individual plot without permission.
- You may not erect buildings without permission. Some agreements state the maximum size of a shed and greenhouse permitted and also state that you can have two small items such as a cold frame and a compost heap.
- You can't place a caravan on the plot.
- You can't sleep overnight on the allotment or in any buildings on it (I know it's tempting!).
- You're not allowed to erect barbed wire.

- You can't plant trees or shrubs that take more than 12 months to mature, without permission from the council.
- You can't keep livestock on the site, except rabbits and hens for personal consumption. Some agreements include the right to keep ducks, geese and bees as well, but usually only with prior written consent from the council.
- You can't pass on your allotment in a will. When you die, the plot automatically reverts to the council as landowner. (Councils word it a bit more subtly than that!)
- Inspectors have the right to enter your plot at any time.
- You may not use your plots for business of any kind.
- You may not grow illegal substances on your plot.
- The council may terminate your agreement at any time if you breech the conditions it lays down.
- You must pay rent in advance – failure to do so means you're out!
- Access is granted only to the tenant and his immediate family. No other person can enter your plot without the tenant or family member present.
- You may not in any way cause nuisance to other plot holders and should be a good neighbour.
- If allowed at all, bonfires are usually only permitted in the two hours before sundown and only during still weather. Bonfires must be small and supervised at all times.

Considering health and safety

The mere mention of health and safety makes many people tense up with dread, and conjures up the idea of reams of silly rules that actually make life more difficult. Allotments contain many hazards, however, so you have reason to be health and safety conscious. If you think about it, if you were in a workplace that involved hazardous chemicals and trip hazards, and your job involved using sharp and sometimes dangerous tools, the firm's health and safety officer would have a field day filling in assessment forms and investing in insurance policies to keep your employer covered. I'm not saying allotments are dangerous places, but hazards exist that you need to be aware of.

WARNING!

Here are a few pointers to help you keep safe:

- **Carry a mobile phone.** You should always carry a mobile phone – if you have one – when you're on the plot, just in case of emergencies.
- **Always tell someone where you are.** This sounds silly, but allotments can be very quiet places at times, and if you come a cropper and don't make it home, at least somebody'll know where to find you.

- **Keep your tetanus vaccinations up to date.** Tetanus is a nasty disease spread via tiny bacteria in soil, particularly soil treated with manure. Symptoms include a high temperature, muscle rigidity, headache, sore throat, sweating, rapid heartbeat, extreme sensitivity to touch, bleeding into the bowels, and diarrhoea. Tetanus can be fatal, so it's crucial for you to be vaccinated.
- **Treat power tools and rotavators with respect.** With all power tools – hedge trimmers, strimmers, hole borers and turf cutters, for example – make sure that you read the manual and all the related safety warnings in detail. *Rotavators* are large, powerful machines with a spinning blade to whip through the soil: they can be dangerous bits of kit if used incorrectly. They take some getting used to but, with practice, are extremely handy for cultivating areas quickly. Keep your feet well clear of the spinning blades and wear appropriate safety gear like goggles, ear protectors and safety shoes. Goggles are really important when using tools with spinning parts, because stones and other debris often whip up without warning.
- **Wear safety boots.** It always amazes me to see people at the allotment in sandals, wielding a fork with gusto – this is just crazy! Make sure that you wear a decent pair of tough boots, ideally with a steel toecap, to protect your plates of meat.
- **Keep chemicals and fuels in clearly labelled containers and out of the reach of children.** Strange-looking bottles and liquids seem to be magnets to children, so store your containers in a lockable cupboard or box hidden in the shed or other secure area. Fuels should be kept in suitable containers that are approved for holding petrol and in a fire-proof store box; these can be bought from office furniture companies and are usually called flammable storage cupboards. Check your tenancy agreement in case the allotments have rules regarding the storage of fuels, chemicals and fertilisers, so you comply with their demands.
- **Clear rubbish safely.** When clearing an allotment site, be wary of hazards such as broken glass, needles, sharp bits of metal and so on, and dispose of them in the correct and safe way, preferably in a sharps bin at your local council tip.
- **Discourage rats.** Rats carry the dangerous Weil's disease in their urine. Your crops are a magnet to rodents, so be on the lookout for any signs of rodent damage. Turn your compost heap at least twice a year so rats do not nest in your heap, and have a shovel ready to exterminate any escapees! Also make sure to harvest fruit as soon as it is ripe, so you enjoy it and the rats don't. Every plot holder is responsible for making every effort to limit rodent infestations. If rats are a real problem, let the council or allotment association know about it, and it will act quickly.
- **Warm up properly.** Gardening can be great exercise but it's well worth warming up your muscles and joints to avoid strains and injury.

- **Look after your back.** Digging and lifting put strain on your back. When lifting heavy items such as compost bags, be sure to keep your back straight and bend your knees as you lift.

Disposing of your waste

Most of the green waste on your allotment can be recycled on your compost heap and turned into rich organic matter for your plot (see Chapter 6). However, you're sure to find other bits of rubbish that you can't easily dispose of. Do be wary of composting perennial weeds and plants that have been sprayed with pesticides, because these contaminate your compost heap. Many allotments allow skips on site, and you may well find it necessary to use one if you get your hands on a really untidy plot, but in most cases this shouldn't be necessary. In fact, if the plot is in a really bad way, the council should be able to arrange for the rubbish to be taken away at its own expense, although the cost may ultimately come out of the allotment's annual budget. Any hazardous waste should be disposed of via the proper channels. The main thing to remember with allotment waste is to try and reuse whatever you possibly can and recycle, recycle, recycle.

Sites sometimes provide skips for allotment waste that can't be composted. Using these skips for household and other rubbish is illegal and you risk losing your tenancy for doing so.

Living with livestock and bees

Livestock is often a contentious issue on allotments, but the rules may say that you can keep certain animals such as chickens, rabbits, geese and ducks for your own consumption. Some sites don't allow this, but many do as long as you can provide a safe enclosure that contains your livestock and ensure that they're well looked after. Some allotments even allow pigs, and I well remember one old lady who took hers for walks around the site. If you want to keep any livestock, you should write to the council or whoever runs your site and get written permission. Give exact details of what animals and how many of each you want to keep. The council then gives you the go ahead – or not.

Allotment holders don't have a statutory right to keep bees on their plots, but some sites do allow it. Bees simultaneously help crop pollination and provide great-tasting honey. Make sure that the entrance to your hive faces south-east so that your bees are warmed by the rising sun and are ready for action as early in the day as possible.

These basic rules are more than likely to apply to your plans to keep bees on your plot:

- You must become a member of the British Beekeepers' Association (BBKA) and be insured through it.
- You must qualify as a beekeeper by attending the relevant courses and passing the basic standards regulated by the BBKA.
- You need to agree with other plot holders who want to keep bees about the number each of you is to have. A maximum of three hives is permitted to each acre of land.
- You need to force your bees to fly above head height and not across paths. Traditionally, bees kept in an urban environment are housed in hives on roofs so that their line of flight avoids people and the inevitable stings. You can use willow hurdles or similar as screens to direct your bees' flight path.
- You must be aware of how to deal with swarming. Bees naturally swarm between April and July but can also do so at other times. During the swarming season, you need to check your hive at least once a week for the signs of swarming, which include more bees than usual climbing around the front of the box, agitated behaviour and forming a conical shape on the bottom of the hive. If you are going to be away, always arrange for someone to look after your colony, especially during the usual swarming period.
- You need to make sure that your bees have a source of water. Sometimes they find a favourite place and keep on going there. If this is another plot holder's pond, he may well get annoyed. If you encounter this problem, ask the plot holder to cover the water source until your bees find an alternative. Or just try and educate the person with the pond about the fact that bees are usually pretty harmless and, if left alone, won't be a problem.
- You need to put your name and contact details on your hive so you can be contacted by anyone who has concerns or in an emergency.

Before even considering becoming a beekeeper, research the subject thoroughly. Read books on the subject and befriend a beekeeper if possible. Beekeeping is a huge subject that can't be covered simply in the few lines that I've written. The world of beekeeping is a complex one that requires skill, knowledge and a keen sense of responsibility. Bees are endangered, and if you do decide to take up the challenge, you'll be looking after a really important investment, not only for yourself but the wider environment as well. Bees search for food over ranges of 5 kilometres, so their pollinating powers benefit not only your allotment site but the surrounding areas too.

Taking care with pesticides and chemicals

Most people these days tend to try and garden organically, especially when it comes to food crops, but some gardeners do resort to chemical control when they deem it essential. If you can buy the chemicals over the counter, you're allowed to use them on your plot. Most allotment contracts contain clauses and directives on the safe use of chemicals. Along with these rules, a certain etiquette exists with regards to the use of chemicals on your plot. These unwritten rules are pretty much common sense: for example, always use pesticides and chemicals on still days, because wind will carry the spray over to other people's plots, and the plot holders may be trying to be organic. I look at chemicals in more detail in Chapter 5.

Putting in ponds

Many allotments allow small ponds on plots, and these offer fantastic little havens for all sorts of beneficial creatures, especially frogs. Frogs love to eat slugs, so they really help if you have a slug problem. You can buy a ready-formed pond; you simply dig a hole and pop it into the ground. These are quite inexpensive and much easier than using a pond liner. For a small pond – which is all you'll want on the allotment – these ready-formed ponds are by far the best option. It's best to wait for frogs to arrive of their own accord, because you risk transmitting disease by transferring spawn from another pond. Add some oxygenating plants from your local garden centre to keep the water clear. In addition, it helps to get a bucketful of pond water from an existing pond to pour into yours, because this old pond water contains all sorts of little creatures that will help your pond come to life.

Ponds can be really dangerous for young children, who can drown in the shallowest pool of water. If you involve children on your plot, install a heavy-duty metal grille over the top of your pond to ensure that no little ones can fall in! The holes in the grille should be large enough for frogs to get through but small enough to provide a safe cover.

Kitting Yourself Up with Tools and Equipment

When it came to tools, my granddad – a lifelong allotment gardener – always had just the bare essentials. The only tool I remember that he always carried was a good bone-handled pocket knife. It was his pruning tool, harvesting tool, cane-cutting tool – he used it for everything. The only other tools he used were a rusty old spade that weighed a ton and a fork that was very similar. Nowadays, though, lots of tools exist that make life down at the allotment much easier and save a lot of back-breaking work and precious time. In this section I look at what's needed and what isn't, and decide whether it's really worth spending loads on all the gadgets on the market.

Investing in the basics

The spade, fork, hoe and rake are the obvious tools, and are the basic essentials for any gardener. Choosing tools sounds simple, but many products, variations on a theme and gimmicks exist – for all budgets. Consider the following:

- **Spades.** These come in all different shapes and sizes from tiny 'lady spades' to big, heavy, industrial-sized monsters. What you go for is all down to personal taste, but I always feel it's worth spending a decent amount on one that'll last. I prefer a wooden-handled spade with a stainless steel lower shaft and blade, although you can get handles made from all sorts of materials and fancy ergonomic handles that look like space-age weapons. You can buy stainless steel blades or carbon fibre ones that are easy to clean. Always opt for the best quality you can afford. Some spades have a foot tread designed to make digging easier and also protect your footwear, but these are usually a bit heavier. I have a load of old tools that I've inherited from my granddad, and they lasted him a lifetime. I'm sure they will outlast me – they don't make them like that any more!
- **Forks.** These are used for cultivating the soil, lifting plants and roots, and teasing out plants that would otherwise be damaged when dug up with a spade. They're also really useful when turning compost heaps, lifting organic matter – such as straw – or for moving cut garden material around the plot. A fork is the best tool for fluffing up hard soil and for incorporating organic matter, *top dressings* (a surface layer of compost or other feed) and *green manures* (fast growing crops that are dug into the soil as a manure). They're also useful when you use two to prise roots apart when dividing *perennials* (plants that grow during the growing season, die back over winter, then grow back each year). Just like spades, forks are available with a range of handles; the best policy is to go and pick some up and see which one suits you the best. You can get forks in different sizes from small border forks to normal-sized forks or large potato forks ideal for lifting delicate spuds.
- **Hoes.** Hoes are useful tools for weeding, creating *drills* (channels for growing vegetables in) and working closely between rows of plants. Many different types of hoe are available, from the classic Dutch hoe, which is the traditional type most people use, to triangular and draw hoes. The best policy is to go and look at a few and see which suits you. You can also get combination hoes, which are meant to be suitable for chopping at weeds and drawing earth up, but other more basic tools like spades can do this job, so save your pennies.

- **Garden rakes.** Particularly useful when preparing plots for sowing seeds and planting, garden rakes can be used to level soil, break up soil, and collect debris from the soil surface. You can get rakes in all different sizes from those only 15 centimetres (6 inches) wide to 1-metre-wide giants for working large areas. One is usually enough, so I'd go for a simple garden rake with rigid teeth and a wooden handle that'll suit all your needs.
- **Lawn rakes.** This type of wire rake is ideal for collecting leaves and keeping paths and other areas free from garden debris. It's not essential on the allotment but can be worth having around.
- **Trowels and hand forks.** Available in a baffling range of sizes, they have multiple uses such as close-up work when planting, weeding, and working with small plants and bulbs. You can get trowels with narrow blades that are useful for planting bedding and transplanting seedlings but, to be honest, all you really need is a normal trowel and hand fork that'll suit all your needs.
- **Garden knives.** These are really useful for light pruning and for harvesting some fruits and vegetables. They can also be used for cutting twine, grafting, and taking cuttings. A plethora of different knives are available for different application in the garden, but unless you're a specialist, a good sharp pocket knife will be fine!
- **Secateurs.** Used for pruning stems under about 1 centimetre thick, secateurs are ideal for trimming fruit bushes and trimming back flowering stems and seed heads. Secateurs are available to suit all budgets, and they come in different sizes and weights to suit every gardener.
- **Loppers and shears.** Loppers are used for cutting woody stems over 1 centimetre in diameter, and can be useful when pruning fruit trees and bushes. Shears are used mainly for trimming hedges and shrubs. Loppers and shears are both worth having but aren't essential bits of kit.
- **Watering cans.** Often an allotment essential, since many sites operate hosepipe bans, and watering cans may be the only way of irrigating your crops. Don't bother with a small one that involves continual trips to the water supply; get one large enough to make each trip worthwhile! But remember you have to carry it, so be sensible. You may also want a smaller one for use in the greenhouse – one with a long spout can be useful so that you can reach plants easily. It's also essential to have a separate watering can if you use pesticides and other chemicals on your plot, so that you don't cross-contaminate containers. Mark it clearly with a big red X or skull and crossbones, or something equally obvious! You can get metal or plastic cans. The metal ones may look nicer and be a more authentic accessory for your new wholesome look, but the plastic ones are much lighter and easier to handle!

- **Sprayers.** Use these for spraying pesticides, herbicides and fertilisers, and for misting plants. The small ones are quite cheap, and all you do is pump them up until they're full and spray where needed. You can usually adjust the mist from fine spray to one sustained jet. Never store a sprayer full, and dispose of its contents safely. It's also advisable to have separate sprayers for different uses.
- **Wheelbarrows.** Without wanting to sound too obvious, these are useful for moving compost, bags, heavy plants and garden rubbish around the plot. They also have a great use when upended, as a place to sit and drink a cuppa or a wee dram! Don't fret too much over which type to get: a good builder's barrow is large enough for all purposes and should do fine. You can get barrows with ball-shaped wheels that are supposed to be easier to move around and more stable. Don't get one with solid tyres, because they get stuck in wet mud quite easily and don't have the bounce of inflatable tyres.
- **Multi-head tools.** A number of systems of multi-headed tools are available, and they're usually really good and a great space-saving bit of kit. You buy the handle and then choose from a variety of additions that simply click on the end, such as rakes, hoes, saws, tree loppers and so on.
- **Propagators.** Not essential items, but propagators are very useful when it comes to raising plants from seed earlier than you can outdoors. They're also useful for certain types of seed that require a more controlled environment. The cheapest options come most often as a simple plastic tray with a clear plastic lid. These are great for some seeds, but are a little limited because you can't control the heat in any way. The propagator must be placed in a sunny spot, and the temperature fluctuates with the ambient conditions. Heated propagators are the better option because you can set the ideal growing temperature. If you buy one that's thermostatically controlled, the ambient temperature won't affect the temperature within the propagator, so it remains constant, offering the best results. You can purchase simple propagators for around a fiver, but heated ones with a thermostat start at around £25–30.
- **Pots and trays.** All sorts of pots and trays are around that have different uses for growing plants. You'll grow many seeds directly on your plot, but some need a head start or special conditions in order to get going. Pots measuring 7 centimetres (3 inches) are really useful for sowing many types of crop indoors, such as tomatoes and cucumbers. Seed trays are good for starting off seeds before transplanting them, and seed modules are available with 6–12 cells, which are also suitable for this. You can also buy biodegradable pots, which are ideal for plants that hate being transplanted, such as peas, beans and sweetcorn. These plants can stay in the pots and be planted directly onto your plot.

- **String lines.** These are useful for marking out straight lines on your plot, especially when it comes to planting out and preparing drills. Strung between two canes, a string line ensures that everything is nice and straight and neat. You can use any string, but I find some decent nylon brick line (available at builders' merchants) lasts well, and is often bright orange, which makes it easy to see and follow when sowing.
- **First aid kit.** Your first aid kit is absolutely essential and should include all the usual plasters, swabs, steri strips and an eye bath with liquid. You'll be surprised how often these get used (or maybe I am just really clumsy!) and you need to restock it regularly.

Going for optional extras

As well as the basics (outlined in the previous section), lots of other tools are available to the allotmenteer. Some prove useful, and some don't. In fact, many optional extras remind me of those kitchen gadgets like egg slicers, apple corers and juicing machines that seemed a good idea at the time but now sit tucked away at the back of your kitchen cupboard. As long as you have the basic kit, you won't really need anything else, but let's face it, tools are cool and great fun to collect. Consider these:

- **Dibbers.** These have been used since Roman times and are simply pointed sticks used to make a hole in the ground in which to sow a seed. Not an essential bit of kit, seeing as a stick can do the job just fine, but because you'll be sowing seeds all the time, it's nice to have a good dibber if you want it. Dibbers come in all sorts of guises from simple wooden pointed ones to heavy steel versions useful for heavy soils. Some are straight, whereas others are T-shaped with a handle. Possibly one to ask for as a nice Christmas gift!
- **Widgers.** Useful for transplanting seedlings and inserting cuttings into compost, widgers look exactly like a pointing iron used for brickwork – in fact one of these will do the trick just as well!
- **Hammers and mallets.** Always good to have lying around for tapping in stakes, attaching netting to supports and so on.
- **Asparagus knives.** Available in two main designs, the first knife is like a small, less-curved sickle with a saw blade that you push into the ground and, as you pull, the saw teeth cut the asparagus under the soil. The other type resembles a chisel head on the end of a long prong, which you simply push into the ground, where it slices the spears. Both types work well and can be lovely looking tools for the avid collector!
- **Pruning saws.** You can buy all sorts of sizes of pruning saw, from small folding ones to large bow saws. You may well need one occasionally if you have any woody plants on the allotment, but you won't use one often. Only buy a pruning saw if you find you need one for large shrubs and small fruiting trees on your plot.

Looking after your tools

Tools are an investment and can last a lifetime if looked after correctly, so here are some ways to ensure that they stay in tip-top condition:

- **Keep them in the shed.** This way they don't rust and get ruined by the weather. All too often you see spades, rakes and other tools left lying around allotment sites, rotting and rusting and simply going to waste.
- **Oil them.** Keep a can of oil in your shed or greenhouse and use this regularly on your tools, especially secateurs and other tools with moving parts. Also oil the blades of your spades and other tools to keep them protected and rust free.
- **Keep digging tools clean.** Remove any soil residue from tools every time you use them to keep them clean and effective. If you don't practise proper tool-cleaning, you can cross-contaminate disease from one bed to another.
- **Wipe blades after use.** Wipe knives, secateurs, loppers and shears after using them. Disease can easily spread via dirty blades, so wipe them after moving from plant to plant.
- **Sharpen tools regularly.** You're wasting your time working with blunt tools. If you work with blunt secateurs, for example, you have to squeeze much harder, crushing as opposed to cutting the stem, and possibly damaging the tool itself.

TIP

Make a wooden box about 40 centimetres by 40 centimetres (with a lid) and keep it by the door of your shed. Fill it with sharp sand and every time you use your spade or fork, push it into the sand, removing any soil left on the blade or prongs. It cleans them up a treat. People used to pour old oil from their cars into the sand, which helped clean the blade and oil it at the same time. I'm not so sure how you'd dispose of the oily sand when it came to changing it, but if kept dry, it lasts for years.

Choosing protection for your plants

As an allotment gardener, you're at the mercy of the weather almost at all the time. The first and last frosts determine everything you plant and when you can plant. Protecting your plants – not only from the weather, but from pests and disease as well – is a vital part of gardening. Greenhouses are usually the first ports of call for allotmenteers, and are ideal as places to sow and grow seeds, and to grow more tender plants. Polytunnels are also a brilliant way of offering protection and controlling conditions to a certain extent, thus greatly extending the growing season.

Greenhouses

Greenhouses are ideal for sowing and propagating seeds to be planted out early in spring. On the allotment, you're more than likely to have a non-heated greenhouse, but it can still offer good protection from the weather and allows you to grow tender vegetables such as tomatoes, cucumbers and aubergines, and also some delicate fruits such as peaches, kiwis and grapes.

When choosing a greenhouse for your allotment, you'll be restricted by the rules as to how big it can be. I would recommend getting the largest one you can, which will offer you the greatest flexibility and growing room. Also, the smaller the greenhouse, the hotter it gets, which can cause problems and damage plants.

You have to get permission from the department of your local council that deals with your allotment site before erecting a greenhouse or shed, and you usually have to fill in a form describing exactly what greenhouse you want to erect. This includes what type of foundation, size, style and often a photo. You're not usually allowed to have concrete foundations, but you don't always need them for simple greenhouses, and you need to be able to plant through the floor anyway.

The greenhouse should be positioned in an open sunny spot that gets plenty of sunlight, offering the most warmth to your seedlings and other plants. An allotment is not a posh garden, so don't worry too much about where the greenhouse looks best, simply think about where the ideal spot is.

Don't place a greenhouse under a nearby tree; not only does a tree limit the light and therefore the growing conditions, but falling branches may well damage the glass.

Often, though, a greenhouse can get too hot in the height of summer and can benefit from some kind of shelter. If you have deciduous trees planted on the sunny side of the greenhouse, they'll keep it cooler in the summer and, as the leaves fall in winter, they let through precious light and warmth to keep things warm. Just make sure that the trees are planted at a safe distance so no branches can fall and damage the glass. You can also buy a selection of blinds and shades that you can install to offer protection from too much sun.

Applying a whitewash shading is the age-old and tested method of keeping a greenhouse cool in summer, and simply involves whitewashing the glass on the outside during hot weather to cool things down a bit. You can either whitewash the whole thing or just the sunny side, depending on how hot it gets. Allotment holders usually use a water-based white matt paint, watered down to about ten parts water to one of paint. Apply this to the glass on the outside, and it will slowly wash off over the summer into the winter.

Sheds

The shed is the most important part of the gardener's realm; it's your tool store and fertiliser and chemical store – and possibly your refuge!

Your shed needs to be absolutely secure, so vandals and thieves can't get at your precious tools. In addition, it needs to be large enough to keep all your kit inside in an orderly fashion. Ideally, there should be room on one side to have some kind of bench for potting up and transplanting plants, and room for that all-important folding chair for well deserved tea breaks and the odd snooze. The size of your allotment shed may be restricted, and on some sites sheds are not allowed at all, so check your tenancy agreement for details. The norm is a maximum floor area of 1.8 metres by 1.2 metres (6 feet by 4 feet).

Timber is the usual material for shed construction, but many people opt for galvanised steel sheds that are more secure and vandal-proof. Many people actually make their own sheds out of old pallets and bits of wood. I love these cobbled-together sheds – they look the part and are a great use of recycled materials. Some people even give the shed a name and hang a plaque above the door! You'll be amazed at how much thought goes into some sheds: some are works of art, whereas others are simply recycled old Anderson air-raid shelters made from corrugated metal sheets. But the simple fact is they are a gardener's 'hub' – somewhere to store tools and the all-important cheeky bottle of something warming.

Polytunnels

Polytunnels are temporary structures consisting of hoops of metal with a simple plastic covering. They range in size from cheap, mini polytunnels that are about 15 centimetres (1 foot) high and a few metres long, costing a tenner, to huge 9.1 metres by 4.2 metres (30 feet by 14 feet) polytunnels that would even suit professional growers and cost about £700.

A polytunnel is the ultimate growing tool for any fruit and vegetable gardener, offering perfect growing conditions for many plants. A polytunnel protects plants from the cold in spring and keeps them warm during the summer months. They're not insulated at all, so are very cold in the winter, but they do warm up quickly in the spring. If you're looking to erect a large polytunnel, you need to check with your allotment authority first, even though polytunnels are temporary structures. You can also buy pack-away tunnels that are large enough to walk in.

Consider these advantages offered by polytunnels:

- **Cost.** They're far cheaper than greenhouses per square foot, so for the same money they give you far more covered growing space.

- **Portability.** They're moveable, unlike a greenhouse, so you can shift them wherever you want, every few years. The soil in a greenhouse can easily become infested with diseases and pests and therefore needs to be dug out and replaced, whereas a polytunnel can be moved as part of a crop rotation system (see Chapter 7) to minimise this problem.
- **Temperature.** Polytunnels are warm and humid in the summer – the perfect growing conditions for many plants that otherwise you may not be able to grow (or grow so well) outdoors, such as aubergines, peppers, cucumbers, kiwi fruits, melons, sweet potatoes and grapes.

  The warmth and humidity of polytunnels can cause problems with fungal disease and mould, so monitor your plants carefully.
- **Extended season.** Polytunnels warm the soil quickly in spring, so you can plant earlier and extend the season right into autumn and winter in some areas.
- **Plant protection.** They offer effective protection from wind, frost, pests and diseases. They also provide you with somewhere to stay dry, so you can keep working in the rain.
- **Overwintering and drying potential.** Many plants can be overwintered in polytunnels, keeping them safe from frost and cold wet winters. Onions, shallots, beans and other vegetables can also be hung from the cross members in the ceiling to dry (but not during hot and humid months).

Bear these tips in mind if you're considering a polytunnel for your plot:

- **Big *is* better.** Always get the biggest polytunnel your plot and pocket can manage. You can get them in all sorts of dimensions, but remember that, ideally, there should be a path down the middle with enough room either side for a good range of plants. Also, get one with a door at each end so you can ventilate your polytunnel well during warm summer months.
- **Get the best you can afford.** Scrimping is never a good idea with polytunnels, because you get what you pay for. Cheap ones usually come with flimsy polythene covers that won't last for more than a few years, whereas a decent cover lasts up to seven years. Also make sure that the frame is of good construction, because allotments can be windy places, and an inferior tunnel won't stand the test of time. You can get polythene covers that allow up to 90 per cent of the light through, and also some even more techno ones that filter out ultraviolet (UV) light. This is particularly good, because many pests rely on UV light to be able to see. If there is no UV light inside the tunnel, the pests are effectively blind when they enter. Also, with no UV light, mildew and *botrytis* (a fungus that affects many fruiting plants) are far less likely to attack.

- **Be considerate of your neighbours and site it carefully.** Make sure that your polytunnel doesn't cast shade or block views. Also think about water, because the plants inside rely on you for it; if you can place your tunnel near a water source, this is ideal.

Cold frames

Cold frames, also known as mini greenhouses, are ideal for *hardening off* your plants. Hardening off is when you gently get plants used to being outdoors, using the cold frame as a halfway house to the great outdoors. Plants go into shock if you simply take them from a nice warm greenhouse or window sill and stick them straight in the ground, so a cold frame is ideal. You can use cold frames to protect tender plants in the winter, and also in early spring and autumn for sowing seeds that can be damaged by frosts.

A vast range of cold frames are available. Some are simply like a metal shelf with a plastic cover. These are cheap but don't offer much protection. You're better off with a wooden-framed version that's double-glazed and so retains more heat and offers better protection. The downside is, it costs more. They come in a variety of sizes, so choose one to suit your space. You usually place a cold frame next to the greenhouse as a plant hotel before the big move onto your plot.

Cloches

A cloche is the simplest method of protecting a plant and warming a small area of soil in the spring. Cloches can be really cool-looking glass domes (bell cloches) or simply small plastic greenhouses that you place over individual plants. You can also buy *cloche tunnels*; these are basically miniature polytunnels that can be placed over drills before and after planting to protect young and growing plants and also warm up the soil prior to sowing. Cloches offer the same kind of protection as polytunnels and greenhouses but have the added advantage of being easy to move and simple to use.

Chapter 4

Deciding What to Grow and When

In This Chapter

- Working with the seasons
- Sowing seeds and planting established plants
- Getting the timing right
- Extending the growing season

As a new allotment gardener, the first and most important lesson you have to learn is patience. Rushing to the garden centre, buying loads of seeds, chucking them in the ground, crossing your fingers and hoping is tempting. Well, this may work for some plants, but long term is a recipe for disaster. A successful vegetable garden takes planning, planning and a bit more planning! What you grow and when is dictated by the seasons and your location. Every site can become productive in some way or another, and even the most inhospitable plot can usually be turned into a vegetable garden.

This chapter looks at when to plants things, how to get the timing spot on, how to choose between sowing seeds and buying ready grown plants to save time and, most importantly, how to create your own tailor-made planting calendar. Eventually, you'll discover how to eat seasonally and will become tuned in to working with the seasons to your benefit.

Choosing What to Grow

One of the first decisions you have to make before you start planting up and sowing seeds is to decide what to grow on your plot. This should be a simple case of simply deciding (and asking your family) what you and they like. You may well decide that your plot is best dedicated to more unusual fruit and vegetables that aren't so easily available or are too expensive to buy on a regular basis. Alternatively, you may have made the decision to become more self-sufficient, in which case you'll want to grow as much as you possibly can in as great a variety as possible.

My advice is to grow the stuff you like and, secondly, not to dedicate too much space to the staples (get them from your local market!), but simply grow treats like peas, sweetcorn, sprouting broccoli and all those things that don't travel and store for long. That way you can eat the freshest produce around. I'm not saying that you shouldn't bother with your spuds (home-grown are simply the best!), just don't dedicate half your plot to them when they're cheap and easily available from local farmers and markets.

Of course, the conditions on your plot dictate what you can grow, but most allotments are on open ground where they receive plenty of light, so the range of fruit and veg you can grow is enormous.

Realising that timing and location are everything

When you can plant your produce is wholly dictated by factors such as *latitude* (distance from the equator), height above sea level, *aspect* (view in a specific direction) and how exposed your plot is. Your planting schedule is determined by calculating how many days each year are suitable growing days. Fruit and vegetables only grow when the average temperature during the day rises to above 6 degrees centigrade.

The arrival of spring in southern parts of the United Kingdom comes a good few weeks earlier than in more northerly regions and, likewise, at the end of the season, autumn draws in faster in the north than the south. This means that the entire growing season in the north can be up to a month shorter than in the south, thus affecting greatly what can be grown and when. This is no big deal in terms of growing decent crops, but you just have to go about it slightly differently and time your seed sowing according to where you live. The usual guide to planting in the spring is based around when you expect the last frost of winter to be. You should aim to plant most seeds and seedlings around or after this time.

Deciding on growing from seed or buying plants

Whether you decide to grow your vegetables from seed or buy ready grown plants is dependent on many factors. First there are the time considerations. Obviously it's far easier to just to go out and buy a plant and plant it in the ground, but you pay dearly for the privilege. With seeds, you have to sow them, thin them out and transplant them, all of which can be a time-consuming process (but really satisfying!). With ready grown plants, you're restricted in terms of which varieties are available to you, but if you grow from seed, the options are almost limitless.

Location, location, location

When you have drawn up the list of fruit and veg that you want to grow, you'll probably have to lose the odd item when you look more closely at where you live. Some vegetables and varieties need longer days and a longer season to mature than others. Many *cultivars* (cultivated plants that have been selected and given a unique name because of desired characteristics) have been specifically bred to adapt to shorter days and cooler climates, so it's vital to choose varieties that are well suited to your area. Many vegetables aren't frost-hardy and need a certain amount of time to mature ready for harvesting, so you must plant them so that they have time to mature well before the onset of the first frost date in your area. For example, in the far north of Scotland, you can expect the last frost to be as late as early June and the first frost as early as mid-October, whereas down south, the last frost can be in late March and the first in mid-November. That means the growing season is far shorter the further north you go, in fact anything up to six weeks shorter at the extremes. Areas near the coast, especially in the south, often escape hard frosts and sometimes get no frost at all, which extends your growing season, meaning you can plant things earlier in the year to make the most of the season.

Sowing from Seed

To grow successfully from seed, the first and most important stage is to read the seed packet in detail. This gives you all the information you need to grow that particular plant.

All that seeds need to *germinate* (sprout) is the correct temperature, enough moisture to get them going, and air. Many seeds can germinate on a piece of blotting paper with nothing more than some warmth and a splash of water. Of course, you can give them a better start in life than that, and if you can create the perfect conditions for germination, their chances of success are far higher.

Often when you sow seeds, not all of them germinate, so a common practice is to sow more than required and closer together. You can do this in a container or on open ground. When the plants reach a size large enough to handle, they need *thinning out*, which just means removing the extras (often the weaker-looking ones). In some cases, these can be replanted to carry on growing, or you can discard them. It's important to make sure that you thin out your plants to the appropriate distances, because they're all competing for light, water and nutrients, and if they're too close they battle with each other to their detriment, often causing them to *bolt* (produce a flowering stem). Pumpkins, for example, need up to a metre or more in all directions to grow to maturity, so you usually plants three seeds a few inches apart in the correct place. As soon as they germinate and reach the two- or three-leaf stage, remove the weaker two plants to allow the strongest free rein.

Sowing in containers, trays and modules

Nearly all vegetables can be grown from seed, and many gardeners aim to give them an early start ready to be planted out just after the last frost. To do this, you need to grow most seeds inside in trays, modules or in pots, in a greenhouse, conservatory or on a bright window sill. Many vegetable seeds need a bit of warmth to germinate. Around 20 °C is ideal, but as long as they're above 10–15 °C they can usually get going, so the warmth of the sun through a window is often enough to start off most seeds.

TIP

Buying a few *propagators* (covered plastic boxes for growing plants in) is certainly worthwhile. I use the ones that aren't heated, and they're very cheap, but you can also buy heated ones that are designed to create the perfect conditions and temperatures and can be adjusted accordingly. They also help keep moisture in the compost you use, making it far easier for you to keep tabs on the watering. See Chapter 3 for more on propagators.

Nothing beats the satisfaction gained from raising plants from seed. To get going with sowing in containers, you need some essential pieces of kit, which are all fairly cheap and easily available:

- **Compost.** A huge range of different types of compost is on the market, but in most cases multi-purpose compost will suit all your needs. Many gardeners make their own and have various recipes they swear by for different applications. A lot of composts contain peat, a fantastic moisture-retentive ingredient but taken from unsustainable sources. You should really avoid compost containing peat. When buying compost, be sure to buy it fresh, because its nutrient content diminishes over time. Also store open bags in a dry place out of the rain, because rain washes all the goodness out of it. Also, weed seeds can find their way into open bags. For more information on making your own compost, see Chapter 6.
- **Containers, pots and trays.** You need an assortment of these to suit different sowing and growing needs. Trays are used to sow seeds ready for moving (*transplanting*), usually into larger containers, before planting out. Seed cells or modules are trays divided into small sections suitable for sowing seeds in their own little zones ready for transplanting. Plastic pots can be used for most plants and those seeds that need a little more room when they're sown. You can also buy (or make from newspaper) biodegradable pots that are great for all plants, but especially those that don't like root disturbance when they're transplanted. Figure 4-1 shows a seedling being transplanted.
- **Perlite and vermiculite.** These are little bits of volcanic rock that can be added to compost to improve its water retention. You can also use these minerals to cover sowings to protect them from direct sunlight and stop them drying out.

- **A watering can or a mister.** This is an essential bit of kit when sowing seeds, whether indoors or outdoors. It must have a fine rose that gently waters your seeds without disturbing the soil surface too much.
- **A propagator.** Not vital, but it's useful for germinating seeds and rooting cuttings (producing new plants from cuttings taken from established ones). You can create similar conditions by using cling film or clear plastic bags placed over pots and trays.

Figure 4-1: Transplanting a seedling.

To sow your seeds in containers, follow these steps:

1. **Cover your bench or table with newspaper and then tip some compost onto it.** Crumble the compost between your fingers to make sure that all the large lumps are broken up.
2. **Fill your containers with compost and gently tap them on the counter to knock out any air pockets.** The compost should almost fill the containers and just leave a little space at the top. Firm the compost gently but don't press it down too hard, because doing so compacts the compost too much.
3. **Water the containers using fresh water.** Use a fine rose on the watering can, or a fine mister. Watering the compost not only creates a nice moist new home for the seeds but also settles the compost ready for sowing. Allow to drain. Watering beforehand avoids the potential pitfall of washing small seeds deep into the pots, where they can't grow.
4. **Sow the seeds according to the instructions on the packet.** Some seeds are sown thinly simply by sprinkling them over the compost, whereas others are sown at specific depths. It is always advisable to sow more plants than you think you need. Some won't germinate, and some will be lost to disease, damping off (see point 7 below), drying out, pests or other problems than can occur.

5. **Cover the seeds with compost as directed.** You can also use perlite or vermiculite as a covering – this is ideal for seeds that need light to germinate, because these materials let light through whilst retaining moisture.
6. **Place the seeds in a warm place to germinate.** You can use a propagator or cover the pots with plastic bags or cling film with some holes poked in the top. Some plants are fussy about what temperature they'll germinate at, and this is where a heated propagator comes into its own. Most fruit and veg seeds need a temperature of around 20 degrees centigrade to germinate, but some such as peas are cold-season crops that prefer lower temperatures to germinate. Others such as aubergines like it even warmer; they require temperatures between 20 and 30 degrees centigrade. The best idea is to check the seed packet for directions and check out the sections on the individual plants in this book.
7. **Keep a close eye on your babies!** If the soil surface starts to look dry, you may need to water the compost again, so check this daily. But do be careful; too much water can cause the seedlings to *dampen off.* This means that fungal diseases present in the soil contaminate them. The ideal way to water seedlings is to place the containers in a shallow dish of water for up to an hour.

Most seeds start to show quite quickly. Lettuce and spinach can show in as few as five days, but most seeds appear within a month and during this time may well need watering to keep them moist. As soon as the foliage appears, move the plants into a light place, otherwise they start searching for light and grow tall and spindly.

REMEMBER

Not all vegetables are suited to being grown in trays for transplanting. For example, beetroots, carrots and parsnips are best grown directly on your plot. You may be able to transplant some successfully, but the loss rate will be so high that it's not usually worth it. If you're prepared to wait, most seeds can be sown directly onto your plot as soon as the soil warms in spring and then throughout the growing season into autumn.

Thinning out

Thinning out is usually done when the first true leaves are showing at the top of the seedling. You must thin the seedlings at this point before the plants become too large and start to tangle into each other, when they're likely to be damaged. Thinning out is also known as *pricking out* and must done gently so as not to damage the plants in any way, especially the delicate stems, which if broken kill the plants.

To thin out and transplant your seedlings, follow these steps:

1. **Cover your bench or table with newspaper and gather together everything you need.** Find some pots or seed modules, compost, a *widger* (a tiny fork for lifting seedlings) or pencil, and a watering can with a fine rose attachment.
2. **Fill the pots or trays with compost.** Follow the instructions in point 2 of 'Sowing in containers, trays and modules', earlier in this chapter.
3. **Lift the seedlings.** Do so gently with a *widger* by gently prising the seedlings out of the soil, holding the leaves and not the stem. If the roots are entangled, carefully prise the seedlings apart. You'll soon find a method that works, but a gentle approach is essential. Most seedlings come away easily and fall away from each other with no bother.
4. **In the pots or seed cells, make holes in the compost with your dibber.** Hold the seedlings by their leaves and lower them into the holes. Gently push the compost around them.
5. **Water the seedlings using a fine rose.** Place them out of direct sunlight for a couple of days so they can get over the whole experience. You may notice some of the little plants flop over, but they'll soon recover. When they perk up, move them back to a bright spot to carry on growing ready for transplanting when the time is right.

If the seedlings are going to be in their new temporary home for more than a few weeks, it's a good idea to give them some general-purpose liquid feed once every two weeks. This gives them the strength to jump into life when you move them onto your plot.

Transplanting

Transplanting in horticultural terms simply means moving a plant from one place to another. This may be just moving a plant to a new site on your plot, but more often than not refers to the process of transplanting plants and seedlings into a larger pot (*potting on*) or onto the allotment. This may be necessary for several reasons:

- So you can get your seedlings growing before the last frost arrives, giving the plants a head start in spring.
- To avoid problems with pests and disease until plants are strong enough to cope outdoors.
- To ensure enough seedlings have germinated to fulfil your needs.

Most plants that have been grown indoors in sheltered conditions will need to be acclimatised to the outside for a period of a few weeks before they can be planted out; this is known as *hardening off.*

Sowing directly into the soil

Often the best policy is to sow seeds directly onto the plot in the place where they're to spend the rest of their lives. Most root crops are happier like this. The key to successful growing is in the preparation of the soil. This also applies to successful sowing. If the soil is poor, you need to add copious amounts of organic matter to improve the soil structure and nutrient levels whilst also improving its water-retaining qualities. Chapter 6 contains everything you need to know about preparing and maintaining the soil on your plot.

Many root crops such as carrots, parsnips and beetroot don't do well on recently manured soils, where they're likely to become misshapen and forked. You can get away with planting these root crops if the manure or (even better) compost is well rotted down and only lightly spread as a surface dressing.

To sow directly into the soil, follow these steps:

1. **Prepare the soil for sowing.** Fork the area over then rake it to a *fine tilth* and a fine texture with no large lumps and stones. Also ensure that you remove all traces of weeds.
2. **Prepare a drill ready for sowing.** A *drill* is simply a straight shallow trench created using a hoe, stick or anything that can be dragged along the ground to create a channel. These drills need to be spaced out depending on what you're planting. Before sowing the seeds, water the drill well unless the soil is already moist.
3. **Sow the seeds.** You need to sow most seeds thinly, about 1 centimetre deep, but larger seeds are usually sown in couples spaced according to needs of the specific plant. Cover the seeds lightly with soil and gently firm down with the back of a rake, and if the soil is dry, water the seeds using a fine rose. When the seeds start to grow, you need to thin out the seedlings to the appropriate spacing, according to the guidelines on the seed packets.

Figure 4-2 shows you the steps.

Many seeds and seedlings are particularly vulnerable to attack from rodents, birds and slugs, and may need protection. Also, plants that are planted early need protection from the cold. Cloches, polytunnels even plastic drink bottles cut in half provide a great way to protect your seedlings and seeds. Alternatively, you can erect cages with netting, or cover plants with fleece to offer protection. For more on protecting your plants from attack, see Chapter 7.

Figure 4-2: Sowing seeds into the soil

Buying Plants

Nowadays many companies supply a great range of ready grown little plants that you simply pop in the ground and look after until they produce an easy crop. A lot of these companies take the whole thought process out of the allotment calendar for you and offer a month-by-month supply delivered to your door ready to put straight into the ground. This is ideal if you're pushed for time or simply don't have the space or inclination to grow from seed.

Many garden centres and DIY stores also supply grow-your-own plants, but I find the best option is to buy direct from the growers via mail order or, if you're lucky enough to live near one, buy from the grower direct.

Knowing what to look for

You need to look out for a number of things when buying plants, to ensure that you're getting a good, healthy specimen. Healthy plants should have strong, healthy looking foliage that's not discoloured, withered or wilted in any way. The compost should be free from weeds and the pots not too heavy, which can be a sign of over-watering, or the soil too dry. For larger seedlings in pots, check the bottom of pots to make sure that the plants aren't *root bound*, that is with lots of roots growing out of the holes. You can even ask nursery staff to take the pots off and check the roots aren't too heavily packed together and that the plants have plenty of *fibrous roots* (fine hairy roots, which maximise the uptake of water and nutrients).

Buying fruit trees

When buying fruit trees and bushes, it's always best to go to a specialist or a garden centre you know and trust for good quality.

Many fruit trees and bushes are supplied *bare rooted*, which means they're dug up in their dormant season and sent out during autumn and winter with bare roots. These, surprisingly, often do far better and become established with greater success than plants supplied in pots, and they are often cheaper too. When you take delivery, you should unpack the plants as soon as possible and, if the roots are dry, soak them in a bucket of water for a few hours before planting them out.

When planting, dig a hole at least two or three times the size of the root ball and then incorporate plenty of good compost into it with the excavated soil. Ensure that you plant the tree or shrub to the same level it was in the nursery or in its pot by placing a pole (the handle of your hoe is good) across the hole and lining up the tree to that level. There should be a ring around the trunk marking roughly the level at which it was planted before. Gardeners call this the *nursery mark*.

Most trees and shrubs are best planted during the autumn and winter whilst they're dormant, but you can buy them in pots all year round. Most garden centres have limited selections. Sometimes you can get something decent, but you're usually better deciding on a variety and finding a good supplier rather than going somewhere and hoping they have something you may like to try. Hundreds of varieties of many different fruiting trees and bushes are available, and not all will be suitable for your allotment. The rules and regulations you get when you become a plot holder will contain details of how many and what size fruiting trees you can have, so careful selection is vital. Check with your allotment association what you can do.

Some plants are better not grown from seed, because they often fail or take too long. Rhubarb is a good example; it can be grown from seed but it takes at least three years until it's large enough to be cropped. It's far easier to chat to a fellow plot holder and get her to donate a clump of an established plant that can easily be replanted, or buy one ready grown. Another good example is asparagus, which is a perennial (a plant that lives for more than two years). Asparagus takes three years to produce a crop from seed, so you're often better off buying a ready grown *crown* (little clump). You can usually get asparagus plants as one-year-old crowns, which are best planted and left for a year before cropping, in order to build up strength in the plant.

Even if you decide to grow everything from seed, ready grown plants may well still be of use to you. More often than not, and for no apparent reason, a crop may fail or all your seedlings may suddenly just perish out of the blue. This is a sad fact of vegetable growing and something you have to get used to. But if it does happen, you can always grow a *catch crop* or replant using bought plants that can fill the hole.

Catch crops

Catch crops are grown when the ground is empty, and are usually sown in between crops that have completed their life cycle. Catch crops usually grow fast and don't take up the ground for long, so you literally squeeze them in between main crops. Radishes are the traditional choice, but pak choi, oriental mustards, leaf beet, corn lettuce and herbs like parsley and coriander are suitable for filling the gaps. You can even grow some flowers between crops, because many attract beneficial insects onto the plot that can help all the fruit and veg pollinated by bees. Try cosmos, larkspur and *annuals* (plants that germinate, flower and die within one year) such as marigolds and candytuft.

Heritage varieties

When trawling through seed catalogues and websites, you often see seeds mentioned as being heritage (sometimes called heirloom) varieties. *Heritage varieties* are basically old-fashioned varieties that have been around for donkey's years, many of which are very rare and have been saved from the scrap heap by enthusiasts and plant collectors. Most of these varieties are the predecessors of the modern plants most of us grow today.

Some people insist that heritage varieties are far superior in flavour to modern varieties, and in some cases this is true. Quite a few companies and organisations dedicate their time to collecting and preserving these heritage seeds. This is of great importance in terms of preserving the heritage, origins and history of modern-day plants, and it's also great fun to grow rarer varieties to show your allotment buddies. With all the messing about with plants we humans have done over the years, we may well lose track of what the parent plants once were – and you never know, it's possible we'll rely on these old varieties to start over again one day. If they're lost, we can never get them back.

In essence, nothing is wrong with heritage varieties, but through modern breeding techniques and hybridisation (I discuss this later in this chapter), the best traits of these original plants have been kept whilst the flaws have been bred out. This may mean that the great flavour of an old-fashioned tomato has been kept whilst its susceptibility to blight has been bred out, or it has been bred to mature faster in a cooler climate.

Selective breeding and hybridisation

These days, large companies (and also enthusiasts) spend millions of pounds and lifetimes respectively developing new vegetable varieties to offer hardier, faster-maturing veg that produce larger yields and are easier to grow. This is sometimes at the cost of flavour.

Selective breeding doesn't mean that the plants are chemically interfered with, and hybrid varieties are merely varieties that have been crossed with other varieties to produce plants with more sought-after traits such as disease-resistance. This is great news for organic growers, because these new, tougher plants don't require chemicals to protect them and keep them healthy.

Hybridisation is a naturally occurring phenomenon when the pollen from one variety pollinates the flower of another, creating a brand new offspring. It's not rocket science or anything to fear. Plants that are compatible with each other for cross-pollination have often failed to do so previously for geographical reasons or because they flower during different times of the year. Through human intervention, various cross-breeds have been developed to our benefit.

Strangely enough, many hybrids have improved vigour, and this common trait is really beneficial to the allotment gardener.

Selective breeding is the main way that growers breed the beneficial characteristics into a plant. Growers only collect seed from cross-bred plants that have the characteristic they're wanting to keep – for example, pink flowers. Over a number of years, all the plants that produce, say, yellow flowers are destroyed before they can cross-pollinate with the pink-flowered ones, so eventually all the offspring will be pink. This is what is known as a hybrid. An *F1 hybrid* is a cross between two plants that have already been selectively bred – so in effect an F1 hybrid is a cross between two other hybrids. With F1 hybrids, you always know what you're going to get and every seed that germinates does exactly what it says on the tin!

In simple terms, here is an example of an F1 hybrid. Breeders create two hybrid carrot varieties, which are called the *pure line*. One is resistant to bolting and tastes great; the second tastes great and is low in chlorogenic acid, making it less attractive to carrot fly. The two hybrids are crossed, and the resulting new carrot is bolt-resistant, tastes great and is low in chlorogenic acid, making it carrot-fly-resistant too, and an F1 hybrid is born. The new F1 plant has been bred to adopt the best characteristics of both hybrids.

The offspring of F1 hybrid plants won't produce seeds that are true to type, which means that the seeds will actually be those of the parent plant and not the new cross. Only by keeping these pure line varieties together and crossing them can F1 seeds be produced. You must therefore buy fresh seed every year for F1 hybrids. They're more expensive, but only because of the effort it takes to produce them.

Creating an Allotment Calendar

An allotment timetable or calendar is a vital tool that all but the most experienced gardeners must produce to keep things to plan. The gardener's year on the plot is a constant mission of sowing, planting, harvesting, digging, weeding, manuring, feeding, clearing and sowing again. Planning your year with military precision is vital.

The easiest way to prepare your vegetable calendar is in a notepad. Allow a page for each week of the year and note down exactly what you need to do each week. This may sound a bit boring – and believe me it is – but as soon as you've finished your calendar, your year ahead will be much easier to tackle. The main things to include are what you're going to plant and when. This is especially useful for successional crops such as lettuce, peas and French beans that can be planted every week or so, because you can very easily forget these.

You can also create your own personalised planting grid like the simple one shown in Figure 4-3. This can be as detailed as you like. Include whatever fruit and veg you want to grow, with as much detail as you want. Figure 4-3 shows the vegetables – when to sow outside and under cover, and also when to harvest. You may also want to include planting distances or any other details you need to remember such as critical watering periods, when to earth up (a technique used to raise soil levels around certain crops to produce pale stems or heavier crops), when to offer protection, and so on.

Invest in a vegetable planning wheel. You can buy one online or in a garden centre. A vegetable planning wheel is a wheel that spins around showing vegetables, sowing dates for both indoors and outside, planting distances, soil requirements and when you can expect a harvest. This is an invaluable little tool that offers all the basic information in an easy-to-read way. Lots of planting calendars exist to simplify and demystify the whole planting year. Try one.

Figure 4-3: An example planting grid.

	January	February	March	April	May	June	July	August	September	October	November	December
Beetroot			Sow under cover	Sow under cover Sow out	Sow out	Harvest	Harvest	Harvest	Harvest	Harvest	Harvest	
Broad beans		Sow under cover	Sow outside	Sow outside Remove growing tips	Remove growing tips	Harvest	Harvest					
Runner beans			Sow indoors	Sow outside	Tie into supports	Check pollination and hand pollinate if necessary	Harvest and water	Harvest	Harvest			
French beans				Sow under cover	Sow outside	Sow out	Harvest	Harvest	Harvest			
Brussels sprouts			Sow under cover	Sow outside	Transplant seedlings					Harvest	Harvest	Harvest
Carrots			Sow outside	Sow Thin out	Sow Thin out	Sow Thin and Harvest	Sow out, thin and Harvest	Harvest	Harvest	Harvest		
Leeks	Harvest	Harvest Sow indoors	Sow out doors under cover		Thin, transplant	Water	Water	Earth up	Earth up	Harvest baby leeks	Harvest	Harvest

Chapter 5

Preparing Your Plot

In This Chapter

- Taking stock of your plot
- Organising your plan of attack
- Eradicating weeds
- Designing and setting out your plot

By far the most vital stage in developing a productive allotment garden is the preparation of your plot. Having a well planned allotment with good soil makes life as an allotmenteer far easier in the long run. Resist the gung-ho approach and tackle your new plot methodically, planning every stage with military precision. The time of year when you inherit your plot and the condition it's in will greatly influence the order in which you tackle the preparations. You're aiming for a well set out, tidy plot that's properly organised, weed free and has rich nutritious soil.

Maintaining a Tidy Allotment

In order to be productive, an allotment garden needs to be kept as tidy as possible. When you finally get your green fingers on your plot, the first thing to do is clear the site of any rubbish, weeds, unwanted plants and other debris. Of course, if you are lucky enough to have inherited any healthy plants of value, such as an area of currant bushes or a herb garden, don't dig these up! Regulations usually require that your allotment is kept clean and tidy, and if you don't adhere to these rules you can face the possibility of being turfed off your plot. This isn't only for aesthetic reasons; a messy plot is a magnet for pests, weeds and diseases that reduce your chances of success.

On most allotments, you find two groups of people. First you have the ones with neat, tidy, weed-free plots, with nice neat raised beds and neat paths running between them. Then you have the scruffy group whose plots make it difficult to tell the weeds from the veg. If you want to be productive (and maintain good relations with your neighbours), I strongly advise the neat approach!

Removing debris and rubbish

When I was training to be a garden designer, I used to work for a little garden centre in Walthamstow in London and every day drove past an allotment site to get to work. It used to amaze me what a dump the place was (the allotment, not Walthamstow), with old fridges, rolled-up carpets, half-derelict sheds and brambles everywhere.

If your new plot is scruffy and full of rubbish, you need to tackle it straight away. Rubbish isn't only detrimental to your produce, it affects the ecology of the allotment as a whole. First, carefully remove any rubbish that you find and dispose of it safely.

You never know what you're going to find, so please look with the utmost care and beware of any hazardous materials you may find. In the past, I've found hypodermic needles, broken bottles, razor wire and all sorts of dangerous waste, so just be cautious. Your allotment has rules and regulations regarding recycling, so when it comes to disposing of rubbish you should observe these rules with care.

Sorting out the undergrowth

The most likely scenario when you get your plot is that it'll be fairly clear of rubbish but covered in weeds, and more likely than not will have an old rickety shed. Some weeds, such as chickweed, are good indicators that the soil is actually in pretty good shape, so if your plot is covered in tall, leafy specimens, that's not always such a bad thing.

The days of abandoned allotment plots have long gone, and due to the fact that allotments are so oversubscribed these days, the plot you're allocated has probably been productive recently, so the weed cover you see should be fairly new and easy to deal with.

Plot providers in reality only have to provide you with the land and offer no guarantee as to the condition of it, but many pride themselves on supplying a quality service. So if your new plot is in a real state and you need help to clear it of debris, it's worth approaching the provider and seeing what can be done.

Green waste from the allotment (apart from perennial weeds and diseased plant material) should be composted wherever possible. For more detail on this topic, have a look at Chapter 6.

Meeting the Enemy: Common Weeds

Some of you may win the allotment lottery and inherit a plot that's free of weeds, with the teacup in the shed still warm from the previous tenant. Others may have plenty of hard weeding work ahead of them. Weeds compete directly for light, nutrients and water with the plants that you want to nurture, so you need to deal with them. They come in two different forms – perennial weeds and annual weeds – and you'll undoubtedly have to battle with both in your quest for vegetable utopia and weed freedom.

Preventing perennial problems

Perennial weeds are the most difficult and problematic weeds you encounter, because they're long lived and store their food in underground roots that enable them to survive through winter. Some of them are really difficult to get out because they're deep rooted and spread underground, making digging them out a real issue. A good example of this is one of the best known and difficult to eradicate: bindweed. Its roots can grow underground to over 5 metres, so it's almost impossible to get rid of; you therefore have to control its spread. Most other perennial weeds can be eradicated by digging them out; with hoeing and constant cultivation of the soil, you can keep the problem at bay.

Perennial weeds that need beating are:

- **Brambles.** These are a common sight in hedgerows and on scrubland and allotment sites. They are easily recognisable, being the scrambling mass of thorny stems that bear blackberries in the late summer. They're not much of a problem on land that's cultivated frequently, such as on an allotment, because hoeing and cultivation eventually kill off the roots. Problems can arise if you simply cut the brambles off at ground level, because this stimulates the root to send out new shoots, making the problem worse. Ideally, you should dig the plant out completely. If you spray brambles with weedkiller, you then need to dig up the mini forest of brittle brown stems that results. Brambles spread via fruit seeds, which pass through the digestive systems of birds and animals; the excrement in turn acts as a fertiliser helping the seeds to germinate.
- **Dandelions.** The dandelion gets its name from the French '*dents de lion*', which means 'teeth of the lion', and can be identified easily by its distinctive yellow flowers that appear from spring onwards and its deeply toothed green leaves. Dandelions are a total pain on the allotment: they have fleshy tap roots that grow straight down. The best thing to do is dig them up, making sure you remove the entire root; if you leave a

piece of the root underground, it simply grows back. Dandelions also spread via their seeds, which are held on fluffy white seed heads on tall hollow stems. The seeds are like little parachutes and are carried by the wind for miles on windy days. This means that you often find new plants popping up on your allotment – but they're easily dug up and disposed of. Dandelions are edible, the leaves being used as a salad leaf or cooked like spinach. The roots can also be eaten as a vegetable or dried and ground to make a coffee-like drink, plus you can use the flowers in dandelion and burdock wine.

Dig up dandelions when they're young when it's easier to ensure that you get the whole root. Also be sure not to let them set seed, otherwise they spread even more.

- **Stinging nettles.** These are very common, and on the outskirts of an allotment are a really useful companion plant because they provide a great breeding ground for ladybirds and tortoiseshell butterflies. Ladybirds love to gorge themselves on greenfly and black fly, which are constant allotment enemies. Nettles spread via underground rhizomes and can creep around your plot if not kept under control. Some allotment holders allow a small patch to develop for use in composting and to make nettle tea. Nettles can be eradicated by regular mowing that eventually kills them off – or just dig them out. They have one particular use that makes them valuable to the allotmenteer: they're high in nitrogen, so added to a compost heap they act as a useful activator which helps speed up decomposition. Only add the tops, though, not the roots, which would continue to grow on the heap.

  Fill a bucket loosely with nettles and fill to the top with water. Leave it for two weeks, and the resulting liquid makes a potent (although rather smelly) fertiliser. If you water it down to a 1:10 ratio, you can use this fertiliser as a feed for most crops, especially tomatoes.

- **Creeping buttercup.** This invasive weed can be identified by its five-petalled shiny yellow flowers, and also by its lobed green leaves and creeping stems. This weed is a real nuisance, and one single plant can spread over 3–4 square metres in a single year. It spreads via seeds or, as the name suggests, via its creeping stems. These stems root as they grow, creating a thicket of many plants from just one parent. You need to dig creeping buttercups out thoroughly, ensuring that you remove the entire plant and as much of the root as you can. After digging, rake the area over to remove any surface roots that you may have missed.

- **Common couch grass.** This looks pretty much like any normal tuft of grass, but below its inoffensive façade lies a network of invasive roots that can cause problems, especially when entangled in the roots of other crop plants. The tufts on their own can be dug out fairly easily, but you're sure to leave behind some of the roots, and these then quickly produce new plants. On a new allotment plot, I'd seriously consider chemical control methods such as spraying with a weedkiller containing glyphosate, which gets right down into the roots of the plant, usually killing it off in two or three weeks. You may find you need to apply a second dose if growth appears again. You need to spray with the utmost care: direct the spay only on the plant itself, so as not to contaminate the soil or other plants.

- **Greater plantain.** This forms a rosette of foliage close to the ground, and in summer 15-centimetre-tall flower spikes appear that turn brown and felt-like when the seeds mature. On cultivated ground, the greater plantain is a really common weed that reproduces mainly from seed. When ground is freshly dug over, the seeds are disturbed, and when open to the elements, they burst into life. The plants are quite easy to dig out and dispose of and, luckily, don't reproduce easily from the roots, even if you leave a small piece in the soil.
- **Ground elder.** This has to be one of the most annoying weeds that you encounter on the allotment; the key to its elimination is vigilance. It carries vibrant green foliage and spreads via a network of underground stems and sometimes by seed. Its spreading nature is the main problem. In the summer, it bears flower stems up to a metre tall that look like flat plates. It's fairly easy to dig up, but any remaining trace of stem becomes a new plant. You may well think that you've cleared the area and won the battle . . . only to discover a year or two later that it's back to ruin your day! It takes persistence to get rid of it, and chemical control is, unfortunately, often the only viable option.
- **Horsetail.** This is a really cool-looking plant that forms tall stems which can be pulled apart into little sections. As the name suggests, the stem resembles a horse's tail. In spring, horsetails pop up from the ground as single shoots with a cone-like growth at the tip, which carries the spores. These spores spread like crazy. Horsetail is a particularly difficult offender to eradicate, because the roots delve deep into the ground. It's also fairly resistant to weedkillers, so the only real option is to dig out as much as you can and just keep at it; eventually this kills off the root, but it takes dedication to succeed. Horsetails go back 30 million years, and relatives are known to have existed 300 million years ago, making this plant a living fossil. To my mind, if it's survived so long, what chance have we got of wiping it out? So learn to live with it and simply control it!
- **Japanese knotweed.** This weed is the ultimate offender, being vigorous, tall and pretty much indestructible. It's listed by the International Union for Conservation of Nature and Natural Resources as one of the world's worst 100 invasive species, and even had a dedicated alliance set up in 1999 to research ways in which to combat its spread. The plant is actually quite beautiful, bearing large heart-shaped leaves with fluffy white flower spikes in the summer. It grows to around 2 metres tall, and was introduced in the mid-nineteenth century as an ornamental plant. However, people soon realised their mistake as the knotweed quickly swamped areas, preventing other plants from growing. The only effective method of control is using chemical killers, and I'd advise using a specialist company that has access to the right chemicals for the job.

An alternative is to use a systemic weedkiller that contains glyphosate during the flowering season, which may do the job and is cheaper.

- **Creeping thistle.** This weed can colonise 6–12 square metres each year if left to its own devices and is a common problem for gardeners nationwide. It's a tall thistle-like weed with pale purple flower heads followed by fluffy white seed heads, and spreads via underground stems that creep in all directions, slowly engulfing and overpowering any plants in its way. The most effective means of attack is to dig out as much as you can and, if the problem persists, use a systemic weedkiller as a last resort.

Doing away with the annuals

Annual weeds are plants that grow, flower, set seed and die all within the space of one year. Due to the fact they're short-lived, they're often vigorous and are a common problem in cultivated areas such as allotments, where the constant tilling of the soil unearths seeds that germinate and grow quickly. Annual weeds are a nuisance mainly because, as your seedlings grow, the weeds often grow at a quicker rate, smothering them in the process. Due to the fact that they grow so quickly, these weeds drain the soil of precious nutrients and water that your crops need to succeed. If the problem is really bad, it's often worth holding fire on getting planting, and first dig the plot over a few times so as to encourage the seeds to germinate in order that you can remove them.

Below is a list of annual weeds to watch out for:

- **Chickweed.** Best identified as a tangled mess of small green leaves, chickweed can germinate, grow and set seed in a matter of six weeks, so is a voracious little thug. Thankfully it's easy to pull up, and with regular hoeing, the problem should subside over a few years. This weed spreads though seed dispersal, but its reaching stems also take root and start to grow as new plants. It's actually delicious as a salad leaf and can be grown for this purpose, but I don't recommend doing so because of its aggressive nature.
- **Groundsel.** Really common on cultivated land where disturbance promotes seed germination, groundsel can be identified by its toothed green leaves, the yellow flowers that never seem to open, and by the fluffy white seed heads that are similar in appearance to those of dandelions. Importantly, groundsel acts as a host to a virus that causes black root rot in peas, carrots and tomatoes, so it's definitely one to keep under control!
- **Hairy bitter cress.** This is a common annual weed that sometimes can be biennial, lasting over winter into another year. It can be identified by its pinkish green stems, all coming from a central point, with opposite oval green leaves and simple white flowers bearing four petals. It too

is edible and is great in salads. It's part of the mustard family, so has a spicy flavour much like rocket. I never suggest growing it on purpose, though, because it grows easily from seed and carries explosive seed heads that can catapult its seeds several metres in all directions.

- **Purple deadnettle.** This weed has pretty purple-tinged upper leaves and flowers. It's not actually related to the stinging nettle but has a similar appearance; also it doesn't sting, hence the name deadnettle. It forms dense groups fairly quickly. If you're a beekeeper, you may want to leave an area of deadnettles on your plot; bees find the nectar irresistible, and the nettles are often in flower when not much else is and so can be a useful source of food for bees.
- **Annual nettles.** Also known as the small nettle, they're stingers just like the perennial version and they reproduce from seed, which they're capable of producing in abundance. They love rich soils just like that on allotments, and their presence is an indicator that your soil needs an injection of lime. They're common in East Anglia and can be a real problem for sugar beet growers. You can control these nettles best by frequent hoeing.
- **Goosegrass, sticky willy, cleavers, catchweed.** This weed has so many common names I never know what to call it, and each area of the country seems to have its own name. I've always called it sticky willy (who knows why?). It is easily identifiable by its scrambling nature and whorls of thin green leaves that protrude in sections around its long square stems. It's invasive and clings and climbs through other plants quite quickly. It is most recognisable by the seeds that seem to stick to everything, especially dogs that have been out for a walk! Thankfully, it's fairly easy to control as long as you keep hoeing and pulling it up as soon as you see it appear.
- **Shepherd's purse.** A virulent weed that can complete its life cycle over and over in one season. It gets its common name from its triangular seed pods that look like an old shepherd's purse. The leaves are formed in a rosette at the base of the plant, from which shoot spikes, 20–50 centimetres tall, bearing small white flowers and the odd leaf which protrudes from the stem. Shepherd's purse should be treated like most annual weeds and not left to set seed; hoeing regularly should keep the problem at bay.

Killing Off Weeds

You have quite a few options and methods at your disposal when it comes to clearing and eradicating problem weeds from your plot. As a starting point, I'd always encourage you to try chemical-free ways to deal with weeds; any use of chemicals on an allotment should be avoided because of the associated potential health risks and damage to the soil. Admittedly, many allotmenteers do resort to chemical weed control, but only as a last resort. With both perennial and annual weeds, prevention is always the best form of cure, so good practice and thorough weeding from day one pays dividends in the future.

Initial weeding strategy

The time to attack weeds hard is when you first get access to your allotment. If you make a good job of this first attack, you make life easier in the long run. Before you engage in any planting, you must ensure that you clear the allotment completely of weeds. By failing to do so thoroughly, you'll get weeds popping up in the middle of your established plants in the future, and these weeds are the most difficult to get rid of.

You may have noticed or heard of gardeners covering areas of the ground with old carpet or plastic in order to deprive the weeds of light; this can be effective, but the plastic needs to be in place for a least a whole growing season and, to be honest, most of us when we get our plots can't wait that long. So the best method is simply to dig out as many of the weeds as you can and dispose of them.

Bear the following tips in mind:

- **Avoid laying carpets.** Carpets have been banned from many allotment sites throughout the country. Not only do they become mouldy and smelly, but the backing can release harmful chemicals into the soil.
- **Drop the rotavator.** You sometimes see people turn up to their plots with petrol rotavators in hand, ready to get stuck in to their weed-ridden patches. A word of warning . . . don't! The spinning blades shred the roots of perennial weeds such as bindweed into hundreds of pieces that eventually become new plants.
- **Lose the perennials.** Don't add any perennial weeds to your compost heap – they'll just become new plants. Some say you can leave them out to dry and die or put them in water until they rot and then add them to the compost – but why bother? Just get rid of them; it's not worth the risk.

Organic control

Controlling the weeds on your plot by organic means is always best. Try the following methods before you resort to chemical warfare.

Digging and hoeing

This is quite simply the best starting point when faced with any weed problem; all plants need leaves, which absorb light in order to grow, so if they don't have any leaves they eventually die. Annual weeds are fairly easy to deal with, and most can just be pulled up or lightly hoed to remove them. Perennial weeds are a bit more difficult to get rid of and require digging out, making sure that you remove all of the root or, in the case of the more persistent weeds, as much of the root as you can! Some weeds are almost impossible to remove by digging, especially in really heavy soils such as clay, but in lighter sandy soils it's much easier.

If you catch annual weeds before they flower and set seed, you can simply hoe or dig them into the soil, where they rot down, returning precious nutrients to the soil.

Mulching and using weed-suppressing membranes

Mulching is a practice employed by gardeners, which involves covering the soil with a layer of organic matter. This layer acts as a great weed suppressor, helping to retain moisture in the soil by preventing evaporation by the wind and sun. Mulch rots down, too, adding nutrients to the soil. Before applying a mulch, do make sure the ground is weed free, otherwise you are just covering over a problem that may well resurface.

A number of different materials are available for use as a mulch, and some people even leave recently hoed annual weeds (not in seed!) as a layer in between crops to rot down. Wood chip is the most common mulch but should be used with some caution, because as wood rots down it draws nitrogen from the soil as a way of feeding the bacteria that break down the chippings. Because nitrogen is so important to many crops, it needs to be replaced in some way to counterbalance the problem.

Weed-suppressing membranes are basically large sheets of woven plastic fabric that you peg to the ground. Plants can then be grown through holes cut in the fabric, with mulch often spread over the top. The membrane helps suppress weed growth, and due to the porous nature of the material, water and nutrients can still get through to the plants. This method can work really well for particular crops such as celeriac that like the moist conditions and hate being suppressed by competing weeds. But, for other crops, I do not suggest weed-suppressing membranes. To my mind, soil needs to be open to the elements in some way. If it isn't, you run the risk of depriving the soil, which is basically a living substance, of all light and air, resulting in lifeless dust. So membranes should only be used with certain crops that require special conditions.

Burning

One of the most satisfying ways to tackle annual weeds is to hire a flame thrower. You can get them at most hire shops, and they come attached to a gas canister. Flame throwers provide a really effective way of quickly zapping annual weeds, and you get to feel like the terminator for a brief moment! A quick blast is enough to scorch the seedlings into an early grave.

Chemical spraying

A few years ago, it was perfectly acceptable to turn up on your first day as an allotment holder and wipe out the entire weed population with a good spray of powerful weedkiller. This works well and quickly, but not only do you kill the weeds, but most probably any other plants, insects and other useful micro-organisms that are in and around the soil, so it's a practice best left to the history books. Selective spraying may be needed as a last resort for real problem offenders.

You need to understand a few different terms in relation to weedkillers on the market, in order to avoid making mistakes. I cover the basics below, but if in doubt, ask at the garden centre before you buy.

Systemic (translocated) weedkillers

Systemic weedkillers are the nuclear arsenal for the allotment gardener; you spray the foliage of a plant, and the chemical is absorbed into the leaf and transported around the entire plant, right down into the roots. This type of weedkiller is generally really effective in the war against weeds and is ideal for spot treatment, when you have to kill a weed that's close to plants you want to protect. If you need to be especially careful of neighbouring plants, you can paint the weedkiller onto the leaf surface so as not to get any spillage anywhere else. The most common chemical used in systemic weedkiller is glyphosate.

Contact weedkillers

These do exactly what the name says: they kill on contact. Some are suitable for organic growers and are produced using a natural fatty acid that dissolves the protective coating on leaves, which means they dry out and die back. Other contact weedkillers are powerful chemicals that affect only exposed green material on a plant and aren't absorbed into the root system, meaning they're most effective on annual weeds. Diquat is a common chemical used in these types of weedkiller.

Residual weedkillers

Residual weedkillers are better kept well away from the allotment. As the name suggests, the chemical stays in the soil, killing off any seeds that germinate and perennials that pop up. These chemicals are useful on paths and driveways but are counterproductive on an allotment. Diflufenican is a common chemical used as a residual weedkiller.

Selective weedkillers

This is a term for a weedkiller that's specially formulated to target broad-leaved plants and doesn't kill narrow-leaved plants such as grass. This type of weedkiller is most useful for killing weeds in a lawn. Selective weed killers are absorbed into individual plants and will not kill off the narrow-leaved plants nearby. Glyphosate is a selective weedkiller that is also systemic.

Non-selective weedkillers

Non-selective weedkillers destroy broad- and narrow-leaved plants. They can be contact or systemic and are for blitzing and can be used to spot-treat (target) individual weeds. Diquat is non-selective and also a contact weedkiller.

Finally, always bear in mind the following safety tips:

- All chemical weedkillers should be handled with the utmost care, and all safety instructions should be followed rigorously. Many weedkillers are powerful chemicals that are damaging to the natural cycle of life. The laws regarding the use of these chemicals often change, so if you keep a bottle for a number of years, do check current laws to ensure that you're legal.
- You should never use weedkillers on windy or even breezy days, because the wind disperses the spray in all directions and you run the risk of spraying other precious plants on your own and, heaven forbid, your neighbours' plots. Also, you run the risk of the spray being blown back onto your skin or even of inhaling it, which can have damaging effects on your health.
- Wear appropriate safety clothing while spraying; this may include breathing apparatus and protective clothing, so do read the instructions and follow them carefully. Keep children and pets well clear of the area you're spraying and **never** mix weedkillers in drinks bottles, because the liquids can be mistaken for drinks.

Designing Your Space

One of the first jobs you can tackle when taking on a new allotment is the design of your space. In fact, one of the most important elements to a successful allotment is the layout. Every allotment and vegetable garden is different, as too are the external factors and personal requirements that influence them. The starting point in designing your plot is to decide what you're going to grow on it; it's pointless dedicating vast areas to potatoes if you don't really like them. Make a comprehensive list of what you'd like to grow and bear this in mind when you divide up your plot.

Considering your location

Your plot's location, aspect, access to light, incline and climate all affect what you can grow. Consider the points in the following sections when designing your layout.

Aspect

The aspect (whether it faces north, south, east or west) of a plot in my mind really doesn't matter too much. For example, if you have a more northerly facing plot on a sloping site, yes, it takes longer to warm up than a south-facing one, but you can still produce successful crops, and they really won't be that far behind those on a south-facing plot. Each aspect has its own benefits and drawbacks; it's down to the gardener to overcome them and make the most of his plot.

Shade

Light is crucial. Most fruit and veg need lots of sunshine and warmth to reach the optimum state in which they can be harvested. So you need to assess your plot and note if and when areas, or its entirety, are in shade. Hopefully this won't be an issue, but if you're on the edge of an allotment, you may find that shade affects you at some point. Some plants are more suited to a bit of afternoon shade, whereas others require full sun all day to thrive. You should note on your sketch of your plot which areas are in shade and at what point of the day, and plan your planting accordingly.

Lie of the land

The lie of the land also has an impact on your plot, sloping plots usually being more difficult to cultivate. Rainwater simply washes the topsoil downhill and with it all the nutrients in the remaining soil. Sloping sites also make gardening a real chore, so if this sounds like your plot, the answer is to *terrace* your plot. See the later section 'Terracing your plot for more on this.

Climate

What you can grow and when is very much down to which climate zone you live in and when spring arrives and winter descends. Down south, spring arrives a good few weeks earlier than in the far north, meaning that the soil warms up more quickly and that plants can be planted out earlier. Your knowledge of local weather trends is your guide to when spring is likely to appear each year, and this knowledge of your own locality will become like a sixth sense. For example, in the south, you can often put your tomatoes outside in mid- to late April, when the risk of frost has passed, but to do so in the north, with the risk of frost still at large, may well be condemning your plants to an early grave. Spring is arriving earlier each year, but once you get a greater understanding of the seasons, you soon learn how to best judge the situation.

Putting pen to paper

Now that you've thought long and hard about your plot and what you want in it, it's time to put pen to paper. You don't need to be an artist or even be able to draw to do this: all you need is a simple diagram so you're clear in your head what is going where. Being a garden designer, I'm a bit obsessive about measurements and accuracy, but in your case you can simply pace out your plot. Assume that one pace is around a metre (take big steps), or you can measure it properly (which is what I'd do!). On a piece of squared paper, draw the dimensions of your plot. Usually one square on the paper is 1 centimetre, so I suggest each square represents 1 metre or 0.5 metre, giving you a scale of 1:100 or 1:50 respectively. Draw the boundary on the page then draw in where the shed is and any existing features, trees and shrubs that you want to keep. Mark the shade where these features cast a shadow. You should also draw on the plan any neighbouring features that cast a shadow onto your plot. The next thing to do is to draw the path of the sun across your plot. This gives you a guide as to where to plant what. Using a compass, note which direction is north. Figure 5-1 shows a typical plan.

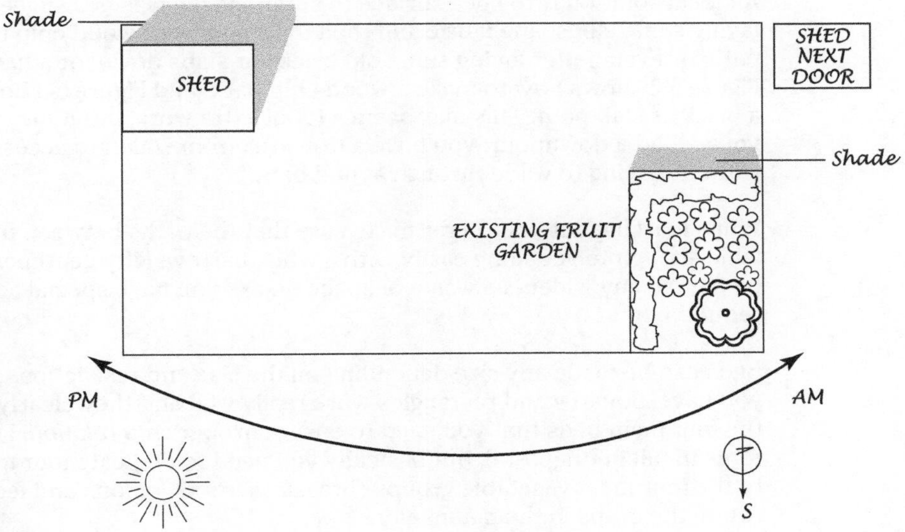

Figure 5-1: A typical allotment plan showing where shade falls.

Using the bed system

The traditional way of laying out a patch is into a succession of beds that are clearly set out for growing, with paths dividing them either side. Ideally, these beds should be narrow enough (a maximum of 1.2 metres wide) so that you can reach the middle of them from either side of the path. This is important because the more you need to tread on your precious soil, the more compact it becomes, damaging the soil structure (soil structure is discussed in Chapter 6). If you can avoid treading on your soil at all, you can aim to create 'no-dig' beds, where annual dressings of organic matter are laid on the ground for soil organisms to take down, rather than you having to dig it in.

Creating paths

The beds can be dug with no edging to retain the sides – in the traditional vegetable garden they're simply dug out in long rows. But by neatly edging these beds permanently, not only do you keep things nice and tidy but you also create a hard edge along which you can create paths. I simply use lengths of treated timber to edge the beds; this edge can then act as retainer for the path on the other side.

Paths can be left as bare soil and weeded as necessary. Many allotment gardens have grass paths running through the allotment that work just fine but do require some maintenance – and I'm all for keeping that to a minimum! All you need to do is lay some turf on bare soil along the paths and water it well during dry spells until it becomes established.

An ideal solution is to lay a surface to suppress the weeds. I suggest either laying some landscape fabric and then topping it with wood chip to create a path, or even better laying some old bricks or slabs down for a hard surface. Figure 5-2 shows how to make a wood-chip path, and Figure 5-3 how to make a brick or slab path. This may seem a lot of extra work, but it means that if you've had a downpour, you have a firm area from which to access the beds without having to wade through a mud bath.

When marking out your beds, make sure that the paths between them are wide enough to get along easily with a wheelbarrow. Fifty centimetres should be plenty; any wider is a waste of space unless you have special access requirements.

Beds can be made any size depending on the size and restrictions of the plot you have. Squares and rectangles work really well and they clearly define the four main beds that you need to ensure proper *crop rotation*. I cover this topic in full in Chapter 6, but basically you need to dedicate four main areas to the four main vegetable groups (brassicas, roots, onions and legumes) and rotate the crops in them annually.

You need not restrict yourself to only four main beds for the main crop-rotation vegetables; you also surely want to include beds for soft and hard fruit, herbs and possibly flowers. In addition, don't forget your shed, greenhouse and compost areas, all of which take up space.

I've seen allotments with all sorts of creative designs, from star-shaped beds to really ornate *potagers* (ornamental kitchen garden plots) divided up with neatly trimmed box hedge, but I prefer to keep it simple and leave the fancy stuff to someone else! Remember, this is a productive garden and there are no gold awards for your design skills (well, some allotments do hold competitions!).

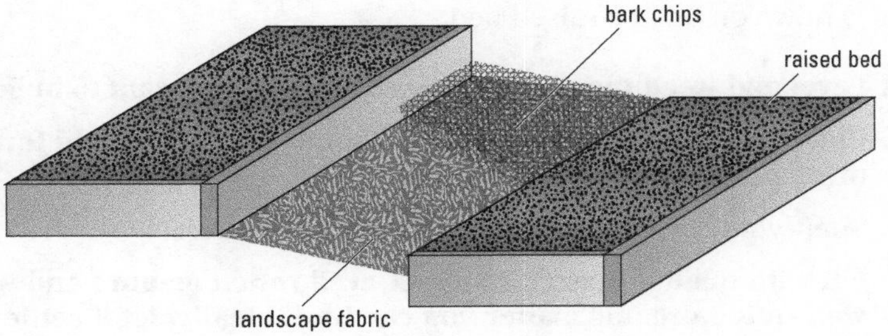

Figure 5-2: How to make a wood-chip path.

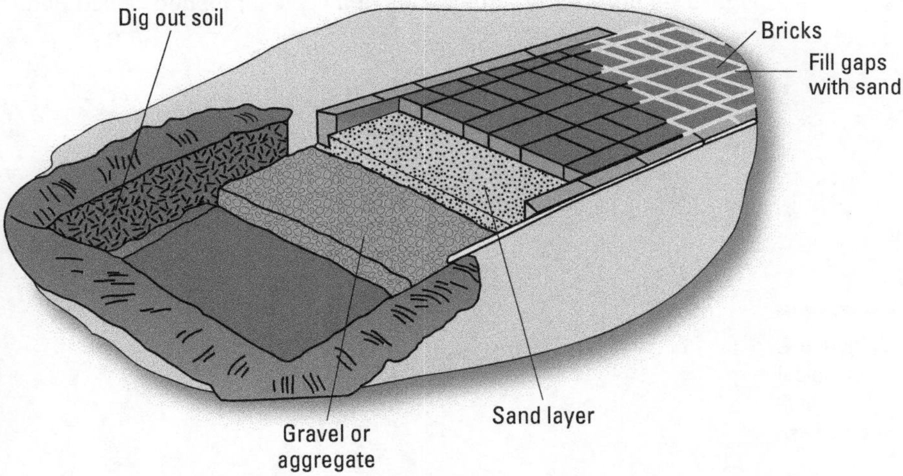

Figure 5-3: How to make a brick or slab path.

Building raised beds

Raised beds are usually created on an allotment using chunky timber, and are usually around 30 centimetres off the ground. Again, as with any bed, raised beds should only be as wide as can be reached from all sides, allowing easy access. Raised beds offer many advantages to the grower and, as so often with allotment gardening, an initial bit of hard work pays dividends in the future.

WARNING!

Reclaimed railway sleepers are not suitable for use on the allotment; they contain creosote, a tar-based preservative that is considered carcinogenic. These carcinogens can leach out of the sleepers into the soil and then be absorbed by the plants and finally consumed by you. EU guidelines state that reclaimed sleepers should not be used anywhere that comes into contact with any foodstuffs, so I don't risk it!

This is how you build a raised bed:

1. **Level and weed the area of bare soil where you want to build your bed.**
2. **Place the railway sleepers directly onto the ground and form a square or rectangle to the size required.**
3. **Simply nail, screw or bolt the timbers together.**
4. **Fill with quality topsoil, compost, well rotted manure and whatever well rotted organic matter you can find. Ideally, let it settle for a few weeks and you're ready to plant!**

Figure 5-4 shows the dimensions of a typical finished raised bed.

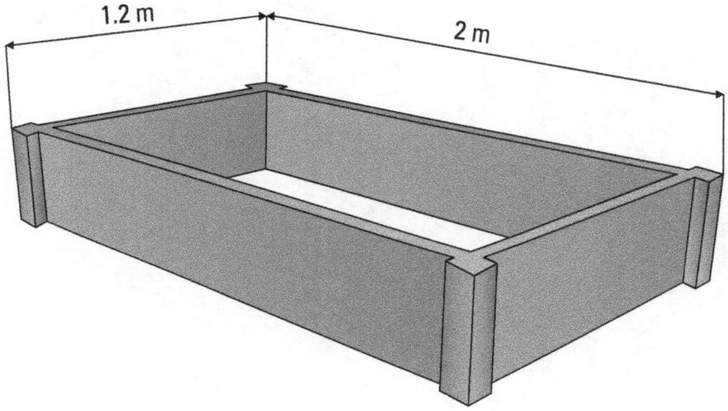

Figure 5-4: A typical raised bed.

The benefits of using raised beds are manifold. First, you can ensure that the topsoil you import is of top quality by buying it from a reputable supplier, and then add as much organic matter as needed without having to dig deep down as with double digging. Second, raised beds greatly improve drainage, because you are starting with new imported soil that has not been compacted underfoot, to which you can add organic matter that will also help the soil's water-retaining and drainage capabilities. Third, you'll have buried any weeds so deep under the beds that the only weed problems you're likely to incur are those brought in by the wind. Fourth, and most vital, in spring the soil warms up much more quickly than at ground level, offering you a more extended growing season than that in level beds.

TIP

My grandfather used to angle his raised beds between 5 and 10 degrees towards the sun, but don't worry about getting a protractor out and being exact – just a slight angle will do. This helps the beds warm up even more quickly in spring and is one of the most effective vegetable gardening tips. Aspect, on the whole, does not matter in the long run, because you can still grow stuff successfully, but if you can angle your beds, you can help the plants get as much light as possible, which is always beneficial.

Raised beds are often employed by organic gardeners, because they aim to disturb the delicate balance of the soil as little as possible. Raising the beds means you don't mess with the soil below, so all the beneficial micro-organisms, bacteria and fungi lay undisturbed. Another bonus is the fact that you have less bending to do – and believe me, anything that makes life easier on the allotment is worth its weight in gold!

Terracing your plot

Terracing your plot is an excellent way to overcome awkward slopes. Create a terrace by starting at the bottom of the slope and digging into the base of it, creating a series of steps. You will need to build retaining walls to stop the soil washing back down each step, and this is show in Figure 5-5.

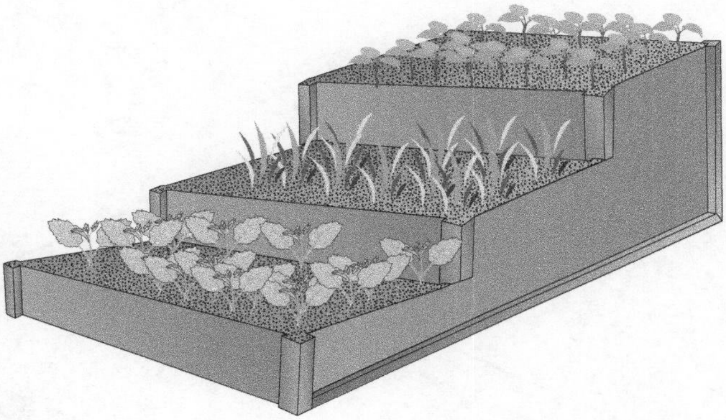

Figure 5-5: Terraced beds can help to overcome awkward slopes.

Creating support for climbers

Every allotment needs some kind of framework or trellis for climbing vegetables to grow up. These can look pretty cool as well and offer some shade for plants that need a little bit of protection during the heat of summer.

Pea and bean supports must be able to withstand the wind, so they do need to be fairly sturdy. The design and quality depends on whether supports will be in place for one season only, such as for peas and beans, or whether you will be growing longer-lasting crops.

For runner beans, the supports need to be at least 2.5 metres (around 8 feet) long, and you can use one of two methods of construction. The first method is probably the easiest:

1. **Push two parallel rows of 2.5-metre bamboo canes into the ground about 50 centimetres apart.** Tie the tops together with some garden wire, crossing the canes over each other to create a 'V' at the top.
2. **Place a horizontal cane along the top, resting in the 'V'.**
3. **Tie each vertical cane to the horizontal cane along the top to secure it in place.**

Figure 5-6 shows the result.

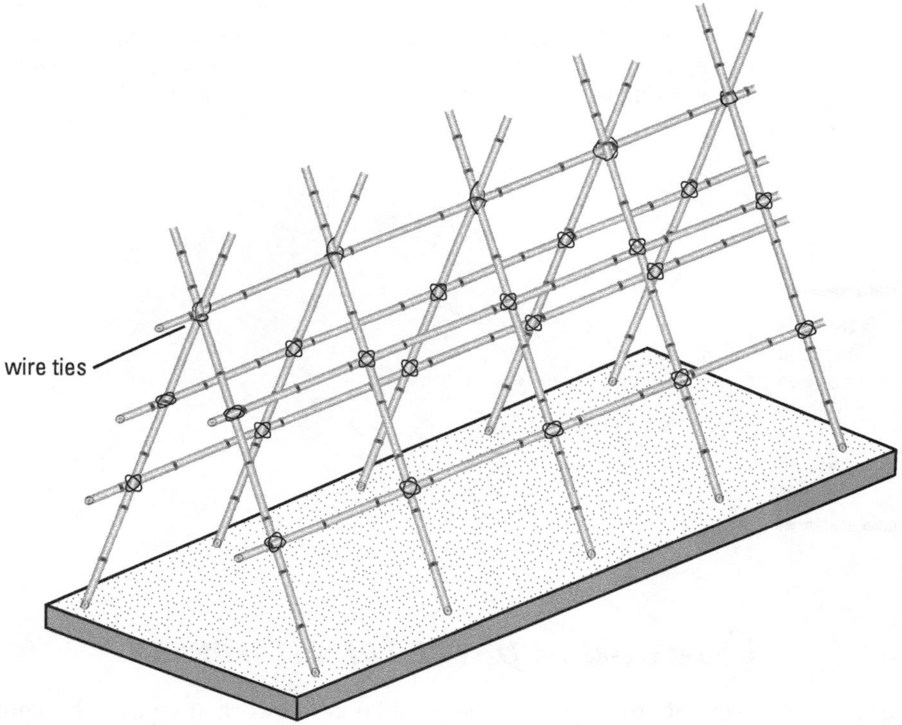

Figure 5-6: A bean support, made from canes.

For the second method:

1. **Ram two 7.5 centimetre diameter-round pointed poles vertically into the ground about 2.5 metres apart.**
2. **Attach a horizontal pole or length of 5–8 centimetre -diameter timber at the top.** Secure it firmly using some screws or simply nail it on.
3. **Attach bean netting with 12.5-centimetre-square holes to the inside.**

You can buy bean netting online or from garden centres; it usually comes on a roll and is bought by the linear metre.

Figure 5-7 shows a netting support.

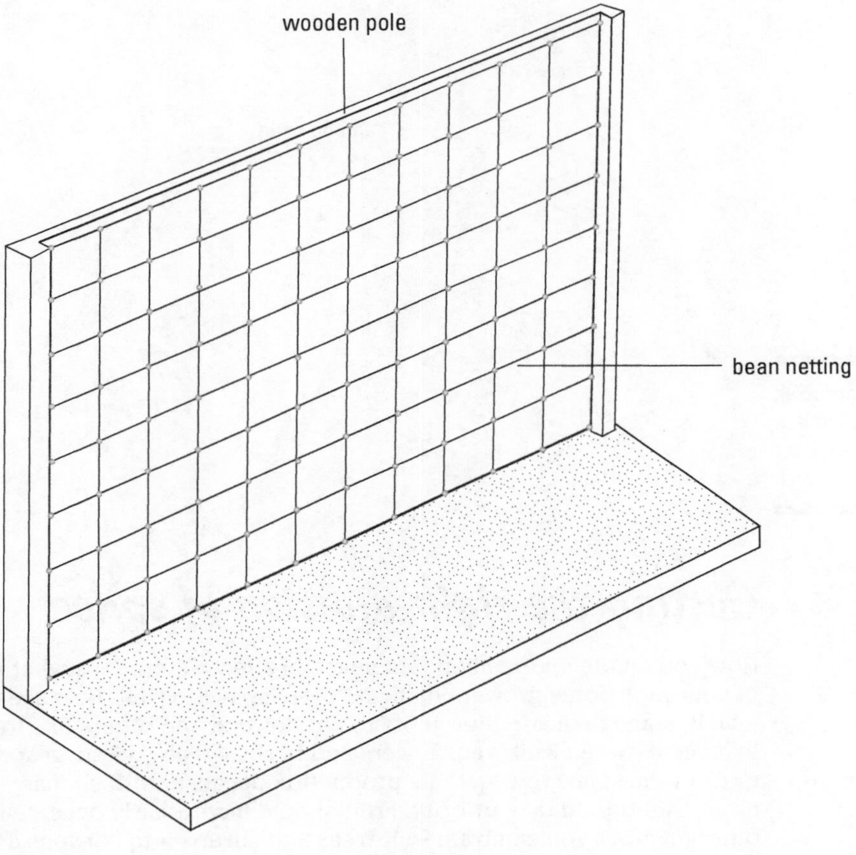

Figure 5-7: A bean support using netting.

If space is very limited, you can erect bamboo wigwams consisting of four or more 2.5 metre upright canes in a 60 centimetre circle tied at the top. See Figure 5-8.

For peas, there's a tried-and-tested method using pea sticks, which you can't beat for simplicity. Pea sticks are simply brushwood twigs, but you can use any twigs that you can find as long as they have plenty of little branches.

Peas and French beans also grow up netting on supports in a similar way.

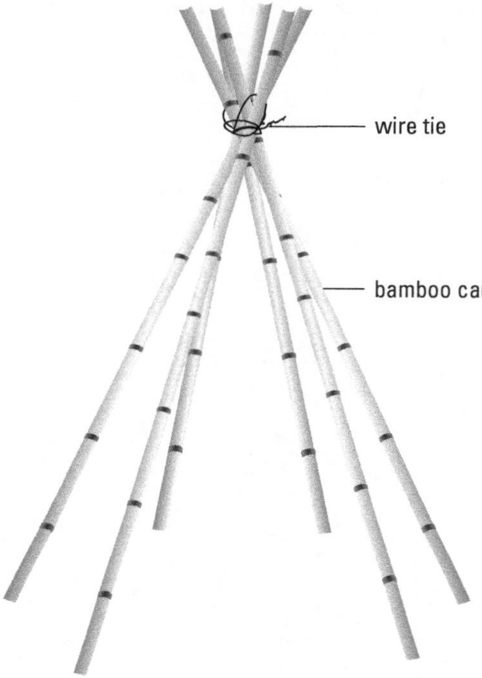

Figure 5-8: A bamboo wigwam for beans.

Getting the right division of space

How you divide up the allotment space in effect determines what you get out of your plot. Some growers dedicate more space to fruit, because they simply love it; some dedicate their plots to cut flowers, and others like to have a balance between fruit, veg, flowers and herbs. I'd always suggest dedicating most of the space to vegetable production because, with so many varieties to grow, this should take priority. Fruit should have a fairly decent-sized area, but remember you can train fruit trees and shrubs into cordons and espaliers in order to save on space, and can even buy dwarf and *step-over* varieties (which are trained no higher than you can step over) for the same purpose. (I cover fruit growing in more detail in Chapter 17.)

I'd divide the allotment into five and dedicate one area to fixed crops such as fruit bushes, herbs and flowers, and the rest become the four main rotating beds. I recommend the four-bed system even if you have a half or quarter share of an allotment, because it doesn't take any more work to make four small beds than one large one. Either position these beds in rows or in a large square or rectangle with a path criss-crossing it in the middle. You decide how much space you dedicate to each type of crop, so you need to have figured out what you want from your allotment.

Chapter 6

Keeping Your Soil Healthy

In This Chapter

- Assessing the soil you've got
- Improving and maintaining your soil
- Creating compost
- Rotating crops

Soil is amazing stuff and should be looked after and treated with care and respect. It's basically made of tiny particles of rock and organic matter, and also contains all sorts of bacteria, other living organisms and minerals. The rotted down *organic matter* is called *humus* and is the most vital ingredient in creating a rich, productive soil. Decent soil is absolutely vital when it comes to having a successful allotment. It provides the food, water and some of the air that plants need to grow, so the quality of that soil determines how well your plants will do. Assessing your soil type is not hard, although improving your soil does requires some graft. This pays dividends during the growing season, however.

When plants grow, they suck up water and, more importantly, nutrients from the soil. If these elements aren't replaced, the soil eventually becomes lifeless and barren. It's therefore really important that you understand what soil is made of and how it works so that you can get off to a good start and if you encounter any problems, you can fix them. This chapter shows you how to figure out what soil you have and provides the recipe for soil success.

Assessing Your Soil Type

Before you begin planting, you need to work out what type of soil your allotment plot has. Soil type affects what you can and can't grow. Although you can add organic matter and certain chemical compounds to alter your soil's composition, in reality you won't be able to change it forever. However, you can vastly improve the quality of your soil. The following sections describe various soil types and how to work out what your allotment is made of.

Discovering what soil is made of

Without the effects of weather, soil wouldn't exist. When rocks warm up they expand, and when they get cold they contract; this constant change eventually causes them to crack. Water then gets into these cracks and freezes, causing the rocks to break up. Wind and rain and the erosive effects of running and tidal waters all help to erode and grind these rocks up into small particles, and this is the basis of what soil is made of. These particles vary in size greatly from large stones down to the very smallest, the particles which make up clay.

The mineral particles don't really add much nutritional value to the soil, because they can't be dissolved in water; it's the dead and decaying animal and plant life that provides most of the nutrients. Plant matter, dead animals and their excrement all add organic goodness to this otherwise infertile rock dust, and it's this organic gold that helps plant life grow and prosper.

Topsoil and *subsoil* are terms you will come across often as a gardener:

- **Topsoil** is the uppermost layer of soil on your plot. It usually contains the most organic matter and can vary in depth from a few centimetres in certain regions to many feet in others. It is usually darker in colour than the subsoil due to its higher organic content.
- **Subsoil** is the layer below the topsoil. Unless you live in an area with very shallow topsoil, the subsoil should not affect you very much. Subsoil is usually lighter in colour and more compact, often containing more stones or, in clay areas, being much more sticky and harder to work. Subsoil can usually be improved with the addition of organic matter.

Understanding different soil types

Your local area will have its own distinct soil type. The rock type in your local area strongly influences the soil on your allotment. Soil is generally classified according to the clay, silt, sand and chalk present in it. These elements affect the qualities that particular soils possess. No two soils are ever exactly the same but, as a rough guide, soil can be classified in the following ways. Figure 6-1 shows you the three basic types.

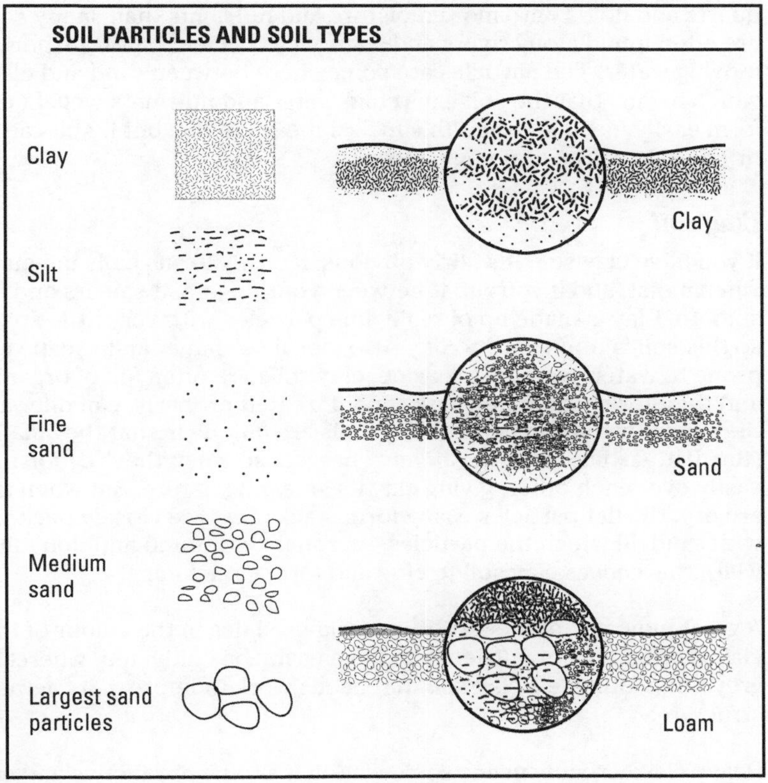

Figure 6-1: Basic soil types.

Sandy soil

This soil type is usually made up of varying levels of ground-up rock such as limestone, quartz, granite and shale. Sandy soil has a gritty texture when you rub it between your fingers. Sandy soils have a few problems that can be overcome with the right treatment. They tend to be *free draining*, which means that they don't hold onto water well and can dry out quickly. Because of this free draining quality, nutrients leach out quickly, often reducing the fertility of sandy soil. But having said that, if you add plenty of organic matter such as well rotted farmyard manure to a sandy soil, you can overcome both these problems and create a great medium for growing fruit and veg. The big benefit of sandy soils is that they warm rapidly in spring, so you can get going with early crops.

Silty soil

Silt soil is often regarded as almost top of the pile (after loam; see below) when it comes to fertility. It has a less gritty texture than sandy soil, feeling a little like flour, and is darker in colour. This soil is mostly made up of quartz and holds onto more moisture and nutrients than sandy soil. Silt soils are often found along rivers and waterways because silt transports easily in moving water. The particles are somewhere between sand and clay in size, which means that the soil can retain water and nutrients well. Lumps don't form easily in silt soil, and this makes it easy to dig, but it still can become dry due to its free-draining nature.

Clay soil

If you have clay soil, it's fairly obvious: it easily forms balls in your hand when moist, and if you rub it between your fingers, it smears and feels quite smooth. Clay is made up of really fine particles with very little space for air, so this soil is often hard to dig. Also, because water can't escape easily, it's prone to waterlogging. This aside, clay soils are often full of organic matter and therefore high in nutrients, and if treated properly, can offer a really fertile soil with good structure. Clay soils are unique in that the small *platelets* (tiny flat particles) are negatively charged, so when they're moist, they slide easily over each other, giving clay its smearing nature. But when the particles are dry, the flat particles easily form stacks that are closely packed (unlike with sand, in which the particles are rough and round and don't fit together well); this causes clay soil to clog and form large lumps.

A great indicator of the fertility of a clay soil lies in the colour of the clay: red clay is often high in nutrients and can easily be cultivated, whereas blue and grey often indicate a clay soil that needs work to improve its aeration and structure.

TIP

Heavy clay certainly needs some work if it's to be productive and easier to work. The best option, as ever, is to add loads of well rotted organic matter in the autumn, which helps improve the structure, which in turn lessens problem wetness and makes the soil easier to work.

Loam soil

Loam is the king of soils and what all gardeners dream of in terms of its fertility, workability and nutrient content. Loam is very roughly made up of 40 per cent sand, 40 per cent silt and 20 per cent clay, giving it all the best characteristics of each of the soil types and few of the drawbacks. Loam soil doesn't get waterlogged but holds on to moisture well; this means that it retains its nutrient content making it ideal for cultivation. Loam soil feels neither overly gritty or sticky and has a fine crumbly texture and often a sweet smell.

Chalky soil

Chalky soil is probably the worst soil for cultivation and needs a lot of work to get right. Chalk is a sedimentary rock high in calcium carbonate, which dissolves easily in water and ups the alkaline levels considerably. The presence of this alkalinity renders some trace elements such as iron and magnesium unavailable to the roots of plants; this often causes mineral deficiency, which can be diagnosed, for example, by the yellowing of the leaves. Chalk soils are usually light brown, fairly shallow and full of stones. All things considered, they are pretty tough to work with.

TIP

Chalk soils can be improved in a number of ways, mainly by adding bulky organic matter to improve the soil's nutrient content and water retention. A wheelbarrow-load dug in every 2.5 square metres should be adequate. This soil type can further benefit from *deep mulching* (spreading organic matter thickly on the surface), which will continue to help the problem.

TIP

A rough guide to the soil type you have in your area is the water that comes out of your tap. If you have limescale problems and find deposits in your kettle and around your taps, you're in a hard water area and probably have an alkaline (limey) soil. If your water is soft, you're more likely to be on an acid soil. This is only a rough guide but can prove reasonably accurate.

Checking your soil's pH level

Acidity and alkalinity are measured on the *pH* scale. Soil has a natural pH level that's measured on a scale from 0 to 14, 0 being really acidic and 14 highly alkaline; 7 (in the middle) is often called *neutral*. In terms of the garden, you rarely find any soil outside pH 4–8.5.

The pH level directly affects the nutrients in the soil and which of those are available for the plant to absorb. Most plants prefer a neutral soil of around pH 7, but others such as strawberries prefer slightly acidic (*ericaceous*) soil, and the *brassicas* (broccoli, cauliflower, cabbage, Brussels sprouts and the like) prefer slightly alkaline (limey) soil. Your soil's pH directly affects which plants you can grow. You can adjust the pH levels slightly to suit certain plants, but in reality you need to work with the soil you have and therefore should plant accordingly.

Using testing kits

pH tests are available in all good garden centres and DIY stores and are really simple to use. I prefer a test tube test, which you use like this:

1. **Dig three or four small test holes in different parts of your allotment.**
2. **Discard the top 8 centimetres (around 3 inches) of soil and take some small samples from deeper within the holes.**
3. **Mix the samples together, crumbling the soil into a fine texture, and spread it on a tray to dry (it dries quickly on a radiator).**
4. **Put some of the soil in the tube provided, together with the powder or chemical in the kit.**

5. **Add some deionised water (available in supermarkets, garden centres and DIY stores) or bottled water (tap water is more likely to affect the test results because of its chemical and mineral content).**
6. **Put the lid on, give it a good shake and leave it for a minute or so.**
7. **Check the colour of the sample against the chart provided.**

Usually, yellow or orange means you have an acid soil, bright green is neutral and dark green is alkaline.

You can also buy electronic probes for reading soil pH. They usually cost a little more than the chemical kits but can be used over and over again, and are quick and simple to use. To check your soil with a probe:

1. **Dig three or four test holes in the garden and discard the top 8 centimetres of soil.**
2. **Crumble up the soil in the holes and get rid of any stones and other debris.**
3. **Fill the hole with water and let it drain.**
4. **Stick the probe in the wet soil in each hole for a minute then read the results.**
5. **Note the readings from each hole, from which you can work out the average pH level.**

You can buy kits that contain everything you need to test the pH and also specific nutrients in the soil. They usually test for nitrogen, phosphorus and potassium, and can be a great guide when it comes to improving your soil. You can also buy very specific tests for trace elements such as boron and magnesium, and these can be useful for assessing specific problems with plants.

Adjusting Your Soil's pH

You can temporarily adjust your soil's pH to a degree by adding certain chemicals, some of which can be organic.

Making your soil more alkaline

If you want to raise pH levels (that is, make the soil more alkaline) you can add lime. This is usually available in various forms in garden centres and can be invaluable on the allotment. At the risk of contradicting myself regarding adding organic matter to soil, doing so may mean you may actually lessen the available nutrients by raising the acid levels. This situation can be counterbalanced by the addition of lime. Lime is alkaline and lowers the pH levels, thus releasing the locked nutrients and making them available to the plants.

WARNING! Avoid hydrated lime, which is caustic and damaging, both to you and to existing plants. Instead use ground lime, which is far safer and can be used around existing plants. The downside is that it takes twice as long as hydrated lime to be effective – six to eight months. Hardwood ash, bone meal, crushed oyster shells and spent mushroom compost can all also raise pH levels.

WARNING! Never use lime and fertiliser at the same time; leave it at least four months, but ideally a year, between applications. When you add bicarbonate of soda to a fizzy drink, you get a very gassy reaction. The same happens to lime and fertiliser: the combination produces a nasty gas called ammonia that takes the nitrogen from the soil and turns it back into gas, which disappears into the atmosphere, undoing all your hard work. Combining the two also renders both the lime and fertiliser useless.

Making your soil more acidic

To lower the pH of your soil and thus make it more acidic, you need to add aluminium sulphate (which is quick working) or sulphur, both of which can be bought at the garden centre. Follow the instructions on the packet carefully to ensure that the product you use is right for your soil type. Aluminium sulphate is the quickest method because it's soluble and instantly increases the soil's pH, but the effects can be short-lived. Sulphur takes longer to be absorbed, and because the process is slower, so too are the effects. The fact is that raising your soil's pH levels is no easy task, and the effects are generally only temporary, whatever method you adopt. You can also try sawdust, composted leaves, wood chip and leaf mould, all of which lower pH and raise acidity.

REMEMBER You can't permanently adjust soil pH levels. You can temporarily improve conditions for certain plants you want to grow and correct things when they go wrong, but these improvement methods take months, sometimes even years. Your best bet is working with the soil you have.

TIP If you want to create zones in which to grow plants that require specific conditions, you can install raised beds using soil created to suit their needs (see Chapter 5 on how to create a raised bed). For example, blueberries and strawberries like a more acidic soil, so by installing a raised bed for them and using an ericaceous compost you cater specifically for their needs.

Assessing Organic Matter

Organic matter is material that was once alive and, in terms of the garden, consists mainly of plant material. As plant material grows, it absorbs goodness from the soil, and so by returning plants to the soil, you're returning valuable nutrients. When leaves fall from plants or when plants die, they begin to rot down into unrecognisable organic matter and continue to rot until you're left with *humus*. This humus is basically the food that the next generation of plants will feed upon. Now this is all well and good in a natural cycle, like that of a forest, but on an allotment this process is never completed, because we consume the plants thus breaking the cycle.

Humus is generally recognised as the dark matter that makes your topsoil black or dark brown, and it's this dark colour that helps your soil warm up in the spring. Humus is full of nutrients and, amazingly, can hold up to 80–90 per cent of its own weight in water. This makes humus essential for your soil, which needs to retain water.

The best way to look at your soil is to consider it a breathing organism that needs feeding and watering, just like a living thing. The complex microbiological processes that help make your soil healthy need to be encouraged and protected if your soil is to remain productive. The micro-organisms and insects that live in the soil work tirelessly, recycling organic matter and moving around in the soil, all of which helps create space between the particles, where water and air can move freely. Ideally, soil contains around 25 per cent oxygen, which means space is needed between the soil particles to make room for the oxygen. Without getting too complicated, beneficial micro-organisms also need this oxygen to survive, and if your soil is compacted, this restricts or even eliminates the available oxygen for plant roots and these creatures. This restriction can in turn render the soil *anaerobic* (lacking air) and infertile.

Maintaining Soil Structure

Soil structure is a term used to describe how the soil clumps together; it refers to how the soil particles are arranged and how easily the soil can be cultivated. Ideally, your soil should have no large clods (lumps) and be light and *friable* (crumbly). The state of your soil structure is directly affected by the ingredients of that soil, such as the clay, sand and organic content. Soil that has a good structure is easy to cultivate because its crumbly nature means roots can penetrate well, seeds can germinate easily in the top layer, and there's plenty of oxygen available to roots and beneficial organisms. Also, water is able to penetrate down to the plants' roots.

Soil structure deteriorates naturally the more the soil is cultivated and tampered with. Compaction by foot and even heavy rain breaks down the precious soil structure. Soil with a hard crust on top adds to the effect of soil erosion, because water can't penetrate and so washes off along the surface, slowly taking with it the precious topsoil. The effect of watering and rain can also wash the fine clay particles present in the soil down to form hard pans of clay below the topsoil. The clay pans can become impervious to water and cause waterlogging problems, so the pans need to be broken up by double digging. Avoid cultivating unimproved wet clay soil with a rotavator, as this can also create more problems than it solves. The blades (if they don't bounce off the surface) will smear the surface of the clods the rotavator cuts through, making them impenetrable to water. This makes the soil structure even worse.

Getting the Low-Down on Nutrients

Nutrients are needed by all plant life in order to grow. The three main elements needed are nitrogen (N), phosphorus (P) and potassium (K), referred to together as NPK. Trace elements such as iron, boron, copper, manganese, molybdenum and zinc are also needed to promote healthy growth. Plants that are only provided with N, P and K will become weak and over the years become less resistant to disease.

In the past, the only available fertilisers were organic ones such as horse manure, which were used in abundance. These are high in NPK but not all the trace elements. This led to problems with disease and overly lush, weak growth, so plants were developed to be more disease resistant and cope with less than perfect conditions. This in the long run is great, because we have now inherited these strong plants. But trace elements are important to the long term health of your plot. For example, if the soil has a lack of boron, your swedes and turnips will suffer with a certain kind of rot in the centre of the root, which can only be rectified by the addition of a fertiliser containing boron. We now know that we need to concentrate on not only the main three elements, but these trace elements as well.

Nitrogen for leaves, stems and shoots

Nitrogen has the most dramatic effect on plants, more so than any other element. In particular, it is responsible for lush leaf growth and helps develop branches and stems. Nitrogen does occur naturally in soil as a product of decomposed plant matter and animal waste products, but most of it exists as a gas in the atmosphere. Most gaseous nitrogen can't be absorbed by plants until it becomes fixed. *Fixing* is a process in which bacteria in the soil combine the gaseous nitrogen with hydrogen from water to produce ammonia. The bacteria work on the ammonia further and it becomes a form of nitrogen that plants can easily absorb. Some plants such as *legumes* (peas and beans) have naturally occurring nitrogen-fixing bacteria on their roots that process the nitrogen and turn it into a form that is available to plants.

You can get nitrogen fertilisers in many forms, some organic and others that are inorganic, but they need to be used with real care. The bacteria in soil naturally fix the nitrogen from the air and also from manures as they get to work on them. By adding artificial chemical nitrates, you undermine the job these bacteria do and eventually you run the risk of eradicating these helpful and important bacteria altogether. This is because the chemicals you add replace the process the bacteria perform.

Nitrogen fertilisers are available in concentrated organic forms such as blood meal and chicken manure, which I always recommend in any garden.

Warnings aside, nitrogen does have some very important uses on the allotment. For example, during spring, any plants from the brassica family that need a boost benefit greatly from a dose of nitrogen-rich feed to give the plants vitality. I always advise that you add nitrogen, but only in the form of bulky organic matter such as well rotted farm manure, a green manure or by growing a leguminous crop that fixes the nitrogen. For the health of your soil, it's always cheaper and better to let nature do the work for you. However, on free-draining soils where the nutrients are washed out readily by rain, you are likely to need to add fertiliser in order to produce good crops.

Phosphorus for seed germination and roots

Phosphorus helps to promote healthy root growth and helps plants to *photosynthesise.* It also helps convert other chemicals such as nitrogen into food. A lack of phosphorus leads to stunted growth and less produce, so it's an important element for the allotment gardener. However, most soils don't suffer from a lack of this element, so it should only really be needed when a specific problem arises.

Animal manure should contain plenty of phosphorus for your plants' needs, but if you find your plants suffer from stunted growth or a lack of productivity, you may need to intervene. Allotmenteers usually add phosphorus in the form of bone meal or superphosphate, both of which can be bought from any good garden centre. But saying that, most compound fertilisers (which contain a mix of nutrients) contain enough phosphorus to cover all your gardening needs.

Phosphates, if used in large quantities, have some negative effects. They can bind with the surface soil and produce a hard cap, which water runs off. In addition, if a lot of phosphorus gets into a pond or lake, for example, it can encourage algae to flourish, suffocating other plant life.

Potassium for fruit and flowers

Commonly delivered in the form of potash, not only is potassium really beneficial for root crops and fruiting plants, it also has other benefits such as toughening woody growth on fruiting trees and bushes, which helps them withstand the cold. Potassium is mainly used to promote flowers and fruit and is usually added in late summer, when it will encourage plants to form flower buds that will open the next year and go on to produce fruit.

Farmyard manure should contain plenty of potassium for your needs, but if you require a dose of potassium, then wood ash from a fire is a really rich source. Alternatively, get some sulphate of potash from the garden centre.

Creeping Around with Helpful Beasts

Your soil needs to be treated as a living, breathing entity that has a complex combination of organic and non-organic matter. It needs to be kept in good health. The soil includes billions of bacteria, and other living organisms, and you need to look after them.

Without these living things, the soil surface would simply be covered in a layer of leaves and organic matter. It's the living organisms in soil that act as a natural recycling plant, returning the organic matter back to where it came from and turning it into nutrients that the plants can use.

Bacteria

Bacteria in soil are absolutely invaluable, and there are millions of bacteria living on, in and around the plants roots. One gram of soil can contain up to three billion of the micro-organisms. Bacteria are single-celled organisms and are responsible for many processes that ensure soil health and fertility:

- They help fix nitrogen from the air and turn it into a form that plants can absorb. See the section 'Nitrogen for leaves, stems and shoots' earlier in this chapter.

- Some forms, in the process of nitrogen fixation, actually create the same amount of free nitrogen and return it into the atmosphere.
- Some, known as *actinobacteria*, are responsible for decomposing organic matter into humus (see earlier in this chapter) , which gives life to your plants. Gardeners often say that great garden soil has a sweet smell; it is the presence of actinobacteria that gives the soil that sweetness.

Fungi

Fungi are present in vast numbers in healthy garden soil; they include yeast and moulds that feed on organic waste thus turning it into food that becomes available to your plants. Fungi spread underground using long white strands called *mycelia* – if you disturb the surface on a healthy compost heap, you see these white strands going through your compost.

Mycorrhizae are a form of fungus that are extraordinary in terms of how they assist other plants to grow. They form a network of fibres under the soil, which, in effect, links the roots of all the plants in your garden. This almost physically links all your plants, effectively creating one vast root and extending the feeding capabilities of the plant. Fungus doesn't photosynthesise, so when it attaches to the roots of plants, its action creates a kind of exchange of labour: the fungus helps the plants absorb more water and nutrients, and the plants turn them into food that the fungus can use.

The only problem with mycorrhizae is that an allotment garden is continually dug over and constantly being cultivated, so this kind of fungus only really works on the no-dig allotment (which I cover in more depth in 'Using the no-dig method' later in this chapter) and more specifically with plants that live permanently on the allotment, such as fruit trees and bushes and some herbs. Mycorrhizae treatments can now be purchased from garden centres and are incorporated into a planting hole or pot. They can greatly benefit plants including tomatoes, pumpkins, capsicum, onions and many other allotment crops and plants in your garden.

Winning with worms

Worms are an allotmenteer's best friends (and you may well find yourself talking to them!). They are scavengers that feast on organic matter and then disperse it through the soil. As they go, they aerate by tunnelling, improving the structure and water-holding capabilities of the soil.

Worms do a lot of the work in your compost heap when it comes to breaking down the organic matter into a state that's suitable to be used in the garden, so it makes perfect sense to have composters that use worm power to produce great compost. This process is called *vermicompost*. Hundreds of different products are available, from indoor wormeries up to 300-litre boxes that are best suited for allotment use. When worms eat organic matter, they leave behind them what are known as *worm casts*, which are basically processed organic matter that's really high in nutrients. In fact, a worm cast has up 11 times the NPK content of the soil that the worm consumed in the first place to produce the worm cast. On their own, worm casts should be used sparingly around plants because they're pretty potent stuff – but probably the best natural fertiliser you'll ever get!

Wormeries need a temperature between 12 and 23 °C to work effectively, so they may need some winter protection to remain active. When you order your wormery, you receive the container, a bag of worms and a medium to which you add the worms to get things going. The container is usually a recycled plastic bin with a tap at the bottom for draining moisture. (This liquid makes a great plant feed or compost accelerator!). Often you're advised to add a layer of gravel and then shredded newspaper to the bottom of the container to help drainage and retain water respectively. You then add the starting medium with the worms, and then add your kitchen waste. You should never add more than 6 inches (15 centimetres) of waste at a time, and it helps to put a layer of damp newspaper or compost on top to help retain moisture. You should let the worms completely devour each layer of waste before adding more, to ensure that the process is effective. You can use the worm compost periodically, as you need it, by sieving out the worms from the top and throwing them back in, but either way once the container is full, you need to sieve the worms out and start the process again.

WARNING!

To encourage great worm castings, you need to avoid a few pitfalls:

- **Don't let the wormery get too hot or too cold.** If the temperature exceeds 35 degrees centigrade for any long period, you'll cook the worms (which is both unkind and stinks!). If they get too cold, cover them with an old blanket to keep them warm.
- **Don't rush things.** It can take two to three months to get the conditions perfect for the worms' new home.
- **Don't put too much kitchen waste in at once.** It's far better to under fill it than overfill it.
- **Don't add cooked food or meat to the wormery.** It'll turn rancid.
- **Don't add citrus peelings or flesh.** These can turn the wormery too acidic.
- **Don't add tap water.** Ideally, collect rainwater; it doesn't contain chlorine, which can affect the organism working within the composter.

Admiring creepy-crawlies

There are all sorts of other insects on and in the soil that forage and consume organic waste; others burrow and dig around, but both add to the nutrient soup and help with soil structure. Take ground beetles, for example. They consume chafer grubs, fruit flies, aphids and even slugs so they play a vital role in the whole circle of life involved in creating plain old garden mud! Some are not so beneficial, such as the chafer grubs which feast on a plant's roots, but as they're on the menu for ground beetles, they too have an important role to play in you soil's ecosystem. So be careful if you resort to chemical sprays to control pests, because they can kill beneficial critters too!

ORGANIC WAY

Unless absolutely impossible, always try adopting an organic and sustainable method of gardening: pesticides and fertilisers all interfere with the careful balance of nature. This applies critically to your soil. If you encourage nature and work with it, nature in turn works for you, feeding, protecting and promoting an all-round healthy plot. This way of working will give you much better results in the long run.

Improving Your Soil

All allotment holders strive to have the best soil they can possibly create, and each one will have her own methods of achieving this. Most soils need improving in some way to boost the nutrient levels or to improve the structure of the soil. Each different soil type needs slightly different alterations to what needs to be added in order to improve its growing potential, but always remember that even the poorest of soils can be cultivated. At worst, you can create raised beds (see Chapter 5) and import new soil.

Adding organic matter

Many different theories exist about how soil should be treated in the allotment garden: some advocate double digging, crop rotation, and intensive cultivation using fertilisers, whereas others advocate the no-dig method and letting nature take the reins.

The basic fact is that plants need a constant supply of the correct nutrients and water, and whatever the method you adopt, this still applies. The best way to provide this is by adding well rotted organic matter.

Where there's muck . . .

You can buy all sorts of organic soil improvers, which can be pretty expensive, so the best option is to find a local source of *manure*. Now this manure needs to be well rotted and dark in colour, and is usually steaming and warm . . . mmmm . . . sounds nice, I know, but this stuff is great! If you search local farms, the Internet or classifieds, you're sure to find a local source. To be honest, it can be a bit of a slog going to pick the stuff up, so if you can pay to get it delivered, I'd certainly advise you to. You can even ask around the allotment and share a load with another plot holder.

If you're starting a new allotment, you won't have an established compost heap, but in the years to come, the one you create will be your source of organic mater.

The best time to establish a new plot and dig in the organic matter is in late autumn before the ground turns hard. If you incorporate the organic matter during this time, the winter frost helps break up the large clods and incorporate the organic matter for you. This applies mainly but not exclusively to heavy soil such as clay, but if you miss this opportunity, don't worry too much, and just dig in a load before planting.

Double digging and single digging

Double digging is the best way to improve drainage and at the same time add organic matter to your plot. Now some people argue that it disturbs the soil too much, so if this is you, don't fret – I discuss the no-dig method later on in this chapter. Double digging is usually done only when you are establishing a new plot, so thankfully you only have to do it once.

Double digging is really hard work and is best described by imagining two layers of soil, each a spade's blade deep. You need to dig the first spade's depth out, fork organic matter into the second layer and then put the top layer back again. This method of digging is ideal for heavy clay soils where the deep penetration of organic matter can significantly improve drainage, nutrient levels and, most importantly, the soil structure. It also benefits sandy soils by improving water retention and nutrient levels, and improves the structure by adding bulk to an otherwise light soil. Follow these steps:

1. **Mark out a large rectangle on the soil surface and then imagine it as a grid with two columns each divided into 30-centimetre-wide sections.**
2. **Dig out the first section to one spade's depth – known as a *spit* – and set the soil to one side.**

3. **Add a spade or two of organic matter and fork it well into the lower layer.**
4. **Dig the next section in front back into the previous section.**
5. **Continue this process until you reach the end of the rectangle.**
6. **Barrow the soil from the first trench you dug into the last and ensure that the area is level.**
7. **Allow the area to settle; ideally you double-dig in autumn ready for planting in spring.**

Figure 6-2 shows how it's done.

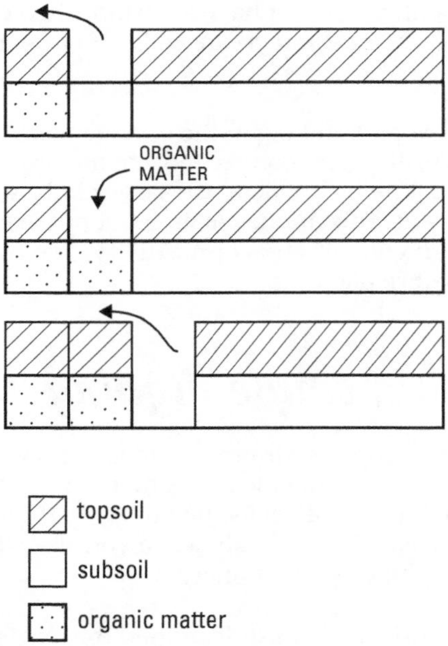

Figure 6-2: Double digging.

Single digging is far more straightforward and involves the same rectangular grid but only working on the top spade's depth. It's ideal when the soil needs a boost of nutrients, and a load of organic matter is required. Follow these steps:

1. **Dig out trenches to a spade's depth and about 30 centimetres wide.**
2. **Place the soil from the first trench on the ground in front and work backwards along the plot, turning the soil from each subsequent trench into the one in front.**
3. **Incorporate organic matter if desired by spreading it in the trench then burying it under the next spit of soil.**

Figure 6-3 demonstrates each step.

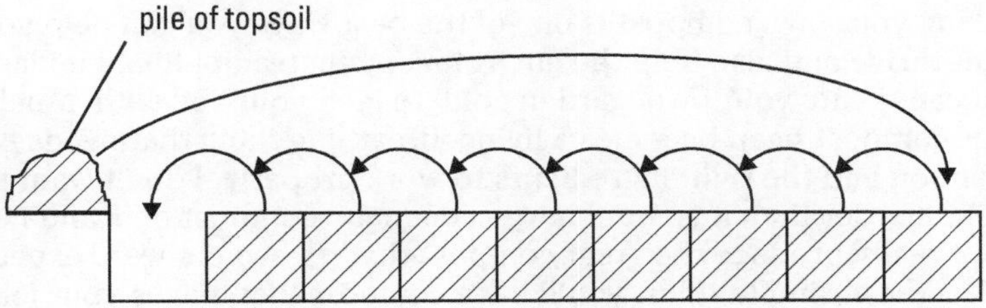

Figure 6-3: Single digging.

Using the no-dig method

No-dig systems work best if you create a bed system with 1.2-metre wide beds, accessed from paths. These beds are double-dug once only; then in future years, organic matter is spread on the surface as described later in this section. However, it's vital that you do not tread on the soil or compact it, otherwise digging will indeed become necessary.

The no-dig method is becoming more popular on allotments all over the country, and in its simplest form involves covering the entire growing area with thick layers of organic matter or compost, year upon year. This layer needs to be at least 5 centimetres deep and is best spread in autumn each year, allowing time for nature to take its course and incorporate it naturally into the soil. This method is often employed by organic gardeners who swear by the fact that the less you disturb the soil the better, because it leaves the micro-organisms and delicate balance undisturbed. On the allotment, these gardeners are often called *no-diggers*, and many have great success with this method. It's ideal for those who can't face the hard graft of double and single digging and for those who are less physically able.

The main problem is the amount of compost that you get through. To cover an entire allotment, involves a huge amount. Considering that an average allotment is 250 square metres in area, covering it to a depth of 5 centimetres would mean using 12.5 cubic metres of compost! You may well not have to dig, but a lot of heavy-duty fetching and carrying is involved. Another problem lies in the cost and where to find all that organic matter. Some no-diggers are lucky enough to have befriended local farmers, but if we were all to adopt the no-dig option, where would all that organic matter come from? Surely not from your compost heap – a compost heap would need to be the size of a small house to create enough for your allotment's needs!

In theory, the no-dig method is simply brilliant. Not having to dig is great, and not disturbing the soil is also great. You also tend to get fantastic disease-free crops year upon year . . . so if you know where to find truckloads of organic waste then this is the option for you!

Nurturing Home-Made Compost

Making your own compost is one of the best ways you can help your allotment thrive and also help the environment: instead of filling up landfill sites, you can create your own 'garden gold' to feed your soil with. Much like soil, your compost heap becomes a living, breathing thing that needs careful attention and the right ingredients to work properly. I don't want to make it sound harder than it is, but I have seen many compost bins and heaps that don't really produce the great compost that its owners were expecting. If you follow these simple rules, you'll have compost that makes your fellow plot holders green with envy.

Choosing a composter

A dazzling array of composters are available on the market, some better than others. The good thing about shop-bought ones is that they're usually dark in colour and well insulated; this helps build up the heat that speeds up the process of decomposition. The bigger the composter the better, because big ones store heat much more effectively, so don't bother with anything too small. Your composter should be open at the bottom. This is so that you can place the composter directly onto the soil, and the worms and bacteria can travel up into your bin and get to work on the contents. A problem with these composters is that although they're great for garden use, to satisfy the hungry soil on an allotment takes at least three large ones, so what I suggest is a properly installed compost area.

I love to see compost heaps on the allotment: they seem as much part of the landscape as an old rickety shed. They can be made really simply using old pallets, old planks or whatever you can find to create a large open-topped box. Figure 6-4 shows you how it's done. Ideally, a compost heap needs good ventilation, so allow some gaps for air to circulate. I'd also install a removable front so you can gain easy access when it comes to turning your pile.

When adding to your composter, you need to bear a few things in mind to make sure that it works effectively. Things you can put in your composter include:

- Uncooked vegetable waste from the kitchen
- Annual weeds
- Teabags, coffee grounds and eggshells
- Garden cuttings from herbaceous plants, dead flower heads, shredded branches and twigs
- Dried leaves, straw and grass

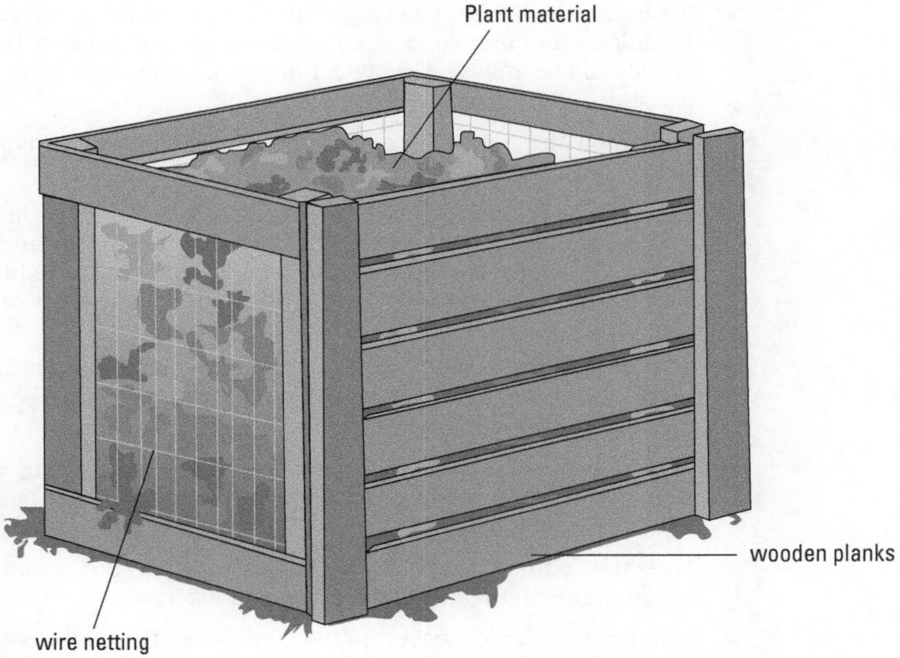

Fig 6-4: A simple timber composting frame.

- Shredded cardboard and non-glossy paper
- Bedding from small domestic pets such as rabbits and guinea pigs.
- Manure
- Wood ash (but not if you burn coal or solid fuel)

Things you **mustn't** put in your composter include:

- Cooked food
- Meat
- Human, cat or dog excrement
- Perennial weeds, especially their roots
- Any non-organic material

Try this list of top tips for top compost:

- For the first level, add a layer of twigs to help air circulate under your heap.
- Don't add great thick layers of one thing at any one time, especially grass cuttings. These are best mixed with other kitchen and garden waste and added gradually.

- The bigger the better. The larger the bin is, the more heat is created and the quicker and more effective the decomposition process is. Ideally, bins should be at least 1 metre x 1 metre, which allows them to really heat up!
- Don't allow the pile to dry out; as you add layers, water them. This helps speed things up.
- Turn your heap over regularly from the outside in and the inside out. This is best done when the heap has been hot for a while and is starting to cool. Turning takes the well rotted stuff on the inside to the outside and puts the not-so-well rotted stuff in the middle where it can build up heat again.
- Be sure not to include diseased garden waste or perennial weed roots. Diseased waste spreads the infection into the heap and may survive the heat and decomposition process.
- Ideally have two or, even better, three heaps or bins: one to store your green waste, a second as an active compost heap and the final one full of ready-to-go compost.
- Cover the compost heap with black plastic, especially in winter, to stop it becoming waterlogged and losing precious heat.
- Be wary of evergreen leaves on the composter: they take forever to decompose and unless finely shredded they aren't worth using.
- Mix drier materials (paper, straw, plant stems) with wet ones (grass clippings, kitchen waste).

Compost heaps need encouraging to start the process of decomposition, and all sorts of activators are around that can aid the process. For a heap to decompose, it needs to contain plenty of bacteria and nitrogen. Green waste does contain plenty of nitrogen, but it never hurts to add some more. Dried fish, blood and bone works really well, or you can buy compost activators in the garden centre that are well worth the money.

TIP

Nettles and comfrey act as fantastic compost additives. Comfrey has long roots that suck the goodness from deep in the soil; the nutrients are then stored in the leaves. Cut some comfrey leaves from the plant and shred them finely into your heap. Young nettles too are great accelerators, are full of goodness and help speed up the process.

Chapter 7

Keeping Your Plants Healthy

In This Chapter

- Feeding your precious plants
- Knowing when to water
- Rotating your crops
- Dealing with pests and disease

Once you've lovingly nurtured your plants and they're safely in the ground you may think you can sit back and simply watch them grow . . . if only that were true! You're now the proud parent of hundreds of little plants, which need love, attention, nurturing, feeding and caring for, so that they can grow up into healthy specimens. You've already given them the best possible start in life by giving them a comfortable new home to grow up in, but now they need your guidance through life, so they can flourish in the outside world.

In this chapter you discover the skills required to keep your plants safe from attack and well fed and watered. In addition, you get to know the signs to watch for when your little ones aren't well or when they've been bullied by nasty pests. Now you're about to become a real allotment gardener.

Using Fertilisers

Plants, especially food plants, are really hungry things and need as much help as they can get to ensure that they get enough of what they need to grow well. Adding organic matter (for details see Chapter 6) does them pretty well to start with, but often specific plants need extra help, and if they start to flag a bit they need a nutrient boost. Professional growers spend fortunes on specific soil analysis and complex combinations of feeds and pesticides to ensure that their crops are in tip-top condition, but for an allotment gardener this simply isn't feasible. If you've done a simple soil analysis (see Chapter 6), you know what type of soil you have, its pH, nitrogen, phosphorus and potassium levels, but it's also beneficial for you to look closely at what certain plants require and how you can provide for their needs. In order to do that you need to understand fully the available options – whether chemical, organic, liquid or granular fertilisers, what they contain and how much your plants need.

Fulfilling your plants' needs

Plants naturally produce their own food by converting the sun's energy into glucose. They do this by combining the energy from the sun with carbon dioxide and water to produce the main food they need, but that's not enough. Plants also require other elements and minerals in addition to their basic food and the dietary supplements they get from the soil, so we have to ensure that they're on the right diet. The nutrients plants need in the greatest amount in order to grow are called *macronutrients* and include the following:

- Nitrogen (chemical symbol N)
- Phosphorus (P)
- Potassium (K)
- Magnesium (Mg)
- Calcium (Ca)
- Sulphur (S)

Plants also require *micronutrients*, commonly known as *trace elements*. They need these in tiny amounts to maintain good health, and they include

- Iron (Fe)
- Manganese (Mn)
- Copper (Cu)
- Zinc (Zn)
- Boron (Bo)
- Molybdenum (Mb)
- Chlorine (Cl)

When the soil isn't rich enough to sustain healthy plants they begin to suffer, and you need to learn the signs to watch out for so you can act quickly to fix the problem. Common problems, such as yellowing of the leaves, are often caused by mineral deficiencies – for example, a lack of magnesium or iron. More obvious problems, like poor growth on leafy vegetables, is usually due to a lack of essential nitrogen.

What do all the numbers and letters mean?

UK law states that the fertiliser manufacturer must show on the packet the nutrient content and the levels at which they are present. These are shown as numbers for the specific nutrients nitrogen, phosphorus and potassium (N, P, K, respectively). These are followed by a number that represents the percentage by weight that each nutrient makes up of the total product weight. For example, one tomato feed that I have in my shed reads N 4, P 4.5, K 8, which means it has 4 per cent nitrogen, 4.5 per cent phosphorus and 8 per cent potassium. Potassium, being great for fruit and flowers, is present in a higher percentage. Of course, you can always apply potash in the form of wood ash or manure, which is nature's answer to providing extra potassium!

On most soils you only really need to worry about the main macronutrients – specifically nitrogen, phosphorus and potassium, known collectively as NPK – and these are the only ones that you need to apply regularly. If you do find signs of other mineral deficiency you need to work out which mineral or combination of it is causing the problem.

Looking over liquid feeds

Liquid feeds are available in a number of different forms: as crystals, powders and concentrated liquids, all of which need diluting in water before application. You can also buy the liquids in a ready-to-use form, but they're much pricier so aren't really worth it! Because the nutrients in liquid feeds are suspended in water, they're instantly available to the plants, which absorb them, with the water, into their roots after application. This means that a plant gets the benefits immediately. The problem with liquid feeds is that they don't stay in the soil long, and are washed away by rain.

I only use liquid feed on my tomatoes and sweet peppers, aubergines and chillies, which benefit from a boost from a specific liquid tomato feed high in potassium.

You can also purchase foliar liquid feed that you spray directly onto the *foliage* (leaves) of a plant. Plants do absorb some moisture and nutrients through their leaves and sometimes it can be beneficial to apply foliar feed to give them a quick boost. This can help plants that are suffering mineral deficiencies due to high pH levels in the soil (see Chapter 6 for details). Foliar feeds are usually very weak concentrates, so they cause no damage to the leaf surface.

As with all feeds you should follow the instructions on the label to make sure that you're providing exactly what the particular feed is designed for. You can weaken the dilution if you're unsure, or wish to feed the plants slightly more often, but I would never recommend making a stronger mix than is suggested on the packet, because you run the risk of damaging the plant. Overfeeding can cause leaf burn, excessive weak growth, and can even kill a plant.

Working with non-organic granular feeds

These fertilisers often contain really high concentrations of nutrients that are chemically produced to give accurate dosing and timed release of the nutrients, for maximum control. They're very often much cheaper than organic-based fertilisers and are easy to transport and store. They can be soluble or in granular form and be applied as a spray or sprinkled across the soil and into planting holes.

These fertilisers also include *slow release pellets*, small pellets coated in a protective layer. These fertilisers are usually quite expensive and over a period of, say, six months, slowly release the nutrients to give a constant and sustained feed. They are simply brilliant for container plants, which only have a small area for their roots from which to draw up all their nutrients. However, over a large area like an allotment, this type of fertiliser is uneconomical and doesn't offer the specific doses to specific plants that are sometimes required.

Looking into organic fertilisers

Granular or solid feeds of organic origin are usually a great option for feeding plants on your allotment and are usually supplied as concentrated forms of organic matter processed into an easy-to-handle form. When they're called *organic feed*, that usually means that they're of organic origin, and doesn't always mean organic or untreated in terms of it production. I'd always use these rather than chemical feeds, because they're of natural origin and usually fairly harmless (see the nearby sidebar 'Compound, general and specific fertilisers'). They include dried fish, blood and bone meal, and also chicken manure pellets, ground dried hoof and horn and seaweed meal. All of these usually contain good reliable levels of nutrients that you can use both during planting and on top of the soil during the growing season.

Organic fertilisers generally release their nutrients slowly, with the soil-borne bacteria doing the work for you by breaking down the fertiliser. Some organic fertilisers are also absorbed in water and in turn by the plants so the effect can be fairly long-lasting. These won't need applying as frequently as liquid feed.

Not for the squeamish?

Some people do have reservations about how safe animal-derived products are to use around food crops, and if you're vegetarian you may well want to look for other feeds. On the one hand such products are great in that they use up what would otherwise be waste products, but it's not always a nice thought having dried blood spread around your cauliflowers and leeks! No records exist of cases involving any health risk caused by the use of such products and I use them happily. All I'd say is wear gloves and wash all your produce thoroughly, but I am sure you'd do this anyway! If you want an alternative, seaweed meal is just as good, if used correctly.

Building up your veg with compost tea

Compost tea is a great homemade feed that is great for growing not only you giant veggies but your other plants too. There are many different ways of making it, and growers all have their own recipes, but in essence they are all pretty similar and involve steeping amounts of compost in water for around five days. The resulting liquid is used as a feed for the soil and can also be used as a pesticide, although there is very little scientific evidence to prove it is effective for this use.

Compost consists of mainly organic matter, but it also contains bacteria, fungi, and all sorts of beneficial micro-organisms that when steeped in water become a rich mixture that acts like a live yoghurt for the soil. Much like the beneficial bacteria in yoghurts help our digestive system, so compost tea helps to improve and enrich the soil where a plant grows by adding live bacteria. The tea helps to speed up the natural process by which bacteria break down the organic matter into a soluble form, that the plants can then soak up into their roots. It also adds some nutrients and minerals.

There are a few ways in which to produce your compost tea. You can simply put a good handful of compost into a large bucket of water and stir it daily for five days, strain, and use. For a more accurate method that is well tried and tested, however, follow these steps:

In a large bucket or waterproof container, mix 1 part compost in between 4 and 9 parts water, depending on the strength required.

Add any other additional nutrients required such as molasses (to aid bacterial growth) or seaweed (to aid the growth of fungi).

Compound, general and specific fertilisers

The world of fertilisers can be very complex and a little daunting, with all sorts of terms and confusing concoctions around. For those of you who tremble at the thought of fertilisers I'd strongly advise using a *compound,* also known as a *general purpose fertiliser.* These contain a broad range of nutrients that cater for most of your plants' needs and do all the thinking for you. *Specific* or *straight fertilisers* do exactly what they suggest, being only one nutrient that's applied for a particular reason, for example, sulphate of ammonia provides nitrogen in a soil and nothing else. These should be used with care and accurately so as not to create a nutrient imbalance in the soil. Dosing must therefore be correct.

Leave at room temperature for 2–20 days, depending on your requirements stirring daily.

Strain and use immediately. The bacteria and other microbes will be most active if used quickly; the longer the tea stands for, the less active they will become.

Compost tea is greatly affected by how long you brew it for; a short brewing time is best for fungal growth, whereas a longer brew will encourage more bacterial growth. For a decent brew I tend to average around 5 days.

You can buy special barrels that introduce fine air bubbles into the water, aiding the brewing process greatly. This method is often used by commercial farmers to produce their teas. You can also buy home kits that do the same. One cheaper way of introducing air is to buy a simple aquarium pump, pop it into the bucket of tea and leave it for 24 hours. This activates the aerobic processes, and you end up with a better all-round compost tea.

TIP

Worm castings are brilliant for making compost tea. They are a really rich source of all the goodies that your plants will thrive upon, especially when activated in compost tea.

The great thing about compost tea is that a little bit of compost will make a lot of tea, so if you only have a limited supply of compost, you will greatly expand its beneficial use by making tea with it.

Tea should be applied either directly to the soil (where it will not need passing through a sieve) or it can be sieved and sprayed directly onto the foliage of your plants. Foliar feeds are absorbed quickly into the plants where the benefits are much quicker, but to be careful and test a few leaves first to ensure that the spray does not damage the plant and remember some plants such as pumpkins do not like foliar feeds so these are best fed at the bottoms.

Dealing with Watering

Using the correct amount of water is absolutely vital for plant growth, especially on an allotment, where much of the produce comprises swollen vegetable roots and fruits that are full of moisture. Water is a precious resource and you need to make every effort to conserve it on the allotment.

The amount of water you use is greatly dependent on the type of soil you have and its structure (see Chapter 6). Sandy soils, for example, drain really quickly, whereas heavy clay soils can become waterlogged easily.

REMEMBER

Effective watering relies greatly on applying a really good soaking that penetrates deep into the roots of the plant. Many people make the mistake of not watering for long enough. If you water frequently in short bursts, the water simply evaporates from the soil surface and doesn't get to where it's needed.

Getting your priorities right

Many plants have different watering requirements but you should bear in mind some special cases.

- Because new plants and seedlings haven't got fully developed root systems, you need to keep the soil moist to ensure that the plants get what they need.
- Fruit trees and bushes need plenty of water in the first half of the growing season while they are producing flowers. and in turn developing the young fruit. If they're starved of water during this time the yield, fruit size and quality are greatly reduced.
- Plants such as chillies, tomatoes and peppers suffer if not kept well watered before and during flowering. A lack of water prevents the flowers from developing properly and the fruit doesn't develop at all.
- Potatoes also need plenty of water when they're forming, otherwise the tubers fail to develop properly and become misshapen, with pits and holes in them.
- Runner beans and French beans become stringy if short of water.
- You must keep large-fruited crops like courgettes, pumpkins, marrows and squash well watered, otherwise they will not develop well and the skins are likely to crack.

If soil moisture levels fluctuate greatly from dry to very wet this too can cause problems, especially with root vegetables like carrots, parsnips, beetroots and radishes. They become swollen when the soil is damp, then dry quickly when drought occurs, causing the roots to split and spoil. This shows the importance of a constant level of moisture within the soil.

Plants in sandy soils should be monitored really closely to ensure that the soil remains moist, and this also applies to container plants.

Many allotments operate hosepipe bans and don't allow their use at all. Some do allow it, but be wary of anyone you may offend. Most established allotment gardeners frown on hosepipe use and employ water-saving techniques to ensure good use of natural resources. So collect rainwater as much as you can and use a watering can.

Watching for the signs of dehydration

When plants become dehydrated the signs come on really quickly. The leaves are the first indicator, and as soon as they start to wilt the speed at which your plants grow immediately slows down. The signs are obvious, with plants looking wilted and limp, and unless you're quick to respond it'll be too late and the plants will perish. The cells within the leaves are usually plump and rigid with water, but when plants become dehydrated these cells can collapse to the point of no return, and aren't able to recover.

Saving water

Saving water and reducing your water consumption are two really important factors when undertaking an allotment. It' s a fact that most of us simply turn the tap on and water comes out – we don't really think about where it comes from or the process involved in getting it the consumer. Water is a valuable and precious resource and I'm sure you have experienced hosepipe bans yourself. When I was younger I remember water storage tanks out on the streets for us to collect water from because the local reservoirs had dried out during summer droughts.

To sustain your garden you need to be on the lookout for ways to conserve and manage your water consumption. Here are some tips:

- **Use mulches.** *Mulches* can include all sorts of things from bark chippings to coconut shells, and from compost to newspaper covered in grass clippings. Mulches protect the soil from the sun and wind, and thus lessen water evaporation. They reduce the water needs of certain crops, and fruit trees, herbs and shrubs can benefit greatly. Organic mulches also help suppress weeds, and in rotting down add organic matter to the soil. Put mulch around plants that are permanent residents on the allotment.
- **Plant through landscape fabric.** This special membrane simultaneously keeps moisture in and weeds out.

- **Avoid watering in the daytime.** Watering when the sun's at its hottest increases evaporation, and water splash can also cause scorching on leaves as the drops act like individual magnifiers. Water when the sun is at its coolest, in early morning or evening.
- **Plant in the right place.** Planting crops in unsuitable soils or positions is pointless. For example, celery and rhubarb need lots of moisture to grow well and struggle in free-draining, sandy soils, so don't waste time and precious water trying.
- **Protect your plants from the wind.** Wind has a dramatic effect on drying out your soil, and also increases evaporation from the plants themselves. As the wind blows on the leaves it evaporates the moisture on them, which in turn speeds up the rate at which the plant sucks up water from the soil, thus increasing water consumption greatly. So for example, you could plant tall runner beans on supports around the edge of your plot to act as a natural windbreak, filtering the wind and thus protecting the other crops (in Chapter 5 I cover how to build supports). If your plot is large enough and you have the space, you can even construct windbreaks using hazel or willow hurdles to act as wind filters
- **Use organic matter to improve your soil.** This is always the answer when it comes to improving the water retention and structure of any soil type (see Chapter 6). In good soil, water is stored in small pores that are usually less than 0.1 millimetre in diameter. Air in this soil is trapped in slightly larger pores, so when a soil is described as moist and well drained, this is exactly what is being described. In clay soils these spaces can be much smaller, and they trap the water and sometimes the air where a plant's roots can't get hold of the soil. Organic matter improves the space between the tight soil particles, allowing more space for water and air. Loamy soils offer the best of both worlds, with a good mix of fine and coarse particles, the coarse offering good drainage and the finer particles holding onto water well so that the plants can get hold of it.
- **Check weather reports, and water and plant accordingly.** There's little point in watering if the weather forecasts predict rain, so plan to save loads of water simply by noting the weather. Also, if you can plant new plants just before a heavy downpour, this satisfies the new plants rather thirsty needs without you having to resort to the tap. Equally, if you can possibly sow seeds where they're to grow permanently, you won't have to transplant them, which saves you watering them in.
- **Keep on top of weeding.** By keeping weeds down you stop them pinching all your precious water and nutrients. All plants compete with each other to gain access to water and nutrients, so eliminate the competition.

REMEMBER

Water established plants thoroughly once every 2–3 days during dry spells, but water seedlings and young plants lightly and frequently. This is because seedlings don't have deep established root systems and need to access water in the top layer of the soil, which often dries out first.

Watering in the right way

This may sound as if I'm stating the obvious but there's a right way and a wrong way to water your plants. Always try and water gently; too powerful a spray or flow can damage plants, resulting in pooling and washing away precious top soil. Ideally create a 'basin' around your plants using the soil in which to catch water and 'guide' it to the plants roots. You'll notice that many plot holders have sunken plant pots with holes in the bottom beside their plants. These act in a similar way to the 'basin' and direct the water down to the plant's roots – you simply fill the pot and it drains into the soil by the plant.

Collecting rainwater

I don't know a single allotmenteer who doesn't collect rainwater. Not only does this save resources but it's better for your plants as well. Tap water is treated with chlorine, fluoride, and all sorts of strange chemicals that can affect your plants' wellbeing. Also, tap water in hard areas is full of calcium and magnesium, which can be detrimental to acid-loving plants by neutralising the soil around the plants' roots.

Rain water does have a tendency to be pH neutral to slightly acid, due to the fact that the atmosphere contains carbon dioxide, which causes rain to become a very weak carbonic acid (not taking into account pollutants, which can have an even greater effect in causing acid rain). But all this considered, the best reason to collect rainwater is the fact that it's totally free and usually much better for plants than tap water.

TIP: Install a couple of water butts (attached to the shed roof, if you've got one) to collect plenty of water for your needs. You can link two or even three of them together with overflow pipes to collect water over the wetter months for use when things dry up, or even to see you through a hosepipe ban! It's really important to keep the butts covered so that algae, mosquitoes and other nasties don't breed.

TIP: Bury a length of leaky pipe or a drip irrigation system and link it to a water butt and bury it amongst your beds so that water is gently drip-fed directly to your plants as they grow.

TIP: A upturned fizzy drinks bottle with a few small holes in the lid makes a great drip feeder for pot plants and especially for individual plants that require a constant supply. Fill it up with water and shove it into the pot or the ground by the plant and it will slowly release its water through the holes.

Rotating Your Crops

Crop rotation is arguably one of the most important techniques a new allotment gardener needs to grasp to ensure a successful new plot. The method involves growing different vegetables on different parts of the plot each year. The benefits are two-fold: rotation groups plants according to their soil and cultivation needs and avoids a build-up of pests and diseases specific to a particular crop.

The worst of these pests are clubroot disease (*Plasmodiophora brassicae*) in brassicas (cabbages and the like) and eel worm in potatoes. By moving the crops each year, you lessen the nutrient losses and limit the development of pests and diseases (although you might not eradicate them).

Two to five beds are workable for the rotation system. Some organic growers even suggest eight, but I feel that any more than five is too mindboggling in terms of noting what plants go where, what feeds to add and when, and so on.

Working out your rotation plan for a typical four-bed system may look complex but in reality is really simple and easy to follow. Here's how it works.

First, write a list of what you want to grow. Next, group the plants together in families. Some of the family combinations may seem a little strange; for example, turnips are in the brassica family, and tomatoes in the potato family.

- **Solanaceae**: Potatoes, tomatoes, peppers and aubergines.
- **Leguminaceae:** Beans and peas.
- **Root vegetables:** Beetroot, carrot, celeriac.
- **Brassicaceae:** Broccoli, kale, Brussels sprouts, cabbages, cauliflowers, radishes, swedes and turnips.
- **Umbelliferae:** Carrots, parsnips, potatoes, peppers and celery.
- **Alliaceae:** Onions, garlic, shallots, leeks, Welsh onions and spring onions.
- **Chenopodiaceae:** Beetroot, Swiss chard, spinach and Good King Henry.
- **Cucurbitaceae:** Pumpkins, courgettes, marrows, squashes and gourds.
- **Asteraceae:** Chicory/endive, Jerusalem and globe artichokes, lettuces, salsify and scorzoneras.

Some families of plants or individual plants can be mixed with others that like the same or similar conditions. If you were to have an individual bed for each family you'd need far too many, so we tend to rotate our crops using the groups set out below. These groups are the fussier ones that benefit most from crop rotation. Here's a guide to what can go in each of your four plots:

- **Plot A:** Legumes.
- **Plot B:** Onions.
- **Plot C:** Carrot and tomato families.
- **Plot D:** The brassicas.

Each year simply move plot A to plot B, B to C, C to D and D to A, as shown in Figure 7-1. Table 7-1 shows a more detailed four-bed rotation.

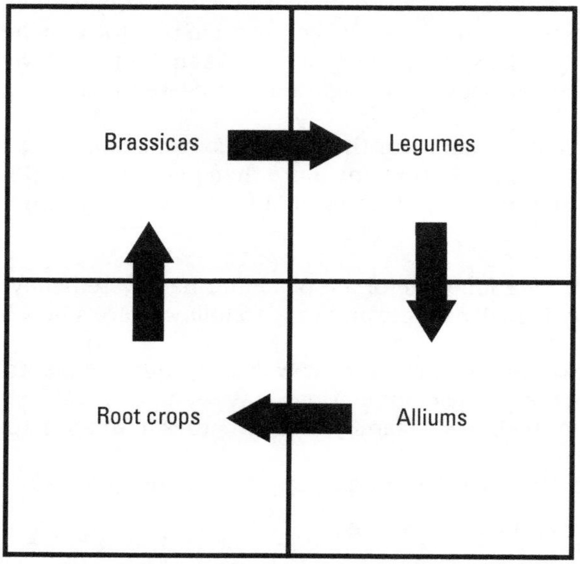

Figure 7-1: A typical four-bed crop rotation

You can plant the other stuff you like in a plot with plants that like similar conditions. For example, you won't want to dedicate a whole plot only to onions, so in the remaining space plant the courgettes, pumpkins and marrows.

TIP

Salad crops and short-lived vegetables don't really fit into the rotation system and can be grown in between other crops as the space is made free. This is called *intercropping*.

The best way of looking at a rotation system is to analyse the state of the soil once a current crop has finished (see Chapter 5 for how to do so). Then select crops that are best suited to the existing state of the soil.

Table 7-1: Another four-bed crop rotation system

	Year 1	*Year 2*	*Year 3*	*Year 4*
Plot 1	Potatoes. (Lime soil afterwards)	Beans (Lime soil afterwards).	Brassicas	Onions and Roots (Add manure afterwards)
Plot 2	Beans (Lime soil afterwards)	Brassicas	Onions and Roots (Add manure afterwards)	Potatoes (Lime soil afterwards)
Plot 3	Brassicas	Onions and Roots (Add manure afterwards)	Potatoes (Lime soil afterwards)	Beans (Lime soil afterwards)
Plot 4	Onions & Roots (Add manure afterwards)	Potatoes (Lime soil afterwards)	Beans (Lime soil afterwards)	Brassicas

Some further rotation planting tips are:

- Potatoes don't like limey soil; legumes and brassicas do, but only after the lime has been in the soil for a year. Thus, for the relevant plot add lime in the autumn, plant legumes in the spring, plant brassicas the following spring, and potatoes the year after that.
- A four-year rotation is best for both potatoes and the brassica family.
- Sometimes you can squeeze into the same plot a crop of brassicas after the legumes have passed by midsummer. Doing so can effectively turn a four-plot system into a five
- You need to have the brassicas growing at the same time ready for transplanting in a holding bed, either on the allotment or at home, but this is a great way of getting the most out of your allotment.

Many problems occur with the crop-rotation system, so a lot of gardeners don't follow the rules strictly. This system dedicates the same amount of space to the four plots meaning that you have to grow the same amount of each crop. For example, you may not like potatoes as much as peas and beans, but you have a whole bed dedicated to spuds! Runner beans can cause problems when you move them around because of the shadows they create as tall climbing plants, but you can usually sort this out fairly by way you orientate them. Also, potatoes tend to take up much more room than other crops, so they do allow space for them.

Some argue that being on an allotment and so close to other plot holders means that you can't avoid cross-contamination from pests and diseases. Well, if everybody adopted the rotation system in some way, they'd be helping to reduce this problem, because keeping crops moving from year to year helps avoid the build-up of specific pests and diseases. The rotation system isn't perfect, but the benefits far outweigh the drawbacks.

Putting Down Pests

A plethora of nasty critters are out there to ruin your day on the allotment, and in this section I show you what signs to look out for and how to deal with the most common pests that attack your plants.

Aphids

Aphids are small, very common pests that can colonise your plants in a matter of days. Aphids include black fly and green fly, and they have really soft bodies that are easy to squish. Ladybirds, lacewings and birds, amongst other creatures, love to devour them, but they are also easy to get rid of with pesticides both chemical and organic, so ask your local garden centre to advise you on a suitable one.

When aphids attack they suck the sap out from plants and this causes many plants' new growth to become distorted.

Cutworms

Cutworms are the larvae of nocturnal moths and can be a real menace. They eat the buds and young stems of plants, and can literally cut seedlings down like little lumberjacks. There is no chemical pesticide to deal with them, so it is a case of seek and destroy by hand.

Rabbits

Rabbits can be a nuisance and will happily nibble their way through pretty much any crop. They also strip the bark from trees in winter and munch your fruit bushes too.

The first and best line of defence is to protect you young trees and fruit bushes with spiral fruit guards that can be bought at the garden centre. But the only real answer is to build fences around your plants to keep them out. This should be done using chicken wire supported on posts at least 80 centimetres high, with 20 centimetres of wire bent along the soil and buried to stop them digging under the outside.

Rats and mice

Rats and mice will also be attracted to the easy pickings on your plots and will head straight to crops such as sweetcorn and strawberries. They are really hard to keep out, and rats are nearly impossible to beat. But if you have a serious problem with rats you should talk to your allotment society to try and deal with the infestation.

Birds

Birds are usually to be encouraged into the garden, but on an allotment some can be a real problem. The main culprits are blackbirds and pigeons. Both are really common and tenacious. Blackbirds love ripe fruit, so the only way to protect your crop is to invest in a fruit cage built over your soft fruit area. This will keep your blackberries, raspberries, currants and strawberries safe from attack. You can improvise a fruit cage by building a simple frame over the fruit and covering this with fruit netting, or simply laying fruit nets over the crops. You can also buy ready made cages from garden centres or online.

Pigeons are a rather fond of your veggies and will peck away at your brassicas (especially the foliage) and will nibble your young pea shoots in spring and winter. So, again, protect them with netting.

Slugs and snails

Meet the most common and annoying pests you will encounter on the allotment. Slugs and snails work under cover of darkness, climbing up plants like mountaineers, sneaking around undetected to devour innocent plants. Although they do prefer the sweet, younger, tender foliage they can also do damage to older plants and will eat fruit, tubers, stems – in fact pretty much any plant material.

Slugs and snails thrive in moist conditions and love organic matter, so they find a well prepared allotment irresistible. But you can use a few methods to fight back

- **Physical barriers:** If you lay a mulch of sharp material around the base of your plants, this gives the slimies a really uncomfortable surface to traverse to get at your plants. This they hate, so they stay away. Suitable materials include sharp gravel, baked egg shells and cocoa shells. Another barrier method is to use a ring of copper wire. This simple method creates a low electric charge around the plants and works like a mini electric fence, keeping the pests at bay.
- **Encourage nature:** Not the easiest thing to do on the plot but if you garden as naturally as possible and work with nature, encouraging birds, hedgehogs and toads onto your plot, they will really help eat any problem slugs and snails on the plot. But they will only help so don't rely solely on their services!
- **Traps:** There are a few methods you can use to trap slugs, and they are all pretty effective. Beer traps are plastic cups buried in the ground to soil level and filled with beer or fruit juice, which the slugs are attracted to, only to fall in and drown. You can also try placing empty half orange or grapefruit skins upside down around the plot. Slugs and snails will and try to devour them. You simply scoop them up and dispose of them. This method really works well but you then have the problem of what to do with a load of live slugs in the morning!
- **Pellets:** The best method for dealing with slug problems, but also controversial. Many believe that pellets are deadly poisons that will kill pets, children and all who ventrure near them. This is simply not true, most slug pellets contain a chemical that dries up the slugs as opposed to poisoning them. They also contain special chemicals that make them taste disgusting, so children and animals will not put them in their mouths. They are only really effective in dry weather, when the slugs dry out more quickly, and should always be used subject to the package instructions. Usually you only need one pellet every 10 centimetres or so, so that they are not in big groups on the ground where another creature could accidentally take a big mouthful of them.
- **Nematodes:** These tiny little creatures are like little worms or microscopic tubes. There are 15,000 different parasitic types but you can now buy special nematodes that are specially selected to attack and kill certain slugs. They are mixed with water and sprinkled around your plants where they will enter the soil and seek out slugs (though not snails), bore into their bodies and eventually kill them. They are only effective when the soil temperature is above 5 °C and can usually be kept in the fridge for up to four weeks. They are not so effective in heavy clay, in which they find it difficult to penetrate the soil, but in an allotment setting usually the soil should have been improved, so they should be pretty effective.

Flea beetles

Flea beetles are tiny black beetles that get their name from the fact that they jump like fleas, hopping away and hiding as soon as they sense your presence. Signs of an infestation are tiny little holes all over the leaves of your plants. They also attack seedlings and can totally devour them, so the plants have no chance of survival. Flea beetles are a pest exclusive to brassicas (for example, amongst others, cabbages, radish, turnips and rocket). They are quite difficult to get rid of completely, but you can make the problem better in two ways. First, flea beetles hate dust, so sprinkle your plants with some bone dry, dusty soil every now and then. Second, get a sticky whitefly trap and pass it over your plants. This startles the beetles and they leap up to meet a sticky end. Flea beetles will only really kill young plants, so try not to plant these out too young if you know of a problem, and offer protection with a cloche tunnel. You can buy chemical spray insecticides to fight the problem but make sure you sneak up stealthily, or the beetles will hop away to safety before you can zap them.

Wireworms

These are the larvae of click beetles, and look like tough, orangey-brown worms (although they're not worms at all). They munch on the roots and tubers of plants and can be a real problem, especially with potatoes. They are very common in areas that have been grassed over for a long time and only recently tuned into a veggie plot. They love nibbling grass roots, and when the turf is gone will swiftly turn to the roots of your crops instead.

Constant digging helps the problem because it exposes the larvae to insect-eating birds, and over a few seasons they will eventually disappear. There is no chemical control to treat wireworms, but you can grow a green manure of mustard that helps speed up the larval stage so they turn into beetles faster and fly away. Otherwise they can stay as larvae for years.

Dealing with Diseases

Plant diseases are conditions that attack your precious plants in various forms, and can eventually kill them. Diseases can be *fungal* (such as mildew and rust) or *viral* (such as cucumber mosaic virus), with the fungal diseases being more common and easier to spot.

Fungal diseases are carried by spores that are often carried by the wind as they travel from plant to plant. They can also be transferred on infected plant material between plots, or even from suppliers, so always check new plants for any evidence of an infection. The signs of an infection are most commonly white or orange dusty patches on the foliage (white for mildew, orange for rust). They also discolour the leaves and can cause foliage loss.

Viral diseases are less easy to spot, and can be a real problem with permanent fruit shrubs and trees in particular. The microscopic organisms attack the plant cells, reducing yields. Viral diseases are impossible to cure, meaning you will have to discard any infected plants. Viruses also attack young plants such as courgettes and cucumbers, and if any signs of infection are present these plants should be disposed of (and not on the compost heap, either).

Healthy plants are less likely to suffer attack from diseases, and you can buy varieties that are resistant to particular diseases, so look out for varieties that can cope. Also plants that have been given too much nitrogen can be subject to attack as well, as nitrogen makes plants produce soft, lush foliage that is not tough enough cope with an attack.

Mildew

Mildew is indicated by a greyish white, powdery residue on the leaves and buds of plants, and eventually causes them to fall off. Mildew is a fungal infection that is caused by dryness or a lack of nutrients, conditions which lead to a less than vigorous plant which is susceptible to infection.

Mildew is carried by the wind and lands on the foliage of plants, where it spreads. It is not usually fatal to the plant, but it can cause the plants to weaken and be less productive.

Powdery mildew is the most common type and affects the leaves of courgettes and other squashes, apples, spinach, leaf beet and cucumbers. Dry soil is usually the culprit, so as long as the plants are kept well watered you should be okay. *Downy mildew* is less common and affects salad crops and onions.

You can use fungicides which will prevent infections from occurring. They will not, however, cure an infection, so use them as a preventative measure at the first sign of an infection.

Rust

Rust is another fungal disease that produces rusty patches on the foliage of plants such as leeks and garlic, but also affects both raspberries and apple and pear trees. Rust does not really affect the edible parts of the plant, but damage the foliage, thereby stressing the plants and causing smaller crops. Rust can cause premature defoliation, and is normally caused by warm, wet summers creating the perfect conditions for it to thrive.

Choose rust resistant varieties as a first port of call but if a problem occurs spray with a fungicide suitable for food crops, before the infection gets out of hand.

As with mildew, rust preys on plants that are fed with too much nitrogen, easily infecting the soft, lush growth.

Viruses

Viruses are sneaky diseases that develop unnoticed, reducing yields and even destroying plants completely. They are usually spread by aphids who suck the sap from diseased plants then fly to another plant and spread the disease. Signs to look for are

- Reduced yields.
- Yellowing of the leaves.
- Weak-looking plants.
- Distorted leaves.
- Yellow spots on the leaves.

A viral infection is a death sentence to a plant, so dig up and dispose of any infected plants. Never put them on the compost heap. Ideally, burn the plant material to reduce the likelihood of it returning.

Plants that may suffer are the soft fruits, so make sure that you buy your plants from a source that can guarantee virus-free stock. Other plants that can get viral diseases are cucumbers and all the members of the squash family.

Damping off disease

Damping off is a disease that affects seedlings and causes the base of the plants to rot away and the seedlings to collapse. You can do nothing to stop it once it happens, and the only way to prevent it is to adopt hygienic growing practices. Damping off is a soil-borne fungal disease, so always use trays and pots that have been disinfected prior to use with chestnut water (available in garden centres) as a fungicide treatment. As soon as you see the signs, remove any infected seedlings, the compost and the surrounding plants in a tray.

Problems with Specific Plants

Some diseases and pests attack plants without prejudice, but there are also ones that only attack a few specific types, so in this section I look at problems with specific plants.

Brassicas

The brassicas are a large and varied group of plants that present the allotmenteer with many challenges in terms of fighting pests and diseases. Some you should expect to have to tackle include the following.

- **Clubroot:** A fungal disease that's spread in the soil from other infected plots. It causes the roots of brassicas to become swollen, misshapen, and often rotten, and kills the plant. Never grow donated plants from other places unless you're one hundred per cent sure they're safe. If you do have a clubroot infected plot, then you can still grow brassicas with some success. Grow young plants in pots and plant them out a little later than usual. If your plants have a larger root ball they will have a better chance of becoming established and growing well before they become affected by the disease. Ideally, always grow your own plants from seed. Bought seedlings from reputable companies, or those grown in seed cells or pots from friends will be safe, just don't transplant from other plots. The disease can even be spread on the soles of your boots if you walk on an infected plot, which just shows how careful you need to be.
- **Cabbage root fly:** These annoying little flies lay eggs around the base of your brassicas, and the maggots that hatch from them bore into the base of the plant. This causes havoc with the plant, turning it a purple colour and eventually causing it todie. The only real method of protection is to put *collars* around the bases of the stems. These are plastic discs that slot around the base of the plant acting as a barrier stopping the maggots getting to the stem. You can buy them in garden centres.
- **Brassica white fly:** These are really common pests that infest the foliage of your plants. They are tiny little white flies which secrete a sticky mucus (honeydew) that sticks to the underside of the plants, this in turn attracts a sooty mould, that uses it as food. This turns the plants sticky and black. The only treatment is to catch them early and kill the flies with an organic or chemical pesticide before they get out of control.
- **Mealy cabbage aphids:** These are tiny little grey aphids. They are hard to spot and they hide in the tips of broccoli and inside your sprouts. They attack young plants and cause distorted new growth. The only method of control is by using an organic or chemical pesticide.
- **Cabbage white butterflies:** These are public enemy number one for brassica growers. There are two types, the large cabbage white and the small cabbage white. The caterpillars of the large variety are yellow and black, and those of the small are green. The caterpillars hatch from eggs laid under the leaves of your brassicas, especially cabbages. When the caterpillars hatch, they devour your crops. They will quickly turn the cabbage patch into nothing but plant skeletons if not dealt with. Netting is a great way to protect your plants, and you can also pick the caterpillars off by hand or use chemical or organic sprays.

- **Pigeons:** These are a pain and during winter are a real problem when there is not much on offer. They will eat leaves, sprouts, broccoli . . . whatever they can find. Old CDs, hung around the plot, deter them well. Netting also works a treat.

Carrots

Carrots are affected mainly by the carrot root fly, which lay its eggs on the soil at the base of the plants. The maggots that hatch out bore into the roots, making little holes. The flies are attracted by the smell that carrots give off, and this smell is released in particular when the foliage is snapped during thinning out, or when you break the roots.

No chemical control exists for this pest, so the only methods of keeping it at bay are preventative ones. Carrot flies have one drawback in their design: they rarely fly higher than 45 centimetres off the ground so we can use this to our advantage. Gardeners often place screens around their carrots that carrot flies cannot fly over, place fleece over the plants or even grow the carrots in raised beds high off the ground all of which will stop the problem.

You can buy varieties that are more resistant to the problem and give off less of an alluring smell, but this is not a guarantee. Many gardeners grow a resistant variety and nearby they grow a normal variety as a sacrificial crop so the flies attack these instead.

Courgettes, squashes and marrows

These are usually pretty simple to grow, and are not often attacked by nasties, but there are couple of things to watch for. Mildew can be a problem but the real bad guys are viral infections. Cucumber mosaic virus is a killer and any plants must be destroyed. It is a viral disease spread by aphids, and causes distorted leaves, mottled yellow leaves and mottled misshapen fruits. One thing to watch for is chickweed, a weed which can harbour the disease, so make sure to keep on top of this weed or you will keep on having to fight the problem.

Cucumbers

Cucumbers are host to many a pest and disease. Most problems are caused by fungal infections, but cucumbers are also attacked by cucumber mosaic virus (as described in the previous section), mites, aphids and whitefly.

- **Stem rot** is the most annoying problem, and is the result of over-watering and cold conditions. The rot attacks the plants at the base and the plants start to wilt. You can try and save plants by drawing soil around the base to encourage new roots, though this is often futile (but worth trying!)
- **Red spider mites** are easy to detect as tiny red pin heads crawling on your plants. They also leave a fine web on the underside of the leaves. They usually only attack greenhouse grown plants, and thrive in dry, warm conditions, so spray the foliage regularly and keep warm greenhouses well ventilated and cool during warm weather. You can spray with insecticides if need be.
- **Green and black fly** will infest outdoor grown plants and can be sprayed with soapy water and then rubbed off the foliage, greatly reducing the problem.
- **Verticillium Wilt** causes the leaves to turn yellow at the bottom, and it spreads up the plant. There is no cure, so remove infected plants and burn them. Wilt is a fungal disease that lives in the soil, and can also affect tomatoes, potatoes, peppers and chillies.

Peas and beans

Legumes have a few nasties of their own. Watch out for signs of any of the following:

- **Chocolate spot** affects broad beans, covering the plant with chocolate brown patches that eventually kill it. Carbendazim fungicides can prevent a really bad infection, and adding lime to the soil and not overcrowding the plants also helps.
- **Black fly** attacks are a certainty on many peas and beans, so spraying with soapy water and wiping off the aphids by hand is often necessary. You can also remove the soft growing tips above the uppermost flowers, as these pests they find these parts the most attractive. You can spray with chemical and organic pesticides, which often helps.
- **Pea moths** are the big baddies when it comes to peas. They lay their eggs on the pods, and then the little maggots bore into the peas. When you pop the pods open, there they are: very annoying! You can sow seeds earlier or later than you usually would, which can help the plants avoid the problem. Spraying with bifenthrin insecticide sprays as soon as the plants have flowered will see off an attack.
- **Pea and bean weevils** are only a real issue with seedlings and young plants. These beetles nibble the edges of leaves, damaging immature plants, but this is rarely a problem with mature plants which will still produce good crops. Offer seedlings protection with fleece or cloche tunnels until they are larger.

Potatoes

Historically, potato problems have been economically and socially devastating. Nothing as drastic will happen on your allotment, but you still have to be on your guard against the pests and conditions which affect spuds.

Potato blight

Potato blight (*Phytophthora infestans*) symptoms are typically dark, pitted patches that develop on the skin with brown stains in the flesh. The first stage of rotting comes on as a dry rot stage that can then develop into a soft, slimy rotten mess. Symptoms can be seen on the foliage as well, as the leaves start to turn brown on the edges, and tips often develop white rings of fungal growth.

The first sign of blight is when the *haulms* (leaves) are affected, so remove any that show the signs and burn them. If you find it starts to affect the whole crop, remove all the leaves and then hope that the tubers haven't been affected. Earthing up (see Chapter 9) helps limit the spores' ability to attack through the soil: they simply wash away in the furrows in-between the rows. The main thing then is to wait at least three to four weeks before attempting to harvest any potatoes. If you lift them before that time, the spores are still on the soil surface, and as you dig the potatoes out billions of spores get down to your precious crop and onto the ones you dig up. If any spores get onto harvested potatoes during storage, the potatoes become infected and rot away. If you get struck by blight, your best option is to leave the potatoes underground after you've removed the foliage. They'll be safer there from infection than those dug up and put into storage.

Chemicals are available to help, but these need to be used really early on, before the infection becomes too rife. One is called Bordeaux mixture, which contains copper sulphate; or you could use fungicide products containing mancozeb. Both need to be applied as preventative measures every two weeks during warm, humid periods. Personally, I try not to use chemicals if at all possible.

ORGANIC WAY

Liquid seaweed fertiliser sprayed onto the top and underside of the leaves can deter the blight spores adhering to the leaf surface. Be sure to use a fine spray and carefully spray each leaf. Do this when the foliage is dry, or it won't work. Seaweed extract mixed with water as a foliar feed, or *compost tea* (made by steeping a good handful of compost in water for a few days and use the resulting liquid) can also help reduce blight attack. Spray every other week during the growing season and after rainfall. Compost tea contains many useful bacteria that can actually aid the plant in fighting off the blight. It's also a great feed, so you get bigger, tastier potatoes as well.

Blight usually strikes from midsummer onwards, when the weather is warm and humid, so early crops of potatoes usually mature and are harvested before blight gets hold. I also strongly advise buying varieties that show good resistance.

Blight-resistant doesn't mean immune to attack, only that the potatoes are better equipped to resist – so always watch out for the signs of blight.

Blight also attacks tomatoes so watch both of them and your potatoes for any sign of infection.

Potato scab

Potato scab is a common bacterial infection that affects your crop, especially in recently limed soil or in soil that's highly alkaline. It produces scabs on a potato's skin that look pretty nasty, but don't affect the potato in any way: You can simply peel them off and eat the potato as usual. Potato scab isn't a problem in well-manured soil, so if you go about things properly it shouldn't be troublesome.

Potato eelworm

Potato eelworm is sometimes a problem on allotments, especially those where crop rotation hasn't been adhered to (see the earlier section 'Rotating Your Crops' in this chapter). Two types of eelworm exist: the *white cyst eelworm* and the *golden cyst eelworm*. They both form cysts on the roots of potato plants and cause the foliage to go yellow, then brown and then fall off. These cysts are the female eelworms, full of eggs which then hatch and infest the soil even more. Unfortunately, no chemical control is available to the allotmenteer and these pests can hang around for up to 20 years in the soil. Earlies may be grown successfully if you harvest them before the eelworms get established on the roots too much. Be sure to burn infected roots as soon as you dig them up. Crop rotation should help avoid the problem, but if the soil is really infested you may have to leave potatoes off the agenda in that area for up to seven years.

A plant called *Tagetes minuta* (Mexican marigold) can help control eelworm if grown as a green manure (green manures are sown on vacant plots and grown to be dug in to improve the soil). Its roots excrete a chemical that's supposed to fool the eelworms into remaining dormant for a season while you grow your spuds. This chemical also helps suppress weed such as couch grass, bindweed and ground elder, so if you have the time it's well worth trying out!

Eelworm can also attack tomato plants, so watch them for the signs as well.

Keel slugs

Slugs are always a problem on the allotment. Keel slugs are up to 6 centimetres long, dark grey in colour and have a distinctive orange or yellow stripe. They're burrowing specialists and bore into potatoes, leaving nasty holes that are open to infection and rot. Because keel slugs are a burrowing species, slug pellets are almost useless as a form of defence. Nematodes can be effective, though (see the earlier section 'Slugs and snails' for more on nematodes). These worms are available from garden centres and via mail order from specialist suppliers. Apply them in water around the plant. The only problem with this is that keel slugs are most common in damp, clay soils, and this is the one place that nematodes of this kind aren't always effective – but it's certainly worth a shot.

Tomatoes

Tomatoes do have a few problems for growers and here are the main ones to look out for.

- **Tomato blight** is caused by the same disease as potato blight, so look for similar symptoms. It only usually affects outdoor plants and will attack plants when they are damp for long periods.
- **Blossom end rot** is a problem caused by a lack of calcium drawn up by the plant. It is common in plants grown in pots or growbags, and is generally caused by a lack of watering. Calcium is soluble in water and can only be drawn up by the plants in this state, so if you don't water the plants they don't get their calcium fix, and sunken patches develop at the bottom and tips of ripe and unripe fruits. The solution is to keep them well watered!
- **Greenhouse white fly** are usually only a problem in polytunnels and greenhouses where conditions are warm and humid. They are not the same as brassica white flies, but are tiny moth-like creatures that secrete honeydew, which encourages mould. They can also spread viral diseases, so they should be dealt with swiftly. Insecticide sprays need to be used often to be effective, and will combat the problem, but the white flies also have a larval stage where they suck the sap of the plants. To beat these the only effective measure is a systemic insecticide absorbed into the plant and ingested when the larvae suck the sap. You can also use biological control, by buying special wasps called *encarsia* (you can find these in mail order catalogues and online). These great little wasps lay their eggs in the young whitefly, and these then hatch and eat the pest: Gory but a great way of dealing with them. Sticky yellow paper sheets are also available: these trap the white fly and this can also work well.

Fruit Pests and Diseases

Fruit is usually pretty delicate and sweet, so is open to attack from many pests which just can't keep away. Many fungal and viral diseases can affect yields and crop quality, attacking the foliage of the plants. These are generally easy to deal with and less of a problem than the more serious infections of the fruit that decimate a crop.

Apples

An array of pests and diseases exist that simply cannot keep away from your apples. Here we go with some of the most common!

- **Codling moths** are a real nuisance. The moths lay their eggs on small fruit at the beginning of summer. These hatch and then bore into the fruit, and when you pick them you get a nasty surprise when you bite in to the fruit. Sometimes you may find a black hole on the fruit where the grub has crawled out and this is a dead give away of a problem. Insect spays are effective when it comes to control, but the timing has to be spot on otherwise you are wasting your time and money.

  Another great method of control is by using *pheromone traps*, little tents conatining chemicals attractive to the moths. Hang these in the affected tree, and they attract the moths to an early demise. Such traps catch the male moths, which then cannot then fertilise the females. This method won't get them all, but as soon as you start catching moths you know that this is a good time to apply insecticides as well.
- **Woolly aphids** are found on the shoots of apple trees in large colonies, where the bark swells around them. They are covered in a mass that looks like cotton wool. To deal with them, cut away infected areas. On shoots or on thicker areas a blast of water will dislodge them.
- **Sawfly** is a pest that leaves ribbon-like marks over the skin of the fruit where the eggs have been laid. The eggs hatch and grubs bore into the fruit, feeding in the middle. They then drop to the ground. Sawfly infestations can be treated with insecticide as soon as the flowers have fallen, and this alleviates the problem.
- **Scab** is more of an annoyance than a massive problem. It is a fungal disease that causes brown scabs on the surface of the fruit. It does not affect the fruit apart from in appearance, and can be prevented with fungicide sprays.
- **Mildew** is a fungal infection that can affect the vigour of young trees. It only affects the leaves, which will have the telltale white powder on them. Cut away affected shoots towards the end of the summer, or prevent the infection by spraying with a fungicide in early summer. Also, seeing as mildew is often caused by soil dryness, keep a 1 m wide circle free of all other plants around the base to eliminate competition for water.
- **Bitter pit** causes the fruits to have sunken brown spots on the skin and a mottled look. This is not a disease but is still worth knowing about. It is caused by a lack of calcium which is in turn caused by a lack of water (in the same way as with blossom end rot on tomatoes), so regular watering should help.

- **Brown rot** is a really common fungal infection that also comes after pears, plums, cherries and plums. It gets in through the skin and basically turns the fruit brown with little rings of beige mould that spread outwards. The fruit then rots. All you can do is remove infected fruits and dispose of them (though not on the compost heap). Any left on the tree shrink and will re-infect other fruits next year, so get rid.

Currants

The big bad foe for blackcurrants is *big bud mite* which are actually tiny and live amongst the foliage, infecting it with *reversion virus*. This causes swollen, rounded buds, fewer flowers and less foliage. This all greatly affects crop yield. Dig up affected plants and dispose of them.

Gooseberries

Gooseberries are my favourite of all so I always make sure to watch out for the following two problems.

- **American gooseberry mildew** is a really serious fungal disease for gooseberries, and a bad infection can cover the entire plant with a white dusty power. By this stage there is nothing you can do but dig it up and dispose of it. If caught early, though, remove any infected areas and spray with fungicide.
- **Gooseberry sawfly** is a real bugbear. The adults lay eggs in the middle of the shrub, where they hatch into caterpillars. These feast upon the foliage and can defoliate the entire shrub. Birds can be of some help but many allotmenteers grow their fruit bushes in cages, and this keeps them out. The only real cure is spraying with insecticide.

Pears

There are a couple of problems that affect pears, and here they are.

- **Pear leaf blister mites** cause yellow raised spots on the foliage, which then turns black. The eventual outcome is that the tree drops all it leaves too early. There is no cure, but removing the infected foliage and destroying it helps.
- **Pear midges** turn young pears black, and they then fall off the tree. The midges lay eggs on the baby fruits, and these hatch into larvae and bore into the fruits. When the maggots are ready to pupate, the pears drop to the ground. The maggots crawl out and hide in the soil until spring, when the adults emerge. There is no really effective chemical treatment, so pick up all the fallen black fruit and dispose of it before the maggots emerge.

Raspberries

Pests and diseases on raspberries are not that common, but some can still be a big issue.

- **Spur blight** is a fungal disease that causes the growing tips on one-year old stems of more common summer fruiting varieties to develop purple patches around the developing fruits. These patches then turn silver, and mould appears all over the upper stem and kills it. The only answer is to remove the infected stem to ground. The plant will recover, but you will have to wait two years for fruits.
- **Raspberry beetle a**ttacks raspberries, blackberries and loganberries. The adult beetles lay eggs on and feed on the flowers. These eggs then hatch and the grubs feed inside the fruit. The only effective treatments are insecticide sprays; apply when the fruit is turning pink.
- **Viruses** of several types can infect your raspberries, but the most common, especially on large allotments, is mosaic virus. This causes the leaves to turn irregular and become covered in yellow patches, so the plants become poorly and unproductive. Because viruses are spread by aphids, this is common on allotments. The only cure is to dig up and destroy infected plants.

Chapter 8
Growing Organic

In This Chapter

- Deciding whether going organic appeals to you
- Choosing organic plants and seeds
- Attracting wildlife

Organic gardening is really quite simple. It's gardening without the use of synthetic chemicals and often without the use of genetically modified seeds or plants, or those of inorganic origin. Organic gardeners look at the garden in its entirety as a living, breathing entity that needs careful nurturing to remain productive and healthy. The soil is the most important element in any garden, and in an organic garden this is the heart of all organic principles.

Organic gardening to grow food seems pretty obvious to me. Why put loads of chemicals on produce that you want members of your family and friends to eat? People are becoming increasingly fussy about what they put into their bodies, and an organic revolution is well under way.

Organic gardening is by no means a new invention and is far better at maintaining *biodiversity* (the range of living things such as plants and animals) and the long-term health of your plot. If you fill your soil with chemicals and all sorts of man-made fertilisers, you damage the delicate balance of micro-organisms and insects that work so hard to maintain and look after your plot. Decomposed organic waste (well rotted manure and home-made compost – see Chapter 6) is the best food for your plants, so dousing your plot with chemicals really isn't necessary.

Deciding Whether Organic Is Right for You

Before the development of chemical fertilisers and feeds, people had no choice when it came to horticulture. Everything was done organically. Pesticides didn't exist, rivers were clean, and soil was healthy. So organic gardening techniques have a more far-reaching history than the comparatively short history of non-organic gardening.

Not such a new-fangled idea

Since Syrian gardeners first cultivated the soil for food production 13,000 years ago, organic gardening techniques have been honed as an art. Organic gardeners know exactly what's going into the soil and therefore onto our plates and into our mouths, whereas chemicals in crop production are a relatively recent development and often shrouded in environmental and public health concerns. Who knows what the long-term effects of chemicals are going to be on both the environment and our bodies?

A good example is DDT, which was one of the first artificial chemical insecticides ever mass-produced; it was banned in 1972 for agricultural use worldwide, after evidence of links to it causing cancer, nerve damage and birth defects, and being acutely toxic to all life forms. DDT also has a half life in soil of up to 15 years, during which it can build up. Nowadays most governments regard it as a significant risk to the environment.

One major factor when considering becoming an organic gardener is the fact that when you buy cheap fruit and veg in a supermarket, you're usually buying uniform specially bred products. They are mass-produced to crop heavily and cheaply, and all with the help of chemicals. The organic produce on offer is always more expensive, deemed to be better quality and more often than not tastes better, so why not grow it? Commercial production on the mass scale adopted nowadays is exceedingly wasteful, with any veg deemed imperfect being rejected by buyers, meaning in some cases simply being thrown away. Imperfection is a fact of vegetable growing (especially organic vegetable growing), and there's nothing wrong with a cucumber that bends too much. Organic vegetables are often less than perfect, and this is just something you will get used to and in the end come to appreciate.

Weighing up the pros and cons

Organic methods are usually no more complex than non-organic, they take no more time, and are cheaper and better for the environment and for your health, but you may well face challenges along the way. Diseases, pests and weeds can be more of a problem, so why bother? Well, you can now look at the pros and cons of both methods.

The whole biodiversity of an area relies on a delicate balance; if you damage even one simple bacterial element of your soil, the knock-on effects can be massive. Many pesticides are intended to be selective, in that they only target certain species of pest. In reality, wiping out even one pest has a knock-on effect via the delicate food chain. For example, you spray a chemical on your plot, and as a result the earthworm population declines; next, the bird population is affected because of the lack of worms to eat.

Unfortunately, this process doesn't stop here; if bird populations decline, the insects and other creatures they feed on increase in numbers, worsening the initial problem and necessitating more spraying.

Organic gardeners have to accept a few certainties that they just have to get along with. More than likely, your plot may not look quite so neat and perfect as those of some of your non-organic neighbours; you may well have to work a bit harder to fend off weeds. You're sure to be more open to attack from certain pests and diseases. On the other hand, if you systematically spray chemicals onto your plot, the long-term effects on your soil quality will be almost irreversible – some chemicals can reside in the soil for ten years or more. It can take that long for the natural balance to be restored.

Arguments have been put forward against organic methods, and although they apply more to organic farming, they are important points that need discussing. Some argue that due to the fact that organic food production uses fewer chemicals, it's a far less efficient means of producing crops. Amongst the claims are that organic crops use three times as much land as conventional food crops. Therefore with more and more land being dedicated to organic growing, eventually more land will be needed to produce the same amount of food. This could be at the expense of rainforests or other important areas that are as yet uncultivated. So it's possible in the long run that organic methods may actually do more harm than good.

This argument isn't of any great consequence to small producers like allotmenteers, however. Although it's often the case that organic crops are a little less productive and smaller in size and so don't feed as many per square metre, give me a good pile of manure over a tub of chemicals any day!

What's in your food?

If you look at studies and chemical analysis of the fruit and vegetable produce you get off the shelf in your average supermarket, the findings can be alarming! Take a look at the Pesticide Residues Committee's website (www.pesticides.gov.uk/prc_home.asp) and you'll find all sorts of statistics that may put you off buying off-the-shelf non-organic vegetables for life. The main issue for me is the list of chemicals that the committee regularly tests food for – it's long (in fact it's vast) and contains all sorts of compounds that most people have never heard of, let alone want to be putting onto their food. Admittedly, the amounts of chemical residue found on the food tested are usually minute, but are still present. The committee comments on many chemicals found on food samples, saying 'None of the residues detected would be expected to have an effect on health'; that doesn't sound too reassuring to me. The fact is that many foods contain a variety of different chemicals, so who can be sure that these 'chemical cocktails' won't cause any harm?

Understanding organic methods

An old gardening adage states, 'Feed the soil, not the plants.' In basic terms, the soil contains a delicate balance of ground-up rock in various size particles, organisms and micro-organisms, and decaying organic matter. When you plant something, the plant sucks nutrients out of the soil; if these nutrients are not replaced, over years the soil slowly becomes 'dead' and infertile. Soil that lacks organic matter has no water-retaining ability and can't hold on to nutrients, because they simply wash away when it rains. So even if you do add chemical fertilisers, they don't stay in the soil for long and leach out into the waterways and surrounding areas.

So it's vital to keep the soil well stocked with organic matter. This organic matter is full of beneficial bacteria and micro-organisms that are responsible for breaking down the dead and decaying plant and animal waste into nutrients that plants can absorb into their roots. It also improves the drainage of your soil and the water-retaining properties, helps warm the soil up more quickly in the spring, and greatly improves the soil structure. Spraying with chemicals can damage these delicate organisms, meaning that the soil works less effectively. For more detailed information on soil and the importance of organic matter, check out Chapter 6.

Embracing nature and the environment

As an organic gardener, you must first choose plants that are suitable for the environment you garden in. You need to assess your plot in terms of soil type, aspect, location and so on in order that you can choose the plants that will thrive best on your plot. Many non-organic gardeners use chemicals to adapt their plots so they're more suited to crops that otherwise wouldn't thrive. By doing so, they're basically working against their environment to produce crops. As an organic gardener, you have to do the opposite and work with your environment or adapt it with non-chemical methods, and grow plants that are suited to it. The fact is that a plant that grows happily and naturally is a more healthy plant, and a healthy plant is stronger and more able to cope with disease and pests that attack it. On the other hand, a plant that's in the wrong environment will struggle, be unhealthy and be more susceptible to attack.

REMEMBER

Organic gardeners takes the view that you must analyse the plot as a whole rather than any individual components of it. This means, for example, that if you have a problem with your carrots, you don't look at the carrots directly but at the reason why the environment in which they're growing isn't right for them. This isn't to say you can't try and figure out individual problems when they arise, but your main aim should be to create a plot where these problems are less likely to happen, creating a balance between you, nature and the environment you garden in.

Recycling has to be at the heart of every organic garden, and by recycling all the suitable green waste from your plot, you not only save the cost of buying expensive composts, but you also help reduce the pressure on landfill sites. Therefore, prunings, old plants (that aren't diseased), annual weeds, kitchen waste and leaves should be returned to the soil as home-made compost. For more on nurturing home-made compost, see Chapter 6.

Getting Practical

In practice, organic gardening is a wonderfully life-enriching process both for you and your plot, but it does involve hard work. You need to be one step ahead all the time and anticipate problems before they arise. For example, if your carrots have been affected by carrot fly, look ahead and choose a variety that offers some resistance to the problem. You can also install a carrot fly screen – because the carrot fly flies low, a physical barrier around 50–60 centimetres tall will keep them at bay.

Another example is growing leaf crops such as cabbages. These need relatively high levels of nitrogen to succeed, so plant them after your legumes (beans, peas and so on) in the crop-rotation calendar (see Chapters 4 and 6 for more on crop rotation), when the nitrogen-fixing bacteria on the roots of legumes have sorted any nitrogen deficit in readiness for your leafy crops. Or if you need a boost of nitrogen, apply a dose of bone meal or dried blood, both of which are high in nitrogen.

Preparing for disappointment and accepting imperfections

Things quite commonly go wrong on the vegetable plot, and this applies equally to organic and to conventional plots. A crop may suddenly fall foul of a hoard of hungry mice or rats, or a swarm of aphids may attack while you are away on holiday, infecting your crop with some nasty disease. But these problems can all be avoided with planning, and a little experience goes a long way. When you first start out, be prepared for these devastating setbacks from the word go, so you can learn to put them down to experience and do things differently next time. The only way to learn is through experience – and as they say, 'Once bitten, twice shy.'

Imperfect vegetables seem to be the hardest thing for new allotmenteers to accept. People are so used to the supposedly perfect fruit and veg that we buy in the shops that when faced with a cabbage with caterpillars on it and holes in some of the leaves, they recoil in disgust. These are normal things that happen to normal vegetables, especially when you don't ply them with chemicals! Just because they don't look as uniform and perfect as shop-bought veg doesn't mean you can't eat them and – surprise, surprise – I'd put money on them tasting better! Don't panic, though – I'm not saying that all your crops will look odd. In fact, once you refine your art, your crops will improve and start to look as good, if not better, than 'normal' veg.

Now you're equipped to deal with imperfections and the loss of the odd plant to pests and disease, you're ready to look at the organic methods employed to counter-attack some of these problems.

Selecting your plants carefully

Choosing suitable plants and, more importantly, suitable varieties is essential when planning your organic allotment. The first point to make is that *hybrid* plants aren't necessarily non-organic: they're simply cross-breeds, bred to possess the best traits possible. Some purist organic gardeners like to stick to *heritage* varieties (see Chapter 4), but I argue that these older varieties are still mutations of older plants and that by ignoring new varieties, these gardeners are simply limiting their options and making life hard for themselves. Hybrid and F1 (again, see Chapter 4) varieties are often highly vigorous, fast growing and disease resistant, and are even resistant to some pests, which makes them ideal for the organic plot. This means that you won't need to spray them with chemicals and pesticides, and because they have what's often known as *hybrid vigour*, they become strong, healthy plants, which is always the ultimate aim.

Resistance doesn't mean immunity, so always be on your guard. It's not just hybrid varieties that have beneficial characteristics, so don't rule out *open-pollinated* types (varieties pollinated by insects and by themselves) or old heritage varieties, which can still offer organic gardeners plants well suited to their individual plots. Open-pollinated plants can cross-breed with other similar varieties on the allotment site, so collected seeds may not always grow to be exactly the same as the parent plant.

Many seeds are treated with chemicals to aid *germination* (sprouting), extend their shelf life and help prevent diseases whilst they're germinating, so if you're a really determined purist, you'll want to source only organic seeds for your plot. Many seeds are available to you. These include seeds from companies that specialise in organic and heritage seeds, but the choice is far more limited.

Saying that, because demand for organic produce is on the up, so is the selection of products and seeds available to organic growers, so you've plenty out there to try. The debate rages over whether organic seeds produce better-tasting plants, and I'm not totally convinced that an organic seed really produces a more organic plant, but the option is there if you so fancy. The only argument I can see for buying organic seeds is the fact that, in their production, no man-made chemicals have been used, and this is better for the environment. One final point is that you can get hybrid seeds that are also organic, so don't rule out the modern options!

Fruit trees are a little harder to find if you're a strictly organic gardener, but quite a few organic growers now supply them, so the varieties available are certainly increasing.

Using organic pest control

If you don't have the powerful chemical weapons available to the conventional gardener, pests and diseases are difficult to fend off, but you have a number of methods to employ that are just as effective as chemical warfare and are much better in the long run. In an ideal world, your plot will be a diverse micro-habitat in perfect balance, with the food chain being complete and uninterrupted so that the predators keep all the pests at bay. This is, of course, just a pipe dream and next to impossible to achieve, but predators can greatly reduce pest numbers, so should be encouraged at every opportunity. Here are some methods that organic gardeners employ to fight back against pests:

Physical barriers are the first line of defence:

- **Netting, cages or fleece.** These can be erected or placed over crops to prevent attack from certain pests. Ideally, build a simple frame over the crops you want to protect, leaving plenty of room above and around the plants so none of the foliage is accessible to large pests such as birds. Use fine netting with holes less that 1 centimetre in width to keep cabbage white butterflies away from your precious cabbages.
- **Cloches.** These act like mini greenhouses that you can place over your crops, and can be really effective in protecting young plants from the cold and from attacks from slugs, insects and birds. They are available either as single cloches to place over individual plants or cloche tunnels that look like mini polytunnels. You can also buy really great-looking bell cloches that are made from glass or clear plastic; these look like glass bells when placed over plants.
- **Collars.** A simple yet brilliant idea, which usually works every time. You can buy collars or, easier still, make them yourself. They're circular bits of black plastic with a diameter of at least 15 centimetres. The collars have a slit from the outer edge of the circle to the centre, and a hole in the middle. Slip the collar around the plant so it sticks out through the middle and the collar sits on the ground. You then bury the edge in soil a little. These collars protect the roots from cabbage root flies and carrot root flies, which lay their eggs on the roots of cabbages and brassicas, and the collar forms a simple barrier that the flies have no way of breaking through.

- **Fences.** Fences may seem a bit obvious, but if you have trouble with rabbits, put up a fine wire mesh fence that's at least 1 metre high and buried 10 and 20 centimetres underground so the little fellas can't burrow into your plot.
- **Barriers for slugs and snails.** Mulches around plants that are targets for slug attacks can protect plants from being eaten to bits. Gardeners use many types such as crushed eggshells, sharp stones or grit, or even copper wires. Mulches deter the slugs, who hate sliding over rough surfaces, and the copper creates a slight electric charge that acts as a mini electric fence.

Other methods to protect your plot include:

- **Removing pests by hand.** Slugs are most active at night, so many gardeners go out with a torch and bucket and collect and dispose of them. With aphids, caterpillars and other visible bugs, you can easily squish them and wipe them off the leaves. Many hide under the foliage, so look closely and get squashing. Just make sure that you don't squish any beneficial or harmless insects – identify them first!
- **Traps.** You can trap slugs in a number of ways. Try beer traps – jam jars sunk into the soil and filled with beer or old milk or even old fruit juice. The slugs love all of these liquids and fall into the traps and drown. You can also buy pheromone traps, which are great for capturing specific pests such as codling moths – which attack your apples and pears – and plum fruit moths.
- **Encouraging wildlife.** Planting flowers and plants that attract beneficial insects to your plot can help with pollination, attracting hoverflies, whose larvae feast on black fly, and also ladybirds, who like black fly too. Getting wildlife on your side means you encourage nature to help look after your plot for you.
- **Companion planting.** This method can really help protect your plants from attack by pests. For example, strong-smelling aromatic plants such as French marigolds, lavender and most herbs are great for disguising plants that aphids like, because aphids are guided by a keen sense of smell. The same applies to carrot flies, which are attracted by the smell of a form of acid in carrots. If you plant strong-smelling plants such as onions or herbs around your carrots, you can create a great 'smelly' foil.
- **Biological control.** You can buy a range of different parasitic insects or predatory insects that can be used to attack unwanted pests. These are usually only effective in greenhouses or sometimes in containers, where they can be kept in one place. For example, parasitic wasps are useful for attacking whitefly in the greenhouse, where they lay eggs. The developing whitefly egg hatches and the baby wasp eats the carcass. It sounds gruesome but it really works! Also you can buy *nematodes*, which are tiny worm-like creatures that bore into pests such as slugs

and eventually kill them. A number of other biological control methods exist out there, for example lacewing larvae that can eat hundreds of aphids a week. They also eat small caterpillars and thrips (tiny, slender insects with fringed wings). And don't forget ladybirds (especially their larvae), which are well known for feasting on aphids and other insects.

- **Organic sprays.** Several organic pest sprays are around, some better than others. Most of them create a soapy film over the pests, stopping them from breathing or basically causing the surface cells on their bodies to leak and dissolve, quickly killing them. The fatty acid in soap is what does the damage, but you need to use sprays fairly often, and can kill beneficial insects in doing so, so do take care. You can make your own soap sprays using household soaps, but be careful because some soaps are certainly not organic and may contain chemicals that can damage your plants, so only use shop-bought sprays or those made with mild soap not detergent.

Utilising organic fertilisers and feeds

Organic fertilisers are fast becoming more readily available, and usually contain: natural rock minerals; seaweed and seaweed extract; fish, blood and bone meal; composted chicken manure; and farmyard and animal manure. Some are also made of extracts of beneficial plants such as comfrey, and all sorts of plant extracts that are designed for specific plants, such as tomatoes. Keep your eye out for these:

- **Rock minerals.** All sorts of rock mineral mixtures are now on the market, including mined volcanic rock that contains nearly all the minerals and trace elements you can possibly need. You can also obtain more specific sources such as ground limestone and ground scallop shells, both of which you can use to sweeten acid soil by raising pH levels and reducing the acidity in the soil.
- **Seaweed.** Seaweed is wonderful stuff containing all sorts of chemicals that benefit all sorts of crops. It contains major elements such as nitrogen, potassium, phosphorus and magnesium, and many minor elements as well. It's available as a dried product, a liquid feed or as seaweed extract, all of which are clean and easy to use. Fresh seaweed has been used for centuries as a soil improver and can literally be dug straight into the soil, where it rots down fairly quickly. It also contains an acid called alginic acid, which, in really simplified terms, combines with certain metallic elements in the soil to create a polymer resembling a sponge. This swells, thereby greatly improving a soil's water-retention capabilities. Seaweed is proven to greatly improve soil structure and helps create the perfect 'crumb' texture that gardeners strive for. Seaweed also promotes a plant's ability to take up existing nutrients in the soil, making it a super food and plant tonic in one.

- **Fish, blood and bone.** These natural (but processed) fertilisers are really commonplace and easily available in all good garden centres and DIY stores. All of them are by-products of the fish and animal food processing industry and contain varying levels of nutrients such as nitrogen, potassium, phosphorus and magnesium, along with some other beneficial trace elements. This type of fertiliser can be used as a top dressing, as a general feed, and is also useful incorporated into the planting hole when planting new shrubs, trees and other plants. Rake it into the soil few weeks before sowing or planting so it can be broken down ready to give new plants a boost. It's effective in giving fast-growing plants a burst of feed and can also be used as a tonic if your plants seem a little lacklustre.
- **Bone meal.** A mixture of ground-up animal bones, a by-product of the meat industry. Bone meal is a slow-release fertiliser that is a good source of phosphorous. It comes as coarse-ground or fine-ground powder, the finer being faster acting. It is mainly used in the early stages of a plant's root development and to help in forming shoots.
- **Hoof and horn.** This is made from ground, cooked hooves and horns from slaughtered cattle, and comes in a ground form that can be applied to the garden. It is a really useful source of slowly released nitrogen, which is best tickled into the surface of the soil. Hoof and horn is ideal for leafy crops, and one application will take about four to six weeks to kick in. It can last up to 12 months in the soil. Hoof and horn can also be used as an additive (known as an *accelerator*) in your compost heap to get it decomposing more quickly.
- **Plant- and animal-based products.** Many products out there combine all sorts of organic ingredients to make fertilisers suitable for all sorts of applications. Many use plant and animal extracts, various microbes and fungi, all of which claim to help plants with their nutritional needs. Some are in liquid form and are fast-acting feeds, others are in granular form (often mixed with poultry manure) and are spread around your crops throughout the season.
- **Animal manures.** I don't know how many times I've mentioned the importance of well rotted farmyard manure so far in this book, but here we are again and for good reason! Animal manure provides nutrients, improves water retention, improves soil structure, improves soil texture, helps the soil warm up in spring, introduces beneficial bacteria to the soil that aid decomposition, and is the life blood of any allotment garden. Ignore it at your peril! Chicken manure provides a great high-nitrogen feed that's ideal for greening up leafy vegetables. Rabbit droppings are higher in nitrogen than even chicken manure and these are great for the allotment, although unless you keep rabbits, are a bit hard to come by!

Considering companion planting

Companion planting isn't just some trendy gardening technique that eco warriors have adopted to add green credentials to their eco portfolio, it's based on hundreds of years of horticultural evidence. But what is it?

Companion planting is based on the idea that certain plants grouped together have beneficial effects on each other. This can be in terms of deterring insects, aiding each other's growth by providing nutrients in the soil (legumes and nitrogen fixing), offering some protection from the weather, or even attracting beneficial pollinators to your plot. For example, many allotmenteers sow spring onion seeds alongside their carrots: the strong-smelling onions help confuse the dreaded carrot fly, who then can't find the carrots on which to lay their eggs.

Companion planting also includes planting crops that are grown as a sacrifice to crops you want to encourage. For example, you can grow a row of soft, succulent, fast-growing lettuces around other crops that are likely to be attacked by slugs. This is also known as trap cropping.

Some people claim that herbs when planted amongst other crops can subtly change the flavour of them. A good example is basil, which is said to improve the flavour of tomatoes when planted alongside them.

Planting to deter pests

Many plants are used in companion planting to keep pests away from your precious fruit and veg. Most of these have strong aromas that confuse pests hell-bent on ruining your crops.

Here are some well known plants to try:

- **Basil:** Deters whitefly, so is good planted near kale and tomatoes, which can really suffer from an attack.
- **Chives and coriander:** Both are excellent at keeping aphids away from most allotment crops.
- **French marigolds:** Aphids and whitefly hate the smell of French marigolds, so they steer clear. French marigolds secrete a natural pesticide from their roots which can stay in the soil for years, even after the plant has died.
- **Rosemary:** Deters carrot fly with its strong aroma confusing the carrot flies and acting as a foil for your carrots.

- **Sage:** Also a good deterrent for carrot fly with its strong smell masking the smell of the carrots which the flies find so attractive.
- **Mint, hyssop and sage:** Plant these amongst your cabbages and lettuces to repel slugs.
- **Leeks and carrots:** Planted together these benefit each other. Leeks help repel carrot fly, and carrots keep the leek moth and onion fly at bay.

Planting to attract beneficial insects

Of course, not all insects are baddies. Attract beneficial insects to your crops by introducing plants that they like. Such plants include:

- **Dill.** Dill attracts hoverflies and predatory wasps, which feast on aphids.
- **French marigolds.** These attract hoverflies into the garden, and hoverfly larvae gorge on aphids.
- **Yarrow (*Achillea*).** Yarrow attracts beneficial insects – both pollinators and predators – to the plot, but are also useful for adding silica, phosphorus and calcium to the soil if thrown onto your compost heap.
- ***Phacelia*.** A lovely looking flowering plant that has many uses. It attracts pollinators, but also lacewings and ladybirds, whose larvae will happily help munch on any aphids on your plot. *Phacelia* is also great as a cut flower and dug in as a green manure to return nutrients to the soil.
- ***Limnanthes*.** Commonly called the poached egg plant, this is great for attracting hoverflies and also bees to your plot, both combating aphids and helping pollination respectively.

Combining two or more different companion plants in particular combinations can reap major benefits. Here are some well-known combinations to try:

- **Brassicas and dill:** The cabbages, broccoli or Brussels sprouts act as a support below the dill, and the dill attracts predatory wasps that feed on cabbage pests.
- **Cucumbers and nasturtiums:** The nasturtiums climb up alongside your cucumbers and the smell deters cucumber beetles. The twining stems make a great habitat for spiders and other predators to hide in.
- **Tomatoes, basil, marigolds and lettuce:** These all work well together: the basil deters whitefly and aphids, favouring the tomatoes, whilst the marigolds attract hoverflies that munch on any aphids that get through, thus protecting your lettuces.

- **Corn, beans and squash:** A classic combination (the 'three sisters') traditionally used in the USA, where corn, beans and squash are grown together, each helping the other out. The corn acts as a support for the beans, the beans help the other plants by fixing nitrogen in the soil, and the squash crawls over the ground, reducing the need for weeding.
- **French beans and sweetcorn:** French beans are great planted amongst sweetcorn, the sweetcorn offering useful protection for your beans as well as something for them to climb up.
- **Nasturtiums and cabbages:** Well known for attracting caterpillars, nasturtiums are great for planting around your cabbage patch so that the caterpillars tuck into them instead of your cabbages.

There are also examples of plants that should not be grown together, such as garlic or chives with beans or peas. It is said that the garlic or chives will stunt the growth of beans and peas, so this combo is to be avoided.

Encouraging Wildlife onto Your Plot

The essence of organic gardening is to embrace nature and guide it to work for you and not against you. By encouraging wildlife onto your plot, you encourage predators to keep pests in check. Admittedly, some forms of wildlife can cause more damage than good. Blackbirds and thrushes can strip your raspberries and currant bushes in minutes, but if you protect the plants with netting, they'll be fine. On the upside, thrushes love to eat snails, hoverflies and some wasp species. Ladybirds love to feast on aphids, and most birds eat insects in abundance, so by encouraging wildlife you not only help your plot but also the environment.

Here are some great ways to encourage wildlife onto your plot:

- **Stop using chemicals.** Chemicals are harmful to all wildlife; this is especially true of insecticides that indiscriminately kill beneficial insects as well as pests. Man-made fertilisers can destroy the quality of the soil, disrupting the delicate balance of life.
- **Install a small pond.** Ponds encourage frogs, which feast on slugs, woodlice and other little nasties.
- **Plant flowers to attract beneficial insects.** Yarrow, marigolds, lavender, poached egg plants, *Zinnia*, catnip, tansy and sweet alyssum all attract hoverflies, bees and predatory wasps, which will help keep pests at bay.
- **Make a log pile.** Log piles provide hiding places for beetles, frogs and toads. Indeed, amphibians often hibernate under them. The slowly rotting logs attract woodlice and other insects on which the frogs and beetles feast.

- **Make a hedgehog house.** Hedgehogs love to eat slugs, snails and caterpillars, so provide a safe, dry home in which they can shelter and hibernate. You can buy all sorts of hedgehog houses, but they're also easy to make. You simply build a wooden box the size of a milk crate, make a tunnel for an entrance that's at least 12.5 centimetres high, and attach some kind of ventilation pipe on the back. Then cover the house with leaves and soil. Be sure to put plenty of straw or shredded newspaper inside for the hedgehog to use as bedding. Also remember to face the entrance away from cold northerly winds. Figure 8-1 shows you how to make one.
- **Grow hedges.** Growing hedges doesn't really apply to allotmenteers, but if you're creating a vegetable garden on your own plot of land, native hedges and plants will attract native species of animal and insects, which is the best way to create a bio-diverse environment for your plot.
- **Buy or make insect homes.** You can buy all sorts of insect homes that encourage insects onto your allotment. You can buy beetle boxes and ladybird and lacewing houses – in fact, houses that suit many insect species. Many look pretty cool as well.
- **Leave an area wild(ish).** Nettles and long grass are great hiding places for ground beetles, who like to eat slugs. Also nettles (both stinging and dead nettles) provide flowers that attract bees and butterflies, which (with the exception of the dreaded cabbage white) are good for your plot. Nettles and yarrow are also good for attracting ladybirds.

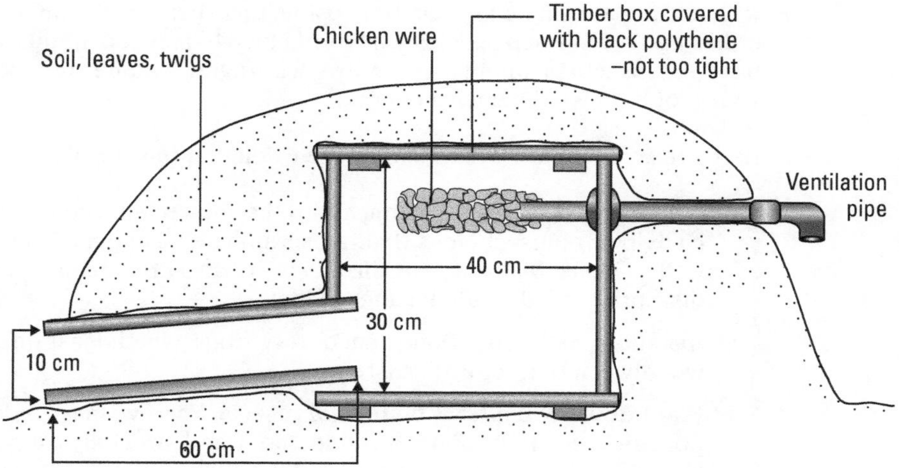

Figure 8-1: A home-made hedgehog house.

Part III
Growing Your Favourite Vegetables

'He said he was specialising in herbs but he didn't tell me what sort they were.'

In this part . . .

This is the part of the book you can really get your teeth into. Here's where I lead you in detail through the preparations and planning you need to undertake to grow perfect veg.

Each chapter deals with a different group of vegetables, taking you through everything you need to do to get bumper crops of all your green favourites. I take you through from sowing seeds, to raising and planting seedlings and right through to successfully harvesting and storing your little beauties. I outline the crops that would be good for you to grow and warn you off the ones that won't really work on your plot.

Chapter 9

Going Underground with Root Vegetables

In This Chapter

- Producing perfect potatoes
- Creating crunchy carrots
- Preparing parsnip plots
- Bringing out the best in beetroot

Nothing is more satisfying than sticking your fork into the soil to lift some potatoes. For me, it's like unearthing buried treasure. Some root crops (such as swede and beetroot, for example) tend to be a little out of fashion on the modern allotment, with many people preferring to grow more expensive and unusual vegetables. Yet roots are packed full of goodness because they are where plants store the starch and sugars they feed on. There are lots of root veg for you to try, such as swede, turnips, celeriac and Florence fennel, but potatoes, carrots, parsnips and beetroot are the obvious first ports of call.

In this chapter you discover all the skills you need to grow great-tasting, nutrient-packed super roots. Most root vegetables are reasonably easy to grow. Some, such as carrots and parsnips, do better in lighter, sandy soils. They can struggle, especially in heavy clay or stony soil, but you can grow them easily in raised beds or containers (see Chapter 5 for more on these). So if you have clay soil or an allotment full of stones, don't despair.

Growing Potatoes

Potatoes (and most root crops) are grouped according to how long they take to mature, using the terms *early*, *second early* and *main crop*. If you grow a selection of all three types, you can harvest potatoes right through the summer from June to October. *Earlies* do exactly what the name suggests, and are ready early on in the harvesting season, from June onwards. Usually known as new potatoes, they're smaller and can be washed and cooked straight from the ground without peeling. Although they're less productive than other varieties of potato and don't store well, earlies mature quickly and offer a great quick crop. *Second earlies* are simply ready a bit later, from late June to August, and bridge the gap to your *main-crop* potatoes, which take longer to mature and are usually much bigger, ready for harvesting from September. Main-crop potatoes store well and will keep your supply of spuds going right into the winter.

Potatoes are one of the most widely grown and popular vegetables on the allotment. They're tender perennials that grow to 60 centimetres in height and the same width. Potatoes are closely related to tomatoes. You may actually discover your potato plants bearing green tomato-like fruit after they flower.

These tomato-like fruits are *not* tomatoes and contain a poisonous alkaloid called *solanine*. Don't eat the fruits or let your children touch them. Potatoes are actually closely related to deadly nightshade. Potatoes turn green when they're exposed to light, and this indicates the presence of solanine; it's the plant's self-defence mechanism kicking in to stop animals from eating it. If you find green potatoes, don't eat them!

Due to the fact that potatoes originate from the tropical jungle regions of South America (in fact all modern potatoes can be traced by DNA to potatoes from ancient Peru), they prefer rich damp soil and benefit from leaf mould that imitates their native habitat. Their tropical origins mean that potatoes are in no way frost hardy and should be started off indoors and grown protected from the frost (you find out how to do this later in this chapter).

The potato is not, strictly speaking, the plant's root. In fact, the potato is a *tuber* – the part of the plant where food is stored to feed the next generation of plants the following year. The plant grows and fattens up the tubers, which then sprout from buds called *eyes* and grow into new plants. Out of sight underground, potatoes reproduce in this way, turning each seed potato into many.

Getting started with potatoes

Potatoes are grown from a seed of sorts, but not like the usual seeds you get in a packet. The green fruit on potatoes do contain small seeds that can be saved and used to grow new plants, but I don't know anyone who actually bothers. Most people grow from *seed potatoes*, which are simply potatoes grown specifically by growers to plant out. Potatoes are very prone to certain diseases and attack from pests, so seed potatoes are generally bred and grown to be resistant. Breeding takes place in areas that are free from the aphids (greenfly) that introduce a virus disease. These areas are usually at a certain height above sea level (where aphids aren't a problem) or in windswept areas where aphids have difficulty flying.

In praise of Scottish spuds

Scotland became a really important source of disease-free seed potatoes during the early 1900s when, in certain areas, English potatoes began to suffer greatly from localised disease problems. Farmers came to realise that when they planted Scottish seed potatoes, the problems ceased. The farmers didn't realise at the time that it was because greenfly couldn't survive and reproduce in the cool and windy climate of some areas of Scotland. This discovery then led to massive development in the Scottish seed potato industry.

Although, after cropping them, you can keep some of your potatoes for planting next year – and do so for a couple of years – they become less disease resistant and less productive each year. You're better off playing safe and buying new certified disease-resistant potatoes each year.

Never plant potatoes that you've bought from a shop. You may well get a decent crop, but you run the risk of introducing diseases to your plot, rendering it useless for growing spuds for the next few years.

Potatoes are fairly easy to grow but do take up a fair amount of space. Some people dedicate vast areas of their plots to potatoes, but if you're using the crop-rotation system strictly (as described in Chapter 7), you're limited by the size of your four sub-plots. Potatoes really prefer a deeply cultivated fertile soil that has been manured heavily the previous autumn. That said, they grow in pretty much any soil type but need organic matter (see Chapter 7) to help them preserve moisture.

Chitting

Chitting is a simple process that encourages a potato to sprout. It should be started about six weeks prior to planting. If you choose to chit, order and buy your seed potatoes and start chitting them from mid-winter onwards. You can plant seed potatoes without chitting; in fact, the process is most beneficial to early crops to give them a head start. Second early crops may benefit slightly, but I no longer chit main crops, and they seem just as good.

Examine your seed potatoes carefully to find the side with the most *eyes* (little marks where the shoots appear). In single layers, place the potatoes in trays so that the eyes are facing upwards – charmingly called *rose end up* – then store them in a cool, frost-free place, out of direct sunlight. Each eye will produce a shoot. As the shoots grow, keep the potatoes cool and make sure that the shoots are looking healthy and plump. Any spindly, weak ones should just be rubbed off with your finger; usually, a new stronger shoot will appear. When the shoots are about 1.5–2.5 centimetres long, they're ready to plant. You'll have firm green shoots that give your potatoes a head start as soon as you've planted them out. You can also buy pre-chitted potatoes, which will save you the bother. Figure 9-1 shows potatoes chitting in a box.

Figure 9-1: Chitting potatoes.

WARNING!

Many gardeners leave their potatoes in a dark cupboard to start sprouting, but doing so produces weak, pale specimens.

Planting out

Early potatoes need to be planted out around late March, second earlies in early to mid-April, and main crops in mid- to late April. This will vary a little depending on where you live in the country.

TIP

If you're an allotment newcomer, ask your fellow plot holders when they plan to plant their potatoes out. Weather conditions and local knowledge are their guides, so learn from their experience.

I tend to plant the first earlies using my grandfather's methodical approach, as follows:

1. **Mark out your first trench with a taut line of string.** For first and second earlies, trenches should be 60 centimetres apart; for second earlies and main-crop potatoes, allow around 75 centimetres.
2. **Dig the trench into a V shape.** I drag a mattock along, and that works the best. Mark out subsequent trenches with string or just score the ground with a stick. The trench should be about 8–15 centimetres deep (depending on the variety of potato you're planting).
3. **Add a generous layer of well rotted organic matter to the bottom and incorporate it into the soil.**
4. **Place the chitted tubers, shoots up, in the bottom of the trench at 40-centimetre intervals.** Cover them with 13–15 centimetres of soil. For second earlies, allow 30 centimetres between each tuber, and for main-crop potatoes, 40 centimetres.

Earthing up

Earthing up means using a rake, hoe or spade to build up soil gently over the developing shoots. This soil protects the delicate new shoots from frost attack. Because the tubers form on the stems of the plant, drawing up soil around them also encourages higher yields. I tend to earth up two or three times during the growing season: early on and a little later. When your plant grows to around 10 centimetres tall, you can then bury the whole plant; doing so simply encourages it to grow more potatoes. See Figure 9-2.

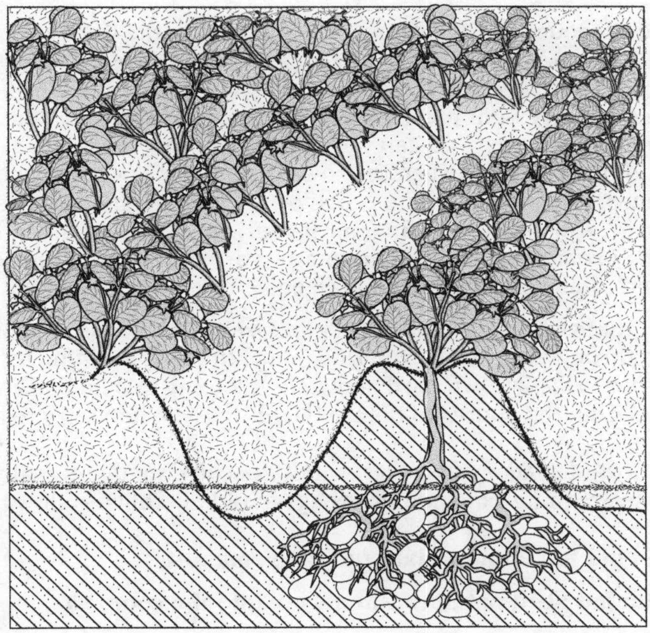

Figure 9-2: Earthing up potatoes.

TIP

Potatoes seem to be far more upright in the early morning and at night. During the day, they can be droopy and limp, which makes earthing up more difficult. Time your earthing up for when your plants are at their most rigid.

Undertaking routine care

Potatoes don't need a lot of looking after, but you need to take a few basic steps to ensure they remain healthy. These are:

- **Guard against frost.** If you expect frost, cover the new shoots with a layer of straw or shredded newspaper, or with *tunnel cloches* made of fleece. (Tunnel cloches are like small polytunnels, are placed over growing plants and can be bought in good garden centres and stores online.)

- **Keep an eye on them.** Monitor your spuds as they grow and make sure that no tubers are exposed to the light, because this causes them to turn green and renders them inedible.
- **Make sure they have enough water.** Keep your potatoes moist once they've become established, otherwise the roots can split or even grow hollow on the inside. Water is particularly important when the tubers are the size of marbles, so if it doesn't rain at this stage, give them a good drink. It is not always easy to tell how well the tubers are forming, so as a guide, simply keep them watered in dry weather and you should not have any problems.
- **Weed thoroughly.** Pull all annual weeds out in the first weeks after planting your spuds. (Later on, the fast-growing potato foliage will smother most weeds.) Potatoes hate competition from weeds, and the rich soil you've built up is a perfect home for weeds, particularly the tenacious varieties. You can (as long as they've not set seed) simply spread the weeds between the rows of spuds to rot down and return goodness to the soil. Potatoes like plenty of sunshine and take up a lot of space, which can work in your favour, especially on a new plot containing problem weeds. When potatoes are fully grown, they cover the ground totally and smother the weeds.
- **Earth them up.** Earth your plants up (see the previous section) a few times through the growing period. Make the final earthing up steep and then pat the soil down hard and smooth; doing this helps protect your tubers from the spores of potato blight that inevitably try to attack.

If you're short of space, you can grow potatoes in containers really easily. You can use anything from compost bags to old dustbins. Follow these steps:

1. **Fill an old bin about a sixth full with compost.**
2. **Plant a few seed potatoes, shoots up, into the compost.**
3. **As the plant grows, but before it flowers (otherwise it is too late and the potatoes are well on their way to forming underground), cover it with compost.**
4. **Continue this process until the plant reaches the top of the bin.**
5. **Empty out the bin when the potatoes are ready to harvest. You will get about 12 spuds for every seed potato you plant.**

You can also grow potatoes in old car tyres. Simply fill one tyre with compost and plant your seed potatoes. As your potatoes grow, keep adding tyres and compost until the pile is between 1 and 2 metres high. To get your bumper crop of potatoes, just empty them out of the tyres.

WARNING! Well over a hundred diseases and pests are lurking out there to scupper your potato success. From the really serious potato blight to keel slugs, you will need to know what to look for. Pests, diseases and other problems are all covered in Chapter 7.

Using the no-dig method

Many gardeners employ the no-dig method for growing potatoes, and I don't blame them, because it is so simple:

1. **Clear an area of all weeds and cover it in a layer of compost 9–12 inches thick. (This uses a lot of compost!)**
2. **Push your seed potatoes into the compost as far as you can with digging, with the same spacing stated earlier in this chapter.**
3. **Cover the area with black landscape fabric and pin it down.**
4. **As the shoots start to push up into the fabric (you will see the little peaks), carefully cut a slit for them to grow through.**

This method helps eliminate problems with slugs and can help keep diseases like blight at bay. The resulting potatoes are usually quite small but they are also clean, so easier to harvest.

Considering varieties of potatoes

Most early potatoes aren't great for storing and are better for those of you who have limited space for growing, because they take up about half the space of main-crop varieties. You usually plant earlies out in mid-March and they take 10–15 weeks to mature, depending on weather and climate.

Here are my top early varieties:

- **Lady Christl.** One of the earliest croppers, offering a really good high yield. It has good disease resistance and firm, creamy flesh that won't fall apart when cooked.
- **Rocket.** A really early salad potato with a firm, waxy texture that makes a seriously good chip as well. May even be ready in ten weeks, hence the name!
- **Premier.** An easy-to-grow variety, ideal for organic growers due to its disease resistance – and makes really good chips.

- **Red Duke of York.** An old variety bred back in 1942 that has always been a favourite of mine. It's a vigorous grower that has beautiful red skin with pale fluffy yellow flesh and produces great bumper crops.
- **Arran Pilot.** A really popular variety and one I often go for. It is high yielding, has a fantastic flavour and is really easy to grow successfully.

Second earlies are gap fillers between early and main-crop varieties and are planted at the same time as early ones. They'll be ready to harvest in 13–15 weeks. Here are the varieties I suggest:

- **Kestrel.** Now a real allotment favourite with growers, who are using this variety more and more. Really easy to grow and really tasty when baked and roasted, it shows good resistance to most pests and diseases.
- **British Queen.** Over a hundred years old, which proves that it's worth a go. It yields bumper crops of delicious floury spuds.
- **Wilja.** A variety that many have seen in supermarkets and which I feel is best for chips and roasts.
- **Picasso.** An ideal all-rounder that produces large crops. This potato is great for storing.

Main-crop potatoes are planted in mid-March and are ready in 15–22 weeks, usually harvested from September onwards. Because they take so long to develop, they're the best types for storing. Just because they take longer to develop doesn't mean they're always bigger – some are, but you can get smaller types as well. Here are my suggestions:

- **King Edward.** Everybody's heard of this variety, and it's popular for a good reason. It's the ultimate floury potato for roasting and making mash. In fact, I used to work in restaurants, and the head chef insisted on this variety for that exact reason.
- **Maris Piper.** Another well known variety, Maris Piper is the most widely grown potato in the UK and is the best all-rounder.
- **Cara.** Another well known variety – a red-skinned potato that's great for baking.
- **Nicola.** Ideal to plant for Christmas. The crop can be harvested when small and used in salads or left to mature for an all-round great spud.
- **Sarpo Mira.** Becoming well known among gardeners for its blight-resistant qualities, it produces loads of large potatoes but does need lots of space for its plentiful foliage. Tests made on it when surrounded by blight-infected potatoes showed it actually resisted attack, so it's great for organic gardeners and beginners.
- **Valor.** Does really well for gardeners on poorer soils, so worth a go if that's you. Good slug and disease resistance, with a mild flavour and waxy texture.

- **Desiree.** Probably the top choice for allotment holders, offering really high yields and good resistance to drought. It can be attacked by eelworms, but that's not a massive issue.

Harvesting and storage

You can harvest early potatoes when the flowers have opened. Second earlies can be left in the ground until as late as September, while main crops should be lifted after the foliage has died back. Lift potatoes carefully using a fork. This is the best bit of vegetable gardening for me. It still amazes me that under the ground these little treasures have been forming over the past 10–20 weeks, and all you need to do is dig them up and eat them. Be careful as you go in with the fork, because if you stab any of the spuds they rot quickly; eat any damaged potatoes straight away (well cook them first!) and don't store them with other potatoes. Early potatoes should be lifted as close to eating as possible, because they're still growing and are full of *carbohydrates* (sugar) which deteriorate quickly. Main-crop potatoes can be left in the soil even after the foliage has died down, but they rot quickly if hit by hard frosts, so they should be lifted before then.

COOKING TIP

When making mash, try whipping the mashed potatoes vigorously with a fork – this really fluffs them up – put in a (large) knob of butter, a drop of warm milk, salt and pepper . . . perfect.

A good idea if you're about to store your late potatoes is to dig them up and leave them on the soil surface, in the sunshine, from a few hours up to a day (no more or they become poisonous see the section 'Getting started with potatoes' earlier in this chapter). Leaving potatoes out for a few hours hardens the skins and helps them keep for longer. Store them in a cool dark place, ideally in a well ventilated box of some kind or a potato sack.

Considering clamps

Clamps are an effective method of storing some main-crop root vegetables such as potatoes and swede outdoors in a way that keeps them for months. This is only worth doing if you've harvested a huge bumper crop that'll go to waste otherwise. Pile your potatoes into a potato mountain on top of a thick layer of straw then cover it with another layer of straw. Draw soil up and over the mountain to cover the entire heap. You should also make chimneys of straw by gathering little bundles and inserting them through the soil into the upper layer of straw every metre or so, to allow air to ventilate into the clamp. These can be placed either on top or along the side. If you store swede in this manner, ensure you pile them up in a small mountain with the cut ends outwards, otherwise they're likely to rot.

So do carrots help you see in the dark?

My grandad was a pilot who flew Lancaster bombers in the Second World War, and he was rationed extra carrots to improve his eyesight – at least that's what he told me! But I recently discovered that these were just rumours circulated by the RAF so that the enemy believed the pilots could see in the dark – a ruse to divert attention from the fact that the allies had developed radar. I can't believe my grandad led the Germans and me on for so long! But there's a grain of truth to the old adage that carrots help you see in the dark. Carrots are a valuable source of *beta carotene*, which the body transforms into vitamin A – great for your eyesight. Beta-carotene-rich foods help prevent a variety of eye ailments.

Cultivating Carrots

Carrots have to be one of the best veggies to grow on the allotment. They're unquestionably superior to carrots you can buy in the shops. Nothing is quite like a carrot straight from the ground to the serving plate . . . if it even gets that far!

Carrots are *biennial*, which means they grow from seed, storing food in their roots (the actual carrot) in their first year. In the second year, they flower then set seed and die. We simply pull them out of the ground before they get a chance to complete their life cycle.

Carrots have been specially bred to have early cropping varieties that grow quickly and others that stay in the ground longer and produce larger carrots. So many carrot varieties are available out there that the choice is bewildering, but your soil and personal preference should help you decide which ones suit you best. Carrots are grouped much like potatoes into early and main-crop varieties.

TIP: If you have clay, stony soil, chalky soil or drainage problems, grow the main-crop varieties that have shorter roots, because they can cope in these conditions much better. Round-rooted varieties are also suitable for growing in containers.

Getting started with carrots

Carrots like a patch that has been manured and has had crops grown in it during the previous year. The soil should ideally be fertile and well drained – for example, a fertile sandy soil. Carrots struggle in clay, but if you have this type of soil, don't worry – it can be improved greatly with lots of organic matter, as long as you add it at least six months before planting. If you grow carrots on freshly manured land, they have a tendency to become tough, watery and forked. If the soil is fairly acidic, you should lime the area well in advance. If you have stony soil, you may well end up with some rather curiously shaped carrots when you pull them up, because carrots tend to grow around obstructions; therefore go for the shorter, stumpy varieties (see the following section 'Considering varieties of carrots'). This an aesthetic issue but one worth bearing in mind.

Carrots can be sown from February all the way through to July, but you're better off waiting until March, when the soil is a little warmer, because the seeds won't germinate if it's too cold. The general rule for sowing carrot seeds is that if the soil feels cold, it's too early to sow. You can warm the soil by covering it with fleece a couple of weeks prior to sowing. I find a layer of fleece and a layer of black landscape fabric works best. The black absorbs heat from the sun, speeding the whole process up.

To sow your carrots, follow these steps:

1. **About two weeks prior to sowing, dig the area over with a fork to loosen the soil.**

   This allows the carrots to penetrate deeply. Don't add any organic matter, because this makes the soil too rich for them.

2. **About a week before sowing, rake the soil to a fine tilth (a fine, crumbly texture) and remove all the stones and other debris.**

   If there are too many stones, these will cause your carrots to fork, because they try to grow around them. This does not necessarily affect how they taste, but it makes them look odd and less visually appealing.

3. **Prepare your *drills*. Make shallow trenches in rows about 1 centimetre deep, closely spaced with between 15–30 centimetres between rows (depending on which variety you're using).**

   Whatever length you've allocated, you can simply use a stick to scour a line in the soil. If you live in quite a dry area, you can sow the seeds slightly deeper (say 2–2.5 centimetres). If the soil is dry, fill the drill with water about ten minutes before sowing, to help moisten the seeds.

4. **Sprinkle the seeds sparingly into the drill. You should aim to have four or five seeds per 3 centimetres.**

   Now admittedly, the seeds are so small that this is really hard to do, but just make sure that you don't overdo the seeding. If you do, you'll have to thin them out later, and this can encourage pests. It helps to mix the seeds with some sharp horticultural sand to make sure that you sow thinly. The sand helps with drainage too.

5. **Cover the seeds with some fine soil and during dry weather, water them well.**

   Don't worry too much if not a lot happens for a while. Carrots can take some time to get going . . . but they will!

6. **Thin out the seedlings. For main-crop carrots, space them 4 centimetres apart, increasing to 8 centimetres later on if you want larger carrots.**

   The further apart they're spaced, the larger they tend to grow. Earlier varieties may also need thinning out, but because they grow more quickly and are generally not as large as main-crop carrots, smaller spaces are fine for them.

WARNING!

When you pull up carrots, they can bruise or break, and this gives off a scent that *carrot root fly* can smell up to 7 miles (11 kilometres) away and they'll come for you . . . well, your carrots anyway! (You can read about carrot root fly in Chapter 7.)

When you thin out your carrots, be sure to gently heel or push the soil back down to flatten the surface and make it harder for the carrot root fly larvae to get to the roots.

ORGANIC WAY

Carrots benefit from potassium, which promotes solid tasty roots. Wood ash is a brilliant source of soluble potassium, which is absorbed quickly by the plants.

TIP

Carrot seeds can take a couple of weeks to germinate, so to speed things up a bit, spread them between two damp sheets of blotting paper and leave them for a couple of days. Be sure to keep an eye on them, because you don't want them to turn white and start to rot. Sow the seeds as normal and you should find that the seedlings appear more quickly than usual.

Considering varieties of carrots

Loads of different carrot varieties are out there for you to try, and they come in colours you may not expect: you can also grow purple, white, red and yellow ones, and also carrots that are almost black. Here are some examples:

- **Adelaide F1 hybrid.** A really easy-to-grow variety, perfect for kids to try, sown under cover (in cloche tunnels) in January and February – you'll be the first on the allotment to have juicy fresh carrots.
- **Amsterdam Forcing.** A really popular choice for growers, which produces uniform cylindrical roots that are deep orange in colour. It's a fast-growing baby carrot that you should thin out to 2 centimetres apart.
- **Autumn King 2.** This main-crop carrot can be left in the ground over winter without the usual problems of the root splitting, so it's a good one for the Christmas spread.

- **Flyaway F1.** As the name suggests, Flyaway F1 is a variety bred to have resistance to carrot flies. It is an ever-popular variety that produces an early crop with blunt roots. It's ideal for more heavy soil types.
- **Honeysnack.** Lives by its name, being really sweet and perfect eaten raw. It's blunt-ended in shape but reaches up to 15 centimetres in length and is a very pale orange colour.
- **Nantes Frubund: Fast Crop.** A brilliant breakthrough in carrot technology. Sow these in the autumn and they are ready for harvesting in spring . . . yes, you heard me right! Have carrots when no one else does. Simply amazing.
- **Kingston F1.** A main-crop carrot and a great all-rounder offering well rounded uniform, slender roots. It's really easy to grow and stores well – and I highly recommend it!
- **Parmex.** This very quick-to-mature, squat-looking carrot forms bite-size round roots. Great in containers, it's a godsend to those of you on clay soils.
- **Purple Haze F1 hybrid.** A main-crop carrot that produces deep purple long, heavy roots that are great eaten raw. It contains high levels of anti-oxidants and vitamin A. Well worth trying, and the kids will love it!
- **Rainbow F1 hybrid.** A new variety that produces carrots that range in colour from almost white to pale yellow through to orange – a bit of an oddity but lots of fun on a plate.
- **Red Samurai.** As the name implies, this carrot has a brilliant pinkish-red colour that stays even after cooking. It grows up to an enormous 28 centimetres in length.
- **Supreme Chanteney Red Cored.** Well known for its stumpy shape and sweet flavour, Supreme Chanteney is great for early sowing and perfect for planting in succession.
- **Sugarsnax 54 F1 hybrid.** This has to be one of the sweetest carrots available. It grows up to 25 centimetres in length and is one of my favourites for eating on the spot, straight out of the ground (washed, of course!).
- **Yellowstone.** Produces pale yellow carrots that are really sweet, especially if eaten raw. They reach about 20 centimetres in length.

TIP

You can now buy carrot seed tapes that are basically rolls of biodegradable paper with seeds spaced along them. They're brilliant in terms of getting the spacing between seeds right and eliminating the need to thin out rows. This really helps by not attracting the dreaded carrot fly!

Harvesting and storage

Carrots are best eaten fresh from the ground – simply grab the base of the foliage and gently tease the roots from the soil. If the carrots prove a bit tricky to get up, try pushing the fork into the soil to one side and then lifting them out in clumps. If you're going to store the carrots, it's best not to wash them, because doing so damages the skin and the carrots deteriorate and rot quickly. They also keep better if you cut off the foliage near the crown.

It's always better to pull carrots methodically from the start of the row and heel in the soil you've disturbed; if you simply pull them up willy-nilly, you encourage carrot flies to infest.

The best long-term way to store main-crop carrots is to lay them in a barrel or crate on layers of sand or old dry compost, making sure that they're not touching and are undamaged. Build up layers and store them in a cool, well ventilated place and use as required. One word of warning: don't store them in the same place or container year after year, because doing so encourages disease and rot.

Producing Parsnips

Parsnips, like carrots, are biennials and are great for growing in dry soil, where the roots can delve deep into the ground in the hunt for water. They're usually the first seeds of the year to be planted and the last to be harvested, because they have a long growing season. Their sweet roots are packed with health-giving nutrients and sugars. They're fairly easy to grow and don't suffer from many pests or diseases – in fact they're the perfect vegetable!

Parsnips actually benefit from being hit by frost: it makes them even sweeter because the starch in the roots turns to sugar. They can be pulled up whilst young and used as baby veg, or they can be left in the ground and used throughout the winter months as a precious winter veg.

Getting started with parsnips

Parsnips are easy to grow and like a light, well dug, stone-free soil, previously but not recently manured, and that had crops on it in the previous year (much as carrots do). They like it if the soil is deeply cultivated so that the tap roots can delve down in their search for water. In shallow soil, I opt for short, stumpy varieties, because the longer ones fork and don't do as well. Just as with carrots, if the soil is really acidic, it benefits the crop greatly to lime the soil in the autumn before you plant in early spring, otherwise you run the risk of parsnip canker.

Parsnips are usually sown in early spring when the soil is cold and often wet. It helps to cover the soil with cloche tunnels (see Chapter 3) or black landscape fabric and fleece to warm it, which really helps with germination. You can sow in April and possibly May, when the warm soil really helps with germination. In really cold winters, cover the rows with 10–15 centimetres of straw held down into the soil with some bent garden wire. This should stop the parsnips freezing and thawing, which they don't like.

To sow your parsnips, follow these steps:

1. **Dig over the intended area two weeks before planting. You need to loosen the soil for the deep-penetrating roots.**
2. **Do a final weed, rake the soil to a fine tilth and create drills. Make small trenches 2–4 centimetres deep and space the rows 30 centimetres apart. Water well.**
3. **Sow the seeds in the drills in groups of three, leaving 10 centimetres between each group. Another method is to sow them every 3–4 centimetres and thin them out to 10–15 centimetres apart later. Cover the seeds with a layer of fine soil and then some fine compost, and walk the seeds in (firm them down with your boot).**

Young parsnips need lots of water, so keep them moist but not waterlogged and be sure to keep weeds under control. Parsnips also benefit from a layer of compost as mulch.

Parsnip seeds are slow to germinate, so I suggest planting radishes in between the rows of parsnip seeds. Radishes grow far more quickly and help keep the soil crust broken, assisting the parsnips as they grow. Another bonus is that the radish foliage acts like a leaky umbrella, allowing water through to the young parsnip seedlings but protecting them from the sun.

Why not add grated parsnip to potato rösti? Grate the potatoes and squeeze out the water then add some finely sliced onion and grated parsnip, chopped thyme, salt and pepper and fry in little patties in olive oil. It's amazing served with a poached egg on top or a dash of chilli sauce, or with an egg, some bacon and maple syrup.

Considering varieties of parsnips

- **Avonreister.** Quite simply the most canker-resistant variety on the market, this small parsnip is good on all soils, even shallower ones.
- **Cobham Improved Marrow.** A late-maturing variety that reaches 15 centimetres in length, is very high in natural sugars and full of flavour.
- **Countess F1 hybrid.** A brilliant variety for first-timers and will give you a bumper crop that's easy to grow and pretty. It's also canker resistant.

- **Gladiator F1.** The world's first hybrid parsnip that revolutionised parsnip growing and reliability. Smooth skinned, tasty and tender.
- **Javelin F1 hybrid.** This tried-and-tested variety grows long, thin and true (hence its name).
- **Tender and True.** A personal favourite of mine and one of the sweetest of all parsnips.

Carrot fly can also threaten your parsnips, so follow the same safety measures as you would for carrots. (See Chapter 7 for more on this problem.)

Harvesting and storage

Parsnips are ready to harvest in about 16 weeks and, as mentioned before, their flavour improves when they're caught by frost. You can harvest them throughout the summer as baby parsnips but it's worth leaving most to harvest over winter and even into spring. The foliage dies back as winter approaches, so I mark the rows with a cane or string line so I know where to dig.

You can store parsnips in the same way as carrots, in layers of sand or dry compost in a wooden tray in a cool ventilated place.

Bringing Forth Beetroot

Beetroot has to be one of the tastiest, most beautiful vegetables around and is racing back into fashion. It's now seen as a superfood, packed full of goodness. It's high in carbohydrate, potassium and folic acid and is a great source of antioxidants.

As a child, I hated beetroot because my grandma would just boil it for days and store it in vinegar, but you can do so much more with this fantastic vegetable: slow roasting intensifies its flavour, served with chilli it's a treat, and what about the Russian soup, Borscht? Fantastic.

Beetroot is part of the same family as Swiss chard, spinach and spinach beet, and they were all originally plants found growing in coastal areas. The leaves are tough, heavily veined and have a sheen that protects the plants from coastal weather but also makes them easy to grow, because they're as hardy as can be, making them great plants for the beginner. Beetroot is a biennial plant grown as an annual. It forms swollen roots that usually are reddish purple but also can be yellow and a dirty white. The leaves are also edible and are best eaten when young.

Getting started with beetroot

Beetroot likes an organic, rich but light soil with plenty of nitrogen. It grows better in cooler climates and does best on a plot that's been manured in the previous season. The best thing is to apply some kind of feed high in nitrogen before sowing and again once during the growing season. Simply use bone meal or chicken manure pellets to give the plants a boost of nitrogen the natural way. Beetroot grows in most soil types, preferring a sunny position. It will grow in poorer soils but not so well: its roots either become tough and woody or simply don't grow as big.

Beetroot seeds are actually pods that contain two or three seeds together. When planted, these seeds need to be thinned out to give the plants room to grow. You can now get seeds from plants that have been bred to produce only one seed so no thinning is necessary. Beetroot seeds should be sown from March, as soon as the soil has warmed, right up to early summer.

To sow your beetroot, follow these steps:

1. **Fork the area over a couple of weeks before planting and rake the surface to a fine tilth.**

   This loosens the soil, allowing good-size roots to form.

2. **Sow the seed in drills with 30 centimetres between rows, 1–2 centimetres deep and between 6–10 centimetres apart, depending on the eventual size of the mature plant.**

   Basically, for small varieties, plant them closer together than large main-crop ones that need more space.

3. **Cover the seeds and water them really well.**

   It can be useful to place a sting line and label the rows, so you don't lose track of what you have planted and tread on the seedlings by accident.

4. **Prick out carefully when the seeds have germinated. Leave only the strongest-looking seedlings.**

   Do this as soon as the first true leaves appear (usually the second pair). Beetroots don't like being too close, when you run the risk of them having distorted roots.

5. **Keep the plants watered through dry spells, giving a thorough soaking about once a week.**

   Drought can cause beetroots to *bolt* (send up a flowering shoot) or the roots to become woody.

Start early crops in a propagator or in seed modules inside. (See Chapter 3 for more info on this method.) Plant out under cloche tunnels when the plants are 5 centimetres tall. This allows you to prepare the seedlings earlier and plant them out early in spring with the added protection of the cloche tunnel. Then plant at intervals of 2–3 weeks, right through until midsummer if you want a constant supply.

Make sure that you hoe regularly to keep weeds down; the foliage of the beetroot soon smothers any weeds, apart from the most persistent. Beetroots growing in dry conditions are likely to bolt, so apply a mulch and water them well during dry spells to prevent this.

Considering varieties of beetroot

Many varieties of beetroot exist. Here are a few to try:

- **Albina Vereduna.** Worth growing not only for a bit of fun but as a brilliant more tasty variety, Albina Vereduna is a great white beetroot. The top leaves are an absolute delicacy as well and full of vitamins and minerals, so make a space for this variety if you can!
- **Alto F1 hybrid.** This is the first cylindrical hybrid beetroot on the market and has a lovely sweet flavour. It's easy to cultivate and a great space-saving variety that grows a little above the soil level. Being uniform all the way up, it's good for slicing and pickling.
- **Bietola da Orto Paonazza d'Egitto.** Yes, that's its real name. I had to include this one simply to up the word count in this book! Fantastically named, it's a variety that matures quickly and can be sown early. It produces unusual squashed roots with a sweet flavour and deep red colour.
- **Boltardy.** A beetroot that's been around for donkey's years and is as reliable as can be. Great for early sowings and bolt resistant.
- **Burpee's Golden**. A tried-and-tested variety that has a delicate golden flesh and a lovely polished brownish-gold skin. It's best harvested small, but can be left to mature without becoming tough. The tops can be eaten like spring greens in stir fries or simply steamed.
- **Detroit Dark Red.** Developed over a hundred years ago from a long line of beetroots, Detroit Dark Red has perfectly formed typical beetroot roots with smooth skin and a lovely dark red colouring that intensifies when cooked. It is early maturing and good for storage. If you can't track down Dark Red, go for Detroit 2, which is easier to find.

Monogerms are a relatively new development in the world of beetroot – instead of producing seed pods with two or three seeds in them, they produce single seeds, which means you don't have to thin them out . . . genius! Here are some examples:

- **Solo F1.** Ideal for baby beets, with good uniform colour and nice smooth skin.
- **Moneta.** Has nice coloured pinkish flesh and smooth skin, and can be harvested over a long season. When young, it's also good for its edible tasty leaves.

Harvesting and storage

Beetroot can be ready to harvest in as little as seven weeks for small sweet treats, or may be left much longer to mature for larger roots that are good for storage. If you're sowing for storage over winter, sow at least 10–12 weeks before winter frosts, so the beetroot have time to develop.

In warmer areas, you can leave beetroot in the ground over winter in well drained soil until the following spring, but the roots can become a bit woody and tough. Roots left in need mulching deeply with 15 centimetres of straw before the first frosts arrive.

Beetroot should lift pretty easily when you pull on the foliage. Twist the foliage off (this stops the roots bleeding out red juice) and store them in boxes of compost in a cool but not frosty place. If I were you, I'd wear gloves whilst handling the beetroot, otherwise your hands will be dyed bright purple!

Beetroot can also be stored in clamps in the same way as potatoes. See the sidebar 'Considering clamps' earlier in this chapter.

Chapter 10

Exploring More Root Vegetables

In This Chapter

- Considering roots other than spuds
- Going for glamorous varieties
- Discovering how to harvest and store your veg

Chapter 9 covers the big four root crops: potatoes, carrots, parsnips and beetroot. This chapter looks at other root vegetables by which you may be tempted. Some, like the humble turnip, are really unglamorous, while some such as celeriac are fit for the most regal palate. These veg are all easy to grow and offer some surprising flavours and textures, both cooked and eaten raw. Here's how to expand your root vegetable repertoire!

Turning Your Hand to Turnips

Turnips are a much undervalued vegetable with an image problem. It's time for an allotment revolution and for the turnip to come out of its shell and soar with the other allotment favourites. Turnips are traditionally thrown into stews and soups or mashed served with butter, but when harvested young they can be shredded into salads or finely sliced and used in stir fries. Young turnips are nice and sweet and have a refreshing taste that's surprising from such a 'boring' vegetable. They also grow quickly, their young foliage being a great alternative to spinach. In fact, what are you waiting for? Go plant some!

Getting started with turnips

Turnips, surprisingly, are members of the brassica family, which includes broccoli and cabbages. Like all root crops, turnips prefer a light, deeply cultivated soil that allows them room to grow. They like a neutral to slightly alkaline soil, so if your soil is too acid, it may require liming (see Chapter 6 for more on soil types). If you live in a hot climate, you should sow turnips early in spring, because they don't like too much heat, or late in the summer so they can happily grow on into the late autumn. They mature in between 60 and 80 days, so are a fast-growing crop.

Boron deficiency

Turnips and swedes are great indicator plants for a lack of the micro-nutrient boron in your soil. They're usually the first crops on the allotment to suffer from such a problem. Even though you're unlikely to encounter this problem, it's useful to know what the signs are. You notice in the centre of the vegetables a greyish-brown mass forming that begins to rot and stink to high heaven! You can remedy this fairly easily by feeding with a fertiliser that contains boron as a part of its make-up. Most general-purpose fertilisers contain small amounts of these trace elements, and that should do the trick. To correct a boron deficiency organically, ensure that the soil pH is between 6.0 and 8.0, spray the plants with seaweed extract and then sow a green manure crop of clover to be dug into the soil.

Turnips are an ideal *catch crop*, which means they can be planted after one main crop has finished, as a quickie to squeeze in before the next main crop. Catch crops are fast-growing crops that are usually grown in late summer before the frosts of winter arrive.

To encourage turnips to grow quickly, grow them in an area that's been manured the previous year. If you live in a particularly rainy area with heavy soil, plant turnips on ridges to allow excess water to run away without causing waterlogging.

Sow turnip seeds in spring to be able to eat young roots; I tend to plant in succession between late March and June to ensure a constant supply of young, tender turnips. Sow main-crop turnips in late summer to allow them to mature into larger ones into the winter. Turnips are quite easy to grow – just follow these steps:

1. **Prepare drills (shallow trenches) 2 centimetres deep, and plant early turnips in rows that are 23 centimetres apart. Sow main-crop turnips in drills 30 centimetres apart.**
2. **Cover the seeds with soil, and water them well.**
3. **As soon as they start to shoot, thin early turnips to 10 centimetres apart and late ones to 15 centimetres apart. Turnips don't like being crowded, so thinning needs to be done fairly early on.**

Although they'll now grow on happily and pretty much care for themselves, during dry spells you should water turnips to keep them from *bolting* (sending out flowering shoots) and ruining the tasty roots. And as with all plants on the allotment, keep the growing area weed free!

The easiest way to thin out seedlings is to stand parallel to the rows and, using a hoe, weed out the extra plants, leaving the correct gap between the ones you want to grow on.

Considering varieties

Four varieties of turnip you might like to try are:

- **Tokyo Cross.** This is a really fast-growing variety that matures in 35–40 days. It's best eaten when about the size of a golf ball, and really nice eaten raw. The leaves too can be eaten, so try them in a stir fry.
- **Oasis.** A pretty new variety that's fantastically sweet and has a hint of melon flavour. It's great eaten raw straight from the ground or try it grated in a salad.
- **Rapa Bianca Lodigiana.** This one looks as if it's been squashed, because it's flatter that your usual turnip. It has tasty leaves and can be sown like most turnips at intervals for baby vegetables or left to mature a little longer.
- **Golden Ball.** Highly rated by allotmenteers as one of the best main-crop turnips, Golden Ball has edible leaves and keeps well. It has yellow tasty roots that are extremely tender.

Harvesting and storage

Turnips are best eaten young and are ready to harvest in as little as six weeks. I like them when they're small, the size of a golf ball. When they get older, they're not so sweet and tender, but still quite tasty and suitable for stews and soups. Many varieties are sown for their edible leaves – these can be cut off with a sharp knife and they'll shoot again. Turnips won't last long in the ground over winter, so lift them before the frost hits. You can store turnips in boxes of sand or dry compost in a cool, dry, well-ventilated place.

Getting Sweet on Swedes

Swedes deserve a place on the allotment as a valuable winter crop. Swedes are known by many names throughout the world: in Scotland they're called *neeps*, with other names including *yellow turnips*, *Swedish turnips* and *rutabaga*. They're a cross between a cabbage and a turnip, and in Sweden they call them *kålrot*, which translates as cabbage root. Swedes thrive in cold climates, which is why they became so popular in Scandinavia, especially in Sweden, and this is where they get their common name.

Hallowe'en before pumpkins

Before pumpkins arrived, people in Britain celebrating Hallowe'en used hollowed-out swedes with a burning coal placed inside. Folklore would have us believe this represented the damned soul of an unsavoury chap called Stingy Jack, who was allowed into neither heaven nor hell. As a result, he wandered with his lantern lit by a coal from hell that the devil had given him . . . hence the name jack-o'lantern.

COOKING TIP

A dish my mother and grandmother (both Swedes, but not the vegetable type!) used to make when I was a child was a Swedish dish called *rotmos*. It consists of mashed roots such as potatoes, carrot and swede with cream and butter. I make it all the time and serve it with a Sunday roast – my kids love it! Swedes are also good mashed on their own with some grated nutmeg and a glug of olive oil – simplicity itself!

Getting started with swedes

Swedes like exactly the same conditions as turnips (see the section 'Turning Your Hand to Turnips' earlier in this chapter) and are also members of the brassica family. They don't like acid soil, so on these soils you should lime the area well in advance of sowing. They like a light humus-rich soil and benefit from an application of fish, blood and bone a few weeks before planting – a handful every square metre should do the trick. As with turnips, swedes should be sown on soil that's been manured the previous year.

Swedes are a slow-growing crop and take 20–27 weeks to reach maturity. They are easy to grow as long as you keep them well watered. Sow swedes in early spring in cooler areas, but if you live in a warmer area, leave sowing until early summer.

To sow your swedes, follow these steps:

1. **Create shallow drills about 1 centimetre deep and 45 centimetres apart.**
2. **Sow the seeds thinly. When the seedlings have three leaves, thin them out to between 15 and 20 centimetres apart.**
3. **Keep the swedes well watered, otherwise they will grow small and tough – and more than likely crack. They may well also bolt (put out a flowering stem).**

Considering varieties

Some swedes can be bitter tasting, so always opt for a sweet variety. Because they take so long to grow, it's disappointing to have put in all that work if the results are not up to scratch. Some varieties to try include:

- **Angela.** A classic sweet-tasting variety with nice purple colouring on the top.
- **Best of All.** An favourite with allotmenteers, this old variety isn't as heavy cropping as modern varieties but has a nice mild flavour and low water content, so cooks quickly.
- **Bora.** With its nice purple top and lovely yellow flesh, Bora is the perfect bitter-free variety, which is mildew resistant. It lasts through the winter and well into January.
- **Invitation.** Great for a really late crop that lasts right from December until the end of April.
- **Marian.** A heavy cropper that grows quite large, it has a delicious sweet flavour and the bonus of being mildew and clubroot resistant.

Harvesting and storage

You can harvest swedes as soon as they are large enough to eat. I personally think the younger, smaller ones are more tasty, so don't feel you have to wait for them to reach full size, when they can become a little tough and woody. Unlike turnips, you can leave swedes in the ground over winter and harvest right through until spring. In spring, they will reshoot, and the young tender leaves can be used as spring greens, after which they should be lifted and stored in boxes of damp sand or compost in a cool dark place.

Rearing Radishes

Radishes must be the simplest vegetable on the planet to grow. Some have a spicy fresh flavour that enlivens the summer salad plate, and others are very mild and can be eaten as a cooked vegetable. They don't just come in the red we all know: you can get white ones, purple ones and even a white-skinned variety that's magenta on the inside. You can also grow daikon and mouli, which are oriental radishes – and great fun – and they can grow up to 30 centimetres in length. Radishes are great for first-time gardeners and especially fun for children to grow in pots and containers, because they're so quick to grow. Some are ready just a month after sowing, and there's even a type called *podded* radishes, which are grown for the seed pods, which you eat like sugarsnap peas.

Getting started with radishes

Radishes prefer moist, fertile soil but can be easily grown in growbags or pots. They grow in most soils but don't thrive in poor free-draining ones, which you can easily improve. (See Chapter 6 on improving your soil.) To grow radishes, follow these steps:

1. **Lime the soil a month in advance. Radishes, like all members of the brassica family, don't like acid soil.**
2. **Before planting, dig to a depth of 15 centimetres and mix in some home-made compost and a couple of handfuls of bone meal.**
3. **Create a drill 1 centimetre deep.**
4. **Sow the seeds every 1 centimetre; the seeds are quite large, especially for such a small vegetable, but this makes it easy to space them.**
5. **Backfill the drill and water the seeds in well.**

Plant short rows weekly to ensure a constant supply; salad radishes mature quickly and should be eaten fresh. Winter radishes are usually larger and can be grown more like turnips and simply left in the ground to mature. White ones should be sown in late spring and harvested in autumn, and the others towards the end of the summer ready for late autumn.

Growing radishes really is that easy, but for larger varieties, be sure to space the seeds as stated on the packet. If they're too close together they won't mature properly.

TIP

Radishes grow best when the weather is slightly cool, so avoid sowing in the height of summer in full sun; a semi-shaded spot is better. Otherwise sow in early spring or late summer for the best results.

Radishes are useful for growing in vacant 'lost' corners of the allotment or for inter-cropping (planting in between other plants) for a fast, tasty snack. You can also use them as a catch crop when a plot becomes vacant after cropping.

WARNING!

The only real pest that threatens radishes is the flea beetle, which attacks the foliage. Usually a heavy downpour or good soaking with a hose dislodges them.

Considering varieties

There are so many varieties of radish it's impossible to list them all, but here are some of the best to try. First, the summer radishes:

- **French Breakfast.** This is a super-quick variety, ideal for children to grow; it grows fairly long and is red with a white tip. Great in salads.
- **Amethyst.** A pretty, new variety with metallic purple skin, Amethyst is easy to grow with crisp white flesh.
- **Rudi.** This radish is a brilliant little performer that tastes fresh and crisp and is good on poor soil.
- **Flamboyant Sabina.** Pretty, peppery, cylindrical and fairly long, this variety is perfect for spicing up a salad. I love it simply dipped into salad cream.
- **Cherry Belle.** A perfect-looking little radish that is sweet and crunchy. It's very early and fast-maturing, so get it in as soon as you can!
- **Pink Slipper.** A pink-skinned variety that can be sown at intervals from March right through until September. It adds a lovely colour and flavour to dishes.
- **Ravanello Il Candela di Fuoco.** Who could resist a radish with a name like that?! It's a fast-growing, long radish that can be ready in five weeks.
- **Red Head.** Another attractive-looking radish, white-skinned with pink marbling.

Autumn and winter radishes usually take longer to mature; some are eaten raw and others cooked. A popular misconception is that winter radishes are all really hot and fibrous. This isn't the case, because many are sweet and tender, and if they're hot, this usually disappears totally when you cook them. Try these:

- **Black Spanish Round.** An interesting-looking, black-skinned variety that has really crisp white flesh. Sow in June to August for harvesting from October onwards.
- **Minowase.** This Japanese mouli radish forms a long, crisp, white radish that can reach a 30 centimetres in length. It's a mild radish that is fantastic in stir fries. Sow from June to August and harvest from October onwards.
- **Munchen Bier.** An interesting radish grown for its edible seed pods more than the root (which you can also eat). The crisp, stringless seed pods are a little like sugarsnap peas with a bit of a kick and can be grown outside all the way from late February until September. The roots are best harvested as a winter crop from late summer and autumn sowings.
- **Rosa.** Definitely a radish for hardcore radish fans. It's long and orange, much like a carrot in appearance, and has a very strong peppery taste. Sow in July and harvest from October onwards.

- **Mantanghong F1.** A wonderful Chinese variety that has white skin but a deep magenta inside. It grows to the size of a tennis ball and has a nutty, fresh taste and crisp texture. This variety really brightens up a winter salad. July and August are the best times to sow the seeds outdoors, when the temperature is nice and warm, and the radishes will be ready in around eight or nine weeks.

Harvesting and storage

Harvesting summer radishes is as easy as growing them: simply pull them up, give them a wash and use. If you have too many (which you probably will), give them to neighbours and friends, who are sure to appreciate them. White winter radishes should be harvested at the end of the autumn and stored like carrots, but the others can stay in the ground to be used when needed.

COOKING TIP

Try some finely sliced red radish with soba noodles, drizzled with a dressing of sesame oil, soy sauce, lime juice, honey and balsamic vinegar. Serve with finely sliced spring onions, coriander, a sprinkling of toasted sesame seeds and some pickled ginger or Japanese pickled vegetables to garnish. A real fresh summer treat!

Savouring Scorzonera and Salsify

Scorzonera and salsify are both members of the daisy family and are grown mainly for their long, thin, tasty roots. They have the same growing requirements on the allotment and are similar in appearance, but scorzonera has black skin and salsify has white. They both have a long growing season and are grown in a similar way to carrots (see Chapter 9). They're harvested as annuals from October onwards, or you can leave them in the soil, where in spring they'll shoot and produce edible leaves and tall flower heads (yellow on scorzonera and purple on salsify).

COOKING TIP

The flower heads open in the morning to greet the sun and are best picked before they open and cooked like asparagus. The young tender leaves are also great fried in butter and served on toasted bread.

Salsify is commonly known as the vegetable oyster because it has an oyster-like flavour. It looks much like a hairy parsnip and, like a parsnip, benefits in flavour from a frosting in winter.

Scorzonera has a similar flavour to salsify but has multiple long, parallel roots. The roots are usually washed under cold water then cooked and peeled, but they discolour easily so prepare them quickly and cook instantly. I see them as a 'Marmite' vegetable: you love them or hate them! So if you like the unusual and want to impress at the dinner table, these are right up your street.

Getting started with scorzonera and salsify

Always use fresh seeds bought recently and sow straight into the ground, where they'll take at least four months to mature for harvesting. They need a well dug, deep soil, much like carrots and parsnips. They can fork as well, but salsify is more prone to this than scorzonera. Follow these steps:

1. **Sow seeds in shallow drills 1 centimetre deep in rows 20 centimetres apart.** This should be done when the soil has warmed by mid-spring. You can cover the soil with long cloche tunnels for a couple of weeks prior to sowing to warm the soil for earlier sowings.
2. **Thin out to 10 centimetres apart.**
3. **Water well during dry periods.**

Considering varieties

Few varieties of scorzonera and salsify are available, which is a shame if you ask me. Growers usually respond to public or commercial demand, and as these aren't popular vegetables, they don't bother to develop new varieties. So get whatever variety is on offer where you shop. Below are the most common varieties:

- **Russian Giant.** This scorzonera is easy to grow and has a mild flavour.
- **Sandwich island.** This salsify produces long tapering roots that are pretty easy to grow.
- **Giant.** This salsify has a flavour like oysters crossed with a hint of asparagus.

Harvesting and storage

Scorzonera and salsify are both ready to dig up from autumn onwards. Ideally, leave them in the soil and lift them as required. They can be dug up and stored in the same way as carrots and parsnips (see Chapter 9). Be careful when lifting them, because the roots snap easily underground. Tease them up with a fork by loosening the surrounding soil and pulling them up gently by the foliage. They keep well in the ground and improve in flavour when hit by frost.

If you have any left in the ground by spring, they'll produce leaves and flowers that are edible and quite tasty. The best time to pick the flowers is in the morning with 8 centimetres of stem, before they open in the sun. Treat just like asparagus (they're just as good!).

Scorzonera and salsify are relatively free from pests and diseases, so are ideal for organic growers. Scorzonera is also said to be a useful companion plant for carrots, helping deter the dreaded carrot fly. (There is more on companion planting in Chapter 7.)

Growing Celeriac

Celeriac is one of the tastiest root crops around. Under its rough, mean exterior is a wonderfully versatile vegetable that can be grated, baked, roasted, creamed or sliced. The leaves can also be used as flavouring for stews and soups and are useful as a garnish. Celeriac, as the name suggests, is a kind of celery, but instead of growing edible slender stems it forms a swollen 'bulb'. Celeriac isn't as popular as other root vegetables and is often quite expensive in the shops.

Celery is fairly difficult to grow, but celeriac is much easier, and to me, it's the tastiest of all roots – so for these two reasons deserves a spot on the plot!

Getting started with celeriac

Ideally, celeriac likes a free-draining, moisture-retentive soil that's been manured the previous year. It has a low nitrogen requirement and if planted in nitrogen-rich soil, produces too much foliage to the detriment of the 'bulb'. It struggles in dry and sandy soils that haven't been improved (see Chapter 6 on how to improve your soil). That said, celeriac usually grows in most soils, but a rich, well-drained soil produces the biggest and best crop. Celeriac can also be grown in light shade, as long as it's kept nice and moist.

Celeriac takes a long time to grow – around six months from sowing to harvesting. I like to sow the seeds indoors to give them a good head start; frost damages the young plants, because at this stage they're not hardy at all. Germination is a bit hit and miss, so sow a few more than you actually need just to be safe (any extra can be offered to your allotment chums).

To sow your celeriac, follow these steps:

1. **Sow seeds in early spring in large-module seed trays, with two seeds per section. The seeds germinate in about 20 days – don't let them dry out. They do better if kept at a constant temperature of around 20 degrees centigrade.**

2. **In each section, remove the weaker seedling to allow the stronger one to flourish.**
3. **Once the seedlings are 7 centimetres tall they should be *hardened off* (slowly acclimatised to the outside by placing the plants outside during the day and inside at night for a couple of weeks) and then planted out in their final positions 35 centimetres apart. Be sure not to bury the plants too deep and to keep them at ground level.**
4. **Mulch the plants well after planting and water them well. During dry spells, be sure to keep them well watered.**
5. **Towards the end of summer, remove a few of the outer shoots to encourage a nice neat, bulbous root. Many new varieties don't shoot from the sides, so you won't need to do this, but keep them in check.**
6. **Before the first frost, mulch around the base of the plant with a good thick layer of straw, about 15 centimetres deep, to protect the crowns.**

TIP

Celeriac seedlings don't like being transplanted, so do so with care so as not to disturb the delicate roots. It's advisable to sow the seeds in compostable pots that you can plant directly into your plot when the time is right.

Celeriac is affected by the same pests and diseases as celery, but the main ones to watch out for are slugs, celery fly (leaf miners) and also carrot fly.

Considering varieties

There are only a limited number of varieties of celeriac available to the allotmenteer, and most places only sell one variety, but some I like to use include:

- **Alabaster.** A nice smoother-skinned variety that produces a heavy crop.
- **Monarch.** The variety you'll most probably be able to find; it's easy to grow and doesn't produce the side shoots that may give misshapen bulbs.
- **Prinz.** Having a delicious flavour and crisp white flesh, Prinz is ideal grated in a winter salad.

COOKING TIP

Celeriac makes a fantastic soup. Gently fry some onions in butter until soft then add a whole celeriac cut into small cubes and gently fry for five minutes. Cover with hot vegetable or chicken stock, season and simmer for 25 minutes. Whizz it with a hand blender, add a good glug of cream and season. You can add more stock and cream until the soup is the consistency you like. This works really well with some thinly sliced chorizo fried in a little olive oil and thrown on top (oil and all) – simply amazing!

Celeriac makes a brilliant addition to coleslaw or, as the French call it, remoulade. I use a mixture of finely sliced red cabbage, carrot and an onion, with shredded celeriac, all mixed with mayo, a bit of lemon juice and salt and pepper. Best served with a really good steak and chips.

Harvesting and storage

The bulbs are ready to dig up when they reach between 8 and 15 centimetres in diameter, and can be harvested from early autumn to the following spring. Celeriac is best stored in the ground over winter, covered with deep straw mulch, under which it can withstand temperatures down to –10 degrees centigrade for short periods. However, if you live in a really cold area, I recommend that you lift the roots and then trim off the leaves, leaving a small tuft. Store them in layers in boxes of damp but not wet compost or sand and keep them in a cool place where they should stay good for a few months.

Growing Florence Fennel

Unlike ordinary fennel that's grown for its leaves and seeds, Florence fennel forms a swollen bulb-like base that's delicious eaten raw or cooked. Florence fennel is a highly prized food source, especially in the Mediterranean, where the bulb is commonly used raw and used in a variety of dishes from stews to salads. The foliage and seeds are all edible too, and the plant is used as a herb to flavour many dishes. The stems can be cooked in a similar way to celery. With so many options, this has to be one of the least wasteful of all allotment plants. Culinary uses apart,. It's a good-looking plant, and planted in a block is one of the highlights of the allotment during midsummer; it's also a great addition to your garden at home.

Getting started with Florence fennel

Florence fennel is an easy-to-grow plant, with some varieties reaching heights of up to 2 metres with a 40–50 centimetre spread. It originates from the Mediterranean, and like many plants from that region, is quite tough and adaptable. It grows in most soil types and tolerates cold and warm climates; it can even withstand short periods of gentle frost if necessary.

Florence fennel thrives in fertile, humus-rich soil that's well drained yet moist (go back to Chapter 6 for more on soil) and enjoys plenty of sunshine. It doesn't like the soil to be dried out, so keep your plants well watered during dry periods.

Once established, the plants are easy to grow but they do have a tendency to bolt if anything shocks their growth. They hate being transplanted and may also bolt if sown too early in the season, when they can be freaked out by the cold nights and set seed. If you live in a northerly cool area, wait until midsummer to begin sowing. If you live in a southerly area, you can sow from spring through until late summer for an autumn harvest.

Florence fennel is best eaten in its prime and has a short period of being at its best, so sow seeds every couple of weeks to ensure a steady supply.

To sow your Florence fennel, follow these tips:

1. **Prepare the soil two weeks before sowing, by adding plenty of organic matter. Dig it in trenches about 30 centimetres wide and 40 centimetres deep to give the plants a good rich environment in which to grow.**
2. **Sow seeds thinly in shallow, well watered drills about 1 centimetre deep and cover with moist soil. You can do this at intervals from spring to late summer.**
3. **Thin out the seedlings when they start to appear and form leaves. Thin them to between 25 and 30 centimetres apart.**
4. **Water well; the plants bolt if they get too thirsty.**
5. **Weed carefully between rows, because the plants don't appreciate competition. Be careful, because the delicate forming bulbs are easy to damage, so it's a case of slowly, slowly does it!**
6. **Earth up when the bulbs begin to swell nicely; this involves drawing the soil up halfway around the forming bulbs (see Chapter 9 for more details). This turns the bottom half of the bulb white, and gives it a more tender texture and better flavour.**

Florence fennel is great for organic plots because the bulbs are disease and pest free, so need no chemicals to help them thrive. The only real problems arise when the plants don't get enough water, get confused by temperature change or are moved, all of which cause them to bolt. Older, more traditional varieties are more likely to bolt, so opt for new hybrids for an easier life.

Considering varieties

Here are my recommended varieties of Florence fennel:

- **Victorian F1 hybrid.** This fairly new variety forms lovely fat bulbs with a strong aniseed flavour and has the bonus of improved resistance to bolting.

- **Romanesco.** Probably the best one I've tried, this forms quite tall, large bulbs with a great flavour. Best planted from June onwards to harvest from September, it's also bolt resistant.
- **Zefa Fino.** Good for cooler-climate sowings, it's good at resisting the urge to perpetuate by bolting, so you can plant it early, and it's also good for a quick late crop.
- **Amigo F1.** A good option for a fast-growing early crop that produces squat bulbs and also has some bolt resistance.

Harvesting and storage

Florence fennel is ready to harvest any time from 12 weeks after sowing, but usually in about 15 weeks. It doesn't keep long once cut, so only harvest as and when you need it. You can dig the whole plant up and use it as required or, using a really sharp knife, cut it off just above soil level. The base that's left then usually shoots again with the soft feathery foliage that you can use as a herb for flavouring.

Chapter 11

Bringing Home the Brassicas

In This Chapter

- Growing brilliant brassicas
- Knowing the difference between broccoli and calabrese
- Exploring unusual varieties

With so many vegetables available to grow on the allotment, it can sometimes seem daunting to try and fit them all in. In this chapter you're going to look at expanding your repertoire on the allotment by adding more of the basic vegetables that I'm sure you want to grow. The largest group is the brassicas, which is one of the most important families of vegetable and includes cabbages, Brussels sprouts, broccoli, cauliflowers, kohlrabi and kale. It also includes swedes, turnips and radishes because they grow underground as root vegetables. (Read more about these in Chapter 10.) Most brassicas contain a chemical called *sulforaphane* that is believed to have powerful anti-cancer properties, so not only do they taste great, they are extremely good for you too!

Brassica Basics

Brassicas are usually biennial (they grow over a two-year period). In their first year of growth, they concentrate on building up and storing reserves of nutrients and water in their leaves or roots (in the case of turnips, swedes and radishes) before flowering and then setting seed in their second year. With brassicas such as cabbages, we interrupt this cycle, harvesting them as annuals before the plants flower, and then consuming them with all the nutrients they've worked so hard to store. Cauliflower and calabrese go to flower and then we harvest them as biennials.

Brassicas are really important because they can offer the allotmenteer fresh produce every single day of the year. This is especially important in the period from autumn to early spring, when many other veg are in short supply.

Brassicas are usually eaten cooked, but many can be eaten raw; cauliflower, for example, is great in salads. I am sure we all have awful memories of disgusting grey and watery cabbage served with school dinners, or broccoli that disintegrates on the plate. Most brassicas are best gently steamed to retain their goodness, or cooked quickly in stir fries for added crunch.

Getting started with brassicas

Brassicas are a really diverse group of vegetables, but because they're all so closely related, they have very similar growing requirements. They need full sun with a rich deep soil that's well drained and moisture retentive; they also like it if the soil is firm, and so can be planted on un-dug soil after a previous crop – though cabbages are an exception. Ideally, the autumn before planting out, spread a barrow-load of manure on each square metre of land and leave it over winter for the elements and worms to do their work. This provides all the humus and nitrogen that your plants need in the coming year. Then in spring, fork over the top few centimetres of soil to incorporate the manure well.

In early spring, I suggest you carry out a pH test. Brassicas don't like acidic soil, so if your soil is on the acidic side, add some lime to counteract this. The ideal pH is 7, so you should aim to add the right amount of lime to bring levels up. Look at the packet and work out how much you need to correct the pH of your soil type. (See Chapter 6 for more on balancing your soil.)

Never lime and fertilise in the same year. Doing so produces a nasty gas called ammonia that takes the nitrogen from the soil and turns it back into gas. This gas then disappears into the atmosphere, undoing all your hard work and rendering both the lime and fertiliser useless. Because brassicas need plenty of nitrogen to produce lush foliage, losing the nitrogen is a disaster!

Keeping your brassicas at their best

If your brassicas seem to be struggling during the growing season and aren't diseased in any way, I'd put money on the reason being a lack of nitrogen. It's easy to rescue your crop by adding some fertiliser that has a high level of nitrogen. For a short-term boost, use a liquid fertiliser that gives the plants a dose they can absorb easily, or top dress with a slower-releasing fertiliser for a more long-term effect. (See Chapter 7 for more on nutrient deficiencies.)

Brassicas are vulnerable to attack from pests and diseases, some attacks being disastrous, which is why brassicas should be part of the crop rotation system (see Chapter 7 on how that works) that helps reduce these problems.

Other pests and diseases that attack the brassica family are the cabbage white caterpillar (and other caterpillars), cabbage root fly, cabbage whitefly, flea beetles, mealy aphids, birds (especially pigeons), whiptail on cauliflowers and slugs and snails. You can read more about these other problems in Chapter 7.

Because brassicas are so open to attack from all sorts of nasty little creatures, a good idea is to invest in some form of plant protection. You can buy fine netting that can simply be placed over your crops and pinned down into the soil, or you can build cages around your crops using cheap timber batons and cover these with netting. Whatever method you use, do fasten the netting securely and stretch it taut, or birds could become entangled.

Many brassicas take up valuable space for quite some time, so most gardeners start them off in a *seed bed* before planting them out into their permanent positions. This basically means having a small area of your plot dedicated to growing young seedlings, and then transplanting them when an area becomes vacant. This way you can maximise the crops you grow efficiently.

So now it's time to meet the important members of the *Brassicaceae* family.

Don't Call Me Broccoli: Growing Calabrese

Many people don't bother noting the difference between calabrese and broccoli, but now that you're discovering the skills of being an allotmenteer, you need to know the difference. Calabrese grows quickly and matures in a matter of four months, offering a really quick, tasty crop for summer harvest. Broccoli grows much more slowly and is frost hardy. You plant it one year, and in the following spring it (usually) produces the flowering sprouting heads that we eat. Growing two different varieties will enable you to harvest over a longer period.

Getting started with calabrese

To sow your calabrese, follow these steps:

1. **Sow calabrese indoors. Start it off in modules in a propagator, in a greenhouse or on a well-lit windowsill if you want a crop to harvest in early summer.**

   When the soil has warmed in spring, you can sow the seeds directly into it.

2. **Plants grown in modules should be transplanted into moist prepared ground as gently as possible.**

Calabrese hate being transplanted, so do this really carefully, disturbing the roots as little as possible. Protect plants with fleece until the danger of frost has passed.

3. **Plant out in rows 45 centimetres apart, spacing plants within a row 30 centimetres apart.**

   Alternatively, you can plant in groups 22 centimetres apart on all sides. Different spacing affects the size of the flower heads – the more room they have, the bigger the flower heads become. Calabrese is good for home freezing, but the smaller flower heads are more suitable, so many allotmenteers grow plants close together for this reason.

4. **Weed the area well and don't allow your plants to suffer from drought – water well during dry periods to ensure a good crop.**

Considering varieties

Many varieties of calabrese are available: some that produce large flower heads, and others that produce smaller, more tender flower heads in spears. Personal preference dictates which you go for, but I like the smaller heads picked young – they're so good and tender and, if you ask me, are as much of a delicacy as asparagus.

- **Belstar F1 hybrid.** A good dual-purpose calabrese that produces one large flower head, which, when removed, is followed by multiple lovely-tasting side shoots. Belstar is good for repeat planting right up to early summer for autumn crops.
- **Kabuki F1 hybrid.** Ideal for small spaces, being bred to be planted closely. Kabuki gives you one large head followed by multiple smaller side shoots, which are great for freezing.
- **Olympia.** Works really well late in the season, offering a late summer treat.
- **Ironman F1.** I'm sure most of us have bought Ironman in our local supermarkets, sold under the guise of 'broccoli'. It's vigorous and disease resistant, so a good choice for organic gardeners. Also it has a long shelf life (hence why shops love it!) but, trust me, the stuff in the shops is nowhere near as tasty as freshly picked.

Harvesting and storage

Calabrese is a fast-maturing crop and is ready to harvest in as little as 11 weeks. Plants form one main head (the *terminal bud*), which should be cut off when it's around 8 centimetres across, before the flower buds open. This then causes the plant to produce shoots on all sides, which then develop into smaller, delicious flower heads. These should be cut off when they're about 10 centimetres long.

Calabrese and broccoli can be frozen and kept for up to three months. The best way to do this is to blanch them in boiling water for a couple of minutes and then plunge them into iced water. Dry them off and store in freezer bags.

If you don't freeze it, Calabrese should be eaten as soon as it's harvested and is best steamed or quickly cooked in stir fries. Cooking it quickly retains its glorious green colour and its vitamin content.

Raising Broccoli

Broccoli isn't the large green flower heads you usually see in the shops. *Sprouting broccoli* (I'll call it that from now on) is a much slower-maturing crop that offers you tasty spearheads in spring from plants sown the previous year. This crop is really worth growing because you harvest it when there's not much else around. Another great reason to grow it is that in the shops it costs a fortune, probably because it takes so long to grow. So it's an ideal money-saving crop to have on your allotment.

Getting started with sprouting broccoli

Sprouting broccoli enjoys exactly the same conditions as other brassicas but unlike calabrese, is frost hardy. It's widely grown in the UK because it's tough as old boots and can even survive down to –12 degrees centigrade. The only real problem with it (apart from pests and diseases) is the fact that it hogs its space for a whole year, from sowing to harvesting.

To sow your sprouting broccoli, follow these steps:

1. **Sow seed from spring to midsummer in modules or pots, ready to be transplanted. Ensure that you keep the seedlings moist at all times.**
2. **When the plants have four or five leaves and are 10 centimetres in height, give them a good watering, wait a couple of hours and then transplant them straight into their final home, spacing them at least 60 centimetres apart. Plant them deeply to help stabilise them (they can reach up to 90 centimetres in height) and firm the soil around each plant well.**
3. **Keep the plants well weeded and watered.**

Sprouting broccoli is best not started off in the seed bed, because it dislikes being transplanted. I tend to grow the plants in small biodegradable pots and plant them out when they are large enough. Or just be really careful when transplanting, so as not to disturb the roots too much.

TIP

Because it grows so tall, sprouting broccoli may need staking to offer each plant some support later in the season. The plants benefit from a high nitrogen feed during the summer, but avoid doing this nearing winter, because it encourages lush foliage growth that can be damaged by hard frosts.

Considering varieties

Varieties to try range from the usually purple-headed varieties to the (according to some) more superior-tasting white types. It always amazes me that supermarkets rarely sell the white varieties and only stick to the purple; in fact, most people have never even seen white broccoli.

- **Claret F1 Hybrid.** An outstanding variety producing a vigorous crop. One of these plants produces as many spears as two lesser varieties. This makes it a good choice for those of you with less space, or simply means you can have double the crop you get from less prolific varieties.
- **Nine Star Perennial.** A great choice for the lazy (sorry, busy) gardener, Nine Star produces a crop each spring for two or even three years, saving you from replanting. It's a delicious white sprouting variety that takes up a lot of space, so give it at least 90 centimetres between plants.
- **Early Sprouting Rudolph.** As the name suggests, this plant is one of the earliest to bestow its wonderful spring bounty, producing nice purple spears as early as February, even in colder areas.
- **Bordeaux F1.** Bordeaux F1 gives you an abundance of purple sprouting spears from summer all the way through autumn. Unlike other broccoli varieties, you sow it in spring for harvest later the same year. It isn't winter hardy.
- **Early Sprouting White Eye.** An early-cropping variety of white broccoli that's ready for harvesting from March or April.

Harvesting and storage

Sprouting broccoli is a *cut-and-come-again* vegetable that just keeps on giving. Give your plants a dose of general fertiliser in spring to help them produce healthy florets, or use seaweed extract or comfrey tonic. Many people get bored waiting for the florets to appear and lose patience with their plants, lifting and composting the plants before they are ready. Broccoli can take almost a year to mature ready for harvesting, but the long wait is well worth it! The best way to harvest is to remove the uppermost large floret when it has matured, which will stimulate the plant to produce many more smaller florets. Then simply pick them from the top down as you need them. The florets must be picked quickly before they produce flowers, which can happen in as few as three days after the florets are produced.

Broccoli is best picked fresh as eaten as soon as possible, although it will last for a good few days in the fridge. To freeze, blanch the florets in boiling water for a minute or so, plunge them into iced water to stop them cooking, then place them in freezer bags in the freezer until required.

Cultivating Cabbage

Cabbages are a valuable source of food, and simply the best all-year-round performers you can plant on the allotment. Per weight, they must be the most productive vegetable around: 1 acre of land can produce 40 tonnes of cabbages! Not that you have the space or the need for so much, but it shows what an important crop they are. Cabbages are grouped according to when they're in season and ready to be harvested: spring, early summer, summer or winter. For simplicity, you're best to regard them in these groupings, although there are some crossovers and exceptions.

Cabbages come in different colours and shapes and with different leaf textures – in fact, I could write a whole book about them. The usual colours are dark green, light green, bluish green, white and red. You can get smooth cabbages and, of course, the all-time favourite: the crinkle-leaved Savoy.

Getting started with cabbages

Cabbages like the same growing conditions as most brassicas: fertile, moisture-retentive and humus-rich soil with a Ph of around 6.5–7, although they'll grow in most soils, but not quite as well. They like plenty of nitrogen and lime in the soil, so treat them accordingly. Cabbages are different to other brassicas in that they thrive best in a deeply dug soil as opposed to a firm soil. They do well following on in the plot rotation from legumes. Before planting, add some general fertiliser such as fish, blood and bone to the soil. This helps boost the level of nitrogen a little – although you'll have already dug in plenty of manure earlier in the season, rain washes some of the nitrogen out of your soil. The fertiliser also adds other nutrients that may well not be needed by the cabbages but will wash away or stay in the soil ready for the next crop.

Most cabbages can be grown directly into the ground on your allotment and should be planted in drills (small trenches) spaced according to the cabbage type. Just wait until the soil has warmed up in spring. I find that they tend to do better if started off indoors, and this way you can start them off earlier than if sown outdoors.

If you want cabbages all year, split them into the respective groups for harvesting, and sow accordingly. To sow your cabbages, follow these steps:

1. **Sow seeds in modules or individual pots in the greenhouse or at home in a cool bright place. Sowing times for each type are as follows:**

   Early summer varieties are sown from late winter to very early spring onwards in modules in the greenhouse. These are mainly the round-headed varieties.

   Summer varieties are sown in early spring in the same way, just a little later on. If sown later in spring, they'll harvest well into autumn. Again, these are usually the round-headed varieties.

   Winter varieties are sown in spring. These include blue, green and Savoy varieties. Winter varieties suitable for storage are sown in early spring and are usually the smooth white cabbages.

   Red cabbages are also sown in spring and will mature for harvesting in late summer, autumn and winter.

2. **Cover the seed with a thin layer of compost and water well.**
3. **When the seedlings reach around 5–8 centimetres high, which usually takes between five and six weeks, plant them out in the cabbage bed, ideally in full sun.**

   Plant them deep with lots of room around them and firm down well. Water the seedlings an hour or so before transplanting and again when you've moved them in. Space them apart as follows: early summer and summer cabbages 40–45 centimetres apart; winter cabbages 50 centimetres apart; spring cabbages, which need less room, 30 centimetres apart; and red cabbages, 40 centimetres apart.

4. **Winter cabbages may need earthing up (see Chapter 9 for more on this technique) as they mature. They can develop tall main stems that benefit from the added support.**

   Most cabbages should be protected under cloches, fine netting or fleece to keep pests at bay. Spring cabbages benefit from being protected by cloche tunnels.

5. **Keep the area weed free and water regularly in dry spells.**

TIP

You can vary the size of the heads of most cabbages by playing around with the spacing. If you space them far apart, most will produce a large head. The closer together they are, the smaller the heads will be.

Considering varieties

Try the following spring varieties:

- **Duncan F1.** Can be sown in autumn for spring harvesting. Forms a pointed heart and is very uniform in shape.
- **Pixie.** A fantastic pointed cabbage that has a dense compact head, is early to mature and can be closely planted.
- **Greensleeves.** Bred to be headless, great for spring greens and easy to grow. It has quite a strong flavour.
- **April F1.** Sown in late summer and ready for harvesting in April. It has a small to medium pointed heart that's good for close spacing.

Summer varieties include:

- **Derby Day.** A compact, round, green cabbage that's early maturing and ready by Derby day (early June) if started in the greenhouse.
- **Primo.** Easy-to-grow variety and ever popular, Primo produces a really compact tightly formed round heart and can be harvested from June to August.
- **Hispi F1.** Hispi is in the early summer cabbage category but is adaptable and can even be sown in autumn, over-wintered in a cold frame, and planted out in spring for a really early crop. It's best sown in spring in succession right through until midsummer.
- **Spitfire F1 hybrid.** A beautifully formed pointed cabbage that grows pretty large. It can be sown in situ from March onwards and is ready from June to December if you stagger planting.

Winter varieties include:

- **Tundra.** The hardiest winter cabbage around and really reliable, this cabbage is a little Savoy-like with crinkled foliage. It's ready from late autumn right through until spring.
- **Savoy January King.** A really tough Savoy cabbage that's not bothered by frost. I've seen its green heads popping out of the snow before, and they still survived, so lasts right through to spring.
- **Deadon F1.** With gorgeous red-tinged leaves, this is a pretty new variety of winter Savoy.
- **Robin F1.** A great winter cabbage with pink flush leaves and a lovely flavour. An old-school-style cabbage that withstands winter well.
- **Holland Winter White.** A really dense white cabbage that's good for shredding raw into coleslaw. Sow in April or May for harvesting in October and November.

Red varieties include:

- **Ruby Ball F1.** A fast-maturing dense red cabbage that you sow in early spring, maturing for harvest by late summer.
- **Red Rookie.** Another early-maturing cabbage ready from mid-August onwards. It's pretty resistant to splitting and is really tasty.
- **Rodeo F1.** Has a dense, medium-size head with a lovely reddish-purple colour. It provides a good crop from July until December. Great for pickling.

Harvesting and storage

Cabbages are best harvested and eaten as you need them. Older varieties of spring and summer cabbages don't last long in the ground when they become mature, but the modern hybrid varieties have a better in-the-ground shelf life. The quick-maturing summer varieties provide a good starting point if you're new to vegetable gardening.

You can get most cabbages to crop again by cutting a cross in the top of the cut stem when you harvest your cabbages. From this cut the plant will produce smaller tender shoots that can be used just like spring greens.

Bringing Forth Brussels Sprouts

People love or hate Brussels sprouts. Personally, I think sprouts are an excellent winter vegetable, keeping going right through the cold winter months until spring. They have a fantastic nutty taste and, if cooked quickly, don't resemble the greeny grey soggy balls that we were served at school. They're definitely best harvested whilst small and tender. When you grow them on the allotment, you have the pick of the bunch, whenever you want them.

Brussels sprouts are ruined by over-cooking. Traditionally they're boiled (more often than not over-boiled), but if you do, do so lightly. They can also be sliced and fried in butter and olive oil to crisp up the edges. Try them with thinly sliced smoked streaky bacon, with a few chopped chestnuts thrown in. Or make bubble and squeak using left-over sprouts mixed in with mash made with your home-grown potatoes. Consider adding crispy bacon: mix together with the sprouts and mash, season well and allow to cool. With your hands, form patties and then coat them in flour. Fry the patties for a couple of minutes on each side and finish in the oven until heated through. Brilliant served with roast monkfish, spinach and a creamy wine sauce.

Getting started

Brussels sprouts grow well in any good soil and rely on a good frost to make them tasty. They're best grown in well dug, well manured soil that's firm and non-acidic, so lime well in advance if your soil is acidic. (See Chapter 6 for more on soil types.) Brussels sprouts are generally grouped according to their time of maturation: early, mid-season and late. The earlier ones are usually dwarf varieties that aren't as hardy. F1 varieties are usually more hardy and offer a far more upright and uniform plant with more perfect rounded sprouts. Because they tend to mature all at once, it's a good idea to plant a few varieties that mature at different times.

TIP

Not many people use them, but the top leaves on the plant are also really tasty. When the plant is mature, these leaves can be picked off and eaten. Doing so also encourages the plant to concentrate its energy into producing better sprouts.

To sow your Brussels sprouts, follow these steps:

1. **For an early crop, sow in modular trays or small pots in the greenhouse or at home in a bright place in late winter. Otherwise, sow outside in a seed bed from early to mid-spring.**

   Timing depends on the variety you choose, so read the packet carefully. For a really early crop, sow under glass. The seeds don't do so well in seed modules and produce better plants if sown in one place and then transplanted into their final position.

2. **Transplant the seedlings into their final place when they have four or five leaves, and space them 75 centimetres apart (check the correct spacing on the seed packet for dwarf varieties).**

   Brussels sprouts need plenty of space in which to mature properly, and the soil should be firmed really well around the plants.

3. **Earth up the bottom of the growing plants to help stabilise them as they grow.**

   As the plants get taller, they may need staking to add extra support, especially on exposed and windy sites.

4. **Keep plants weed free and watch out for pests.**

   Snails, slugs and rodents love the young foliage of sprouts, so the plants will need protection from all of them. (See Chapter 7 for more details on pests.)

WARNING!

Squirrels can decimate your crop overnight – they simply can't resist the young, sweet sprouts as they emerge. If you're aware of a local population, make sure that you cover your crop with some kind of netting as protection. Squirrels also hate the smell of moth balls, so bury a few around the plants and this should also help keep them away.

Because the plants are so well spaced out, rainwater readily reaches their bases. As a result, they rarely need extra water, but do always keep an eye on them during really dry periods. Also, be sure to remove and dispose of any dying yellow foliage, as this may harbour diseases that can easily spread to the whole crop. Your crop may, in late summer, look as if it's struggling a little. If this is the case, give the plants a liquid feed high in nitrogen to give them a boost into autumn and winter.

TIP

Brussels sprouts take up lots of room on the allotment, so it seems a shame not to use the space to the maximum. You can grow salad crops in between the seedlings and harvest them before the Brussels sprouts cast too much shade. You can also grow cabbages in the spaces; some people swear that this actually produces better results for both crops. I like to sow a row of French beans (a dwarf variety works really well), radishes or even kohlrabi (see 'Alien Invasion: Growing Kohlrabi' later in this chapter).

Considering varieties

Try these varieties of Brussels sprouts for the best results:

- **Bitesize F1.** Produces medium-sized sprouts that remain firm on the stem for a long period. Small and tasty.
- **Bosworth F1.** A great British variety of early-maturing sprouts; the individual sprouts are spaced evenly on the stem.
- **Falstaff.** Produces gorgeous red or purple sprouts from late autumn into winter, which taste and look great.
- **Igor F1.** Shows great frost resistance and offers lovely firm dark green sprouts.
- **Trafalgar F1.** One for those of you who don't like sprouts – this variety is really sweet, firm and delicious. A great fairly new hybrid variety that is pretty easy to grow, with few problems.

Harvesting and storage

Sprouts take about 20 weeks to mature and should be picked as soon they're big enough to eat; I like them small, so I tend to pick them early. It's a fact that sprouts taste better after a hard frost, so most varieties are regarded as a winter vegetable. Some plants produce as early as September and do taste good, but after a frost they taste really good! Start picking them off at the bottom, and the upper ones continue to develop nicely. If you're in an area where winters are severe, pull the plants up before the ground freezes hard, and store them in a cool place where they'll keep for a good few weeks.

TIP: As soon as the plants have finished, it's best to dig up the whole root to reduce the risk of disease building up in the soil. The roots of sprouts are tough and don't compost well, so let out some frustration on them with a hammer and smash them up a bit, which helps them rot down more quickly.

Getting a Head with Cauliflowers

Cauliflower isn't the easiest vegetable to grow, but is one of the most satisfying. It's basically a biennial plant that has been bred to complete its life cycle in one year. So it germinates, stores food and then flowers all in one season, and is therefore fairly greedy and won't grow in poor soil. Cauliflowers like a heavy, moist, humus-rich soil, so do really well on organic rich clay. If you're planting after the legumes in a rotation system (see Chapter 7), don't remove the roots, simply hoe them off. If you pull them up, you disturb the soil; caulis like a really firm soil. They like lime, so the autumn before planting, check the pH and, if the soil is too acidic, add the required amount of lime stated on the packet to bring the Ph to between 6.5 and 7. (See Chapter 6 for more on balancing your soil.) A couple of weeks before planting, *top dress* (sprinkle on the surface) some fish, blood and bone, and gently rake it into the soil without too much disturbance. Your caulis will also benefit from a good dose of potash feed.

Cauliflowers grow best when they're given really stable conditions, and careful selection of variety will greatly influence your success rate. Ask your fellow plot holders for advice: a bit of local research goes a long way. Newer F1 hybrids help make cauliflower-growing less of a lottery, but it may be a case of trial and error with a bit of guidance along the way.

Cauliflowers are available in winter, summer and autumn varieties, with some winter varieties suitable only for frost-free areas. Some surprising varieties come with green or purple flower heads. If you live in an area that often suffers from summer drought, go for quick-cropping varieties such as fast-maturing mini cauliflowers.

Getting started with cauliflowers

You can get an early crop of caulis ready to harvest in midsummer if you sow seeds indoors in mid-winter and transplant them as soon as the soil is warm enough in early spring. For the main crop, sow a fast-maturing variety in mid-spring for harvest in late summer, and at the same time sow a slower-maturing variety. That way, you'll get a late autumn and early winter harvest as well.

To sow your cauliflowers, follow these steps:

1. **Sow seeds in trays or modules and grow on until they have four *true leaves* (true leaves are usually the second leaves to develop, and all others from then on).**

   Seeds germinate best at 21 degrees centigrade. Sow summer varieties during March under cover and sow winter varieties direct in April and May. Or you can sow for a really early crop in winter and keep the seedlings in a protected cold frame or under cloches and plant them out in spring.

2. **Plant out according to the spacing suitable for your chosen variety.**

   Basically, the longer they're in the ground, the larger they become, so leave between 50 and 65 centimetres between them according to the maturing time needed. You can space the fast-growing mini varieties much closer together – say 15 centimetres apart.

3. **Water during dry periods.**

   Cauliflowers must keep growing; any disruption in their growth and they're ruined.

4. **Protect your cauliflowers from pests and diseases: slugs, snails, rodents and all the usual brassica pests.**

   Pollen beetles can also be a problem and can fly in from oilseed rape fields nearby, but you can't spray them, because insecticides also harm important pollinators. So it's a problem you simply have to live with.

5. **Earth up the main stem to offer more support, especially on windy sites.**

   White cauliflowers benefit from having their heads (also called *curds*) protected from the sun, so pull in the outer leaves and tie them gently with some string so they cover the central curd and act as a shield. This can also help plants during winter by protecting them from frost.

TIP

Cauliflower seedlings can sometimes grow *blind*, which means a flower head isn't formed so no curd grows. Check all seedlings to see whether a flower bud is forming and discard any that don't have one.

Considering varieties

With loads of cauliflower varieties to choose from, here are the ones I recommend:

- **All Year Round.** This has to be one of the easiest varieties to grow, a really popular variety that produces large white curds. It's great for succession sowings, sown from February to May. Seventy days later you can harvest. Also good for autumn sowings, overwintered in a cold frame to plant out in March.

- **Nessie F1 hybrid.** An outstanding cauliflower that develops large, really pure white curds. Crop it from August to October.
- **Emeraude F1 hybrid.** Producing green curds that are really nutritious, it crops from August to November.
- **Winter Aalsmeer.** A superb winter-hardy variety producing nice heavy curds. You plant it in May and it matures in April the following year, extending the harvesting season when not many other cauliflowers are around.
- **Graffiti F1.** This cauliflower has a really deep purple curd, full of goodness and great for kids who may turn their noses up at white varieties. Unlike white caulis, sunlight intensifies the colour, so there's no need to cover the curds.
- **Freedom F1.** One of the best and easiest to grow, and great for main crop or mini cauliflowers. Sow them from February to May and they're ready 70 days later.
- **Sunset F1.** As the name suggest, this cauli produces orange curds that are great fun. Colour is most vivid if grown as baby veg, but stays even on mature plants. Sow them from March to May for harvesting from July to the end of September.

Harvesting and storage

Cauliflowers take varying times to mature for harvesting (anywhere from 15 weeks for mini varieties to 40 weeks for winter varieties). Pick them as soon as they're mature. Caulis don't keep well and deteriorate quickly, so cut them while they're still firm. They store in the freezer really well, especially smaller varieties.

COOKING TIP

Cauliflower is delicious eaten raw and thrown into salad. Like most vegetables, it's best lightly cooked so it retains its crunch. Gentle cooking also helps to retain colour and nutrient content – cauliflower is full of vitamin C.

Most people have had broccoli and Stilton soup so why not try cauliflower and Stilton instead? If you ask me, it's even better. Cauliflower works well with cheese and also with curry and spicy flavours.

Keeping Healthy with Kale

Kale is a cabbage with no heart. It's very winter hardy and comes in smooth and wrinkled varieties. Kale is about as healthy a veg as you're likely to find, containing twice the vitamin C of the equivalent portion of orange juice. Kale leaves are best eaten when young, because they can get a bit tough when older, but are still perfectly edible. Modern varieties allow kale to be grown all year round, so it's a useful crop for the allotment. You also get ornamental kales which come in an extraordinary array of colours such as lavender, white, bright purple and red; these are often sold in garden centres as ornamental cabbages, but they are in fact kales. They are edible and just as good as normal varieties, but if you buy ready-grown plants from a garden centre, you never know what they have been sprayed with, so I would not eat them!

Getting started with kale

Kale likes a fertile soil and can grow pretty much anywhere. Frost actually improves the flavour, and the plants can survive down to –15 degrees centigrade, so are useful for growing in exposed and cold plots. To sow your kale, follow these steps:

1. **Sow seeds in trays or seeds beds for transplanting, or sow directly into the soil.**

   Sowings can be made from early spring for summer crops, or later for late summer and autumn crops.

2. **Transplant into fertile soil in full sun when seedlings have five leaves.**

   Dwarf varieties need approximately 30–45 centimetres between them; larger varieties need 75 centimetres.

3. **Weed and water during dry spells.**

   They pretty much look after themselves and need little care. Varieties grown for over-wintering will benefit in spring from a top dressing that's high in nitrogen to promote growth.

Considering varieties

Loads of different varieties are there to try, but curly kale is probably the most popular. Curly kale can be difficult to clean properly, which puts a lot of people off, but it's really tasty and even the dwarf varieties withstand winter well. You can also get purple-leaved varieties that are full of nutrients. These are just some varieties of kale:

- **Black Tuscany.** A really useful kale that can be sown from March to August for tasty young leaves that you can use in salads, or in March to June for mature plants that can be over-wintered and used until spring. You can even sow and grow this variety indoors in pots for baby salad leaves that add a lovely peppery taste to salads.

- **Cavolo Palmizio Senza Testa.** A lovely green variety with Savoy-like foliage. It can be grown as a baby salad leaf or as a winter crop when not many other green vegetables are around.
- **Skarlet.** This kale can be grown for its young tender leaves and also has great winter hardiness. It has colourful curly purple foliage with red veining. Sow from March to August for salad and young leaves, or from March to June if you want mature plants.
- **Pentland Brig.** A smooth green-leafed variety with crinkled edges. Sow outside in April and May and harvest from November through to March. In spring, it produces lovely side shoots that can be picked as spring greens.

Harvesting your Kale

Kale can be harvested at any time as soon as the plants are large enough. Ideally, choose young growth, which is the most tender and tasty, and don't remove too much foliage from each individual plant – just remove a few leaves from each. The more mature leaves are usually pretty tough but are full of nutrients, so worth eating. Kale does not keep well, so only pick it as you need it.

Alien Invasion: Growing Kohlrabi

Kohlrabi is the weirdest looking vegetable, suggestive of an alien cabbage. It's a cross between a cabbage and a turnip, but it grows above the ground, and whereas turnips are swollen roots, kohlrabis are swollen stems. Kohlrabi looks like a spherical smooth turnip with multiple stems coming out of it.

Unfortunately, kohlrabi isn't very popular and is only sold in shops as an oddity. It's best eaten young, and the ones in shops are often large and tough, so it's not surprising that they're not very popular. But I assure you it's actually delicious and looks interesting growing on your plot, so impress your friends by growing this extraordinary vegetable.

Getting started with kohlrabi

Kohlrabi is quite easy to grow and, although it does best in rich soil with plenty of organic matter, it manages in most soil types. It can easily be grown in raised beds and even in pots with multi-purpose compost, but it needs regular feeding with a liquid fertiliser. It grows really quite quickly, so needs a good supply of water and nutrients to form a tasty, crisp specimen.

To sow your kohlrabi, follow these steps:

1. **Prepare the soil with plenty of organic matter the autumn before planting. If you don't have a chance, don't worry – add some a couple of weeks before planting and your plants will be okay.**
2. **Plant seeds in shallow drills 1 centimetre deep. Allow 30 centimetres between rows.**

   Fill in the drills and flatten them down with a rake. Water well if the soil is dry. Seeds can be planted in succession from March to July. You may possibly squeeze in some late sowings in August as well.
3. **Protect seedlings well, as with all brassicas.**

   Slugs, snails and other pests find the young shoots an irresistible snack, so cover them with protective netting. Crushed oyster shells work really well as a mulch-like barrier that keeps slugs and snails at bay.
4. **When they're well established, thin out seedlings to 10-centimetre spacing.**
5. **Keep them well watered and constantly moist to ensure unchecked growth.**

   This leads to sweet, tender vegetables; even the side shoots that protrude are as juicy as the best apples.

Considering varieties

Because kohlrabi isn't the world's most popular vegetable, few varieties exist. That said, the following are great and easy to find:

- **Purple Vienna.** A purple-rooted and leaved variety that's quick and easy to grow. It's best eaten when about 5 centimetres across.
- **Kolibri F1 hybrid.** Super-fast to mature – in as little as eight weeks – it's best eaten small, but still good until it reaches tennis-ball size.
- **Lanro.** A modern hybrid that grows really quickly. With attractive green skin, it's really good raw, grated into a salad.
- **Quickstar F1.** An extremely reliable little plant. Plants can be grown really close together for perfect baby veg: you can plant them as close as 3 centimetres apart, and they'll still grow into beautiful little specimens.

Harvesting and storage

Kohlrabi can be ready for harvest in as little as 10 weeks and is best eaten when no bigger than a tennis ball. Older varieties must be eaten when young, but some of the new hybrids can be left until they're 12 centimetres across before they become tough. Simply cut them off at the base as needed.

COOKING TIP

Kohlrabi is great sliced or grated into salads and makes a really good addition to coleslaw. Older ones can be used in the same way as turnips in stews and casseroles. The leaves too can be eaten, cooked like spring greens, and are also best harvested when young.

Chapter 12

Growing Wholesome Herbs

In This Chapter

- Getting going with growing
- Finding the right home for your herbs
- Putting together the herbal first aid kit
- Introducing herbs for the enthusiast

No better way to add fresh flavours to home-cooked food exists than adding your own home-grown herbs. Most are really easy to grow, and the more you use them, the harder they work for you. Many are happy in pots, and others can simply be planted, left and used year after year. A good starting point is to grow those herbs that you use the most; herbs can be pricey, so growing your own is the best way to save a few pounds and get the freshest herbs available.

In this chapter I show you how to grow your favourite herbs and some more unusual ones. I show you where they like to grow, how to store them and what uses they all have. Remember that fresh herbs have far more flavour than many dried ones, so they really do deserve a space on the allotment.

Knowing Where to Start

Various ways exist in which to grow and nurture herbs for the allotment. None is necessarily right or wrong, but the methods do involve varying levels of effort. You can cheat completely and buy ready grown – either larger specimens or small plugs and seedlings – and then plant them up in pots or in the ground. You can grow many from seed; this is by far the cheapest option but involves a bit of work and plenty of love and attention. Or you can *propagate* (reproduce) plants through cuttings, layering and division; this is a great way of boosting stocks for free and even for sharing with your allotment buddies. I cover all these techniques in this section.

Choosing Which Herbs To Grow

Which herbs you choose to grow depends very much on how much space you have spare and on which herbs you feel you'll use most. You also need to consider whether you want to dedicate an area totally to herbs or simply plant some in amongst your fruit and vegetables.

Planting herbs amongst your vegetables can have beneficial results on the plants nearby. This is called *companion planting* (see Chapter 7 for more on this). For example, parsley is said to be a great companion plant for tomatoes; its flowers attract beneficial insects such as wasps, and these kill tomato hornworm. Also, strong-smelling herbs shield the smell of tomato leaves, which pests are attracted to.

The staples for me are parsley, basil, rosemary, thyme, sage, oregano, dill and mint, because these are the ones I use most in the kitchen. If you want to grow your herbs for medicinal use, your list may be far more extensive. Only grow herbs that you think you're actually going to use, until you become a herb expert and want to expand you selection.

Most herbs are easy to grow, many being basically wild plants that in their natural environment have to fight to survive. As a result, they have to be tough as old boots. So in the relatively comfy and food-rich environment of an allotment, they romp away happily.

Nearly all herbs have flowers that are very attractive to bees, and so help to improve the pollination of many other allotment crops that the bees visit.

Growing herbs from seed

Many herbs can be grown from seed and offer quick-growing, tasty leaves that can be sown throughout the year for a constant supply. Some herbs such as parsley can be sown straight into the soil, even in amongst your vegetables, where they thrive happily. Others, such as basil, need a little more care and attention to succeed. Growing from seed is a great option if you want lots of a particular herb.

The most popular herbs to grow from seed are:

- **Parsley:** Probably the most popular and easily recognisable of herbs, and highly nutritious, parsley is grown as an annual which can be flat leafed or curly. Finely chopped, it adds a fresh taste to most dishes, making it essential to the allotment garden.

- **Basil:** A frost-tender, low-growing annual herb, which requires plenty of warmth to do well. Many varieties of basil exist, from Thai basil to the more familiar sweet basil, which is so widely used in Italian cookery. All are really fragrant.
- **Chervil:** An annual herb with a similar appearance to parsley but with a slightly more fern-like leaf, the flavour of chervil is very mild with a slight hint of liquorice. It's widely used in French cooking, often added to soups, salads, seafood dishes and vegetables.
- **Dill:** This *perennial* herb (a plant that lives for more than two years) carries its yellow flower heads like little umbrellas above its fine almost fern-like foliage. Dill has a very distinctive taste and is often used to accompany fish dishes.
- **Chives:** Not only do they taste great but they look great too, with their purple pompom-like flowers on slender stalks, and hollow straw-like leaves that have a slight onion flavour. They're the smallest member of the onion family, and the flavour works particularly well in potato salad, with fish and sprinkled in soups. Chives are produced from tiny bulbs, and are perennial plants that are really easy to grow.
- **Coriander:** An *annual* herb (it only lives for one year) that carries the feathery green leaves that are associated with Asian and Middle Eastern cuisine. The leaves have a distinct soapy taste and, finely chopped, are added to countless dishes all over the world.

Herbs that are easily transplantable, such as parsley and basil, are best grown in modular trays that are divided into sections known as *cells* (you can get these at any garden centre). Fill the cells with compost, water them well and allow them to drain, then sprinkle a few seeds onto the surface. Cover with a thin layer of compost and then give them a good water. It's a good idea to buy a cheap plastic *propagator*, which resembles a mini greenhouse, and place the cells in there. Alternatively, you can cover them with cling film and put them in a warm bright place such as a window sill. My father often sows his basil in an old oven dish full of compost, leaving a centimetre at the top and then covering it with clear plastic film. He often has more success than me with my fancy propagators!

Most seedlings can simply be left in the cells and transplanted when they're big enough to be moved, usually after between 6 and 12 weeks, depending on which herb you choose. Shrubby perennials need to be thinned out when they're around 1 or 2 centimetres tall, leaving only the strongest-looking seedlings in the pot. Thinning out gives the roots and shoots of each plant room to grow without competition from the other seedlings.

Some herbs such as chervil, dill and coriander are best planted straight into the soil, because they don't transplant well from a cell tray. They're therefore best planted exactly where you want them to grow, perhaps in the open ground on your allotment or in containers. The containers can be anything from piled-up car tyres to bought terracotta pots, but do make sure that the pots are deep enough to accommodate the deep roots of plants like dill and the *tap roots* (roots that look like carrots) of herbs like coriander. You can get a head start and *germinate* (sprout) them indoors in suitable pots, weeks before the last frost, but if planting them outside, wait until the risk of frost has well and truly passed.

TIP

Try buying or making some biodegradable seedling pots. You can make them by simply rolling some newspaper around a small jar and folding over the bottom, removing the jar, and then filling the newspaper pot with compost and sowing the seeds as usual. Once the seedlings are ready to be planted out, harden them off for a week or so by putting them outside in the daytime, and then plant them by digging small holes the size of your paper pots and popping them in, firming down gently. The benefit of this method is that often, when you transplant seedlings, the fine hairs on the roots are damaged, which can set the seedling back weeks. By doing it this way, you can plant them out with little or no root disturbance at all, which leads to a happier, healthier and more vigorous plant.

Growing from cuttings

Herbs such as rosemary and sage usually root really easily from cuttings, and this is great way to improve your stocks and replace tired old plants. During the summer, herbs are putting all their energy into new growth, and this makes it an ideal time to take cuttings. There are many different ways to take cuttings from plants, but for the beginner the simplest way is as follows:

1. **Get your pots ready.** Fill a medium-sized pot to within a centimetre of the top with good gritty free-draining compost and gently firm it down, tapping the pot on a surface to remove any air pockets. Seed and cutting compost is fine to use, but because most herbs like a free-draining soil, it is best to mix in a third by volume of horticultural grit, *perlite* or *vermiculite* (the latter two are expanded volcanic aggregates that are a bit like polystyrene in appearance). Water the compost thoroughly and allow to drain.
2. **Take your cuttings.** Select a healthy new shoot and cut it off between 7 and 10 centimetres in length, or break off side shoots from the main stem. Ideally don't use the newest fresh growth and choose shoots that are slightly firmer from lower down the plant.
3. **Prepare your cuttings.** Remove the bottom leaves to minimise water loss and cut the bottom cleanly to just below a *leaf joint* (where the leaves come from). Dip in rooting hormone to give it the best chance of rooting. (Rooting hormone is available at all good garden centres.)
4. **Pot them up.** Insert five or six cuttings around the edge of the pot, spaced equally apart. Firm the compost gently to ensure there are no air spaces around the stems, and give the cuttings a good drink of water.

5. **Cover them up.** Place the cuttings in a non-heated propagator, or cover the top of the pot using a clear plastic bag secured with an elastic band. This helps retain a humid atmosphere that encourages root growth.
6. **Nurture your plants.** After a couple of weeks, the cuttings should start to set root; you can see the signs when the top leaves begin to show signs of growth or new leaves appear. You should ensure that the cutting stays moist by using a *mister* (a mist-spraying device available at garden centres) every now and then when needed. Watch out for any cuttings that fail to grow and turn brown. Remove them, because they can cause mould growth.
7. **Pot them out.** After about eight weeks, the seedlings will be ready to be teased gently apart and potted on into larger containers.
8. **Plant them.** The following spring, they'll be ready to be planted out into their new homes.

Some of the best herbs for propagating with cuttings are:

- Rosemary
- Sage
- Lemon verbena
- Thyme
- Lavender

Getting More for Your Money

Apart from growing from seed and taking cuttings, you can increase your stocks in other ways. These methods are often employed by professional growers and offer the allotmenteer a great opportunity to multiply her stocks without spending a penny. In fact, the following two methods are really simple, and if we all adopted them, garden centre sales of some herbs would drop dramatically.

Dividing herbs

Herbaceous perennials (plants that die back to ground level at the end of the growing season) and those with bulbous roots can be multiplied by dividing them up into a number of small plants; this is called *division*. In essence, all you're doing is lifting the plant, splitting the roots (as shown in Figure 12-1) and then planting the sections again. The best time for division is in early spring before the plants spring into life or in autumn as they turn brown and die back.

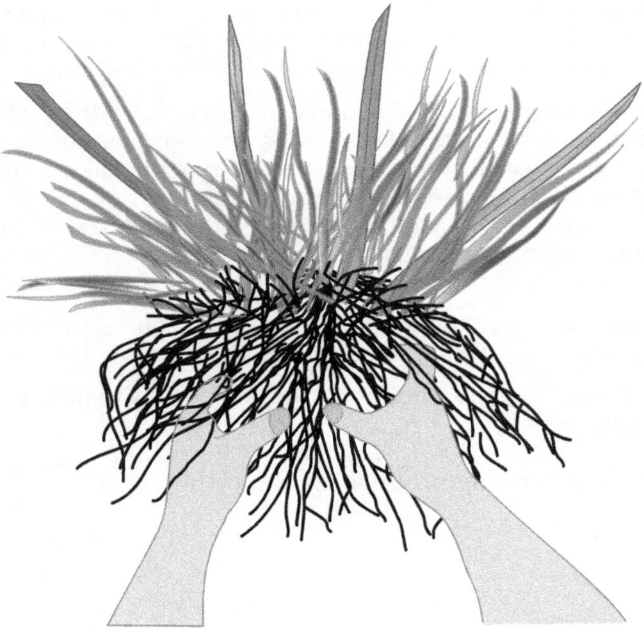

Figure 12-1: Creating new plants by division.

Chives are by far the easiest to treat in this manner, because they have a bulb that forms nice little clumps and can be split easily. You often find chives sold in pots at garden centres and DIY stores. Simply take the pot off, trim the foliage down to half its original height and gently tease the roots apart, splitting the clump into a number of smaller ones. You can then plant these into new compost in pots.

Mint, bergamot and French tarragon, amongst others, can also be divided in a similar way. Once the plant is a fairly decent size, you can simply pull it out of its pot or dig it up and split the root into a number of smaller plants that can be planted into new pots or straight back into the ground.

REMEMBER

Give newly divided plants a really good drink; after the stress of moving house and splitting from their mother plant, they need it!

Using mound layering

This method of *propagation* (reproducing plants from seeds or cuttings) is great for woody or shrubby herbs like rosemary, sage and particularly thyme. You often find that these shrubs become a bit leggy and bare in the centre, so they need replacing every three or four years. In spring, simply pile up a mound of decent free-draining soil around the base, with the top of the plant showing. (See Chapter 6 for more on soil types.) If it rains, ensure that the piled-up soil hasn't washed away; if it has, be sure to build up the level again to support the new growth. What happens is that the shoots that are growing in the mound then develop roots at the bottom, as shown in Figure 12-2. By late summer, they'll have developed enough roots for you to remove them from the original plant.

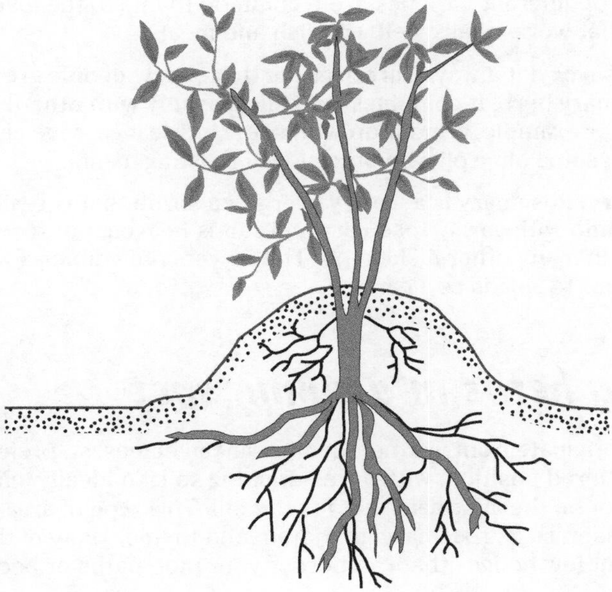

Figure 12-2: Propagating using mound layering.

Once you have some healthy new root growth, gently cut off the new shoots with the roots, using some secateurs, and pot them up or plant them out in the allotment. This is a great way to multiply your stocks for free, and you could even offer some of the new plants to your allotment neighbours, earning you valuable brownie points!

Herbs that are particularly suitable for mound layering are:

- **Sage:** This is an easy herb to grow. It is the perfect accompaniment to pork dishes and often used in stuffing. The leaves are quite strongly flavoured and can be deep fried and used as a garnish. It is a semi-woody shrub that needs replacing every five years or so, because it soon starts to look tired.
- **Hyssop:** This is often grown as a plant in the herbaceous border, because of its really long flowering period. It's great for attracting pollinators onto your plot, and beekeepers often use it for exactly that purpose. The leaves can be dried for storing and can be sprinkled sparingly into strong-flavoured stews and soups, and the flowers over salads.

- **Lavender:** We all know lavender as a garden plant, but not many use it as a culinary herb. The flowers are lovely as a garnish or in salads, but are best popped in a jar of sugar to make lavender sugar, which is good for adding flavour to custards and cakes.
- **Thymes:** Thyme is a classic herb used in many dishes; the small leaves are really fragrant and should be used pretty sparingly. There are a number of different varieties, from common thyme to the lovely lemon thyme that works really well with fish and meats.
- **Winter savory:** It always surprises me that so few people grow this plant as a culinary herb. It combines very successfully with other herbs in mixes. For example, grind it up with some bay leaves, sage and thyme, and with some olive oil, rub onto slowly roasting meats.
- **Rosemary:** Rosemary is a woody evergreen shrub that is really easy to grow. Lamb with garlic, rosemary and salt is heaven, but rosemary can be used in many other dishes too. The flowers are edible as well, and add colour to salads as a garnish.

Growing herbs in a sunny spot

Many herbs originate from warmer Mediterranean climes, so prefer a sunny, open yet sheltered position, with a free-draining soil. So ideally, choose a dedicated spot on the allotment that fits the bill. This type of area suits herbs such as lavender, sage, rosemary, marjoram and thyme. Many of these herbs make excellent low hedges that can border your plot, paths or bed edges.

In a relatively small area – say 1.5–2 square metres – you'd have plenty of room to grow enough herbs to sustain you and your family all year round. Prepare the area in autumn by removing all the weeds, especially perennial weeds. (See Chapter 5 for info on killing off weeds.) Then dig the ground over, leaving the lumps open to the frost over winter. Frost helps break down the larger lumps of soil into finer particles that are more suitable for planting in. Then when spring arrives, again weed the area well and fork in a good load of compost.

Don't add farmyard manure to the herb area of your plot (as you would the veggie plot). If the soil is too rich, it promotes soft growth that's easily damaged by frost and lacks the pungent aroma you ideally want.

The types of herbs that like a lot of sun are usually the tough, silvery leaved varieties or those with tougher green leaves, as described in the following sections.

Rosemary

Rosemary is native to the Mediterranean. It's pretty hardy and is a great addition to the allotment garden because it's evergreen, offering pungent needle-like leaves all year round. It can grow into a pretty substantial plant, up to about 1.2 metres tall, so give it plenty of room. The leaves and flowers can be picked as required, but during winter, pick the leaves sparingly because the new growth won't replace them until spring comes again. Rosemary can be grown from seed but is best grown from semi-ripe cuttings in the early autumn. (See the section 'Growing from cuttings' earlier in this chapter.)

COOKING TIP

Rosemary flowers are edible and are great picked fresh and added straight to a salad. My favourite use for rosemary is to finely chop it with some garlic and a couple of anchovy fillets, then mix it with some butter. Pierce some holes in a leg of lamb and force the mixture into the holes before roasting.

Thyme

Thyme is also from the Mediterranean and is really easy to grow. It actually quite likes poor stony soil but grows in any free-draining soil in full sun. You can find many varieties, some being hardier than others, but *Thymus vulgaris* is a hardy evergreen that's a must for the herb garden. This is a small compact plants that creeps along, low to the ground. Thyme flowers in summer and benefits from a good haircut as soon as flowering has finished, thus encouraging new growth. Thyme can be grown from seed, cuttings or by layering – techniques covered in sections earlier in this chapter.

Sage

Sage comes in a few different varieties, from the plain green ones to purple, and even one with white, yellow and green variegated leaves. It too is from the Med and can reach about 70 centimetres tall in some cases. *Salvia officinalis* is the best one to grow for culinary use, but you can also get a dwarf variety called *Salvia officinalis 'compacta'*, which has the same flavour but only reaches half the height. It's also, in my view, a far prettier plant. Sage takes a long time to establish from seed, so I'd really not bother trying. You're better off buying ready-grown plants and simply planting them directly onto the allotment. If growing from seed, sow in March (indoors) and April (outdoors). When sowing sage, treat in the same way as other herbs: sow in cells and then harden off and plant out.

Tarragon

Tarragon is an herbaceous perennial that sits upright to the height of 90 centimetres in the allotment, carrying slender bright green leaves that are so prized in sauces such as béarnaise. The most readily available variety is Russian tarragon, which grows quite vigorously and is quite easy to grow from seed. In trays or cells, sprinkle the seed onto the surface of the compost and water well. Place the seed trays into a propagator or cover with cling film in a bright place, and in two to three weeks they'll germinate. Transplant when they're large enough to handle into 7-centimetre pots, harden them off for a week in a cold frame, and then they're ready to plant directly into the ground on the allotment. Tarragon likes a sunny spot and grows in almost any soil.

Oregano

Oregano, which is sometimes called wild marjoram, is a ground-hugging semi-shrubby perennial. What pizza or tomato sauce would be complete without it? It's fairly easy to grow, liking routine watering and regular picking. Oregano is a great plant for an allotment because its little pink flowers are magnets to bees and other beneficial veggie garden friends.

Bay

The sweet bay is a vital part of the herb garden and can be trained to be kept compact so it does not take over your plot (bays can grow into 12-metre trees). They are often really expensive, but thankfully they can be propagated from cuttings (see earlier in this chapter) and will reach a decent size within two or three years. They are not the easiest plants to reproduce in this way, but if you take multiple cuttings, some will root. Bays also send up new shoots from the base of the plant, and these can be removed with the roots and re-planted. These will grow much more quickly than cuttings. Many people choose to grow them in pots, especially in colder areas, because they can be damaged by frost, which will scorch the foliage. If you plant them in pots, you can put them in the greenhouse during winter to protect them.

Selecting herbs for semi-shade

Some herbs are far happier out of the intense heat of the midday sun; these are generally the more delicate, softer-leaved varieties such as chervil and mint. Most herbs like plenty of sunshine, but some happily tolerate a semi-shady spot. Consider growing the herbs described in the following sections if your plot lies in the semi-shade.

Chervil

Chervil is a much underused hardy *annual* (a plant with an entire life cycle of only one year) that offers a slight aniseed twang to cooking. It's widely used in French cooking in soups and stews. Grow it as a herb to add to salads. I think it's also fantastic chopped over fish and barbecued meats. Chervil is best sown from seed at three-weekly intervals straight onto your allotment, because it doesn't like being moved.

Sow the seeds from spring right throughout the summer at regular intervals for a constant supply. Sprinkle the seeds in rows 1 centimetre deep and 30 centimetres apart in plain, simple garden soil that's been raked over until it's fine in texture. Once the seedlings are 4 centimetres tall, thin them out to 15 centimetres apart. Chervil is ready to use as soon as six to eight weeks after sowing, so is great if you're impatient for quick results!

Mint

Mint can be (in fact *is*) a total hooligan in the garden, and can spread like wildfire soon after planting. Many different varieties of mint are available (in fact you can buy whole books dedicated to the plant), ranging from simple garden mint (*Mentha sachalinensis*) to apple mint (*Mentha suaveolens*). Check the back of seed packets to see which type you'd prefer.

TIP

To keep mint under control, grow it in a pot or bury it in a heavy pot in the allotment to stop those adventurous roots seeking out new territory to conquer.

Sweet cicely

This fantastic hardy herbaceous perennial likes a spot in semi-shade and a good bit of moisture. The leaves resemble finely cut ferns and have a similar taste to chervil. It's a really useful herb because, as well as the leaves, its unripe seeds and roots are all edible. Cicely readily self-sows but can be sown from seed in autumn or propagated through division at the start or end of the growing season. To stop it going mad in your allotment, it's worth removing the flower heads before they set seed.

COOKING TIP

Chop cicely leaves and seeds and add them to salads and fruit dishes. The roots can be peeled and steamed and are great served with a simple béchamel sauce. The seeds are often used in baking and tart fruit dishes because their sweetness reduces the amount of sugar needed.

Homing in on healing herbs

Plants have been used for the purpose of healing for as long as mankind has walked the earth. In fact, herbal remedies such as hyacinth and yarrow have been dug up next to Stone Age skeletons. Many modern-day medicines are derived directly from plants, from which selected chemical compounds have been extracted.

You can grow hundreds of plant remedies on your allotment, and herbs can complement mainstream treatment to great effect. Check out *Complementary Medicine For Dummies* by Jacqueline Young (Wiley) for more on how to get the best health benefits from your herbs.

WARNING!

Never ever eat or prepare any herbal remedy unless you're completely sure of what you're taking.

The following sections describe herbs that can be used for medicinal purposes.

Angelica

Angelica is usually grown for its towering and striking appearance, and is a real show-stopper in the cottage garden, but it offers much more to the allotmenteer. *Angelica archangelica* is used prolifically in herbal medicine, with a vast list of benefits. The roots contain all sorts of vitamins and minerals such as B12, zinc and iron, all of which are beneficial. An *infusion* of the roots (some roots brewed in water just like tea) is said to aid digestion, and can also be used as a face wash to prevent acne. Other uses are to relieve muscular spasm in asthma sufferers and soothe bronchitis; it has also been shown to relieve menstrual flow and rheumatism.

It's easy to grow angelica from seed: simply sow in rich moist soil in spring or autumn. It tolerates both full sun and moist shady areas. It also self-seeds freely and spreads.

To avoid angelica self-seeding and spreading all over your plot, remove the seed heads before they ripen in summer.

Basil

Basil is native to India, Africa and Asia, and has also been grown in the Mediterranean for thousands of years. The herb is, of course, well known for its culinary uses, but it also has very important medicinal powers. Its main use is to reduce blood sugar levels, and it is helpful in preventing peptic ulcers and other stress-induced conditions such as hypertension, colitis and even asthma. An infusion of basil can be used as a cold remedy and to reduce nasal congestion, fever and aching joints. Basil also has strong antibacterial and anti-fungal powers and can be used to relieve itching, insect bites and other skin complaints: simply crush the leaves and rub on the affected area.

Marigold

Marigolds are said to flower on the first day of every month (the calends), which is where they get their Latin name. Marigold is known as the best herb for treating skin problems; infusions of the petals are used for lessening swellings and soothing sprains, reducing varicose veins, and for soothing stings, burns, rashes and sunburn. To make an infusion, *steep* (soak) a handful of petals in boiling water for about 15–30 minutes. Allow the liquid to cool, and apply as a skin tonic.

Marigolds can be sown easily from seed either in pots inside, six to eight weeks before you expect the last frost, or once the risk of frost has passed, straight into the soil. Prepare the soil by raking it until it's fine in texture and then sprinkle the seeds in rows, 12 millimetres deep and 30 centimetres apart, and cover gently with soil and water. When the seedlings start to shoot, thin them out so that they're 15 centimetres apart. In pots, simply sow them to the same depth, and when the plants are large enough to handle, thin out as necessary. They like a spot in full sun.

TIP

Marigolds flower more freely if you *deadhead* them regularly – that is, cut off the flowers when they fade. Deadheading encourages the plant to concentrate all its energy on producing new flowers.

Chamomile

Of the different varieties of chamomile around, the most widely grown is *Chamaemelum nobile*. This evergreen perennial forms a dense mat that creeps slowly and spreads. It carries white daisy-like flowers. Chamomile grows wild throughout Europe and is well known for its relaxing powers; the flowers are known to help digestion, depression and even headaches. They're also helpful in calming the nerves if you're feeling anxious before a big event, speech or exam. To my mind, the best tea comes from the dried flowers (see the section 'Drying' later in this chapter). When steeped in boiling water for five minutes, these make a soothing night-time drink – I know a nice cup of chamomile tea sends me right off to sleep.

Dill

Dill (*Anethum graveolens*) is a herb I'm very familiar with, being of Swedish origin, because in Sweden they use it in everything. It's well known for its ability to relieve wind, stomach problems and in calming digestion, and simply by eating the leaves as a flavouring for food, you can benefit from its calming effects. The seeds, when chewed, are a great remedy for bad breath, and dill is also good at fighting colds and relieving coughs. Amazingly, eating dill helps increase milk production in nursing mothers and can help with colic in a feeding baby.

Dill is really easy to grow and can be sown directly into the ground on your allotment in early spring and summer in full sun and in a free-draining rich soil. (For more on soil types see Chapter 6.) The leaves should be picked in spring and summer before flowering, and the seed heads harvested as they begin to ripen in the summer. Cut the flowering stem off and hang it upside down in a paper bag; in a week or so, the seeds will have fallen off into the bag ready for use. The seeds have a much more intense flavour than the leaves and have the same anti-colic effects as the leaves. They're used as a spice much like caraway in soups, breads, in stews and in fish dishes.

WARNING!

Never plant dill near fennel; the two will cross-pollinate, and the resulting seeds will have an impaired flavour.

Fennel

Fennel originates in the Mediterranean and has spread as far as India. Fennel seeds are best used for their flatulence-relieving properties; they also relieve colic, stimulate appetite and aid digestion (collect them as with dill above). Fennel has a calming effect on coughs and bronchial complaints, and when infused, the seeds make a good gargle for soothing sore throats. Just like dill, fennel increases milk production in nursing mothers; it can also be used as an eye wash for conjunctivitis.

Fennel is grown mainly from seed and sown in exactly the same way as dill. The leaves are used as a flavouring in a similar way to dill, and the seeds can be collected in the same way as well.

The seeds are well known as the main ingredient in gripe water, which eases colic in babies. You can make your own by adding a pint of boiling water to a teaspoon of crushed fennel seeds and steeping for 20 minutes. Strain, cool and use as required. Use within 24 hours, before the mixture loses its potency and goes off.

Parsley

Parsley was known in ancient Greece and Rome as a medicinal tool rather than a culinary herb. Parsley was introduced to Britain in 1548 and has the useful ability to mask strong smells on the breath, which is why it's such a common garnish. The leaves are also good for treating urinary tract infections and for eliminating kidney stones.

Parsley is fairly easy to grow from seed but can take two to four weeks to germinate (sprout) without a heated propagator. Sprinkle the seeds in seed cells and cover with 1 centimetre of compost. Water and cover in the same way you do for basil (see earlier in this chapter) and place the cells in a warm spot (an airing cupboard is ideal) until they start to shoot. Then place them on a warm window sill. Once the seedlings are 5 centimetres tall, harden them off for a week or so, ideally in a cold frame. Remove them gently and plant in pots (which need to be at least 15 centimetres across), using compost, or plant them straight out into the allotment.

Make sure that you keep the seedlings moist with regular watering, otherwise they dry up and wither.

Peppermint

Peppermint's origins are unknown, but the dried leaves have been found in the pyramids in Egypt, dating from as early as 1000 BCE. Peppermint didn't become popular in Europe until about the eighteenth century. It's a well known fact that peppermint tea aids digestion and is also ideal for wind relief. It's claimed that peppermint can also help with headaches. Peppermint tea is simply an infusion of the leaves in boiling water; it can be made using fresh leaves straight from the plant, but I find the dried leaves make a better cuppa. (See the section 'Drying'.)

Peppermint is easily grown from seed in trays or cells, but don't cover the seeds, just sprinkle them onto the compost surface then water and cover with cling film and keep moist. They take 7–14 days to germinate. When the seedlings are large enough to handle, transplant them into 7-centimetre pots. When they're established, harden them off for a week or so and plant them into large pots. Mints are really invasive, so I always recommend keeping them in pots or they'll take over the allotment herb garden!

Rosemary

It's claimed that rosemary *(Rosmarinus officinalis)* aids the improvement of the memory, and it has been used for this reason for hundreds, if not thousands, of years. It has also been used as a tonic to give a 'zest for life', invigorating those lacking in vitality. Rosemary also improves food absorption by aiding digestion. It's often used in gargles for sore throats and sore gums, because of its antiseptic and anti-fungal properties.

Rosemary can be grown from cuttings (see the relevant section earlier in this chapter).

Sage

Sage was used throughout history as a medicine to relieve sore throats – one of its best uses to date. The leaves contain fantastic flu- and cold-fighting properties and can help with excessive sweating. It also aids digestion. Apparently, the Romans used sage leaves as a toothbrush, because the texture was perfect for the job.

See the section 'Growing herbs in a sunny spot' earlier in this chapter for advice on tackling sage.

Thyme

Thyme is also from areas around the Mediterranean and was used by the Greeks, Romans and Egyptians. It's still used today in some form (*Thymol*) in mouthwashes, vapour rubs and sore throat lozenges, because of its powerful antibacterial action. It also improves digestion and kills parasites in the intestine . . . very useful stuff! It's easily digested, and you can benefit from its medicinal powers. Made into tea, it eases sore throats and coughs, and relieves phlegm. Just steep a teaspoon of leaves in boiling water and drink like regular tea. (It actually tastes great too!)

The section 'Growing herbs in a sunny spot' earlier in this chapter covers how to deal with thyme.

It's no coincidence that many of the herbs that we associate with food also aid digestion, relieve wind and generally help the absorption of food. This is why and how they've become so important as culinary herbs. The great thing is that they not only help cure many common ills, but have a wonderful flavour too. Most edible and not-so-edible plants have some kind of traditional medicinal use, but on the allotment it's only really worth growing those herbs that have multiple uses. Traditional medicinal herbs such as feverfew (reduces fever), milk thistle (repairs liver damage) and St John's Wort (helps relieve depression) may well have a place in a large herb garden, but unless you specifically want these herbs, I suggest that you stick to the more generally useful ones.

Experimenting with unusual herbs

Hundreds of herbs can be grown on the allotment and in the garden, so unless you have a particular interest in the more unusual specimens, I'd advise growing the ones you know you'll use. But it can also be a lot of fun growing strange and unusual things to simply show off to your new allotment chums, expand your knowledge or simply to try something new. As soon as you get the green-fingered bug, you may well find that you want to explore the wonderful world of plants a bit more. Within all gardeners is something that makes us want to become collectors of the unusual, so when you start to get bored of basil and tired of thyme, here's a list of others to try:

Ammi visnaga

Ammi visnaga (toothpick weed) is a very pretty annual or biennial herb that reaches about 60 centimetres tall. It's really easy to grow, and you eat the fragrant sweet leaves raw. It's an age-old medicinal plant from warm parts of Europe, West Asia and North Africa, so is slightly frost tender, but because it's so easy to grow, you can simply grow it as an annual and plant it every year.

On well raked soil, sprinkle the seeds into 1.5-centimetre-deep drills 30 centimetres apart and cover lightly, water well and keep moist. The seeds germinate in 14 and 21 days, and when the seedlings are large enough, thin them out so that they're 25 centimetres apart. The seeds are harvested in late summer and, according to proven research, can be used as a great muscle relaxant and are effective in relieving the pain caused by kidney stones. I love the look of this plant with its large, white, lacy flower heads above fern-like green foliage – it's sure to set those allotment tongues wagging, and best of all is a great flower for cutting and brightening up your flower arrangements.

Korean mint

Korean mint is a real showstopper of a herb. It's a perennial with square stems that tower up to a metre tall, with leaves that are pointy and green with a hairy white underside. Throughout the summer, it bears fantastic tall spikes of purple flowers. It's part of the mint family but, unlike garden mint, isn't a vigorous thug that needs imprisoning in a pot. The leaves can be used in salads to add an intriguing flavour or in mint dressings, and it makes a decent cup of tea. It's not technically frost resistant, but in my experience can withstand temperatures down to –5 or even –10 degrees centigrade, so I'd say that it was! Definitely one for the allotment show-off, because I very much doubt that many know what it is!

Korean mint can be sown from seed fairly easily, simply sprinkled directly onto the soil and watered well, but I'd buy a couple from a garden centre and plant them up.

Lemon verbena

Lemon verbena (*Aloysia triphylla*) is a wonderfully fragrant lemon-scented herb that's undervalued as both a garden plant and a culinary herb. You do sometimes see it in herb plots in grand gardens, but it's a little out of favour these days. It's an *evergreen shrub* in frost-free areas and is on the borderline of hardiness, so is best in a sunny, sheltered spot. The leaves, as the name suggests, have a strong lemony scent and are used in herbal teas, desserts and pot-pourri. You can easily grow the plants from seed in trays, transplant them into 7-centimetre pots when large enough and then harden them off and plant out on the allotment.

Getting the Most from Your Herbs

Preserving some of your produce for use when the allotment isn't as productive in the winter months is a good idea. This is particularly true of herbs. Some, of course, die back in winter; others such as rosemary have a less intense flavour later in the year. With no new growth through the winter, you also risk over-harvesting. Drying, freezing and bottling your favourite herbs are perfect ways for maintaining your supply.

Drying

Drying herbs is an excellent way to stock up your supplies for the dark winter months, and is really easy to do. The best time to pick your herbs for drying is in the late morning when the dew has dried from the plants. Herbs are generally at their most flavoursome just before their flowering season starts, so this would be the ideal time to harvest them for drying. When harvesting for drying, it's really important to pick only healthy leaves and shoots that show no sign of disease or insect damage, and to treat them with care after picking, because any bruising or damage lessens the flavour and wastes the aromatic oils. Most herbs are suitable for drying, but it works best with the tougher ones such as rosemary, bay leaves, thyme and oregano, because their flavours don't fade over a period of storing. They have lower water content than softer herbs such as basil, which you can dry, but I wouldn't bother.The simplest method is *air drying*. Choose a well ventilated room that's out of direct sunlight. A good place to do this is in your shed at the allotment or in an airing cupboard. It's important not to wash the herbs, because doing so encourages mould. To dry your herbs, follow these steps:

1. **Run some wires between the joists in the ceiling from which to hang the herbs.**
2. **Pick the herbs.**
3. **Gather into small bunches using elastic bands.**
4. **Hang to dry (usually takes between 10 and 16 days); if the shed or room isn't well ventilated, a small fan works wonders.**
5. **Store in airtight containers or, ideally, ceramic pots that don't let the light in.**

WARNING!

If, when your herbs are dried, you find condensation in the container, it's a sign that you didn't dry them for long enough.

Drying can also be done in a microwave, as follows:

1. **Wash and pat dry the herbs.**
2. **Place them on a sheet of kitchen roll.**
3. **Put the microwave on full for a couple of minutes or more if needed.**
4. **Store in the same way as air-dried herbs.**

WARNING!

To avoid heat spots, which can cause a fire, be sure to move the herbs around a couple of times during the time they're in the microwave. Also check every 30 seconds to ensure that you don't overdo it!

To dry herbs in the oven, follow these instructions:

1. **Wash and pat dry the herbs.**
2. **Turn the oven on to its lowest setting.**

3. **Place the herbs on some baking paper on a metal tray, leaving them well spaced.**
4. **Place them in the oven to dry, leaving the door ajar to let the condensation escape.**
5. **Keep a close eye on them, and remove when dried. They are dry when they crumble easily between your fingers.**
6. **Store in the same way described for air-dried herbs.**

Freezing

Freezing is a great way to store softer varieties such as chives, basil and coriander. These herbs tend to lose a lot of their flavour when dried and just look like dead dried-up leaves. You can freeze flowers such as borage, mint leaves and basil sprigs in ice cube trays, which then come in handy as garnishes or in drinks.

Chop herbs such as basil and parsley, sprinkle them into an ice tray and add water to make an ice cube. Simply pop one out when you need it in cooking. Or pick whole sprigs of parsley and tarragon and pop them in freezer bags and store them in the freezer, from where they can be used directly just as you do with fresh herbs.

Bottling

Herb vinegars are really simple to make; herbs such as thyme and oregano are perfect, with their strong flavour being preserved in vinegar. They give added flavour to salad dressings or to marinades for barbecued meats.

Get a glass jar and loosely fill it with some chopped herbs; warm some cider or wine vinegar in a pan, and pour it over the herbs. Then place in a sunny spot for a couple of weeks for the flavours to infuse. After this time, remove the herbs and strain the vinegar, throw in a sprig of the fresh herb and store in the jar. Don't use a container with a metal lid, because the vinegar will corrode the lid and make the vinegar useless.

You can find recipes for *herb oils* on many an Internet site, but I never attempt to produce herb oils at home. This may sound like scaremongering, but herb oils carry the potential to produce the bacteria which can cause the deadly condition known as botulism. Although it's possible to make safe herb oils, it's just not worth the risk.

Chapter 13

Cultivating Everyday Essentials

In This Chapter

- Meeting the onion family
- Greeting gorgeous squashes, pumpkins and gourds
- Cavorting with courgettes
- Living with leeks
- Gallivanting with garlic
- Tipping your hat to tomatoes

In this chapter I introduce some allotment essentials for developing your skills as a gardener. You'll meet the onions – a bulb vegetable in the same family as lilies, a family which also includes leeks, spring onions and shallots. I also reveal the secret of growing squashes, pumpkins and gourds, which are brilliant plants for children to grow – what could appeal more than pumpkins ready to carve for Hallowe'en? They're fairly easy to grow into absolute giants that are sure to have the kids hooked for life!

I also look at growing garlic. Fresh garlic is one of the best treats you can grow that's also not readily available in the shops. The natural partner for garlic and onions is tomatoes, so I cover those too. You'll discover all the tricks of the trade of growing tasty toms: you've not lived until you taste the wonder of a freshly picked sweet tomato that you have lovingly grown yourself.

Getting to Know the Onion Family

With a bit of planning and the right storage methods, you should be able to have home-grown onions available for cooking pretty much all year round. They are, of course, one of the most important allotment crops, and are used in a huge variety of dishes, both cooked and raw, so they must deserve a space on your plot. Standard onions are grown from seed or more reliably from *sets* (immature onion bulbs). Sets simply grow larger until ready to harvest. Onions grown from seed take longer to produce a crop. You can either sow onions together in small clumps or in rows, thinned out to grow as individual onions. The one disadvantage of growing from sets is that there are fewer varieties available to the grower, whereas with seed there are many.

If you're new to allotment gardening, start by growing onions from sets rather than seed. Growing from sets is by far the easiest and most reliable option.

Shallots are very similar in appearance to onions (albeit smaller) but are slightly different in that when you plant a whole full-sized shallot it forms a number of new ones, which can then be harvested. Shallots too can be grown from seed.

Leeks are a tall and slender member of the onion family, ideal for squeezing in between other crops, and dead easy to grow. They are ideal if you're just starting out. Unlike onions, the edible parts don't grow entirely underground – leeks are grown for their mild oniony stems. The white part of the stem is created by deep planting or earthing up (covered in detail in Chapter 9). Many other 'spring onion'-type onions can also be grown: oriental bunching onions, pickling onions, and European Welsh onions, all of which offer slightly different harvest times, flavours and uses.

Growing Bulb Onions

Your success with bulb onions greatly depends on your soil type and local conditions (see Chapter 6 for more on this). The first rule of growing onions is to seek the advice of a neighbouring plot holder who's obviously good at it. Some techniques work better in certain areas; for example, in areas that have cool, damp summers, seeds are best sown in spring. Being armed with this local knowledge aids your planning.

As a general rule, bulb onions like a fertile rich soil that's not overly acidic. They do grow on poor soils, but the resulting onions will be smaller. Bulb onions have really shallow roots, and as long as the top 10 centimetres or so of soil has been sufficiently manured the autumn before (or, even better, contains your own well rotted compost), they'll love it. Onions don't like acid soil, so lime well in advance to correct pH levels to around pH 6–7. (See Chapter 6 for how to work out your pH levels.) Onions also appreciate some general purpose fertiliser like fish, blood and bone raked in before sowing, at a handful every square metre or so. A feed high in potash also helps to produce stronger-tasting onions, which many growers like.

Onions like firm ground. If the soil sticks to your boots, it's too damp, so wait a day or so until the area has dried out.

Getting started with onions

When you've followed your neighbour's advice regarding what works best in your area and then decided which variety of onions to grow (see the later section on 'Considering varieties'), you have a few options open to you.

Sowing your onion seeds indoors

In late winter and early spring, sow seeds under glass (in a greenhouse or at home in a propagator).

1. **As the seeds grow into seedlings, transplant them as one unit into the ground, where they'll form a clump of onions.**

   These may not grow as large as individual ones, but will be just as good. (If you want, you can thin out, leaving only one seedling.)

2. **If you sow the seeds in trays, transplant them individually into seed cells when they've formed a couple of leaves and are about 1.5 centimetres tall.**

   The ideal temperature for *germination* (the seeds sprouting) is between 15 and 19 degrees centigrade, and they should germinate in around 21 days.

3. **Plant out when the seedlings have matured enough, probably in March.**

   Harden the seedlings off (acclimatise them to the outside) for a week then plant them into prepared beds 15 centimetres apart and, for units of plants, 25 centimetres apart.

Sowing your onion seeds outdoors

In March and April, you can sow onion seeds directly into the soil. For this method, the soil needs to be warm. Ideally, leave the area after winter so it can dry. The soil also needs to be fairly firm, so don't dig the area over; just rake it at the final moment before sowing.

1. **Sow the seeds thinly in drills (trenches) 1.5 centimetres deep and 25 centimetres apart, and cover with a layer of soil and compost.**

   If you expect really cold weather, cover the drills temporarily to protect the seeds and seedlings from hard frosts.

2. **As the seedlings grow, thin them out, depending on how large you want them to be.**

   For a high yield of medium onions, thin to 5 centimetres apart; for larger onions, thin anywhere from 6–10 centimetres apart.

Planting out onion sets

In March and April, you can sow sets directly onto your plot:

1. **Run a string line across the plot and, using a dibber, make holes every 15 centimetres apart along the line, or simply dig a small hole with a trowel.**
2. **Push an individual set into each hole, covering it with soil and firming it down really well.**

   Some people like to leave the tops showing slightly, whereas others cover the tops with the soil. The latter helps to hide the sets from the birds that may confuse the top shoot with worms peeping out of the soil surface. The birds then uproot the sets! I've tried both methods and found that burying the sets out of view seems to help.
3. **Keep the sets well watered and don't plant them out until you're sure that the worst winter weather has passed – drought and a sudden cold snap can cause the plants to bolt (set seed).**

Sowing late

In late summer and early autumn, sow sets in the same way as spring-sown ones and cover the rows with a tunnel cloche to offer winter protection.

Late sowings can be useful in areas where winters are warm and wet, which can cause the seeds to rot, rather than cold. You need to get the bulbs formed before early spring, when warm weather may cause them to *bolt* (prematurely produce a flower stem). The plants then mature over the summer. In spring, thin out the rows to 15 centimetres apart and use the thinnings as spring onions. Timing is vital with late summer and autumn sowings: too early and they mature too quickly and are more likely to bolt; too late and they won't mature enough to see them through the winter. This sowing period with onions is for the more experienced onion grower who is in tune with the seasons and local climate (another case for asking local experts!).

TIP

You can buy onion sets that have been heat treated. This kills off the flowering capabilities of the plant once grown, meaning that your crop will be far less likely to bolt. The one disadvantage is that sets are more expensive, but they are definitely worth the expense, especially if you're new to growing onions. Heat-treated sets are available in early spring.

Beating the weeds

Onions need to be kept free from weed competition; they need all the water and goodness they can get in the early stages. I like to pull annual weeds (as long as they've not set seed) out of the ground and lay them on the soil surface around the plants as a mulch. They rot down, adding valuable nutrients, and help to retain moisture in the soil. You can even buy special onion hoes that have a small half-moon-shaped blade that is used to slice through any weeds with ease.

TIP

Any flowering stems that appear on maturing plants should be removed gently as soon as you can. If you leave them, they can bolt. This means that the plant puts all its energy into flowers and seeds instead of creating nice swollen bulbs.

Considering varieties

You have a wide choice of varieties of onion to try and many different ways of growing them. Onion sets are often more reliable than seeds and far easier to manage, so this is where I suggest beginners should start. Sets, however, are more prone to bolting and not so many varieties are available, but heated-treated sets offer the ideal introduction to onion growing. Main-crop onions are sown in spring, and you also can get those which are more suited to autumn sowing.

The following are the main-crop onions grown from seed that I recommend:

- **Ailsa Craig.** A variety named after the Scottish island and a good exhibition onion for those of you who want to get serious about growing huge onions. It is a really versatile variety that can be planted in autumn, winter and spring. Can be sown outdoors in early to mid-autumn and protected with a cloche tunnel over winter, or sow indoors in mid- to late winter, ready to plant out in spring, and sow outdoors again in March and April; harvest in late summer.
- **Cipolla Ramata di Milano.** A beautifully named variety that produces attractive fawn-coloured onions that have a really nice pale inside and are great for cooking and storing over winter. Sow seeds between February and March under glass and plant out between April and May, or sow directly into the soil during between March and April.
- **Bedfordshire Champion.** Still very popular with growers as it has been for over 100 years, the reason being that this onion is ideally suited to our climate. Sown in the middle of March to April, these lovely golden bulbs will be ready in late summer.
- **Paris Silverskin.** This onion produces lovely spring onions if harvested young. If left to mature, it'll produce small white onions ideal for eating or for pickling. Really easy to grow, it's a good starting point for first-timers.
- **Red Baron F1.** An onion that produces top-quality shiny red onions that keep for several months. Sow in late winter indoors, and in spring directly into the soil, ready for harvesting in September. Also available as sets.

ORGANIC WAY

- **Marco F1.** A main-crop onion that often lasts right through until March. It's a reliable cropper that performs well on most soils and has really good disease resistance, so is great for organic gardeners.

- **Owa.** Resembling a large teardrop in shape, with nice brown skin, Owa is a lovely long onion that's ideal for slicing into salads.
- **Pink Torpedo.** Another long teardrop-shaped onion (sometimes sold as a shallot), this one has attractive red skin and is really sweet, so is good to eat raw. Also, it works especially well in mustard, white wine and cream sauces over grilled pork.
- **Canto F1.** The ultimate onion for storage, it crops quite early in August for harvesting and will store right through until June the next year. Its really thick brown skin offers great protection to the tender pale inside. One of the best around!

Here are some great autumn-sown sets to try:

- **Electric Red.** Produces lovely shiny red onions; the young shoots can also be used like spring onions in early spring.
- **Radar.** A well known autumn-sown onion, producing nice mild onions from May and beyond.
- **Senshyu.** A Japanese onion that produces a large flat bulb that matures in late June the following year.
- **Troy.** A reliable hybrid onion that produces perfectly shaped onions with a shiny skin and mild to medium-strong flavour.

Here are some other onion sets to try for spring sowing:

- **Golden Ball.** Available as a heat-treated set that is less likely to bolt. Golden Ball produces an excellent crop of golden-brown onions quickly and easily that keep really well.
- **Hyred F1.** Producing gorgeous red shiny onions that have a powerful flavour and store really well, Hyred F1s are heat-treated for bolt resistance.
- **Jet Set.** An award-winning onion set that produces quickly and easily for a decent early crop and also stores well.
- **Setton.** An improved version of a really popular onion called Sturon, Setton produces thin-necked, medium-sized bulbs that have excellent storage potential.
- **Sturon.** A popular onion that keeps well once lifted, and is always productive and consistent, hence its popularity.

Harvesting and storage

When your onions are mature, the leaves start to turn yellow at the tips. Spring-sown onions are ready in around 13–19 weeks, whereas those sown in summer take as long as 40–42 weeks. Many gardeners bend the foliage over to one side, breaking the neck of the onion slightly to stop leaf growth, but I tend to simply let them die back naturally, because bending can cause neck rot if the join between the stem and the bulb gets cracked and wet. Loosen the soil around the plants slightly with a fork to disturb the roots, which helps ripening as well, but be careful not to damage the skins while doing so. Then carefully dig the onions up with all the foliage attached and leave them in the sun for ten days. You can lay them on a wire rack off the ground or on an upturned crate. Alternatively, make a mesh trampoline to lay them on or, as many gardeners do, simply leave them on the ground from which you've dug them. It's vital that they dry free from rain, so if it rains, dry them in a greenhouse or just cover them. When they're fully dry, you can string them together in bunches, place them in crates or string bags, and store them in a cool, frost-free, well ventilated place, where they'll keep for as long as six months.

Bull necks are onions that have formed a thick neck where the foliage has grown. These are no good for storage but perfectly good for eating straight away, so use them first.

Onions should be part of a rotation system (see Chapter 7). If onions are grown in the same spot year upon year, diseases such as onion white rot can develop and remain in the soil for up to eight years. First the foliage turns brown and dies off, and then when you lift the bulb, you see a white furry growth on the base of the bulbs. This is not good news, and you will more than likely lose the entire onion crop. There is no cure available to the home gardener, so the only way to get rid of the disease is to leave the plot empty of any members of the onion family for up to eight years.

Eelworms can also be a right pain in the bulbs! They bore into the stalks, leaf stems and bulbs and cause the plants to become distorted and swell in size. There is no real cure, so dig them up and leave the patch bare for three or four years.

Onion fly can also be a problem; they look like small grey house flies and lay their eggs near the onions and leeks in spring and summer. The eggs hatch and the maggots bore into the plants causing havoc. Young plants are the most vulnerable, but sets seem to do better. Remove any infected plants and destroy them, making sure you get rid of any maggots that fall onto the soil.

Growing Shallots

Shallots are a chef's best friend: they're smaller and more delicate than regular onions, offering a sweet, mild alternative. They have yellow or red skins and, once harvested, can keep for up to a year if stored carefully.

Getting started with shallots

Shallots are far easier to grow than their big brothers and less fussy over the soil they grow in; in fact, they seem to grow better in slightly poorer soils. But in general, they should be grown in exactly the same way as bulb onion sets. Plant sets, just as with onions, in early spring or in late winter in warmer areas. Space sets around 18 centimetres apart. Each set grows new bulbs attached to it as a clump. You can plant sets in autumn that mature in spring to be used like spring onions.

Considering varieties

Here are some shallots for you to try:

- **Delvad.** My top choice for growers, producing on average ten bulbs from each set. It's an award-winning French variety that's outstanding in every way.
- **Golden Gourmet.** A fairly large shallot derived from a variety called Giant Yellow and producing larger, more bolt-resistant shallots.
- **Jermor.** Another long variety producing the classic teardrop-shape shallot the French call Jersey longue – the perfect sweet, mild shallot for creative cooks.
- **Longor.** Another French variety that produces really long shallots prized by chefs. It has a really sweet and hearty flavour, making it a popular choice, and it also stores for ages.
- **Pikant.** A Dutch variety of red-skinned shallot that produces multiple shallots from sets. It's small with intense flavour and long shelf life.
- **Prisma F1.** A fairly new shallot with reddish-brown skins that's grown from seed, each seed producing one shallot. Sow in March and April to harvest from August onwards. Prisma is really disease resistant and therefore a variety that's ideal for organic plots.

Harvesting and storage

Shallots are harvested in the same way as onions and can be stored in the same manner. You need to lay them out to dry and ripen before you string them up for long-term storage.

Spring onions

Spring onions or salad onions are sown from March until July for use between June and October. They are a pretty quick crop to grow, and some can be sown in the late summer for harvesting the following spring. Many main-crop onions and sets can be used as spring onions, and most gardeners simply use immature onions if they require some.

Getting started with spring onions

Spring onions should be sown in the spring or autumn. Do it like this:

1. **Sow seeds in short shallow drills 13 millimetres deep with 10 centimetres between rows. Repeat sowings every three or four weeks for a constant supply.**
2. **If sown in autumn, cover them with a cloche over winter to protect from severe frosts, and they will shoot into life come the warmer weather in spring.**

You can thin the seedlings out to 3-centimetre spacing if you want larger spring onions, but I don't bother – just let them grow. That is it – spring onions are really simple to grow and a quick crop to produce.

Considering varieties

There are quite a few spring and salad onion varieties for you to try, so why not try a few different ones to find a favourite. A few good ones include the following:

- **Ishikuro.** A new variety that grows straight all the way along, can be left in the ground for ages and can grow as thick as a carrot.
- **Pompeii.** A small, round spring or pickling onion that grows really fast. It can even be grown well in pots. Well worth a try!
- **White Lisbon.** A common variety that grows really quickly; sharp and sweet with a flavour that intensifies the longer it is in the ground.

Harvesting

Spring onions can be pulled as soon as they reach a suitable size, usually around the size of a pencil or thinner. Some varieties can be left in the ground for long periods and allowed to grow larger. Spring onions do not store well.

Growing Leeks

Leeks have to be the easiest member of the onion family to grow, being able to produce a good crop in most soils and situations, although they prefer a rich free-draining soil with plenty of organic matter. You can treat the soil just as you would for onions (see the earlier section 'Growing Bulb Onions'). Because the roots grow deeply, leeks like deeply dug soil. If you have really hard ground, it's advisable to create a *leek trench*: simply dig a trench to one spade's depth and mix in plenty of well rotted muck or home-made compost. Leeks also like a slightly high pH, so they do well in a bed that's been limed. (See Chapter 6 on working out your soil type.)

Getting started with leeks

Leeks need a fairly long growing season and do best in moisture-retentive richly organic soil in full sun. Leeks also benefit if, before sowing, you give the soil an application of fertiliser that's high in nitrogen, because leeks have a high nitrogen requirement.

Leeks don't really benefit much from being sown earlier indoors in trays. You can do so if you want to grow summer leeks, but these generally lack the flavour of those that mature in winter. I like to sow leeks directly in the seed bed ready for transplanting.

To sow your leeks, follow these steps:

1. **Sow seeds directly in the seedbed, in rows 1 centimetre deep, when the soil is warm.**

   Don't bother sowing before March, because later sowings work just as well, if not better.

2. **Water using a watering can with a really fine rose, so you don't disturb the seeds.**
3. **When they start to shoot, thin the seedlings, giving each about 1 centimetre in all directions to grow on. You can replant the thinned seedlings.**
4. **Transplant when the seedlings reach about 20 centimetres tall into holes prepared using a dibber. (I use an old sharpened rake handle.)**

   The holes should be around 15 centimetres deep and 25 centimetres apart in all directions. Don't fill these with soil, just pop the plants in, top the holes up with water, and allow the soil to gently fall in as the seedlings grow.

5. **Keep well watered and weed free at all stages until the leeks are well established then weed routinely and only water in very dry conditions.**

Leeks can be attacked by all the usual onion foes – stem and bulb eelworms, onion fly, rust and white rot – but, in all honesty, I've never had any problems with these, and leeks are usually pretty problem free. One more common problem you may see evidence of is *leek rust*, which is a fungal disease identified by round and elongated rust marks on the foliage. A mild infection does no real harm as long as you remove the infected leaves or plants and destroy them, but if the problem gets worse then it can kill off the plant and spread easily to the entire crop. Good hygiene is vital, so wash your hands after touching infected plants. Leek rust can be prevented by crop rotation, early detection and swift action, adequate spacing between plants, free-draining soil (the fungus likes damp conditions) and by growing resistant varieties.

Some people, as they transplant the leek seedlings into dibber holes, trim the bottom couple of centimetres off the roots and also the top 2 centimetres of foliage. This is supposed to make them easier to plant and encourage root growth. I've tried this and didn't notice any benefits, but many gardeners swear by the technique, so it may work for you – there's no harm in trying.

TIP

Leeks, when transplanted deeply, have a longer, whiter stem than those that have been shallow planted. You can earth up (see Chapter 9 for details of this technique) around the growing stem to *blanch* (drain the colour from) the leek as it grows; do this gradually from the middle of August onwards. Make sure that you don't get soil between the upper leaves, because this stays between them as they grow and you end up with gritty leeks.

Considering varieties

Different varieties crop over different periods, so select one or two so that they mature over a longer period. Here are some leeks for you to try:

- **Autumn Giant 2 Argentina.** A superb choice sown early or late, and produces over a long season. Sow in spring for transplanting directly into the soil for early summer where they'll grow and stay happily until May the following year.
- **Bulgarian Giant.** Funnily enough, this variety grows giant leeks that have really long stems of lovely pale green. It can be harvested over a long season.
- **Carlton F1.** Being a hybrid, this leek has a steely determination to do well – and usually does. It's a main-crop variety that has long stems and fast growth. Harvest it from September onwards.
- **Edison.** A truly outstanding leek that's best when harvested young, when it's a truly tender contender. Alternatively, leave it to mature: it will last well from October into February.

- **King Richard.** A really early variety to mature that can be ready from early sowings as soon as June. Ones sown later last until Christmas. This leek develops long white stems that don't need blanching, and the plants are good grown close together for a crop of baby leeks.
- **Musselburgh Improved.** A new version of an old classic leek that most allotmenteers have had encounters with in the past. It is really hardy and grows into solid, thick leeks. It originates from a Scottish variety from around 1834 that at one time became very rare.

Harvesting and storage

Leeks are usually ready for harvesting in around 16–20 weeks but can be harvested any time during the growing season from when they're the size of spring onions. From summer into winter and beyond, you should have a great crop that can withstand all but the harshest winter, with some really hardy varieties lasting well into spring. Protect the ground from freezing around your leeks with a thick layer of straw around the plants to help them through the winter.

TIP

If you find you need to dig up your leeks to make room for another crop, you can do so and *heel them in*. First dig a V-shaped trench in a vacant area of your plot. Second, dig up your leeks, lean them against the wall of the trench, and cover the white parts with soil. Third, push the soil down gently. They'll happily store like this until needed. Figure 13-1 shows heeling in.

Figure 13-1: Heeling in leeks.

Growing Garlic

It often comes as a surprise to people that you can actually grow garlic. Garlic is a member of the onion family and is fairly easy to grow. Even though most of the garlic we tend to buy in the shops is from warm Mediterranean countries, garlic only needs a period of a couple of months at a temperature of 0–10 degrees centigrade to germinate and grow well, so is an ideal crop in our climate. You can grow garlic by selecting the best bulbs bought from a supermarket, but I strongly recommend buying new bulbs grown specifically for sowing in your local climate.

Getting started with garlic

Garlic isn't overly complicated to grow, and is normally sown in November to make the most of the following cold snap that helps germinate the bulbs. If your soil is poorly drained, though, wait until spring, otherwise the bulbs will just rot. A week before planting, it helps to apply a handful of fish, blood and bone per square metre and rake it in to boost the new plants. A number of varieties can be sown in spring that work just as well as winter-sown bulbs and which are better on heavier soils.

To sow your garlic, follow these steps:

1. **In a well drained, *not* recently manured plot, use a dibber to make a row of holes. These should be three times as deep as the cloves are long and 18 centimetres apart, in rows 30 centimetres apart.**
2. **Pop the individual cloves into the holes, pointed side up, backfill and water.**

Then you just sit back and wait. Garlic takes between 20 and 35 weeks to mature and should grow without many problems.

As with shallots, with garlic birds can be a problem. They pull the shoots out of the ground when these first appear, thinking they're worms or grubs. Just gently push the shoots back into place and they should be fine. Put a protective net over the top to protect them.

Considering varieties

There are quite a few varieties of garlic on the market; just try to choose a variety that is suited to the time of year you will be planting. Here are a couple to try:

- **French Arno.** A spring-planted variety that has a papery white outer skin and white-skinned cloves.
- **Lautrec Wight.** Is suitable for autumn planting and has a white skin with large purplish-pink-skinned cloves.

Harvesting and storage

Lift your garlic bulbs as soon as the foliage starts to yellow, otherwise you run the risk of them shooting again – bulbs with shoots don't store well. Lift the bulbs with a fork, carefully, so as not to damage them. Dry them in the same way you do your onions; make sure they're totally dry before storing them in plaits using the dried foliage (simply leave the foliage on and plait the bulbs together) or loose in well ventilated trays. They'll store for up to nine or ten months.

Getting to Know Pumpkins and Squashes

Pumpkins and squashes have to be one of the more impressive vegetables you can grow, but they are frost tender, so are grown exclusively during the warmer months of the year. My daughter Ashley planted a pumpkin seed last year and spent the following few months eagerly awaiting the fruits of her labour. The result was a great big beautiful orange pumpkin that she was as proud as punch of – she's now hooked! Pumpkins, squashes and courgettes are all members of the very diverse Cucurbitaceae family. You can grow giant pumpkins that can flatten a small child and tiny little squashes that fit in your pocket.

Squashes are generally divided into two groups: summer and winter varieties. The summer varieties grow fairly quickly, have thinner skins and include courgettes, marrows and squashes, all of which are real gems on the allotment. The winter varieties are much slower growing, have thick skins and include, amongst others, pumpkins, butternut squash, Hubbards and buttercups. All of them are from warm climates and aren't hardy, but are grown in spring and summer to mature in time for winter.

Growing Pumpkins and Winter Squashes

Pumpkins and winter squashes are slow-growing plants that can take up a lot of room on your plot. They usually come as trailing plants that have very large leaves, but some varieties are smaller and more compact. They all carry pretty star-shaped flowers, and the young shoots and foliage can be cooked and eaten, with the flowers being edible as well. Some varieties are also cultivated for their edible seeds.

Getting started with pumpkins and squashes

All pumpkins and winter squashes like the same soil type: a moisture-retentive but not waterlogged soil, full of organic matter – particularly well rotted manure. Although pumpkins and winter squashes grow on any soil as long as it's free draining, and even on poor unmanured soil, plenty of muck is the ideal. In fact, probably the best place to grow them is directly on your compost heap!

To sow your pumpkins and winter squashes, follow these steps:

1. **Spread some general purpose fertiliser a few weeks before planting out.**
2. **Prepare the ground by digging a pit 40–50 centimetres deep and 60 centimetres wide, and fill it with compost or well rotted manure, then mix in the top soil, creating a small mound or hill.**
3. **Sow your seeds on top of the mound, outdoors, in spring, as soon as the risk of frost has passed. Cover them with a cloche (or even a jam jar).**

   I tend to plant two seeds in each spot, in case one decides not to germinate (sprout), and then remove the weaker one once the seedlings show. Alternatively, you can sow seeds indoors a few weeks before the last frost in trays, seed modules or peat pots, and plant them out when the frosts have passed and the soil has warmed up. Allow anywhere from 1–3 metres between pumpkins, but for smaller varieties check the package for spacing instructions.
4. **Train the plants into neat circles as they grow by pinning the long trailing growth around the area in which it grows or up very strong supports such as trellis. The fruit can be very heavy.**

Pumpkins and squashes are hungry feeders, so you also have to feed them regularly during the growing season to give them a boost. Also mulch around the plants with a load of compost or any other organic matter to help retain moisture in the soil.

Water well in really dry periods. Most pumpkin and squash plants have deep roots and can easily source water in a well improved soil, so only water if they need it.

Any foliage shading the fruits should be removed to allow the sun to ripen the fruit. If you want to grow whoppers, remove all but one fruit. This will encourage a giant fruit. If you just want a few bigger ones, leave only two or three. For more on growing giant vegetables, see Chapter 19.

Slugs adore the young shoots of pumpkins and squashes, so to protect them from attack, cover the seedlings with a cloche to keep the little monsters at bay! Also cucumber mosaic virus can be a problem when plants are small. (See Chapter 7 for more on diseases.)

As the fruits develop, place them on small plates or on bricks to keep them off the ground, as they're likely to rot if they touch the soil.

Considering varieties

Here are some pumpkins to try:

- **Dill's Atlantic Giant.** This has become the leading variety for those of you who want to break records. It's an enormous pumpkin that amazes the kids and is actually a nice pumpkin for eating and carving too. (For more on growing giant vegetables, see Chapter 19.)
- **Full Moon.** A ghostly pumpkin that's a pale cream colour and grows to between 11 and 22 kilograms in weight. When it matures, it starts to turn a brownish orange, so to keep the pale colour, don't let the sun get to it – cover it with some foliage.
- **Hooligan F1.** A small pumpkin with mottled orange and white skin. Hooligan has lovely tasting flesh – you simply cut out the lid and pop the pumpkin in the microwave for three to four minutes.
- **Jack of all Trades.** One to grow for Hallowe'en, with perfect orange skin, nice round shape and a flat bottom to sit on. It tastes good too.
- **One Too Many.** A brilliantly named pumpkin with skin that has the look (albeit pale orange and not red) of a bloodshot eye after a hard night on the tiles. It grows to about the size of a basketball and is easy to carve and eat.
- **Rouge Vif de'Estampes.** This variety is believed to be the one Cinderella's carriage was based on. It's a deeply ribbed pumpkin with dark orange skin, and grows pretty enormous – so get ready for a lot of pumpkin pie!

Here are some winter squash varieties for you to try:

- **Avalon F1.** A butternut squash that is very early to mature, harvesting from August onwards. It's tasty simply cut in half and baked in its skin, drizzled with olive oil; this intensifies the sweet flavour.

- **Barbara Butternut F1.** An odd-looking butternut squash that has green striped skin. It has a delicious sweet taste and keeps for ages. The 'core' where the seeds are stored is really small, which means that it has lots of flesh.
- **Burgess Vine Buttercup.** This very popular variety produces round greenish fruits that keep really well and are probably the best tasting of all! They have really sweet dense flesh and peel easily. They're good for those with less space, because the plants don't grow as large as other varieties.
- **Golden Hubbard.** A classic squash that, in all honesty, looks pretty ugly with its orange golden skin covered in warts, but it tastes sweet and delicious, is easy to grow and stores really well. Blue and green varieties are available as well.
- **Harlequin.** This smallish *dumpling squash* (a term used for many small squashes) matures early to offer attractive green, gold and yellow-striped squashes. It has a lovely sweet flavour.
- **Hasta la Pasta F1.** An unusual addition to your range, and a type of spaghetti squash. This variety is grown for its stringy flesh, which, when cooked, you fluff up with a fork to literally make 'vegetable spaghetti'. It sounds odd, but is really tasty and a great way to impress dinner guests and even the children. Simply cut in half and boil for five minutes and then scoop the 'spaghetti' out.
- **Honey Bear F1.** A type of *acorn squash* (so called because it's acorn shaped) that's so sweet even the kids ask for it again and again. Each squash is the perfect size for one person and only takes up the same space as a courgette plant, so it's good for space-saving gardeners.
- **Jaspée de Vendée.** You can even eat this one raw. It's a ridiculously sweet squash that's similar in appearance to a pumpkin but slightly elongated, and it stores well.
- **Turks Turban.** An interesting-looking oddity that produces fruits that look like two squashed squashes piled on top of each other with the top one being smaller in size. They're usually grown for ornamental purposes, but I think they taste good, and they keep well.
- **Uchiki Kuri.** Sometimes called the onion squash because of its onion shape, it has thick tough skin that makes it ideal for storage, and has a lovely nutty taste.

Harvesting and storage

You can pick the fruit when they're small or you can wait until they're fully matured – it's totally up to you – but the fruit (especially pumpkins) do taste better when they've developed fully and are cut and left to ripen for some time. I wait until the foliage has died back and then cut off the fruit, leaving as much stalk on the fruit as possible. Fruits can be left on the plants for as long as possible and need to be removed before the frost arrives, which ruins the fruit.

All pumpkins and squashes grown for storage should be left to ripen in a bright place. I leave mine in the conservatory, and they ripen in a week or so. Or you can simply cut them and leave them on the plot, protected from frost. This process helps the skin harden and improves the shelf life dramatically. Pumpkins and squashes are best stored in a cool, dry place such as a garage, where they'll keep for months.

Growing Courgettes and Summer Squash

Courgettes have to be one of the most popular allotment vegetables out there – they're easy to grow, fast to mature and crop heavily. During the summer months most allotmenteers have so many, they hardly know what to do with them all.

Courgettes and summer squashes are actually quite a diverse group of veg, with all sorts of weird shapes and colours available, so you don't have to stick to the long green varieties you may well be used to. Courgettes, of course, come in green, but you can also get yellow ones and pale green and spherical ones, with the summer squashes offering varieties such as the smaller *patty pan* types – small, squat and yellow – and *crookneck* types, which are large and crooked.

Getting started with courgettes and summer squashes

These are really easy-to-grow vegetables but do require decent soil with plenty of organic matter dug in (just like for winter squashes). They need plenty of nutrients and moisture, so add lots of well rotted manure in advance of planting to ensure a good crop.

To sow your courgettes and summer squashes, follow these steps:

1. **Sow seeds in small pots of compost indoors, four weeks before the last frost.**

   Place a couple of seeds in each pot and remove the weaker seedling when the seeds germinate, to keep all but the strongest seedling. Then place the seedlings on a bright window sill or in the greenhouse to grow on.

   You can also sow your seeds straight onto your plot when the soil has warmed in spring to at least 16 degrees centigrade.

2. **If sown indoors, plant out after around three to five weeks from sowing when you're sure no frost will return.**

   Courgettes and squashes are not frost hardy in any way! Space the courgette plants 90 centimetres apart and the trailing squashes 1.2 metres apart, depending on the variety.

3. **Mulch the area well using home-made compost or similar to help retain moisture in the soil.**

   You can also plant seedlings through landscape fabric (readily available from numerous websites, garden centres and DIY stores) to help keep weeds at bay and keep moisture in the soil.

4. **Protect your seedlings from pests with a cloche.**

   Slugs and snails simply adore the sweet young foliage and will decimate your beloved plants in an instant. Also watch out for cucumber mosaic virus (see Chapter 7 for more details).

TIP

Sometimes, in cold seasons, you may find that your courgettes don't grow full fruits. They're usually insect pollinated, so if insects are in short supply, you have to do the job instead. To do this, you have to find the female flowers that have a wee fruit at the base (this bump is the unfertilised fruit) and then find the male flowers that have no undeveloped fruits. Remove the male flower and take off the petals then rub the flower stamens together – this gets the pollination process going and your courgettes growing a treat!

Considering varieties

Here are some courgettes to try:

- **Ambassador F1.** Widely used commercially, it gives you loads of lovely dark courgettes.
- **Black Hawk F1.** A trailing courgette variety that can be trained up trellis. I've seen this variety grown up a trellis against a shed and which I thought was a great idea.
- **Defender F1.** Gives you a terrific bumper courgette crop early on and just keeps on producing right through the summer.
- **De Nice a Fruit Rond.** Produces nice round courgettes that taste good and are easy to grow.
- **Early Gem.** This heavy cropping variety can be planted under glass and transplanted gently onto your plot for early harvesting.
- **Midnight F1.** A lovely courgette that's nice and compact and can also be grown in containers (if kept well watered).
- **Orelia.** Producing abundant fruits, this is a marvellous yellow courgette variety.

Here are some summer squashes to try:

- **Bennings Green Tint.** Produces small scalloped squashes – patty-pan-style fruits – that are abundant on this compact plant.
- **Early Golden Crookneck**. A little like a bent courgette with one swollen end resembling a club, this variety has a buttery taste and is a prolific bush variety that will keep you well stocked over the summer.
- **Polo F1.** A white patty pan that's easy to grow and resistant to downy mildew (a common disease on this family of plants).
- **Yellow Bird Scallop.** Another patty-pan type that grows in a bushy habit and doesn't take up too much space. It produces lovely yellow fruits, best eaten young.

COOKING TIP

The best way to cook a marrow is to cut it in half lengthwise and scoop out the seeds, fill with chopped tomatoes and a touch of garlic, and sprinkle with some chopped marjoram, salt, pepper, capers, red wine vinegar and olive oil. Then bake slowly until cooked through. This is one of my favourite veggie dishes!

Harvesting and storage

Courgettes are all pretty quick plants to grow, and can be ready to harvest in as little as seven weeks. They're best picked when they're young and small, because they taste much better like this. Pick them before they get too large and watery. You can eat the flowers as well, but make sure that you only pick male flowers (the female flowers have an immature fruit behind them) after the females flowers have *set* (started to produce growing fruits). Most courgettes don't store well, but some squashes such as patty pans keep for a few months in cool conditions. Most produce heavier crops if harvested regularly, which encourages more flowers and fruit.

You will usually have courgettes coming out of your ears and be so sick of them by the end of the season that you will not want to store any for winter, but you can freeze them if you want to. Choose small fruits and wash them well. Chop them into 1 centimetre squares and blanch them in boiling water for a minute, then cool and freeze. The flesh will last a few months in the freezer, but frozen courgettes are nowhere near as nice as when fresh.

Growing Tomatoes

Tomatoes are the holy grail of all allotment produce. Everyone wants to grow them, there being nothing better than plucking a big, juicy, home-grown tomato from your own bush. Shop-bought tomatoes have admittedly got better over the years, with people becoming more demanding about what they eat, but home-grown tomatoes straight from the vine taste blooming marvellous! Many shop-bought varieties are forced to ripen off the vine using special techniques that reduce the flavour and give them an odd texture. To get decent-flavoured tomatoes in the shops, you have to pay over the odds. Tomatoes are fairly easy to grow, so if you're going to have an allotment, you'd be crazy not to give them a go.

You don't only have to grow round red tomatoes, loads of cool varieties are available that will introduce you to a more exciting place where tomatoes are green, yellow, black, pink or striped, and come in all different sizes from tiny sweet pea hybrid varieties to huge. When on holiday in the Mediterranean, you're sure to have marvelled at the delicious tomatoes they grow. Well, you too can achieve the same results in the UK, and this is how you go about it.

Getting started with tomatoes

Baby tomato plants are readily available in garden centres and DIY stores – and even in petrol stations – but the varieties are limited, so I suggest sowing from seed.

Tomatoes are originally from tropical regions where, in their own climate, they are actually perennial (they live for more than two years). In cooler climates, they're grown as annuals because they won't survive frost.

Tomatoes grow in a greenhouse really well, or in polytunnels or simply directly on the plot. Each method has its advantages and disadvantages, but tomatoes all need a sheltered spot and plenty of direct sunlight to grow successfully. They need at least 14 weeks of decent summer weather to do well, so if you live in a cool area, you can start them off under glass to give them more of a chance of success. Tomatoes do well in most soils, but as with most fruit and vegetables, they like plenty of organic matter in order to thrive. My grandfather taught me the following method of pre-planting preparation:

1. **Dig holes on the plot about 40 centimetres deep and 40 centimetres wide where you intend to plant the tomatoes.**
2. **Fill each hole with well rotted compost or manure and top it off with some soil.**

Over the next five or six weeks, as the seedlings grow, the compost in the holes will settle and sink a little (which helps to collect rainwater), and you can then transplant the seedlings directly into the prepared holes.

Unless you live in a really warm part of the country, you need to start your tomatoes off indoors to give them a long enough growing season to thrive. To get your tomatoes going, follow these steps:

1. **Sow the seeds indoors, in trays, six to eight weeks before the usual date of the last frost. Sow the seeds about 2 centimetres deep in any good seed compost.**
2. **Ideally, place the tray in a propagator and keep at 21 degrees centigrade.**

   If you don't have a propagator, just keep the tray in a bright, warm place at above 15 degrees centigrade.
3. **Transplant seedlings into pots when the pair of seedling leaves are well formed. The pots could be biodegradable pots that can then be planted out directly, but any 5–7 centimetre pot will do.**

   Plant the seedlings quite deep, leaving just the top of the stem and the leaves showing. Tomatoes develop new roots from the stem, which give the plant extra vigour. Keep the seedlings in a warm, bright place and keep them watered, but slightly on the dry side.
4. **After a month, start to harden the seedlings off by gradually introducing them to the outside.**

   Put them outside during the day and bring them in at night. If you have one, put the seedlings into a cold frame; keep the lid off during the day and on at night. If you're growing your plants in 7-centimetre pots, plants are likely to need potting on into a larger size before going outside.
5. **Plant the seedlings out into your plot when they develop the first spray of flowers (usually the *lower truss*, which is a flowering lateral stem).**

   Tomatoes are naturally sprawling plants and therefore need some support during their growth. When you plant them out, insert a cane near the base of the plant so you can tie the plant to it as it grows. Be careful not to disturb the delicate roots as you do so.

   Space the plants between 60 and 90 centimetres apart, depending on the variety. If you live in a cooler area, they should be planted closer together, and in a warmer area, further apart.

As tomatoes grow, tie them gently to their stakes and keep doing so regularly. If you tie them too tightly, you'll damage the delicate shoots. It also helps to pinch out any shoots that develop at the base of each leaf. If you don't, you end up with lots of small fruits that won't ripen by the end of the season. Pinching out stops the plant becoming bushy, and the plant concentrates its efforts into growing fewer larger fruits that ripen more quickly.

Tomatoes benefit from an even supply of moisture. If the plants are left to dry out or are watered irregularly, the fruits crack or develop blossom end rot and other disfigurements, especially when grown in pots or growbags.

With blossom end rot, your developing fruit develop a sunken area on the tip that starts off as some small brown spots that eventually join together in one sunken brown patch. It is caused by calcium deficiency, which in turn is caused by dry compost or soil. Calcium is absorbed by the plants only when the soil is moist, so when it is dry, they suffer a shortfall of this vital element and this causes blossom end rot.

The foliage on tomatoes often becomes yellow and dies, especially around the base of the plant. Don't worry about this; simply remove any foliage that dies back. It actually helps to remove the foliage from the base of tomato plants because this lets the sun in – the warmer the roots are, the better and earlier the crop will be.

You can use chicken wire tubes to support your tomatoes – quite a common site on allotments. Roll a tube about 40 centimetres in diameter and drop it over your young plants; the tomatoes then use the tube as support. This is a far easier method of supporting your plants than constantly retying them to stakes, but it can make harvesting a little awkward at times.

Tomatoes planted outside are open to attack from the dreaded blight, which is the same disease that attacks potatoes and can decimate a tomato crop really quickly. If you see any signs – which are pretty obvious, such as the foliage dying back and turning brown and the tomatoes rotting – remove and destroy infected leaves and fruit, and keep an eye on the rest of your crop.

Using growbags

Many people like to grow tomatoes in *growbags* (plastic bags of ready-made compost), and this can be really useful if you are short of space or simply would rather grow your tomatoes at home instead of on your allotment. Trailing varieties can even be grown in hanging baskets. To sow in a growbag, simply follow the techniques described in points 1 and 2 in the numbered list above and then follow these steps:

1. **Shake the growbag around to loosen the soil.**
2. **Put the growbag in a sunny spot where you want the plants to grow.**
3. **Cut three holes in the bag: one at either end and one in the middle.**
4. **Plant your seedlings into the growbag deeper than you would in a pot to encourage the stems to set more roots. Water in well.**
5. **Stake each plant and tie the plants in gently as they grow.**

Follow the same techniques to care for your plants as with tomatoes grown in the ground, but you need to be sure to water them more often. Give them a liquid tomato feed every other week to give them the nutrients they require to grow.

Watch out when watering that you don't overdo it, because growbags can become waterlogged. It can also help to push three empty pots into the soil by each plant, then use these as spouts. This helps to stop the compost being washed away when you water.

If growing in growbags, you can also try a method known as *ring culture*. Plant your young plants in 10- to 12-inch (25- to 30-centimetre) pots, cut away the bottoms of the pots and insert them as they are into holes the same size in the growbag. The main problem with pot- and growbag- grown tomatoes is keeping them moist enough; this method increases the amount of compost they grow in and therefore lessens the need for constant watering.

Using liquid manure and fertilisers

The absolute best way to water and feed your tomatoes is to use liquid manure. This is an old-school method that actually beats all others.

To make liquid manure, simply fill a net bag with some well rotted manure, drop it into a drum of water and leave it covered for a month or so. The resulting liquid can be used, diluted to the colour of tea, around the base of plants as a brilliant 'tonic'. Don't get this foul-smelling liquid on your hands, and keep a pair of gloves specifically for handling the stinky stuff! It can be used around other plants on the allotment as well, but don't let it get in direct contact with plant parts that you want to eat – use it only to water the base of plants.

You can also buy special fertilisers designed for tomatoes, and these are really worth looking at. You can get both organic and man-made versions, but both generally contain high enough levels of potassium to help produce healthy flowers and fruit. These are usually liquid feeds that are applied after the first fruits have formed and then every other week during the growing season.

Considering varieties

Tomatoes fall into two main types: *indeterminate* and *determinate.*

- ***Indeterminate* types** are generally classed as vine tomatoes, and are trained as a *cordon*. Cordons are plants encouraged to grow on a single stem reaching up to 1.2 metres, or in grown in a glasshouse reaching even further, and can even be trained up and over wires to the ceiling. If left to grow untrained, vine tomatoes create a sprawling mess that produces loads of small fruits, most of which won't ripen. These tomato types are great if you live in a cool area, because they mature more quickly and crop earlier than the second type.

- ***Determinate* types** are generally bush varieties, which are more compact forms that produce fruit over a shorter period, giving you a load of produce all at once. These varieties are easier to handle, but you'll probably end up with a glut. In warm areas, these types of tomatoes, when they start to produce fruit, can keep on producing for months on end, in fact if perfect conditions can be maintained, they keep producing for a year or more!

A huge range of tomatoes are available, especially if you're willing to grow from seed. From beefsteak to tiny cherry toms, there is something suitable for all tastebuds and skill levels, so go on – grow a taste of summer!

Cherry tomatoes

Cherry tomatoes are small, sweet, juicy little jewels that are easy to grow and bountiful. Here are some varieties to try:

- **Apero F1.** Another candidate for the tastiest cherry tom on the market, and can be grown in the greenhouse or in a warm spot outside. It has a slightly elongated shape and produces lovely red fruit.
- **Black Cherry.** An intermediate and prolific variety that produces a lot of tasty black fruits. It can be grown either in a greenhouse or in a sunny spot.
- **Gardener's Delight.** Give you a real taste of old, just what a tomato should do. The fruit are small bites-size treats that you can simply pop into your mouth!
- **Sun Cherry Premium F1.** This has to be the sweetest cherry tomato on the market. It's best suited to the greenhouse, but does well in a sunny spot. Grow the plants in pots in the conservatory or greenhouse and then move them outdoors during the heat of the summer for great results. Just make sure that you water and feed them regularly.
- **Sungold.** This classic yellowy orange cherry tom produces masses of sweet little fruits. But for an alternative variety, try **Golden Cherry F1**, which is proving even better.
- **Tumbler F1.** Tumbler has to be one of the best of the well known varieties out there, and is ideal for tubs, pots and even hanging baskets. It's a bush variety that offers loads of really sweet cherry toms.

Cherry plum tomatoes

These are becoming very popular for good reason: they offer small, really sweet fruits that are as tasty, if not more so, as cherry toms. Try these:

- **F1 Santa.** A really well known variety that's been tried and tested, and produces literally hundreds of sweet red fruits per plant. There's also an orange variety available called **Orange Santa TZ4111 F1**, which is equally good! Both are indeterminate varieties.

- **Ildi.** A fruitful variety that produces massive trusses of up to 80 little pear-shaped fruits, with up to four trusses per plant. It's one of the indeterminate varieties.
- **Rosada F1.** As good as F1 Santa, Rosada F1 is really worth a punt because it's just as productive and is suitable for indoors and outdoors. Grow it as a cordon.
- **Sweet Olive F1.** This is a really easy cordon to grow, simply needing a stake for support, with little or no training required. It's good for beginners and children, and produces masses of olive-shaped fruits with a full flavour.

Beefsteak tomatoes

Beefsteak tomatoes are usually large juicy tomatoes with excellent flavour. I say *usually* because they often taken a long time to mature and ripen. I don't mean to sound pessimistic, but they're pretty tough to grow well, and yields are far lower than with other types. So it's best to grow them as a challenge and if you get good results, pat yourself on the back and do the same next year! Consider these:

- **Big Boy F1.** Offers nice big tasty fruits and is easily obtainable. For best results, grow it in the greenhouse – it's an indeterminate variety.
- **Brandywine.** This one has to be included on any list of beefsteaks; it's a really old classic variety with one of the best flavours of all. If conditions are good, it offers a decent crop of large gorgeous-looking and tasting tomatoes.
- **Pomodoro Costoluto Genovese.** Amongst the best-looking beefsteak tomatoes around, it has a really bulbous cushion shape and a wonderful bright-red colour. It can grow gigantic in perfect conditions, and can be a really good cropper. It's one of the indeterminate types of tomato.
- **Roncardo F1 Hybrid.** A reliable-to-ripen beefsteak that has superior flavour to the rest. Definitely one to go for!
- **Super Marmande.** A cool-looking ribbed beefsteak that has a wonderful flavour. It has the classic cushion shape with a pink tinge on top. It's a semi-determinate variety.

Plum tomatoes

Plum tomatoes were actually bred mainly for making sauces; they're usually drier than other varieties with fewer seeds. I love them and personally prefer them to the 'traditional' tomatoes, even in salads and sliced, but as ever it's always down to personal choice. Here are some to try:

- **Health Kick F1.** A great plum for sauces, producing loads of really nice large fruit. It gets its name from the fact that it contains 50 per cent more of the cancer-fighting chemical lycopene than other tomatoes contain.

- **Roma VF.** Probably the most widely available plum tomato, both for home growers and in supermarkets. Roma VFs are really prolific growers that produce a bountiful crop and are in the semi-indeterminate category.
- **San Marzano.** Regarded as the best sauce tomatoe available to humanity (by snobby chefs that is) and, in all seriousness, really good for that purpose and gives a good heavy crop. It's in the semi-indeterminate category.

Standard tomatoes . . .

Finally, here are some standard tomatoes to cast your eye over:

- **Ailsa Craig.** This is one of the best known tomato varieties there are and has been around for ages for good reason. It tastes great, looks great and is pretty easy to grow. It's an indeterminate variety.
- **Alicante.** A really popular older variety that produces an early crop of lovely tasty toms and works very well in growbags. It's one of the indeterminate varieties.
- **Black Russian.** A great black (well more like mahogany) compact variety with a unique flavour. It's an indeterminate variety.
- **Glacier.** As its name suggests, Glacier is capable of withstanding colder weather than most others. Sown early under cloches it produces one of the earliest crops of tomatoes around. It's a semi-determinate variety.
- **Matina.** This is a good variety for growing outdoors, and has really rich red skin and a delicious flavour.
- **Moneymaker.** Another indeterminate variety, Moneymaker is a long-standing gardeners' favourite that offers trusses heavy with fruit (that, in my mind, lack flavour). Nevertheless, it's really popular.
- **Shirley F1.** A variety that's really suitable for the greenhouse and offers an early crop of tasty toms – a good, disease-resistant tomato, great for organic gardeners.
- **Tamina.** An excellent potato-leaved variety that produces a bumper crop of great slicing tomatoes. It can be grown indoors, but develops a better flavour if grown outside. It belongs to the indeterminate category.
- **Tigerella.** Again, an indeterminate, Tigarella is a really great-looking tomato with distinctive yellow stripes like a tiger. It's easy to grow both indoors and out, and has a lovely zingy flavour that works perfectly with a salad.
- **White Tomesol.** Produces the palest of the white tomatoes, with skin that's almost translucent. It has a tangy citrus flavour.

. . . and some non-standard ones

Other interesting types of tomato exist that will extend your knowledge and range:

- **Currant tomatoes.** Quite a few varieties of these are available. They produce tiny fruits (more like berries) that are fun to grow and taste good. Two varieties to try are Currant Red, which produces tiny red fruits, or Currant Yellow, which produces . . . you guessed it . . . yellow fruits.
- **Pear-shaped tomatoes.** These are, of course, pear shaped and are usually slightly larger than cherry tomatoes. Of the many varieties out there, try Red Pear and Yellow Pear.
- **Sausage tomatoes.** These are similar to long plum tomatoes and are also best used in sauces. Many thrive well in the greenhouse but also grow happily outdoors in warm summers. One variety worth a try is Green Sausage.

Harvesting and storage

Your tomatoes are ready to harvest as soon as they become ripe. This is when they turn red or whatever other colour for the variety you've chosen. Cherry tomatoes are prolific croppers, and you'll probably end up overwhelmed with a glut. I suggest growing a variety of tomatoes so that they ripen at different times, giving you a steady supply. When picking tomatoes, do so gently to avoid damaging them, and leave the stem on the fruit.

If you end up with too many tomatoes, don't waste them. Either eat them quickly or make them into soup and sauces, which are suitable to freeze.

Ripening your tomatoes

A common problem with tomatoes is not ripening in time. This is usually down to the weather rather than anything you may have done. It's not necessarily a lack of sunshine but a lack of the plant having had enough warmth. You can help the plants by keeping them upright, so the roots are exposed to as much heat as possible, and also by not allowing the plants to get too large. If you find you keep suffering from this problem, it's worth stopping your plants growing when they have set a maximum of four trusses of fruit. This may sound a bit drastic, but by doing this, you at least end up with four decent trusses on each plant rather than loads that won't ripen. To do this, nip off the tops of the plant above the trusses as soon as four have set (when they start to produce fruit).

The variety you choose also affects your success: smaller cherry tomato varieties ripen much more quickly than large beef varieties, so careful selection helps. If your tomatoes still haven't ripened by autumn, don't despair. You can encourage them using one of three methods:

- Remove the stake, lay the plants down on a bed of straw, and cover them with a cloche.
- Lay a sheet of cloth in drawer or box and position a layer of green tomatoes so they aren't touching. Then lay another piece of cloth over the top and another layer of tomatoes and one final layer of cloth. Close the drawer or put the box in a dark place.
- Put the unripe tomatoes in paper bags in a dark place.

Eat the tomatoes as soon as they ripen, because they won't keep long.

TIP

When fruit ripens, it gives off a gas called ethylene, which triggers other fruit to ripen. Bananas give off quite a lot of this gas as they ripen and can be used to speed the ripening process of other fruits. That's why you should never keep bananas in the fruit bowl. But this can be used to your advantage with tomatoes: by placing a ripening banana in the draw, box or bag with your tomatoes, you can help them ripen more quickly.

COOKING TIP

Finally, if all else fails, you can turn your green tomatoes (and excess red ones) into the most fantastic chutney. Chop your green tomatoes (1 kilogram) and add to ten fried shallots and a few chillies. Throw in some chopped apple (225 grams) and some raisins. Then pour in some sugar (225 grams) and finally half a pint (284 millilitres) of malt vinegar. Simmer until the sugar dissolves, and cook down to a nice thick chutney. Store in sterilised, labelled jam jars.

Chapter 14

Growing Leafy Greens

In This Chapter

- Preparing your plot for sowing
- Growing great salad leaves
- Giving spinach and its alternatives a go
- Producing unusual leaves

Some of the most rewarding crops you can grow on your allotment are leafy green vegetables. Most are quick to mature, easy to grow and full of health-giving nutrients and vitamins. Many are eaten raw, which is the best way to eat any vegetable, because as soon as you cook them, they instantly lose some of their nutritional content. Many can be grown as baby salad leaves, offering a really quick crop that can be grown in even the smallest of spaces. Some can be grown as *cut-and-come-again* crops, which means you simply cut off what you need and more grows back for future use. In this chapter I show you the huge range of leafy green veg you can grow, from simple iceberg lettuce to more unusual oriental leaves that can be used both in salads and in stir fries.

Savouring Salad Leaves

When I was young, salad for dinner meant soggy butterhead lettuce, some quarters of tomato and a squirt of salad cream on the side. My grandfather grew only butterhead lettuce; forget baby beet leaf, mizuna or rocket. Everything was grown to maturity; size was everything. Picking small produce was just a waste. Pea shoots, sorrel and endive were fancy twaddle. Oh, how wrong old-time gardeners had it. Thankfully, times and tastes have changed, and today salads are more of a party for the tastebuds – by turns peppery, acidic, sweet or bitter.

The bonus with growing your own salad leaves is that you can shave quite a bit of money from food bills: bought salad is fairly expensive, especially washed bags of nice mixed leaves. These don't last long. If you were to buy each type of leaf from the bag individually, it would cost you a fortune, but on the allotment, you can simply pick what you need, when you want it, ensuring you have the freshest salad available.

Growing Lettuces

Lettuces require soil that's been fairly recently manured and had time to settle, so do the manuring in advance of sowing. Most lettuces like cool, moist conditions in which to grow well, so manuring ensures that the soil maintains a good level of moisture for your plants. Add as much as half a kilogram for every square metre, which may sound a lot but will give you great results.

Most books say that lettuces require full sun, but in my experience they actually grow best in semi-shade, where they're kept cool and sheltered. They do grow well in full sun but tend to *bolt* (prematurely send up a flower stem) if they are under stress from lack of water. Lettuces struggle in heavy soils, so if you have heavy clay, you need to prepare the soil for at least two years to improve its texture and structure ready for growing salad. Alternatively, you can grow lettuces in raised beds. (See Chapter 5 for more on making raised beds.) Lettuce and other salad crops are ideal small-space veg, because they also do well in pots and window boxes. They like a soil pH of between 6 and 7 for ideal growing conditions, so liming may be needed to correct levels where necessary. (See Chapter 6 for more on analysing and improving your soil.)

Surprisingly, lettuce seeds won't germinate (sprout) in hot dry conditions, but prefer cool moist conditions. For *successional sowings* (sowing the same crop several times, so as to stagger your harvesting) in the height of summer, it's often better to sow seeds indoors in seed cells that can be kept in a shady spot for transplanting when they're at the three- or four-leaf stage. Lettuces don't transplant particularly well, but this may be your only option in the height of summer when the weather is dry. Growing in cell trays is the best option, to minimise root disturbance.

TIP

Using the following technique, you can force lettuce seeds to germinate and help them cope with hot dry weather:

1. **Sprinkle the seeds on a sheet of moist blotting paper and lay another moist sheet on top.**
2. **Place the blotting paper in the fridge for up to five days before planting the seeds.**

Lettuce seeds soak up lots of water in the first few hours, and if they subsequently dry out they won't germinate. This technique gives them a head start and they should shoot even in quite dry conditions.

Lettuces can either be grown on your plot or in pots and growbags. You can sow them outside from late March onwards, but be aware of the local weather patterns and wait until winter has turned its back somewhat. It's worth considering using cloches, fleece or polythene to warm the soil first, or to protect new crops. Spring lettuces can be started off indoors in the late winter and transplanted as soon as the weather has warmed a little in early spring. Winter lettuces should be sown in early autumn directly into the soil to mature for a quick crop. You can also sow spring lettuce in the autumn to be left protected by cloches over winter, where they'll remain dormant until spring the following year.

To sow your lettuce seeds, follow these steps:

1. **Outside, sow seeds in rows about 25–30 centimetres apart and 1 centimetre deep. Cover with a thin layer of soil and water well. In seed trays, plant three seeds in each cell and water well.**
2. **Protect the seedlings from snails and slugs right from the moment the lettuces appear as seedlings. Use either a cloche tunnel or grow them under some really fine netting.**
3. **Thin those sown in rows as soon as they are large enough to handle; you can transplant these thinnings into other rows to carry on growing. Before transplanting lettuces, it is a good idea to give them plenty of water a good few hours before, and to transplant them last thing on a cloudy day.**
4. **Keep the lettuces weed free at all times. A layer of organic mulch (see Chapter 7 for details) will help suppress the weeds and also helps to keep the sun's rays off the soil and keep your precious crop moist.**

TIP

Lettuces thrive in cool conditions, especially when they're young. If you don't have room for the thinnings from Step 3, simply put them in a salad and eat them up!

As lettuces bolt really easily in hot weather, it's advisable to plant little and often so that you're not faced with a sea of lettuces and not enough time to eat them before they set seed.

Lettuces are generally grouped into four main groups: loose-leaf, cos, butterhead and iceberg.

Loose-leaf

Loose-leaf lettuces are types that you generally find in supermarkets in different combinations in bags, washed and ready to eat. Supermarkets have it made with this type of product, because they're easy to grow and fast maturing, and retailers can charge a fair packet for them. You can grow many in pots or they're just as happy in situ on your plot, but I can't stress enough how easy they are to grow. As they're one of the best money savers, they simply must have a space on your plot.

Loose-leaf lettuces grow really well in pots filled with good-quality compost. Because they're fast-growing and get picked young, they take up little space. Why not grow some at home in pots and also have some on your plot? If you need a quick salad when you get home from work, all you need do is open the back door (or window – they also work in window boxes!).

Being such a fast-growing crop makes this type of salad ideal for successional planting, so sow every four weeks to maintain a steady supply throughout the year and to avoid a glut at any one time. You can harvest loose-leaf lettuce throughout the growing season by cutting the central core and leaving the outer leaves in place. Within a week or two, a new plant develops that can then be cut, usually once again. Be sure to keep the plant well watered after the first cutting to ensure the healthy development of a new plant.

With many varieties, you can harvest individual leaves from a number of plants and they simply keep on producing new leaves without weakening the plant. The leaves of these lettuces are best harvested whilst young. Others are more like the larger lettuces that can be cut off once and grow back just once.

Considering varieties

Try the varieties of open-leaf lettuce below:

- **Lollo Biondo.** A lovely loose-leaf lettuce that forms a pale green frilly head and is perfect for cut-and-come-again or left to mature.
- **Lollo Rossa.** A great loose-leaf lettuce that doesn't produce a heart. It's a very well known variety with crinkled red foliage, and it's easy to grow. It can be harvested lightly throughout its growing season and keeps producing new foliage, or it can be left to mature as a larger specimen.

Many cut-and-come-again crops are suitable for sowing in amongst other crops to fill spaces or in unused areas of your plot. Because many grow so quickly, you can even sow them during times when areas are vacant between other sowings. For example, in the late summer when your brassica bed is emptying, sow some cut-and-come again salad leaves as a quick crop before winter arrives.

Cos

Cos lettuces are small, crisp and delicious. An essential ingredient to many a summer salad, they're also known as romaine lettuces. They produce a firm head of elongated leaves with a crisp rib down the middle. The rib produces a milky sap that can taste really bitter in the older leaves, so it's better to cut off the leaves if they get too large. The inner pale leaves are sweet and crisp, with the outer leaves being darker in colour. As most lettuces are made up mostly of water, they hold very little nutritional value.

Cos lettuces come in many different shapes, colours and sizes:

- **Corsair.** A large cos that forms a good, solid butter-coloured heart. Corsair is a really tough little treasure that can take all the abuse the British weather can throw at it.
- **Little Gem.** The variety you most probably know from the supermarkets, it produces lovely sweet little lettuces that always produce the goods. It is reliable and good for intense cropping, with the lettuces planted close together.
- **Lobjoits Green Cos.** Probably the most popular variety around, it grows a nice firm little lettuce that's sweet and crisp. Sow every two to three weeks for a succession of perfect little delights!
- **Nymans.** An interesting cos that's bright red-wine coloured with green lower down. Shows good bolt and disease resistance.
- **Parris Island.** A romaine-style cos that has elongated crisp leaves up to about 25 centimetres (10 inches) long. Parris Island is a well known, reliable variety that won't let you down.

Butterhead

Butterheads used to be the staple salad that all gardeners grew before the advent of the new, more exciting cos, iceberg and loose-leaf varieties. Butterheads are still available in most supermarkets, generally sold as cheap 'value' salad leaves. They're quick and easy to grow, and shouldn't be dismissed, because they taste pretty darn good too. It's best to sow them in spring and late summer, because they don't like the midsummer heat too much. The foliage is usually less crisp and refreshing than other types of lettuce, but the soft velvety leaves offer a great contrast to crisper leaves in the salad bowl.

Have a go with these butterheads:

- **All-Year-Round.** A popular variety that's readily available and reliable. It produces soft buttery leaves in a solid compact heart, and is really hardy and dry-weather tolerant, so is good for the lazy gardener!
- **Buttercrunch.** An all-time favourite, offering vigorous heads that are an attractive dark green and weighty. It offers good performance from a really tasty lettuce that lasts for ages in the ground.
- **Cassandra.** One of the most reliable and disease-resistant varieties around, and therefore ideal for the organic gardener. It's perfect for growing all year round and offers excellent flavour.

- **Tom Thumb.** This is probably the smallest butterhead around, so is aptly named. The plants can be spaced as close as 15 centimetres (6 inches) apart, so this variety is ideal for those with smaller growing areas.

Iceberg

Iceberg is a type of crisphead lettuce; it forms a hard, dense and heavy heart of really crunchy leaves. The iceberg lettuce is probably the most widely bought lettuce there is, offering brilliant shelf life, and has a wonderfully crisp, refreshing bite. I have to admit that I simply love the stuff. I know it's not the most trendy lettuce out there and can taste rather bland, but for added crunch in salads and used in sandwiches, nothing comes close. It's easy to grow for harvesting in summer and autumn. As icebergs are 90 per cent water, they're not high in nutrients, but still deserve a space on your plot.

Considering varieties

Some iceberg lettuces to try include:

- **Lakeland.** This is an easy-to-grow iceberg that forms the classic crunchy heart.
- **Miluna.** Bred to be as tough as they come, Miluna is a hybrid that is resistant to most diseases and has the vigour expected of a hybrid. It's ideal for organic growers, because it's so tough that you don't need sprays or chemicals to protect it.
- **Pablo.** An unusual crisphead with purple-red outer leaves, Pablo is easy to grow and tastes great.
- **Reine des Glace.** A lettuce that'll get all your neighbours' heads turning, this one is about as pretty a crisphead as you are ever likely to find, forming a large dense crunchy heart, with really frizzy outer leaves. Simply outstanding!
- **Webbs Wonderful.** A true garden favourite that I remember my granddad used to grow when I was a child. This isn't a true iceberg and has been around far longer than genuine iceberg varieties, but is often sold as an iceberg type. It has a firm crisp heart and slightly crinkled leaves, grows in both wet and dry summers, and is unlikely to bolt.

Harvesting and storage

All lettuces can be picked and eaten at any stage during their growing season. Whichever type or types you decide to grow, they won't all keep for long after they have reached maturity, and should be eaten as soon as they become ready. Lettuces that form a heart are ready as soon as a tight ball has formed within the outer leaves. Lettuces should be picked at the peak of freshness. They keep in the ground only for a week or two after they've matured. They soon bolt when the weather's hot, and they deteriorate in wet weather.

Winter lettuces

You can also get winter lettuces that are well suited to being grown during the colder months of the year; some can even be grown in winter (with protection). Most gardeners don't bother growing winter lettuces, but they are easy to grow and offer very few difficulties to the grower. Most are best grown in the greenhouse or in polytunnels or cloche tunnels, but some can survive even outside in milder areas; some people simply roll some fleece over them on cold nights. Most winter lettuces are cos, loose-leaf and butterhead types. Varieties include:

- **Lattughino.** A really productive, pretty hardy, frilly-edged loose-leaf lettuce with red-tinged leaves. Great for a taste of summer in winter.
- **Winter Density.** A brilliant choice for growing over winter, producing a cos-like lettuce that is ready in spring after being sown in autumn. Shows great winter hardiness but is best given some protection.
- **Valdor.** An all-time classic, having been around for what seems like forever. A butterhead lettuce, forming a nice medium head, Valdor will be ready for Christmas if planted in August. Usually grown in a greenhouse, it will be okay outside in warmer areas.

Growing Other Salad Leaves

Recent years have seen a salad revolution, with new exotic leaves becoming available, from hot, peppery rocket to sophisticated chicory. Many varieties are available to try, such as claytonia (miner's lettuce or winter purslane), celtuce (grown for leaves and its crisp tender stem), corn salad, and the strange-looking ice plants. Consider giving some of the ones in the following sections a go.

Endive

Endive is not that popular in the UK, but in the rest of Europe it's a mainstay of many a salad plate. Endives are fabulous-looking plants that offer the chef an opportunity to really excite the eyes and the taste buds. Endive comes in both smooth-leaved and frilly-leaved varieties. The frilly types are quite common in bags of mixed salad, but the smooth types are rarely seen in the shops. Endive has a unique bitter yet fresh taste that works really well with sweeter flavours, and I think works particularly well with sweet seared scallops.

Endive requires the same type of growing conditions as most lettuces – that is, a nice free-draining moist soil, rich in organic matter. So the autumn before, dig in plenty of manure to prepare the soil. For baby leaves, sow from mid-spring into early summer, but for full-grown leaves, sow in late June and August so that they can mature during the cooler tail end of the summer. Endive likes cool conditions. It bolts in the height of the summer, so keep your plants well watered to combat this. To sow your endives, follow these steps:

1. **Sow seeds in drills 1 centimetre deep in late summer and cover lightly. Be sure to sow them quite thinly so as not to be wasteful.**
2. **Thin the plants as they mature to 20-centimetre spacings.**
3. **Keep plants weed free and water them during dry spells.**

Both broad-leaved and frilly endive benefit from blanching before they're picked to help reduce bitterness. This basically means that for a few days before harvesting, you need to cut out all light to the plants, so they turn pale. You can do this in a couple of ways. Either place pots over them and leave them for around ten days until they're pale in colour, or partially blanch them by placing a large saucer over the centre of a plant for around ten days. This has the same effect as the first method and turns the foliage pale and less bitter. Some varieties to try include:

- **Indivia D'Estale A Cuore Giallo.** A frilly endive, which may be a mouthful to say, but once you have taken a mouthful you will grow it every year. Blanch the centre for a milder taste, but the whole plant adds texture to any salad.
- **Moss curled.** Is called *chicorée frisée* in France, and is much like the frisée we get in many pre-packed salad bags.
- **Natcha.** Is slightly less bitter than the curly types and has a nice crisp white blanched centre. Is the most widely grown of the smooth-leaved types for good reason: it is easy and quick to grow (ready in as little as ten weeks) and tastes divine.

Chicory

Lots of different types of chicory are available, but all have a really distinctive bitter taste. Confusion between endive and chicory exists; although we call it chicory, in Belgium it is often known as *witloof*, which means white leaf, and in the USA it's called Belgian endive.

Types of chicory

Three main types of actual chicory exist:

- **Radicchio.** Sow between April and May for a summer crop, or from June to July for an autumn crop. Sow in 25-centimetre rows thinned to 25-centimetre spacing. Radicchio can be left to mature fully and be eaten as required, or it can be picked as cut-and-come-again. It forms a heart similar to sugarloaf and once cut, regrows a second heart for harvesting later.
- **Sugarloaf.** Is best sown in June and July in 30-centimetre rows thinned to 25-centimetre spacing. Sugarloaf chicory can be harvested as a cut-and-come-again crop by picking individual leaves, but is best left to mature. Then harvest the inner heart (looks like a cos lettuce) by cutting if off at the base, leaving a stump that usually produces another heart. Sugarloaf can also be grown in polytunnels and under cloches from August onwards, offering a great winter salad crop.
- **Witloof.** Sow this between May and June in 20-centimetre rows thinned to 10- to 15-centimetre spacing. Witloof chicory is usually grown for forcing inside over winter to produce *chicons*, the torpedo-shaped baby leaves that for me are one of the highlights of the allotment year.

Keep the plants of all three varieties well watered to avoid bolting. All varieties of chicory require a site in full sun that's been manured the previous year. Don't plant chicory on recently manured land, because doing so causes the tap roots to fork.

TIP

Don't waste the leaves that have been thinned out – they're great used in salads.

Forcing witloof chicory

Witloof chicory is usually forced and blanched. Follow these steps:

1. **Allow the plants to grow without cutting them back until the first frost hits.**
2. **Dig up the large tap root when the first frost arrives.**
3. **Remove the foliage to within 1 centimetre of the top of the tap root and trim the tip so that the root is about 15 centimetres long.**
4. **Replant up to seven roots in a large pot, pouring compost in and firming well, leaving the ends just showing. Water really well.**
5. **Keep the pot in a dark, warm place (not less than 10 degrees centigrade) and exclude the light completely.**
6. **Don't allow the plants to dry out – water them regularly.**

Within a month, you'll have some fantastic pale chicons to liven up your autumn and winter salads or use as a cooked vegetable.

Witloof chicory is great served in the classic French dish *chicons au gratin*. Steam some chicons until tender, place them in a gratin dish and pour over some béchamel sauce with some small chunks of good ham in it; I like to add a touch of grated nutmeg. Grate some good cheddar over the top and pop it under a grill to warm and crisp up the cheese . . . delicious.

If you carefully break the chicons off, you may well get another crop sprouting soon after. Pick them right before you need them, because they start to droop fairly quickly after harvesting.

Considering varieties

A couple of varieties of witloof you might like to try are:

- **Apollo.** A great chicory for forcing, and gives you lovely pale chichons that taste fantastic.
- **Zoom F1.** A popular forcing variety that's easy to grow and is also good left to mature.

And here are three radicchio varieties:

- **Palla Rossa.** A lovely red chicory that you can eat in salads or stir fried as a vegetable.
- **Rossa de Treviso.** The pride of Italy, it even has its own website promoting itself. This lovely radicchio can also be forced in the same way as witloof chicory can be.
- **Treviso Precoce Mesola.** A variety sown successionally for salad leaves or in June and July to be allowed to mature for larger heads. It's lovely and crisp and tasty.

The best sugarloaf chicory to try is Bianca di Milano – a great little sugarloaf that forms small dense heads, much like a cos lettuce. Its crunchy green outer foliage conceals pale hearts that work well in salads.

Rocket

Rocket has to be the culinary A-lister of recent decades, racing its way to the top of the salad charts during the 1990s. Before then, it hadn't generally been cultivated commercially, other than in Italy and a few other countries. It was usually collected as a wild salad plant until its popularity in trendy restaurants launched it to commercial superstardom. Rocket is so easy to grow it's almost a crime that people actually go to the shops and pay for it ready washed in bags. I always plant a couple of pots at home and some rocket in the beds – one cheap packet of seeds keeps me going all summer and into late autumn.

Rocket can be harvested at all stages from when the plants are tiny to when they reach 15–20 centimetres tall, but the older and larger they get, the hotter the flavour becomes. They do have a tendency to bolt, but if you sow seeds in succession, this doesn't matter at all, because you'll have other plants growing to replace those that have bolted. I actually really like them when they've bolted, because the flowers are edible and the leaves have a real peppery kick.

Rocket can grow pretty much anywhere, so a good idea is to sow it in succession right from February through until late August and even into September (give seedlings protection from frost during cold periods). Sow seeds under cover from February to March and transplant the seedlings as soon as the risk of frost has passed. From spring onwards, sow directly into the soil at fortnightly intervals in small amounts to keep a constant supply and to avoid a glut. Sow the seeds in rows, 1 centimetre deep, and thin the seedlings to 15 centimetres apart.

Rocket can be harvested as soon as you think it's big enough. You can usually harvest it as a cut-and-come-again crop that'll re-sprout from the base. Simply pick the leaves as required or cut the whole plant at the base leaving 2 centimetres at the bottom – it then re-shoots quickly.

Rocket seeds are easy to collect, and each plant produces loads of seeds that can be planted next year to save you a few pounds. Rocket flowers from the top to the bottom, and the seeds take a couple of months to mature after flowering begins. Once the seed pods begin to split, remove them and pop them into a brown paper bag, where the seeds will fall out for collection. Keep the seeds in a marked envelope ready for planting next spring.

Flea beetles can be a nuisance with your rocket (and also your brassicas). Evidence of an infestation is little holes all over your crops. Flea beetles are easy to see and are often there in vast numbers; when disturbed, they hop off like fleas to hide. They emerge from hibernation in spring and start to feed on young tender foliage before laying eggs, which hatch in late summer. You can get chemical sprays to deal with them, or get a piece of card and paint some glue or sticky grease on it. Pass the card over the tops of your plants a few times, and the flea beetles will hop up to escape but stick to the card to meet their doom!

Considering Varieties

Rocket is available in many different varieties. Some have rounded leaves, and others (usually sold as wild rocket) have toothed leaves. Both sorts have a very peppery taste.

- **Apollo.** A salad rocket that grows fast and is less likely to bolt. Peppery and delicious.
- **Discovery.** A really popular toothed-leaf rocket that is fast and easy.
- **Skyrocket.** Produces large toothed leaves that taste like wild rocket but grow really quickly, like the salad varieties.
- **Wild.** Wild rocket has a more potent flavour than other salad types, so if you like it spicy, this is for you.

Other leaves to try

These salad plants do not fit easily into any other category in this chapter. Have a go at the following, for a bit of a change:

- **Corn salad.** Grows wild in its native North Africa and western Asia, proving that it is a determined little leaf that is easy to grow. It is useful as a winter salad leaf, so sow it in September and use it over winter. Don't harvest the whole plant – pick a few leaves from each and it will keep coming back.
- **Ice plants.** A really unusual addition to the salad bowl, they're quick-to-grow perennials in warm climates, but in cool climates are grown as tender annuals. They have tender stems bearing quite fleshy leaves that have the appearance of being covered in ice crystals. Their slightly salty taste contrasts brilliantly with the taste of other leaves. Ice plants can be picked in as little as four weeks after sowing and are best picked regularly to encourage new growth.
- **Purslane.** An unusual salad leaf that's gaining popularity. The two varieties, winter and summer, are entirely different from each other but both can be used in salads or indeed cooked like spinach. Winter purslane is a hardy annual that's also known as *miner's lettuce*. It can become really invasive and prolific because it self-seeds all over the place, but is easily lifted. It contributes to great salads, offering its leaves, stems, shoots and flower heads as a mild, interesting alternative to the norm. Summer purslane is a half-hardy semi-succulent plant that can be used in salads. It comes in two types – green and yellow – with the yellow-golden forms being more popular for their flavour.
- **Salad rape.** A member of the brassica family that has mild mustard-flavoured leaves. It's a useful winter salad leaf, being hardy down to at least –10 degrees centigrade. Fast growing when conditions are right, it can be first harvested in as little as ten days, then keeps shooting over a few months.

Growing Green Leaf Vegetables

Green leaf vegetables have to be the most nutrient-rich, vitamin-laden produce you can grow on the allotment. It's no coincidence that Popeye gained superhuman strength from spinach; it's full of iron, calcium and a whole cocktail of vitamins, making it a proper super-food! Swiss chard is an extra-simple vegetable that is also packed with goodness, and it amazes me that more supermarkets don't seem to sell it. It's often called seakale beet and is, in fact, a beetroot that sends down narrow roots instead of producing a swollen one. Or you could try Good King Henry, which isn't such a common sight any more, but in yesteryears was a common garden vegetable. Also known as poor man's asparagus, Good King Henry produces spinach-like leaves and stems that are edible too.

Spinach

Spinach is a bit of a funny old veg: some people love it whilst others (usually children) seem to hate it. It's usually easy to grow and absolutely full of goodness, but it bolts really easily so can be difficult to grow to maturity. However, sown often in succession, it will reward you with plenty of young foliage that is super tasty (to me, anyway). Spinach is best eaten cooked gently, and you need a lot of it to feed one person, because it seems to disappear during cooking. I don't add any water during cooking, because spinach contains a lot, so simply cook it gently in a pan until it reduces. After cooking, it's vital that you squeeze out the excess water, otherwise you end up with soggy spinach water all over the plate.

One of the best ways to cook spinach is to fry a shallot in some olive oil and then throw in some spinach. Season with salt and pepper and then grate a little nutmeg onto it – fantastic served with any cheese-based dish or with a poached egg and hollandaise sauce. Or use it raw in salad for extra flavour and added health!

Cultivating spinach

Spinach grows much better in a cool climate, and in the heat of summer it bolts really easily. It does better if grown in semi-shade and likes an rich organic moisture-retentive soil that, well in advance of planting, you need to have dug down to around 30 centimetres deep.

Sow seeds little and often from spring onwards right up until the late summer, ready for picking over winter (they need cloche protection). Spinach hates being transplanted, so is best grown in situ in rows 25 centimetres apart and thinned to 8 centimetres (for plants grown for young foliage), or spaced at 15 centimetres for larger plants.

Keep well watered during dry spells and free from weeds. Also, if you can apply a good mulch of compost, it helps keep the plants moist and less likely to bolt.

You can harvest spinach as soon as the plants are big enough, but this can be a laborious task. It's better to pick leaves individually, a few from each plant at any one time. This keeps them growing well, but can take ages. So if you're growing lots in succession, it's often worth just shearing a good bunch of leaves when you need them – they may grow back if you don't cut all the foliage off, but if not, it doesn't matter if you have more plants nearing readiness.

Considering varieties

Three good varieties of spinach to try are:

- **Bordeaux F1.** A fairly new variety that has red stems and green foliage. It's brilliant as a salad crop or just as good gently steamed as a side dish.
- **Rhino F1.** A really easy-to-grow spinach that produces abundant leaves over a long period. It has good bolt resistance too.
- **Scenic.** A revelation when it comes to growing spinach with good mildew resistance, and it produces loads of lovely leaves perfect for salads and cooking.

Swiss chard and spinach beet

Swiss chard and spinach beet (also known as perpetual spinach) are good beginners' alternatives to proper spinach because, especially from late summer, sowings are far less likely to bolt, and from just one or two sowings, as opposed to many sowings of spinach, you can have enough to last the whole year. Swiss chard is really easy to grow and, due to the fact that you can pick it and it grows back steadily, makes it an exceptionally productive leaf vegetable. It also has the added bonus of being frost hardy, so can survive frosts during the winter.

Getting started with spinach beet and chard

Spinach beet, like all members of the beet family, likes a deeply dug soil, but unlike beetroot it likes lots of fresh manure. There's no threat of roots *forking* (splitting into two or more smaller roots), as there is with most root vegetables; with spinach beet, so you can add as much muck as you like without risk. Spinach beet won't tolerate acid soils, so if you have that soil type, you need to add lime well in advance of planting to help correct levels. (See Chapter 6 for more info on analysing and balancing your soil.) Spinach beet plants can stay in the ground for up to a year, and being leafy vegetables, use up plenty of nitrogen. Use a feed high in nitrogen, applied in slow-release form. Use dried blood or bone meal as top dressing, or apply a liquid feed high in nitrogen throughout the season if necessary. A lack of nitrogen in leafy vegetables such as chard causes the foliage to turn yellow around the edges, and in severe cases the whole leaf turns. Plants suffering nitrogen deficiency will not grow with enough vigour, so you end up with a smaller crop – nitrogen is vital for a good crop. (To spot the signs of nitrogen deficiency, check out Chapter 6.)

For an early crop, sow directly into the soil in early April in rows 45 centimetres apart with seeds spaced at 3 centimetres. For a winter to spring crop, sow in July and August.

When the seedlings are well established, thin to 15 centimetres apart and keep them free from weeds. When it's established, your crop will also benefit from a decent mulch.

Harvesting can take place in as little as 8–10 weeks after sowing. Simply cut off leaves from the outside of the plant first – but don't harvest them all, otherwise new foliage won't grow back easily. When the leaves get too large they become tough and not good to eat, so throw them in the composter. Also if you see any flower heads developing, remove them immediately.

Considering varieties

Swiss chard and leaf beets can be used in two ways: the leaves can be separated from the stalks and used like spinach, and the stalks can be cooked separately, much like asparagus. Here are some Swiss chard varieties to try:

- **Brightlights.** Has yellow, red, pink, orange and green stems – some are even multicoloured. A colourful addition to the allotment and the table!
- **Lucullus.** Considered by many to be the most tasty of all Swiss chards, Lucullus is a really vigorous variety with pale stems and lush rich green leaves.
- **Rhubarb Chard.** A leaf beet with ruby red stems which can be used like any other chard.

Good King Henry

This rather out-of-favour vegetable is making something of a comeback on allotments around the country. Not only has it got the best Latin name on the block (*Chenopodium bonus-henricus*), it also offers the grower spinach-like leaves year upon year because it's a perennial (it lives for more than two years), so requires little attention when established. Many see this much-under-loved plant as a weed, but I'm backing a campaign to get Good King Henry back on the throne! Seeds are fairly easy to find and well worth seeking out.

Good King Henry can be cooked exactly as you do spinach, with the new leaves being picked and gently steamed. The young shoots too are really good and are a little like asparagus, hence its common name of poor man's asparagus.

If harvesting the young shoots in spring and early summer, be sure to leave some to develop, otherwise you won't have much foliage to use later on.

Good King Henry is really easy to grow and is happy in almost all soil types, although it prefers a well manured rich soil in order to thrive. You can sow seeds in modules and then transplant them, or sow them direct on the plot where they're to grow, leaving 20–30 centimetres between them. They need a season to establish before they're ready to harvest, so give them a year in the ground for harvesting the following year.

Established clumps can be divided really easily in autumn, and if clumps are fairly large they can be replanted directly. If they're small, plant them into pots and overwinter them in a cold frame for planting the following spring. Or you can even offer some of your divided plants to some of your neighbouring plot holders to spread the word about Good King Henry.

There is only one variety of Good King Henry *(Chenopodium bonus-henricus)*, so if you want to try it, just look for that name!

Growing Oriental Leaf Vegetables

Some of the more exciting vegetables of recent years come from Asia, and these are often easy to grow, super tasty and well worth exploring. The oriental mustard leaves are excellent in salads and add great flavour to stir fries. Consider mizuna and pak-choi, choi sum, tatsoi, tsoi sim, and Chinese cabbages – especially good in stir fries and clear soups. Also, look out for komatsuna greens, which are like spinach with a mustard kick and which you can also use in stir fries and soups. You can also get oriental broccolis such as kailaan and nabana, which are easy to grow and really tasty. Most are members of the brassica family and suffer from the same diseases and pests, so check out Chapter 7 for more information on this.

Mizuna

Mizuna is a type of mustard green that is best used use in salads, and is similar in appearance to salad rocket but with a milder peppery or mustard flavour. It grows to around 27 centimetres tall and is used in salads, stir fries and any other use that rocket has, such as on top of pizzas or pasta dishes. It's about as easy to grow as breathing is – so a good choice for beginners! Mizuna also has attractive leaves and makes an excellent edging to veg beds.

Growing mizuna

Mizuna grows in most soils and requires little encouragement to thrive. Best sown in late summer, it can also be sown in spring or even autumn if given some winter protection. The main issue with it is that if the weather gets too hot and dry, it bolts like a startled horse. So it's best sown to mature in the cooler parts of the year either side of summer. It prefers a well drained, fertile soil, but grows pretty much anywhere. If you do risk planting it in the summer, plant it in the shade to reduce the likelihood of bolting. But if you find yours do bolt, don't despair: the flowering stems are delicious and can be cooked like broccoli.

Seeds can be sown indoors in trays a week before the predicted last frost of winter (experience will have to be your guide, or check local weather trends on a local weather website), if you want a head start. Or they can be sown outside when the risk of frost has passed, when the soil has warmed in spring.

If you sow mizuna in modules, harden off the plants and plant out in rows 10–15 centimetres apart or further apart for larger plants. If you sow in the soil, sow seeds thinly in rows, thinning plants to the same distance apart as for module grown plants.

Mizuna matures in as little as three to six weeks and can be harvested as a cut-and-come-again vegetable or left until fully mature in about eight weeks after sowing. You can cut the whole head off at the base or alternatively cut individual leaves off to encourage new foliage from the base.

Mibuna

Another very similar vegetable to try is called mibuna, which likes exactly the same conditions as mizuna and is treated in the same way – just give it a little more room to grow, because it reaches a height of around 30–45 centimetres. It tastes very similar to mizuna and produces tight tufts of serrated leaves that work well in salads and stir fries or simply cooked as a side dish.

Mustard greens

Mustard greens are another member of the brassica family and are simply the foliage of the plant from which you get brown mustard seeds. The foliage has the same flavour that is associated with mustards. Plants come in a number of different varieties. Often used in Indian and Asian cooking, mustard greens are frequently mixed with other milder leaves to make 'mixed greens'. There are a number of varieties available that include standard mustard greens, other varieties that look more like headless cabbages, and some that resemble curly kale. They are usually quick to mature and are ready to harvest from three weeks for baby leaf and in around eight weeks for mature plants. They're easy to grow and the mustard flavour increases with maturity.

Sow mustard greens thinly 1.5 centimetres deep in rows 25–40 centimetres apart from April through until August (some can be grown in polytunnels and greenhouses all year round). Keep well watered, especially until they emerge, and thin the seedlings out to 10–30 centimetres apart, depending on the variety. Keep weed free and water during dry spells to prevent bolting.

Mustard greens are best harvested whilst still young, otherwise they become really powerfully flavoured. Many can be left to mature, and these are best cooked, which lessens the intense mustard flavour. Harvesting mustard greens is simply a case of cutting the foliage from the base as required. Some produce new shoots like a cut-and-come-again crop, and some can be matured and cut as a whole. If you plant them late in the summer, you can cover any remaining for the winter, and in spring they'll jump into life again and can be used as spring greens. Many are ready to use as baby leaf veg in as little as three weeks, whereas others take up to eight weeks to mature. Either way, they're fast-growing, easy plants that are really prolific and rewarding.

Many mustard greens produce quantities of seeds which, if allowed to set, can sprout up all over the place. If you want to avoid this problem, simply cut the plants down before they set seed.

Considering varieties

Some varieties I suggest growing include:

- **Giant Red.** Looking like a headless cabbage, Giant Red produces large heads that, if sown in late summer, last well over winter if offered protection such as a cloche.
- **Golden Streaks.** A feathered-leaf type, great for salads and for cooking in stir fries and other mixed green dishes. It also looks attractive as a decorative border plant in the garden.
- **Osakara Purple.** As the name suggests, this mustard produces purple-veined green leaves that are brilliant for salads and stir fries. It has lovely tender stems that are tasty in their own right.
- **Tender Green.** A subtle-flavoured variety that's easy to grow.

Pak-choi and tatsoi

Pak-choi is one of the most fabulous oriental vegetables you can grow, and its succulent stems and foliage are a real treat. It grows quickly and offers you a really satisfying crop to be proud of. Pak-choi is a pretty fussy customer, in that it bolts really easily if conditions aren't just right, but saying that, it grows fairly quickly and easily if you can keep it happy. Tatsoi is like a milder mustard green with a texture more like pak-choi; it too is fairly easy to grow.

Both pak-choi and tatsoi are packed full of minerals, vitamins and antioxidants, which promote good health.

These are both cool-season crops that like temperatures between 15 and 20 degrees centigrade if they're to do well, otherwise they tend to bolt. They're both members of the brassica family and require similar growing conditions, and suffer the same pests and diseases (see Chapter 7). They like a moisture-retentive rich soil that has a pH of between 6.5 and 7. (See Chapter 6 for how to work out your soil's pH level.) Getting the pH right helps fend off the dreaded club root (see Chapter 7).

Sow pak-choi and tatsoi seeds in modules, growbags or directly into the soil throughout the growing season as soon as frost risk has passed. Thin seeds or transplant to 10 centimetres apart (for smaller varieties) and up to 40 centimetres apart for larger ones. Keep well watered and if grown in bags, feed weekly with a nitrogen-rich liquid feed.

These plants grow at a rate of knots and have shallow roots, so they require careful watering to ensure that they don't dry out. Many people like to grow them in growbags so they can closely monitor the plants' needs and ensure sufficient watering. Both varieties are, unfortunately, snail and slug fodder, so offer protection such as sharp grit.

Considering varieties

Good varieties of pak-choi and tatsoi include:

- **Pak Choi Hanakan F1.** Fast growing, dark green and gorgeous.
- **Pak Choi Ivory F1.** An easy-to-grow variety that has nice white central stems on tasty green foliage. Grow closer together for smaller baby leaves.
- **Pak Choi Joi Choi F1.** Grows larger than most types, so give it a bit more room to grow. Still only takes 50 days to mature.
- **Tatsoi.** Forms a rosette of spoon-shaped compact leaves and is great in salads and stir fries, fast growing and easy.

Komatsuna greens

Komatsuna greens are also known as spinach mustard and are a really popular veg grown in Korea, Japan and Taiwan. They're an easy-to-grow, fast-to-mature and really tough allotment leaf veg that's really worth trying. The flavour is a cross between cabbage and spinach, with a mild mustard kick that strengthens with age. They're great sown in late summer into the winter, during which they withstand temperatures as low as –10 to –12 degrees centigrade. Komatsuna greens are less prone to bolt than other oriental brassicas and aren't as reliant on constant moisture to thrive. In fact they're ideal for the beginner, so if you're new to oriental veg, this is a good place to start (together with mizuna). Komatsuna greens are sown in exactly the same way as mizuna (see the earlier section 'Mizuna'). They can also be sown and grown under cover during winter to provide healthy, tasty greens throughout the year.

Plants are ready to harvest as baby leaf vegetables in as little as three to four weeks, but to reach maturity they take eight weeks or longer, depending on the variety. Simply pick the leaves as required and they'll grow new foliage throughout the season.

Quite a few varieties are out there to try; some are more suited to summer cropping, and others are better for the cooler months, so pick the variety to suit the sowing times. Try these:

- **Green Boy.** A really fast-cropping variety that'll be ready in as little as a month in the summer.
- **Tokisan F1.** Another easy-to-source variety that's well suited to the warmer times of the year and can be sown all year round.
- **Torasan F1.** Best sown in autumn to mature during the cooler parts of the year, Torasan F1 is best sown in situ. It has all the benefits of a hybrid variety and is less likely to bolt.

Chapter 15

Planting Beans, Peas and Other Odds and Pods

In This Chapter

- Prepping your plot
- Enjoying success with all the beans
- Embracing the pea family
- Sowing successful sweetcorn

Shelling fresh peas or broad beans straight from your plot is a real pleasure. My children sit happily for hours removing the little jewels from their pods, just as I did. The Leguminosae family is one of the most important groups of plants the self-sufficient gardener can grow. As a vegetable group it includes peas, French beans, runner beans, broad beans, lima beans and soya beans; oddly, it also covers peanuts, which aren't a nut at all but a pulse. All of these peas and beans are full of protein; without this family of plants, vegetarians would be scuppered. This chapter looks at the more easily grown members of the family, including peas, mangetout, French beans, runner beans and broad beans. Sweetcorn also pops up in this chapter. Although it's a cereal crop (maize) and not a legume, on the plate this vegetable goes hand in hand with peas.

One of the most important features of the bean family is the nitrogen-fixing capabilities they posses. Organic gardeners and gardeners that employ crop-rotation techniques (see Chapter 7) benefit greatly from the fact that a crop of legumes helps replace nitrogen in the soil. Bacteria found in little nodules on the roots of legumes take nitrogen from the air (which isn't readily available to plants), combining it with oxygen and then turning it into nitrates in the soil that are easily absorbed by other plants. (See Chapter 6 for more on understanding your soil.) If you dig up a bean plant and look at the roots, you'll see these nodules clearly – they're full of these magic bacteria.

Growing Beautiful Beans

Beans are really easy to grow, and most plants produce prolifically, offering you an abundant crop that simply keeps on producing over a long period. Beans, from low-growing purple beans to tall, far-reaching runners, are suitable for all sizes of garden and plot. And don't forget the unpopular beans that everyone seems to hate until they become adults – broad beans.

Most beans are simply steamed or gently simmered and served when they still have a bit of bite. But beans such as broad beans can also be puréed with peas and pecorino cheese and stirred like pesto through pasta. Or you can serve them with a tender rack of lamb nestling on top. Then drizzle over a rich wine *jus* and you're away!

French beans

We all seem to depend on crops grown in Kenya and Egypt when it comes to French beans. They're often called fine beans as well (so supermarkets can charge a bit more!), but French beans are an allotment essential that should be a seasonal treat, not something we expect all year round. They're simple to grow and come in a far more varied mix than the slender selection of varieties on offer off the shelf.

French beans come in two different types: the *dwarf* and *climbing* varieties. Dwarf varieties are quick to grow, space saving, and crop over a relatively short period. The benefit of dwarf varieties is that they need no support and are therefore really popular with plot holders and people who grow them at home. Additionally, they grow well in pots, offering a decent crop even from only a few plants. Climbing varieties take up more room, but produce bigger crops over a longer period, so are well worth considering.

French beans are best picked and eaten whilst young, but when they mature and become too large to eat they can be dried for eating later. These mature beans, when dried, are often called *haricots*. French beans can also be harvested as shelled beans whilst still immature; these are called *flageolet* beans.

Getting started with French beans

French beans or green beans are really easy to grow. They're best grown in organic rich soil that's free-draining, so all soils should be improved with generous amounts of organic matter. You need to do this the autumn before planting, in readiness for sowing from late April onwards. If you're on heavy clay, it's important that you work the soil well with plenty of well rotted farmyard manure, or your beans won't succeed. Beans have deep-venturing roots and struggle in heavy soil unless it's really well dug over, so incorporate your manure by digging deeply down to at least a spade-and-a-half's depth. Beans also struggle in soil that's too acidic, so lime these soils well in advance to get a pH of between 6.5 and 7. (See Chapter 6 for how to work out your soil's pH level.) Finally, you need to position your beans in a sheltered sunny spot out of strong winds.

A couple of weeks before planting, fork over the soil surface to break it up and create a crumbly texture. Apply a general fertiliser and rake it in.

Beans are extremely sensitive to the cold, so don't be tempted to try to sow seeds too early – they're guaranteed not to make an appearance. Beans need to be sown in a bed that's nice and warm, so even with protection such as a cloche there's little point in trying to get a head start.

To sow your French beans, follow these steps:

1. **If you want an early crop, the best way forward is to plant your seeds indoors on a sunny window sill or in a greenhouse in 8 centimetre pots, or in deep seed modules in early to mid-April.**

   Water them well and keep the temperature above 10 degrees centigrade to ensure germination. Plant two seeds per module and remove the weaker-looking seedling.

2. **Outside, sow the seeds in drills 5 centimetres deep and 15 centimetres apart.**

   A good idea is to plant them closer together towards the end of the row, say every 7.5 centimetres. This is because bean seeds often fail to germinate (sprout), so these extra seedlings can be transplanted into the place of those that fail, or you can plant two seeds together and remove the weaker one if both germinate.

3. **Transplant indoor-grown seedlings into your prepared plot when you are 100 per cent sure that the last frost has passed, which for most will be by late May. It's vital to introduce your seedlings to the great outdoors gently by putting them outside in the day and taking them in at night for a week before planting out, so they don't get too shocked by their change in environment. Plant dwarf varieties in rows of two, 20 centimetres apart, leaving a 40-centimetre gap between rows.**

   Dwarf beans don't require any support and offer a really easy option to the allotmenteer. For climbing varieties, plant them at the base of bean poles 30 centimetres apart (check out Chapter 5 for how to train climbing beans) and make sure that the supports are tall enough, because these plants can reach over 2 metres high in some cases.

When transplanting seedlings onto your plot, plant some more seeds in between them that will grow and mature later than the seedlings. This way you can extend the cropping season with a second flush of tasty beans.

Sow your beans in succession right from April through until the end of June. This gives you a crop in autumn. For early and late sowings, choose varieties that are quick growing and fast to mature, so they won't be caught out by a cheeky frost.

Considering varieties

Literally hundreds of French bean varieties are available for you to try, and often the best way to learn which you like is by experimenting. Dwarf varieties are the most popular with gardeners because they don't need any support, which makes life dead easy. However, they only crop over a short period. Or you could choose a climbing variety that offers you a longer season and a much larger crop.

You can get purple beans, white beans, yellow beans, red mottled beans, yard-long beans, wax beans, adzuki beans, borlotto beans . . . the list goes on. My advice is to experiment and try something new every season, so you get variety.

Dwarf beans come in many varieties, some of which are available as climbers as well. Sometimes called bush beans, they don't usually grow over 50 centimetres tall. Have a go at these dwarf beans:

- **Borlotto Firetongue (also known as Lingua di Fuoco).** A really beautiful red and white mottled bean that can be harvested for fresh beans, whole or shelled, but they really shine if left to dry as haricots. This variety comes in both dwarf and climbing forms.
- **Delinel.** Another stringless 'fine' bean that's popular with growers, because it consistently produces heavy crops for gardeners all over!
- **Ferrari.** An aptly named very fast maturing variety that produces 15-centimetre (6-inch) green beans that taste great and are stringless. They're very disease resistant making them a great choice for the organic grower.
- **Purple Teepee.** A great variety that produces loads of purple beans on small plants that only reach about 40–45 centimetres. They're easy to grow, but one downside is the fact that they turn green during cooking; but they're really tasty! A yellow variety called **Golden Teepee** is worth a go as well.
- **Safari.** This variety produces perfectly straight and slender stringless 'fine' beans that are exactly what you would expect from the shelf of your supermarket.
- **Valdor.** A dwarf wax bean that produces great crops of stringless yellow beans that really liven up the dinner plate and palate!
- **Baroma.** This stringless flat bean produces a heavy crop and is fast-maturing, so can be sown late, even into August, to crop in the autumn.

- **Nautica.** A slender green variety that produces black seeds and a heavy crop.
- **Stanley.** Suitable for early and late sowings, this early-maturing variety bears white flowers and slender green beans with white seeds. Tastes great and has good resistance to disease.

Climbing French beans give you a long period of heavy crops and are really satisfying plants to master. They grow quite tall – up to 2 metres. Here are some climbing French beans to try:

- **Algarve.** Produces lovely flat long green beans that are stringless with a great distinctive flavour.
- **Blue Lake.** An abundant producer of lovely rounded beans that, when dried, are perfect for haricots.
- **Cobra.** A really vigorous variety that produce long pale green beans up to 20 centimetres in length.
- **Fasold.** Quite simply fantastic, Fasold produces bumper crops of perfect long round stringless great-tasting beans. It's also good to grow for early crops started under glass. It's slow to produce seed, so lasts for ages on the plant.
- **Goldfield.** Fast becoming an allotment favourite, the Goldfield variety bears unusual flat yellow pods up to 2 centimetres wide that look simply stunning. I even like to use this variety in the garden at home. Grown up a trellis or even over an arch, it make a really decorative yet edible feature.
- **Limka.** A good early-cropping bean that produces perfect long flat beans, very similar to runners but earlier and easier to grow.
- **Mantra.** This plant produces large flat beans early in the season if sown under glass. Really tasty!

Harvesting and storage

French and green beans are usually grown to be eaten while they're still young. They're best eaten before the pods start to bulge where the seeds inside are forming, but even if they mature, you can always pick them and eat the beans inside as fresh flageolets.

Dwarf varieties start to crop in as little as 10–12 weeks and produce beans over a period of a few weeks, but if you pick regularly and water them well, they'll produce more over a longer period. Simply pick the beans as you need them, while they're still young and tender.

Beating the bees

Gardeners often say that if you've struggled with runner beans, French beans are a good alternative. This is because bees aren't good at getting the nectar from runner bean flowers: they tend to chew the backs of the flowers off to get at the rich nectar, with the result that the flowers aren't pollinated and therefore won't produce beans. With French beans, this isn't a problem: the bees have no difficulty getting to the nectar, and pollination is straightforward.

Climbing varieties produce many more beans over a much longer period and, just like dwarf varieties, you simply snap the pods off when you need them. Or you can leave them to mature for flageolets or dry them as haricot beans.

If you have a large crop left over, it's well worth drying the beans. This is really easy to do: just let the pods mature until they start to split, and then remove the beans and dry them on a tray for a three to four days; store them in an airtight jar.

Raising runner beans

Runner beans have to be one of the most eagerly anticipated vegetables on allotments all around the country. They were first brought to the UK from America in the seventeenth century by Charles the First's gardener, John Tradescant, and they were grown for their beauty as an ornamental plant rather than a source of food. But nowadays they've become a familiar sight in gardens and allotments everywhere.

Runner beans can be more fiddly to prepare than French or green beans, but to many this extra hassle is well worth it for the runner beans' superior flavour. They usually need de-stringing and then finely slicing ready for cooking. But the plants are heavy croppers and fairly easy to grow, so are well worth growing.

When growing runner beans, you'll find it fairly common for the flowers not to *set* (produce fruit), which can cause certain growers real problems. If the flowers aren't pollinated, you get no beans. This can be for a number of reasons:

- The bees aren't very good at getting into the flowers to get the nectar and therefore to pollinate the flowers.
- Birds love the nectar and can ruin the flowers.
- If they don't get enough water, the plants fail to produce fruit or simply produce smaller beans.
- If the summer is too hot, the heat can prevent the flowers from setting.

During hot weather you can help the flowers set by spraying them with water that's not too cold.

Getting started with runner beans

Runner beans like soil that never dries out, so require copious amounts of organic matter to do well. Traditionally, people dug long deep trenches in autumn or winter and filled them with any organic matter they could find, such as kitchen waste and green allotment waste, or anything that would've gone on the compost heap. Then in the spring they'd cover the trench with soil and plant the runners into that. As the 'compost' underneath rotted, the soil level dropped into the trench, creating not only a rich organic home for the beans, but also a depression into which water collected, thereby keeping the plants moist. Many people still adopt this method today because it's really effective, but the main thing to remember is that runner beans require lots of compost to grow well, so as long as you dig the ground deeply in trenches with compost, in advance, or with well rotted manure the autumn before, the beans will do fine. Runner beans don't like acid soil, so liming may be necessary to get pH levels to the ideal – between pH 6.5 and pH 7.

TIP: If you line your runner bean trench with wads of damp newspaper, this can really help with moisture retention of your soil. The paper eventually rots down into the soil.

TIP: Spent mushroom compost is easily available and ideal for improving the bed for your runners. It contains quite high levels of calcium, which helps balance the pH levels if your garden is too acidic, and also helps with the moisture retention that's vital for your runners.

Runner beans can grow up to 2 metres high but, in extreme cases, to over 3 metres. They have large foliage, so they easily blow over on windy sites. They also cast a shadow behind them, which may be an issue for other crops. Recently, dwarf varieties have been developed that don't need support, giving the grower more options.

Runner beans grow best in full sun, but will tolerate a little bit of shade. The general rule for sowing runners is to plant them when all risk of frost has passed. You can sow the seeds a week before the last frost – outside directly into the soil – but this can be risky because any frost will damage the seedlings and you will have to replace them. I tend to start them off indoors and plant them out when the frost has well and truly gone. This depends very much on the area you live in; where I live, this is usually in mid-April, but if you live in a more northern area, this could be as late as early June. If you live in a milder part of the country, you can sow a second crop in mid-June to give you some very welcome beans in October.

To sow your runner beans, follow these steps:

1. **Sow your seeds on their ends in 8-centimetre pots or deep cell trays, 4–5 centimetres deep. Put two seeds in each pot to ensure that at least one of them germinates. You can let both of them grow, prick one out and replant it in its own pot or simply remove the weaker one; it all depends on how many plants you need.**
2. **Alternatively, sow the seeds directly into the soil after the last frost. They should be in double rows about 45 centimetres apart with the seeds spaced at 30 centimetres, or just plant a few seeds at the bottom of a wigwam. Put the bean supports in before planting the seeds or young plants, and plant a seed or two at the base of each cane ready to grow up it. For more on this, check out Chapter 5.**
3. **Transplant seedlings, placing one plant at the base of each cane, and water in well. Before planting, be sure to acclimatise your plants to the outside by leaving them out during the day and inside at night for a week or so. Be prepared to offer protection to your plants from the inevitable attack from slugs – they love tender new foliage. For more information on slug protection, see Chapter 5.**
4. **Keep your plants watered well, especially during dry spells, and apply a thick mulch along the rows or under wigwams to help retain moisture in the soil.**
5. **When the plants reach the top of the canes, pinch out the *apical buds* (growing tips), which encourages the plants to produce lateral growth (side shoots).**

If you're planting dwarf varieties, plant them 30 centimetres apart and don't bother with any support or canes. They're bred to grow free standing, much like dwarf French beans. You can plant them in double rows in the same way as French beans. You should also pinch out the apical buds to encourage side shoots, and once the beans appear, spread a layer of straw around the base of each plant to keep the runners off the soil surface, where they're likely to rot. Many gardeners use dwarf varieties if they are short of space, but to my mind it's better to use climbing varieties on wigwams, because these take up even less space than a row of dwarfs.

TIP

Unless you really want to annoy a neighbouring plot holder, be careful where you position your tall bean poles and runner beans. Runner beans can grow anything up to 3–3.5 metres tall if offered a suitable support, so they cast significant shade. This can be handy if you want to build a wall between you and a nosey neighbour, but in all seriousness it can also cause inconvenience to other plot holders, so do be considerate to others.

TIP

Why not plant your runner beans on a trellis panel trained over the sunny side of your shed? Let's face it, sheds aren't usually the most attractive things, so the lovely large foliage and red or white flowers clambering over your shed can make it look rather pretty, even if it's just for a short while.

Considering varieties

Here are some runner beans to try:

- **Lady Di.** About as popular as the princess was herself, they're grown on allotments all over the place for good reason: they're very attractive and tasty, producing long slender stringless beans.
- **Polestar.** Another great stringless bean that carries a heavy crop right through the summer.
- **Red Rum.** A very popular early variety that's pretty much guaranteed to set, ensuring a good crop.
- **Riley.** One of the best British-bred runners around (apart from Linford Christie, that is). It has unique rose flowers and lovely beans up to 25 centimetres in length, which are stringless when picked young. This variety also produces good heavy crops.
- **Scarlet Emperor.** Produces long dark runners that are great for freezing.
- **Streamline Reliably.** A variety producing very early heavy crops of long really tasty runners up to about 40 centimetres long.
- **Teenie Beanie (also known as Rotbluehende).** Produces bunches of relatively small beans up to 15 centimetres long, with loads of flowers and beans – so keep on picking, and it'll keep on giving. Because this is a 'baby vegetable' the beans remain almost stringless.
- **Wisley Magic.** This is an award-winning runner that produces a really heavy crop over a long period. The beans aren't stringless but they make up for that by tasting great.
- **White Apollo.** Bears white flowers that produce really long (up to 30-centimetre) runner beans that are prolific and tasty.

Harvesting and storage

Runner beans benefit from being picked regularly. If the beans are left to mature, the plants stop producing and your crop will finish pretty quickly. They're really generous plants, and the more you pick, the more they produce. Pick the beans when they're young and tender before they start to swell and produce large seeds. Runner beans can also be frozen and store well like this, so if you have a glut (which you will!) you won't waste any.

Broad beans

Broad beans are simply marvellous straight from the allotment and cooked lightly; they have so much more flavour than the flavourless bullets you usually get in the shops, so they're one of my allotment essentials. They do take up a lot of space on the plot and aren't the heaviest croppers, but on the upside they're really easy to grow – in fact, it's child's play. All other beans are frost-tender plants that originate from the Americas, but broad beans tolerate the cold, so can be sown earlier and can withstand all but the hardest winters.

Broad beans love potash, so if you collect wood ash, throw a handful over every 2 metres of broad-bean bed a week or so before planting. Another interesting tip is to dig in some comfrey; as a green manure, it also adds good levels of potash and aids the water-retaining capabilities of the soil.

Getting started with broad beans

Broad beans grow in almost any soil, but actually thrive in heavy soils – even in heavy clay. However, they won't tolerate waterlogged soil, so the usual advice applies – in autumn, use plenty of organic matter and dig it in deeply, adding some comfrey leaves and potash if you have any around. You can always prepare the bed in spring before sowing and planting, as long as the manure you use is really well rotted. Alternatively, dig some home-made compost deeply into the bean plot. Broad beans are a cool-season crop and grow best at under 15 degrees centigrade, so they're best grown in very early spring or in late summer and autumn to avoid the extreme heat of midsummer.

You can sow broad beans in autumn or spring. Autumn-sown crops develop only a few leaves by the onset of winter; these crops can, if necessary, be protected with cloches from snow and frost. They then shoot into life in the spring. The advantage of sowing in autumn is that the plants develop deeper root systems and therefore healthier, more vigorous plants. For spring-sown crops, sow them as early as you can, from February – although usually March – onwards, as soon as the ground has warmed and is no longer frozen. You can keep on sowing in succession right up until June to ensure a constant supply. Some of these very early sowings may not germinate, but it's well worth trying as early as you can.

To sow your broad beans, follow these steps:

1. **Prepare a 5- to 7-centimetre-deep drill (a flat-bottomed trench).**
2. **Sow the seeds 15 centimetres apart, using a trowel to sow individually, 5 centimetres deep. Cover with soil and water well. You can also sow seeds in 8-centimetre pots in February.**

   Place a couple of seeds in each pot, 5 centimetres deep in good potting compost, and keep them in a bright place indoors to germinate. Keep them moist at all times and they'll be ready to plant out when they reach about 10 centimetres in height.
3. **Protect seedlings from attack as soon as you plant them out or they start to emerge.**

   Mice love to nibble the young plants, as do pea and bean weevils. If mice are a problem, cover the seeds and seedlings with a chicken wire mini tunnel to keep them at bay. Have a look at Chapter 5 for tips on keeping your plants healthy. Plants sown in spring are almost certain to be attacked by black fly.

4. **Earth up (see Chapter 9) the plants a little as they grow.**

   Broad beans, unlike many other beans, don't really need any support, but if you earth up around the main stem a little, this can help support the plant. If you're on a windy, exposed site you may want to insert a stake on each corner of the row and run a string line around the row to offer some support to your plants, but this isn't usually needed.

TIP

Black fly usually attack the tender leaves at the top of your broad beans. These are one of the first 'spring greens' available and can be picked and eaten – so don't let the black fly get them. Pick the tips that shoot above the top flowers as a matter course. If this does not work, you may need to spray the plants to kill off the black fly, using an organic fly spray or some soapy lukewarm water.

Considering varieties

A number of different broad bean varieties are out there to try: long-pod types that grow larger and contain around eight seeds; short pods that only contain around four seeds; and also green- and white-seed varieties. Many consider the green-seeded types and short pods the tastiest, and I'd certainly agree. The disadvantage of the short pods is that they take a little longer to produce crops, but I suggest trying a few to see which works best for your needs. Have a go at these:

- **Aquadulce Claudia.** With white seeds in long pods, it's well known as one of the best for autumn sowing.
- **Bunyards Exhibition.** An all-time classic of the past 100 years, which grows lovely long beans with up to eight seeds in each.
- **Express.** Probably the fastest-growing spring-sown variety, which produces a better crop than all others and will survive as a winter-sown crop as well.
- **Jubilee Hysor.** A variety bearing short pods with white seeds inside. Probably the best yielding of all the short pods.
- **Masterpiece Green Long Pod.** Arguably the best green-seeded long pod around. It produces great-tasting beans that are a real treat and also freeze well.
- **Medes.** An award-winning compact variety that produces loads of medium-sized beans.
- **Stereo.** A white-seeded variety that produce pods much like mangetout that, when young, are delicious. They then mature into wonderful broad beans that taste fantastic.

- **The Sutton.** The Sutton is a dwarf white long-pod bean, good for sowing in autumn, and produces a crop of six to eight seeds per pod. Because of its size, it's ideal for small plots or windy sites.

Harvesting and storage

Broad beans are usually ready to pick between 70 and 90 days after spring sowings or, of course, much longer for autumn-sown crops, which are dormant over winter. Many people like to pick broad beans while they're small and tender; the pod can be cooked whole. Soon the pods become too tough for this purpose, and you can then pick them and pop the seeds out of the pods ready to cook and eat. This, for many of us, is one of the delights of vegetable gardening. The pods open easily and by simply running your finger under the seeds, they then pop off into the bowl. You can eat the broad bean seeds at any stage, from when they're little until they grow much bigger and less tender. Personally, I feel they need to be eaten before they get too large, otherwise they become too tough and chewy. You can eat the mature seeds, but ideally the tough skin must be peeled off first – this is a time-consuming task.

Broad beans are ideal for freezing and last ages, while keeping their nutritional value well. They can also be dried easily for storage over winter. To do this, cut the whole plant down and hang it upside down in a dry, airy place. When they're dry, remove the seeds and store them in airtight jars. The seeds need to soak for at least 24 hours before they're ready for cooking, and are best used in stews and soups, where the slow cooking makes them tender and good to eat.

TIP

As soon as your broad bean plants have finished, cut them down to the ground and put them on your compost heap. They'll rot down, adding lots of nitrogen to the heap. This will benefit the plot in the future. Leave the roots in the ground, because they're covered in nitrogen-fixing bacteria that greatly improve the soil ready for whatever you plant there next.

Playing with Pods

You've now looked at some of the more run-of-the-mill legumes that you can grow on your plot. In this section, you can consider the others that you're sure to want to grow. First peas, which you can find fresh in supermarkets in early summer, sold either in the pod or ready shelled for you, but which never seem to have the wonderful flavour of home-grown. Admittedly, the frozen ones are pretty good. Even so, home-grown peas are so satisfying you must give them a go. In this section, you can look at the wonder of growing your own sugarsnap peas – those little treats that are so sweet and crisp and liven up all dishes from stir fries to summer stews, and mangetout, which I also cover. Finally, you get to look at sweetcorn, which is the only grain really worth growing on your plot.

Peas

Fresh peas are a simple pleasure that many never get to taste fresh from the pod. You can choose from a range of pea varieties that suit all types and size of garden. Some can be grown in pots, and others grow into tall productive plants, ideal for cultivating on the allotment. The plants aren't too fussy when it comes to what soil they like and are quite easy to grow.

Getting started with peas

Peas grow on any soil type but benefit from organic matter, lots of sun and a slightly alkaline soil, so liming may be necessary. Sandy soil warms more quickly in spring, so the plants crop a bit earlier, and in heavy clay they crop later. A rich *loam* (soil composed of sand, silt and clay in a relatively even mix – about 40:40:20) is the ideal (as with almost all veg!) and this can be attained with the addition of plenty of organic matter over the years. Peas are cool-climate plants that dislike the intense heat of midsummer in more southerly reaches, so are best grown in early spring to early summer to do well. In milder areas, you can sow peas in autumn that survive through the winter and shoot into life in the spring to get a head start over spring-sown ones.

Peas are grouped in three main groups (like many other vegetables): first early, second early and main-crop varieties. This basically tells you when they mature with first crop coming first and main crop last. They can all be sown from March through until June (and some in autumn to overwinter in mild areas). To sow your peas, follow these steps:

1. **Make a 5-centimetre-deep drill, place the seeds in the bottom with 5-centimetre spacing between them, and cover them over with soil. Sow in single or double rows, around 40–50 centimetres apart, depending on the variety you go for (check the packet for more detailed spacing advice). For double rows, dig a 5-centimetre-wide drill and sow along each edge, and space the rows 45 centimetres apart, depending on the final height of the plant (the taller the plant, the further the spacing, so check the package).**

   Peas can be sown as soon as soil temperatures reach 10 degrees centigrade or more, which is in early spring for most plots, although at this low temperature, germination is slow and not always successful. I like to sow seeds every two weeks right from March into July, so I can keep on picking young tasty peas throughout the summer.

2. **Place some kind of guard over the young plants to stop birds and rodents getting at them. Sow really early seeds under cloches or cloche tunnels to protect them. (See Chapter 3 for more info on cloches.)**

3. **Support your peas.**

   Most varieties need support when they start to grow. Some only reach 45 centimetres tall, whereas others can grow to 1.8 metres, so you will need to check which variety you have and choose a suitable support. Peas produce little twisting tendrils, which they use to attach themselves to the supports and clamber up. You can support your peas in many ways, from pea netting to pea sticks and wire pea frames to bought frames. See the section on creating supports for climbers in Chapter 5 for ideas. One really effective method is to build a wire tent like an upside-down 'V' and grow your peas up either side – the plants will grow up and most of the pods will hang inside the tent, where the birds have no chance of getting them. (Just make sure that the wire mesh is not too small to get your hands through.) But saying that, the old-school pea stick works a treat and can be made from twigs from your own garden or that you find lying around.

4. **Keep your plants well watered when they're flowering and the pods are fattening up.**

TIP

Seeds can also be sown under glass. Get lengths of half-round guttering and drill drainage holes every 5 centimetres or so. Fill the guttering with compost and sow the seeds 5 centimetres apart and a couple of centimetres deep. Keep the seedlings well watered and when they reach about 8–10 centimetres tall, you can slide them out of the guttering straight into a prepared trench on your plot. This method works well and disturbs the seedlings very little. Figure 15-1 shows you how it's done.

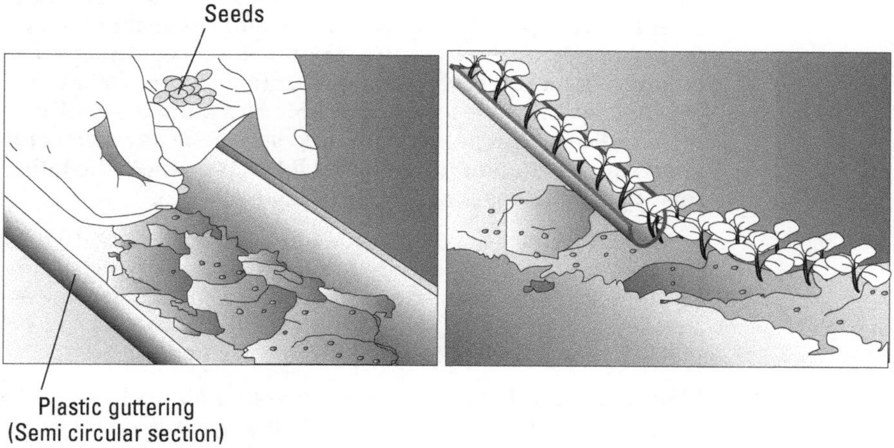

Figure 15-1: Using guttering to slide seedlings into place.

Some peas such as dwarf and semi-leafless varieties can be sown in blocks. Simply push the seeds into the soil to a depth of about 5 centimetres and space them around 13–15 centimetres in all directions in a square block. They will grow and support each other as they grow.

WARNING!

Peas are vulnerable to attack from the minute you place the seeds in the ground. Rodents and birds, especially pigeons and jays, happily swoop on them and gobble them up. They also love the new shoots, which are tasty treats for them. Pea moths are also a problem; for advice on dealing with these, check out Chapter 7.

COOKING TIP

Dried peas are excellent for using in soups. Pea and bacon (or ham) is a classic combination that's sure to please. Fry an onion and some finely shredded bacon in some oil and add a large chopped carrot and a parsnip. Then add bay leaf and a couple of pints of stock and 250 grams of dried peas (soaked the previous night for at least eight hours). Simmer for a couple of hours then add 100 millilitres of single cream or milk and season to taste. Reheat and serve with some finely chopped crispy bacon sprinkled on top and a sprinkle of chopped mint.

Considering varieties

Peas are grouped as first early, second early and main-crop varieties, which is significant if you're going to plant just once or twice in the spring. To provide a constant supply, sow varieties that mature at different times. Many gardeners plant in succession using fast-maturing varieties. This gives you more control and you can have a constant supply of young fresh peas; the early-maturing varieties are much better for impatient gardeners. You also get rounded and wrinkled peas; the rounded peas are generally not as sweet and more hardy, making them better for early sowing, whereas the wrinkled ones are usually much sweeter and less hardy.

Try these first early peas:

- **Avola:** A good-quality very early pea, perfect for autumn sowing, especially in milder areas. Elsewhere, sow in early spring. It reaches about 60–65 centimetres.
- **Douche Provence:** A really early round-pea variety that can be planted from autumn well into winter for a head start in spring, or in spring for successional sowings. It's a dwarf variety – a cross between Meteor and the ever-popular Kelvedon Wonder (see below) – that reaches 45 centimetres.
- **Feltham First:** This is a very early rounded-seed variety that's really hardy, making it perfect for sowing in early spring or autumn. Reaches 45centimetres tall.
- **Twinkle:** This pretty new variety produces tasty peas in heavy crops. It has some mildew resistance and is resistant to wilt (see Chapter 7 for more information). It reaches about 45 centimetres.

Here are some second earlies:

- **Ambassador:** An award-winning variety that offers great-tasting heavy crops in 12–14 weeks. It's disease resistant, making it ideal for organic growers. It reaches 70 centimetres.
- **Jaguar:** A heavy-cropping pea that is ideal for successional sowings from March to June, ready for picking from June to September. It reaches 65–75 centimetres.
- **Kelvedon Wonder:** Probably the most popular variety around, this is a wrinkled pea type that produces prolifically and is ideal for successional sowings. It reaches 45 centimetres.

And finally some main crops:

- **Alderman:** This is a really popular and very tall variety that reaches up to 2 metres in height. Late to mature, it offers heavy crops of great-tasting peas over a long period.
- **Hurst Green Shaft:** Another wrinkled pea type that averages between 9 and 11 peas per pod. It's a really heavy cropper with double pods at each node and tastes amazing! Reaches 70–75 centimetres tall.
- **Oasis:** A British-bred pea that produces massive crops of delicious dark green peas. Gets to 60–70 centimetres tall.
- **Onward:** A popular dwarf pea that produces large pods packed with tasty peas on a 60-centimetre plant.
- **Rondo:** This fantastic variety is undoubtedly a far better option than the very popular Onward variety. It produces ten wrinkled peas per pod in really heavy yields – simply the best! The plants are 70 centimetres tall.
- **Waverex:** A really popular petit-pois type pea that produces the tiniest, sweetest peas around. The plants are 75 centimetres tall.

You may also want to explore the types of pea where you can eat the whole pod. These include favourites such as mangetout and sugarsnap peas, which are just as easy to grow as the regular peas. Try these:

- **Carouby de Maussane:** A French *heirloom variety* (older and non-hybrid) that carries very sweet, flat 'mangetout' pods on pretty plants up to 140 centimetres tall. It also looks attractive in an ornamental garden, with its simply beautiful purple flowers.
- **Delikett:** Produces abundant crops of sugarsnap peas that need no preparation from plant to pot and are really sweet crisp with a lovely crunch. The plants reach 75 centimetres.

- **Oregon Sugar Pod:** Probably the most reliable mangetout-type pea around, and therefore popular. It's ideal for organic growers because of its disease resistance and also has a really sweet, delicate flavour. The plants reach 100 centimetres.
- **Sugarsnap:** A really good variety with young pods you can eat in the same way as French beans. It develops sweet, crunchy pods that are good in salads. The plants are 100 centimetres tall.

Harvesting and storage

Peas are best picked young so they don't become hard and lose their sweetness. Early crops are ready in 11–12 weeks, main crops being a little slower and ready after 13–14 weeks. Harvest mangetout-type peas while the seeds are small and the pods are immature; for peas and sugarsnaps, wait for the pods to swell, and harvest regularly. Peas can be frozen, but to me this is a dreadful waste; eat them fresh if you can. If you have a glut, however, don't waste them. Peas can also be dried for use over winter, and this is done in the same way as for French beans.

Sweetcorn

Sweetcorn is a late-summer treat that should not be missed, and home-grown is sweeter and tastier than anything you can buy off the shelf (I seem to say that about every vegetable in this book, but it's true!). This is because the sugars start turning to starch immediately the cobs have been picked. Sweetcorn is a member of the Gramineae (grass) family, which includes all the cereal crops, but sweetcorn is the only grain that is actually eaten as a vegetable and is harvested when the seeds aren't fully mature and hard. Sweetcorn grows well on any reasonably fertile soil, but it must have a sunny and sheltered site. The other factor critical to success is that sweetcorn must be planted in blocks to ensure good pollination, because unlike most other vegetables, it's pollinated by the wind. Each plant carries male and female flowers. The male flowers are carried as tassels on the top that produce and release the pollen. The pollen is transferred by the wind down to the female flowers – the fluffy, silky tufts lower down the plant – so planting sweetcorn in blocks ensures good pollination.

TIP

Sweetcorn is a quite slow-growing crop, so many gardeners grow faster-growing crops amongst them to make the most of the available space. Most salad leaves can be grown between sweetcorn plants whilst the sweetcorn is small, especially smaller varieties such as Little Gem lettuce. But the most usual is to grow a dwarf French bean that will happily grow amongst the developing sweetcorn.

Getting started with sweetcorn

Sweetcorn takes a long time to grow and mature and requires a long warm period to do well, so the best way to be sure of a crop is to get a head start by sowing under cover. Also, over the years, new varieties of sweetcorn have been developed that mature much faster, meaning that most of us can easily grow our own delicious sweetcorn. Sweetcorn likes a deep, rich loamy organic soil that's well drained and rich in nutrients. It struggles in heavy clay, so the usual improvements need to be made by digging in plenty of organic matter. It will grow in sandy soils, but again the soil needs plenty of manure added to improve the soil's moisture retention and nutrient content. It's best grown in a sheltered, really sunny spot, and needs three to four months of decent sunny weather to thrive. You can, however, get quick-maturing varieties that can handle less sun and warmth if they're planted nice and early to get a head start.

To sow your sweetcorn, follow these steps:

1. **Sow in seed modules or in small pots indoors, four weeks before the expected date of the last frost. Sow the seeds 2 centimetres deep in any good compost, and place two seeds per module; as soon as you spot the weaker one, remove it to allow space for the stronger.**

   I usually sow the seeds in small biodegradable pots, water them and then pop the pots into my mini greenhouse propagator. You can put them into clear plastic bags or cover them with cling film. This helps to germinate the seeds quickly – in 7–12 days – after which you can remove them from the bags and place them on a sunny window sill.

2. **Transplant indoor-sown plants into blocks at 30-centimetre spacings as soon as the threat of frost has well and truly passed.**

   It's best to get sweetcorn acclimatised to the outdoors for a week or two by hardening the plants off outside during the day and bringing them in at night. Sweetcorn doesn't like being transplanted, so be sure to do this as gently as possible so as not to disturb the roots too much. If the plants are in biodegradable pots, plant them as they are in the pots. The plants should be around 16 centimetres tall. Space them 30 centimetres apart in blocks.

You can also sow outdoors, directly on your plot, if you live in one of the milder areas of the country, but the soil must be warm enough first. Sweetcorn won't germinate at temperatures lower than 10 degrees centigrade, so sowing directly in early spring, before the soil has warmed sufficiently, is pointless. You can place black plastic sheeting over the soil to help warm it up in the spring, or even invert halved plastic bottles on the soil like mini greenhouses. If left on the soil for a few weeks, these help warm the right spot. Sow at the spacings given below, placing 2–3 seeds in each station and thinning to leave the strongest seedling.

Sow the seeds in square blocks 2–5 centimetres deep with 7 centimetres between each seed. You normally get two or three cobs per plant, so the size of the block you plant depends on how big a crop you require. A larger block performs better than a small block, because sweetcorn is wind pollinated. As the seedlings begin to germinate and reach 2 centimetres high, thin them to 30-centimetre spacings.

Once the tassels start to form, you must keep the sweetcorn well watered or you run the risk of having a poor crop. Give the crop a mulch to help retain moisture in the soil and improve the crop; doing so can result in the cobs maturing a week or two earlier than otherwise. Some people like to earth up around the main stem as well, which is a simple case of drawing the soil up around the base, helping the plant produce more roots and improving its vigour.

Slugs attack the young plants, so offer your plants protection until they reach around 15 centimetres tall. At that point they'll be tough enough to cope. This isn't a problem for pot-reared seedlings that are planted out after this vulnerable period.

Place netting over your cobs to prevent birds and mice decimating them.

Considering varieties

Of the many different varieties of sweetcorn, some are ideal for a small gardens, only growing to around 1.2 metres tall, but others may reach the heady height of 3.5 metres in perfect conditions. Other 'supersweet' varieties have a special sugar gene bred into them. They contain far more sugar than normal varieties, giving them a longer shelf life and enabling companies to can the corn without the need to add sugar. Grow supersweet varieties at least 10 metres away from other varieties, or they cross-pollinate and lose their sweetness. Try these:

- **Ashworth.** Ashworth is pretty hard to track down but is one of only a few non-hybrid varieties available today. It's an excellent choice for those who want to 'keep it real' and eat crops that aren't interfered with (see Chapter 8 for more on these). Ashworth is an easy-to-grow, adaptable variety that bears lovely sweet cobs that are early maturing.
- **Early Bird F1.** A really quick-to-mature 'supersweet' variety offering good-quality cobs. It can germinate well in cooler soils.
- **Honey Bantam Bicolour.** This lovely sweet variety offers yellow and white kernels and is fast to mature. An absolute winner in all respects!
- **Lark F1.** An easy-to-grow variety that offers kernels with a much thinner skin than other varieties, making it a tasty, sweet, tender treat.
- **Mini Pop F1.** A mini variety that's perfect for stir fries. Space plants 15 centimetres apart.

- **Ovation F1.** This vigorous variety produces abundant crops of very sweet cobs.
- **Rising Sun F1.** A sweet variety that produces large cobs. This variety is known to produce a strong root system, which, coupled with earthing up during growth, makes it a variety ideal for exposed sites.
- **Sundance F1.** Ideally suited to the British climate, Sundance F1 works well during cooler summers.

Harvesting and storage

Sweetcorn takes between 65 and 90 days to reach maturity; baby sweetcorn is ready sooner. You can easily tell when sweetcorn is ready to harvest if you follow these simple tips:

1. **When the tassels at the end of the cobs turn brown, start checking the cobs to see whether they're ripe.**
2. **Gently expose the end of the cob through the husk and push your fingernail against a kernel. If a milky sap comes out, it's good to go!**

Pull the cob sharply down to remove it from the plant then get it straight home and into the pot – as soon as sweetcorn is picked, the sugar starts turning into starch, so the sooner you eat it the better. You can also freeze sweetcorn whilst still on the cob by boiling the cobs for three to four minutes, allowing them to cool and placing them in dated freezer bags in the freezer, where they will keep for three months or more.

Chapter 16

Growing More Unusual Veg

In This Chapter

- Getting to grips with all the artichokes
- Warming things up with peppers and chillies
- Growing the finest asparagus, celery and okra

Some vegetables don't easily fit into the groups described in other chapters in this book. Some have nutty, edible roots and others are tender shoots that feature on the menus of Michelin-starred restaurants. Some of these exotic vegetables are a challenge to grow and can test your gardening abilities but others are child's play. If you want to hone your skills and delight your taste buds, read on.

Growing Artichokes

The term *artichoke* covers many different vegetables, including globe, Jerusalem and Chinese artichokes, and working out the similarities between them, even if they're related, isn't easy. Globe artichokes are cultivated for their large heads, which are flowers surrounded by lovely fleshy, edible *bracts* (modified leaves around the base of the flower), and the fantastic tender heart so prized by chefs. Jerusalem artichokes are grown for their edible tubers, which are formed underground and have a nutty flavour. Globe and Jerusalem artichokes are distantly related, but the latter is more closely related to the sunflower. Meanwhile, Chinese artichokes are totally unrelated to the other two but are also cultivated for their tuberous roots. The following sections describe each in detail.

Globe artichokes

Globe artichokes (*Cynara scolymus*) are statuesque, beautiful and striking in appearance and are grown both for eating and as ornamental plants in gardens. They reach up to 1.5 metres in height, and take up quite a lot of space.

They're only really suited to allotments where they have plenty of space to grow. The good thing about them is that they're perennial, which means once you've planted them they come back year upon year. Even though they look like something from some tropical hideaway, they're actually cool-climate plants that prefer temperatures not exceeding 18 °C (but are fine at a higher temperature when established). They tolerate light frosts and grow best in fertile, well drained soil with plenty of manure dug in. They require an open site but don't like to be too exposed to cold or drying winds.

Globe artichokes are often listed in catalogues as *Cynara cardunculus* but that's actually a close relative, the Cardoon. You also see globes listed as *Cynara cardunculus* 'Scolymus group'.

Getting started with globe artichokes

Globe artichokes are usually propagated through division, which means they're dug up in early spring as they start to shoot and the roots split (divided) into multiple new plants. You must make sure that each new bit has at least two new shooting 'eyes' and plenty of roots so when re-planted will sprout into new plants. But you can also start them off from seed. To sow your globe artichokes, follow these steps:

1. **Sow seeds indoors in 8 centimetre diameter pots in a bright warm place, at around 20 °C. In these conditions they'll shoot quickly.**
2. **Grow on indoors until they are large enough to plant out – when 5-6 leaves have formed. Harden off over a period of a couple of weeks.**
3. **Plant them out with a metre between each plant and offer protection from slugs who nibble away at them happily.**

Water your plants well during dry spells or they'll die, and keep them free from weeds.

Seeds can also be sown outdoors in spring when conditions are warm enough. Success is touch-and-go but you should get some popping up. When you do, you need to thin out to 1 metre apart.

Your plants like a deep mulch to help them retain moisture, and they need watering during dry spells, but apart from that they're easy to look after. On the allotment they need a spot outside of the rotation system (see Chapter 6) because they require a permanent home. During hard winters earth up the base where the stems show just above the ground – it also helps to pile some straw over the top and weigh or pin it down. Globe artichokes need to be divided every three years to keep stocks healthy and to give you new plants to lay out. Only divide the healthiest looking specimens and discard those that are struggling.

Considering varieties

Varieties are limited out there, but this doesn't matter as most are good to eat. Some varieties have little thorns at the tip of each bract which some people remove before cooking. Give the following ones a go:

- **Emerald.** This hybrid variety tolerates both hot and cold conditions so is suited to most situations. It's also thornless.
- **Green globe.** This is the most popular variety and easy to find.
- **Violetto.** A purple-scaled monster that reaches heady heights and tastes great.

Harvesting and storage

Ideally, you should wait until their second year to harvest artichokes. At this point they'll have become well established, but you may get a few decent heads in the first year. They should be cut leaving about 10 centimetres of stem before the scales start to open and the buds are nice and plump. The tallest are the first to be ready. Pick the others as soon as they're ready, before they open into the large, purple, thistle-like flowers – they look great but are no good to eat! Prepare your artichokes by removing the outer scales. Remove the *choke* (the hairy mass inside the globe just above the prized heart) after cooking, and the stem. You can also freeze or pickle your produce.

COOKING TIP

Globe artichokes are great fun to eat; the French simply boil them gently for about 30 minutes and scrape the base of each fleshy bract with their teeth to remove the tasty flesh. You can also eat the inner heart with a spoon once the hairy choke is removed. You can prepare them by removing all the bracts until the white heart is exposed, then peeling away the dark green to expose the tender middle. Quarter the artichokes, to make chokes easy to cut out from each quarter. You can then steam them, fry them in olive oil, pickle them and use them in many dishes from salads to pastas and on pizzas. The only downside is that they're hard work to prepare for such as small amount of food – but well worth it!

TIP

Don't waste a bottle of good wine whilst eating globe artichokes. They confuse your palate, so only drink cheap plonk with them!

Jerusalem artichokes

Jerusalem artichokes are quite easy to grow and aren't that fussy about the soil they grow in, so are the ideal vegetable for beginners and children. The plant is basically a perennial sunflower, but in our climate it doesn't often produce flowers. If it does, they're stunningly beautiful. In perfect conditions Jerusalem artichokes can reach up to 3 metres in height. They can become *invasive* (spreading into areas they're not supposed to be in), so at the end of the season it's worth digging them up and treating them like annual plants, so they don't invade too much.

Jerusalem artichokes are often grown as windbreaks on allotments and in gardens because they quickly produce a tall wall of foliage that's ideal for filtering strong winds and protecting other plants. This is a little ironic, because they're about the worst vegetable for causing flatulence you can possibly come across – if you thought sprouts were bad, wait till you try these little puppies! But please don't let that put you off – they're a delicacy.

Getting started with Jerusalem artichokes

Jerusalem artichokes grow in most soil as long as it's not waterlogged. As with most crops. if the soil is improved with plenty of manure, the crops are superior. Usually, Jerusalem artichokes are kept in the same spot year upon year. As they're perennial, you're unlikely to get all the tubers up every season so you're best keeping them in one spot. You can always mulch with organic matter each winter to keep the area alive.

You always find Jerusalem artichokes available for sale as tubers, not as seeds, and these are either knobbly artichoke tubers or the smooth 'Fuseau' type. You'll be hard-pushed to find any other varieties but many allotmenteers will happily donate you some tubers that may well have been passed around the site for many years, so they could be an old variety.

To sow your Jerusalem artichokes, follow these steps:

1. **Plant the tubers from autumn to early spring, 40– 60 centimetres apart and 12 centimetres deep, in a row. If you have more than one row, plant the rows 70 centimetres apart. One word of caution, though: be careful where you site Jerusalem artichokes, because they easily reach over 2 metres high and can cast a long shadow over your plot. Most people plant them in front of a shed where they don't cause any problems.**
2. **Earth the plants up, like potatoes (see Chapter 9), when they reach 30 centimetres. Doing so stimulates roots at the bottom to grow and increases yields.**
3. **Support them with canes and string: even though may people plant them as windbreaks, the plants can snap on exposed sites. Position them carefully.**

Considering varieties

Try the following varieties of Jerusalem artichoke:

- **Dwarf Sunray.** A dwarf variety that reaches 1.5–2 metres in height.
- **Fuseau.** A smooth-skinned variety that makes for easy peeling and preparation.
- **Garnet.** A smooth variety with red skin.

Harvesting and storage

Harvesting your artichokes is just a case of digging them up when you need them in late autumn. Many gardeners cut the foliage down to 30 centimetres above the ground when it starts to die back, so as to leave as a marker. If you live in an area that suffers from hard winters you're best lifting them all before it sets in, and storing them in crates of moist compost, covered in a cool, dark place until needed. Alternatively, cover them in your plot with a deep layer of straw for protection.

Chinese artichokes

Chinese artichokes are totally unrelated to globe and Jerusalem artichokes and are also known as *knotroot* or *crosne*. They aren't a common sight on allotments and are grown for their edible tuberous roots in the same way as Jerusalem artichokes. They're as easy to grow as Jerusalem artichokes but aren't as big. The plants produce the weirdest-looking tubers; they look like large grubs. Don't let that put you off, though, because they taste absolutely lovely. They're not a popular vegetable for growers, because they're fiddly to prepare. They're so knobbly it's next to impossible to peel them but you can scrub them with a nailbrush, which works just fine. They are only 5 centimetres long so you need lots to feed each person and you sometimes see them on fine restaurant menus.

Getting started

Chinese artichokes are easy to grow. Follow the same steps as for Jerusalem artichokes (see the earlier section) but sow them closer together. They grow best in well manured, free-draining soil in full sun or part shade. They do grow in heavy soils but if grown in heavy clay are very hard to clean, so you may be better off planting them in raised beds with imported topsoil, which makes it easier to clean them.

Chinese artichokes are only ever available as tubers that are ready to plant. They should be planted in February and March, in prepared soil, 30 centimetres apart and 8–10 centimetres deep. Plant them in rows 40 centimetres apart.

And that's it! They spring up and produce lovely spikes of small pink/purpled flowers in the summer. By autumn they are ready to harvest.

Considering varieties

Only one variety of Chinese artichoke exists – *Stachys affinis* – and that's your lot! You can order it from many seed companies.

Harvesting and storage

As well as being easy to grow, Chinese artichokes are easy to harvest. In the autumn cut them down to just above ground level, which surprisingly enough helps the tubers fatten up and grow slightly larger. Then simply dig them up as required. In exactly the same way as Jerusalem artichokes, they'll reappear next year if you don't dig all the little tubers up, but because they don't suffer from any significant pests or diseases this needn't affect your crop rotation system. If they do reappear you get more to eat next year.

Chinese artichokes need to be scrubbed well to remove the skin and any grit from the many crevices they have. They can be used in the same way as Jerusalem artichokes or they can be eaten raw, which is how I like them. You can also steam them very quickly to keep their crunch – overcooking makes them mushy and unpleasant. The Chinese usually pickle them and dye them red using red shiso leaves. This is known locally as *Chorogi*, a traditional garnish served with Chinese New Year feasts.

Growing Simple Yet Impressive Veg

All the vegetables in this section bear fruit. Bell peppers are sweet and absolutely delicious, chilli peppers are hot and fiery and the beautiful aubergine is dark and bitter. They're all easy to grow, and can be real showstoppers. All these vegetables are well suited to Mediterranean dishes and if you grow your own tomatoes, are a match made in heaven. These vegetables are best kept in a polytunnel or greenhouse but you can also sow them indoors and then transplant them outside during a warm summer as long as your site is sunny and sheltered; they just won't grow quite as big and ripen later.

Bell peppers

Most growers fill you with tales of woe when it comes to growing sweet peppers on the allotment, and in many circumstances crops are disappointing; the peppers tend to be small and bitter, and the plants stunted and ineffective. Even so, I've had some great plants in the past simply grown in pots on a patio that produce abundant tasty crops that can save a fortune on shopping bills.

I've even removed the seeds from supermarket-bought sweet red peppers and sown them with great success. Allotments can often be very exposed, which can be problematic for peppers, but if you can provide a sheltered spot with plenty of sunlight they should be okay. They can also be grown in polytunnels, or in the green house where conditions can be more controlled.

Getting started with peppers

Peppers need lots of warmth and plenty of sunshine to produce worthwhile plants and fruits. They grow in most soil types, preferring light soil with plenty of compost, and requiring constant feeding and watering. If you turn your back for more than a day during a dry spell, they wither quickly (although you can get them back from the brink if you're quick with the watering can!). They're slightly hardier than tomatoes, but even in the warmest southern climate are best grown under glass. Try growing some in and some out to compare. To produce fruits peppers need temperatures above 19 °C while in flower.

1. **Sow seeds in potting compost, in modules, six to eight weeks before the last likely frost date, with two seeds planted 1 centimetre deep in each cell. Keep them indoors at this stage.**
2. **Keep the seeds above 20 °C until they start to germinate and show above the compost. Don't allow the temperature at night to fall below 12 °C as this causes the seedlings to become stunted.**
3. **Thin out the weakest seedlings in each module.**
4. **Transplant seedlings into 8 centimetre pots when the seedlings are large enough to handle. Then transplant again into 12.5-centimetre pots when large enough.**
5. **Plant out hardened off plants when the ground has warmed well in mid–late spring. Plant out in well prepared soil with 40 centimetres between plants, in rows 60 centimetres apart. Peppers like to be planted deep, as the roots become easily exposed if they're planted too shallow.**

Water the plants regularly and feed weekly with a balanced liquid feed. Watering is especially important whilst they're young, so the plants grow with enough vigour to support the fruits. Always water the roots and not the foliage or fruits because water on the fruit causes rot. As soon as the flowers open and start to produce small fruits, feed weekly with a liquid tomato feed.

WARNING!

Anthracnose is a fungal disease that can quickly wipe out your entire crop. You can identify it by the circular lesions that appear on the fruit, which quickly spread to other fruits in the crop. You may also notice small spots on the leaves. No cure exists for this, so remove any infected fruit quickly, because rain washes the spores onto other healthy fruits, and the infection quickly spreads. Beans can carry this disease, so plant peppers well away from them or they're more than likely to become infected.

Considering varieties

Quite a few varieties of pepper are on the market. Go out and buy any pepper you like from your local greengrocer and grow the seeds from them: this usually works. But you can also buy seeds, so you know exactly what you're getting and can select a variety that suits your growing conditions. In this country it's advisable to source a fast-maturing type because our summers are so unpredictable and not always the warmest! You can also buy ready-grown plants from many garden centres, but the varieties are limited and you're often taking pot luck. Buying young plants by mail order from specialist suppliers will give you a wider choice of varieties. Try these:

- **Antohi Romanian:** This is an old variety that produces small but intensely sweet red peppers. It can be grown in a container and is a heavy cropper that matures fast.
- **Big Banana F1:** As its great name suggests, it produces big, banana-shaped peppers up to 25 centimetres long that turn bright red. In ideal conditions it produces masses of fruit per plant (up to 50). Best grown under glass but performs well during warm summers.
- **Corno di Giallo:** An Italian long yellow pepper commonly known as Yellow Bull's Horn due to its appearance. These peppers do have a slight spicy edge to their flavour which I personally love.
- **Feher Ozon Paprika:** Produces small orange fruits that can be eaten fresh or is great for making your own paprika. Hang plants to dry and then grind the dried flesh – simple!
- **Jumbo Giant:** Produces massive red fruits up to 25 centimetres long that are bright red or green when young. Jumbo Giant works best under glass but is well worth trying outdoors during a warm summer down south.
- **Sweet Chocolate:** This is chocolate-brown pepper specially bred to mature early in cool climates – definitely worth a shot!
- **World Beater.** A heavy cropper that can be planted outdoors in warm summers, but is best grown under glass.

Harvesting and storage

Peppers take much longer to mature during cool summers, and ripen much quicker under glass. They should be cut from the plants with an inch or so of the stem still attached to the fruit and eaten fresh, but they keep for a week or so in the fridge. All peppers are green before they become orange or red and can be picked whilst green, before they turn. I think they're best picked when fully ripe because this is when they have the best flavour. Many books and articles say that picking them while they're green encourages plants to produce more fruits than if you let them mature. But in my experience they keep on producing no matter how ripe you allow the fruits to become. I've stripped entire plants of ripe red fruits and within a couple of days new ones were appearing.

Chilli peppers

Chilli peppers are so easy to grow and do well even in slightly cool climates. Saying that, they do like really hot summers and lots of sunshine but are so productive you only need a few plants unless you're a chilli-munching monster! Many gardeners only to grow them every other year because a couple of plants give so many chillies they'll keep you going for ages, and they can easily be dried and stored. Chilli plants look cool and grow well in pots, where they won't grow so big but still produce many. Chilli plants look similar to sweet peppers, and the fruits start off being green or purple and turn to yellow, orange and red – sometimes with all these colours on the same plant.

Getting started with chilli peppers

You grow chillies in the same way as sweet peppers (see the earlier section on them) and should treat them in exactly the same manner. They're sown in the same way, so follow the instructions in the previous section to find out how to go about it. Chillis do need plenty of warmth to grow well, and it's best to start them off indoors in the conservatory or green house. When they're large enough, and the weather is warm, move them outside. They are best planted on the plot in well manured, free-draining soil in full sun. Tall varieties may need staking to give them support.

Considering varieties

Chillies come in a massive range of varieties from fierce Scotch Bonnet (*Habaneros*) to the milder, small *Padron* peppers that are picked young and eaten whole as a tapas dish. Some plants only grow to 30 centimetres high, yet others can reach well over a metre and produce literally hundreds of chillies, so choose a variety that fits the space you have and how hot you like them!

Here are some to try:

- **Gelbe Kirschen:** A really unusual variety that produces perfectly round, yellow chillies that pack a real punch. They're quite rare and a real talking point.
- **Inferno F1:** Producing large waxy chillies on neat compact plants, this variety crops nice and early and over a long period.
- **Jalapenos:** Quite a few varieties are available and some do need warmth to mature so they need a long hot summer or to be grown under glass. They have a distinct scarring on the skin that's a unique feature of this chilli. Choose an early maturing variety to get the best results.
- **Meek and Mild:** Just about the mildest chilli you can find and a 'poblana' type ideal for Mexican dishes. Meek and Mild is ideal for growing indoors or out, in pots or in situ.

- **Naga Morich:** Claimed to be one of the hottest chillies on the planet and only for the serious chilli connoisseur. This chilli should come with a health warning and if you do grow it never leave them in reach of children and do handle them with care.
- **Thai Dragon F1:** As hot as a thousand devils, it does best in the greenhouse but thrives outside if summers are warm.

Harvesting and storage

Chillies can be harvested as soon as they're large enough to bother with. You can never strip a plant, as the more you pick the more they grow. On any one plant you may well have chillies at different stages of maturity. The younger green ones are milder, and as they mature and change colour the flavour intensifies and develops. Most people just use chillies for adding heat, but they do have a distinct flavour that can also be appreciated; young jalapeno peppers are a lovely treat stuffed with cream cheese and covered in bread crumbs and fried. The flavour isn't just hot, it tastes of sweet peppers.

TIP

If you like really hot chillies you can *stress* them a few days before harvesting by flooding them with water or allowing them to wilt. This stress causes the plant to increase the heat in the fruits.

The best way to store peppers is to dry them, which is dead easy. You may read about fancy methods of plaiting your chillies and tying them up in all sorts of artistic ways, but I find in the late summer or even in autumn you can simply cut the whole plant down, tie it in a bunch, then hang it up to dry in a conservatory. If the weather's really dry, you can dry them outside in the sun.

COOKING TIP

Dried chillies can be used in exactly the same way as fresh ones, just chopped and thrown into any dish that requires heat. You can also grind them down and store them as dried chilli flakes. A jar of these will last you for years! Alternatively, turn your fresh chillies into a chilli sauce and freeze it for future use.

Aubergines

Aubergines are beautiful vegetables that are impressive and tasty, but in all but the warmest area of the UK are usually suitable for the greenhouse only. Not only is the fruit gorgeous, but the foliage is lovely and the purple, star-shaped flowers stunning. They're perennial plants, and can be grown as such if you never get a frost; if you live in an area that gets even the slightest hint of frost, however, you must grow them as annuals. They need hot summers to do well and like a deeply dug, rich soil – with plenty of manure – that's free-draining and doesn't become waterlogged.

Many books claim that if you can grow tomatoes you can grow aubergines but I'm afraid this isn't the case. Although they're closely related and members of the same family, aubergines need much warmer conditions and humidity to ripen well. Even down south, where conditions are more favourable, you still need to offer them protection and start them off early to have any chance. They require a very sheltered spot out of the wind and in full sun. Saying that, though, they can be a lot of fun and a success.

Aubergines are traditionally sliced and sprinkled with salt and then fried or grilled. In Cyprus they place a heavy weight on top of the salted slices, squeezing out the excess water and helping reduce the bitterness often associated with this vegetable. Aubergines are a vital ingredient in moussaka, in which they're layered with fried minced lamb and béchamel sauce. One invaluable tip when making moussaka is to add dried mint and cinnamon to the mince, which gives the dish a truly authentic flavour. For a perfect béchamel sauce add a couple of egg yolks to make it really rich and another whole egg to help it set. Aubergines are also commonly used in curries and oriental dishes, especially baby aubergines and the small Thai aubergines (also called *pea* or *apple* aubergines) that resemble small berries.

Getting started with aubergines

Aubergines aren't easy to grow; they depend entirely on good soil, lots of warmth and plenty of light. They like soil enriched with plenty of compost or manure and benefit greatly from a good dose of general fertiliser before planting or sowing. To sow your aubergines, follow these steps:

1. **Sow seeds under glass from February to April in a seed module with one seed per cell. Sow seeds in a cold greenhouse in April in the same manner. Try to use a heated propagator, to maintain a constant temperature of 18–21 °C.**
2. **Transplant seedlings. Put March-sown seedlings into 8-centimetre pots in April, and pot April-sown seedlings in May.**
3. **Transplant seedlings when they have four or more leaves into their permanent position outside, or in 30-centimetre pots to be placed in the greenhouse. If outside they need fleece protection if the weather is cool. It's a good idea to build a frame around them that can be wrapped in fleece if necessary.**
4. **Keep the plants moist but not waterlogged at all times. After you've planted them out give them a liquid feed once a week.**
5. **Stake plants to give them support, and gently tie in the stems. As soon as the first fruits set they benefit from a good dose of potash, which helps them form larger fruits (comfrey tea is ideal if you want to make your own; liquid tomato fertiliser is fine as well).**

6. **Pinch out the tips when they reach 45 centimetres in height. Doing so encourages side shoots to develop and the plant to bush out. When you see three or four fruits develop, remove any other side shoots that start to form. This makes the plant concentrate its energy into fattening up the existing fruits as opposed to growing more, smaller ones.**

TIP

Many gardeners grow most of their aubergines in the greenhouse or small polytunnels, and then if they have any extra plants they can plant the rest outside. Aubergines make pretty, ornamental plants and even if they don't produce a good crop they look cool.

Considering varieties

Lots of different aubergine varieties are available to choose from. Try these:

- **Baby Roseanna F1:** A baby aubergine that's ideal in containers, producing small, round fruits on a compact plant.
- **Bonica F1:** Producing large purple fruits on a very early-to-crop plant, this variety is ideal for containers and best in the greenhouse. As with many early plants, it may well succeed outdoors if in the right situation.
- **De Barbentane:** Bred in France specifically for outdoor growing, De Barbentane is a *non-hybrid* (so you can collect the seeds), early maturing variety that can be grown outside even in the UK, but as with all aubergines is better off in the greenhouse. If grown outside, it benefits from some cover. It produces medium-sized purple fruits.
- **Listada de Gandia:** This aubergine bears cool-looking fruits that are pale purple with white strips. You don't need to pinch out the growing tips on this great variety. It's happy in pots, growbags, or outside when the risk of frost has passed.
- **Moneymaker:** A popular variety, being very productive and fairly easy to grow even during our summers. It produces large, tasty fruits.
- **Snowy:** Produces pale green, almost white fruits that mature early, so it's ideal for our unpredictable British summers.
- **Thai Light Round Green:** Produces small 'pea' aubergines that are often used in Thai curries. Also look for 'Thai Pea Green' that's a slightly darker-fruiting variety.

Harvesting and storage

Aubergines should be harvested when they're firm but not too hard and before they start to wrinkle. You can pick them early and eat them as baby veg, but it's advisable to use the appropriate variety or they may well be under-ripe and hard. Aubergines are best used within a week of picking, but in cooked dishes such as moussaka they can be frozen. One of the best ways to use excess crops is to make chutney, paté or tapanades.

To make tapenade simply fry a little onion and a cubed aubergine in some olive oil for five to ten minutes. Throw in 100 grams of pitted kalamata olives and heat through. Blitz it in a food processor or with a hand blender and serve. This works well with any cut of lamb served, with Moroccan spiced couscous.

Cucumbers

Cucumbers are the quintessential English summer crop, used in salads and sliced for dips. No afternoon tea would be complete without cucumber sandwiches. To grow large types, you really need a greenhouse, but you can grow the smaller varieties quite easily outdoors on your plot. Cucumbers of old used to be a pain to grow, with non-hybrid plants bearing both female and male flowers. If the gardener didn't remove all the male flowers they would pollinate the female flowers and produce bitter, swollen fruits full of seeds. Gardeners had to perform this chore every day until the development of all-female F1 varieties. If you grow old varieties, you have this rather tedious task, and you need to stick to it religiously.

You can tell the male and female flowers apart fairly easily. Females have a tiny underdeveloped cucumber behind the flower, whereas the males do not.

Modern cucumbers are quite easy to grow and, surprisingly enough, outdoor varieties are even easier than indoor ones. The main difference is the fact that those suited for outdoors are usually thicker-skinned, ridged varieties with small spines that are nothing like the shop-bought ones you're familiar with. If you want the long, smooth ones then they're best grown in the greenhouse.

Cucumbers can make you belch and eating too many can cause an upset stomach.

Getting started with cucumbers

Cucumbers can be grown outdoors really successfully if conditions are favourable; in fact they're really prolific and will thrive, though for reliable and heavy crops it is best to grow plants under protection in a greenhouse or polytunnel. The smooth indoor types (all but a few new varieties) must be grown in the greenhouse. Cucumbers are bred specifically either for indoor or outdoor growing, so be sure to choose the right varieties.

Cucumbers grown in the greenhouse need a humid environment, plenty of warmth and some shade, or they get too over-exposed. You can grow them successfully in growbags or pots and they love a rich soil that's full of organic matter. They need to be supported and grown up a framework of canes and string lines around which you need to twist them as they grow.

Outdoor varieties are usually called *ridge* cucumbers and can be grown over the ground, although they take up lots of space and are better grown up a trellis or some other support. They like a rich soil high in organic matter. They're usually fast-growing and can be grown in most areas where they'll mature in the summer and fruit well before the damaging frosts come in winter. You should only plant them out when all risk of frost has passed and night-time temperatures aren't dropping to near or below freezing.

Dig the soil to 30 centimetres, with half manure or compost to soil, to provide adequate drainage, moisture retention and nutrients. Position the plants in full sun. Cucumbers work well planted in rows alternated with tomatoes, which like the same conditions outdoors. A good idea is to install a row of temporary trellis, canes or string lines to train them on. However, many gardeners let them flop around freely, which does take up more space but is absolutely fine.

To sow your cucumbers, follow these steps:

1. **Sow seeds in biodegradable pots in April or May. Using these pots means you can transplant them with minimum root disturbance. Sow one seed on edge on the surface of the compost, then cover lightly with compost. Cucumbers like loose soil that hasn't been too firmed. Water gently and place them in a propagator at around 21 °C.**

   Alternatively, sow the seeds outside in their final position as soon as the soil is warmed and nights aren't too cold – cucumbers die at temperatures below 10 degrees centigrade. You can sow them outside early as long as you can offer protection with a cloche (see Chapter 3 for more on protection) but because they grow so fast I wouldn't bother to do this. Simply wait until conditions are right and they'll soon shoot and grow (usually by the end of April).

2. **Plant out seedlings when all risk of frost has passed. Place them straight onto your plot or in large pots and growbags in the greenhouse. Be ready to cover them outside if nights look as if they're getting too cool. Seedlings should have three or four leaves.**

3. **Don't let them dry out but don't overwater as overwatering can cause damping off (see Chapter 7) and underwatering can stop the fruits developing. When the fruits begin to appear start feeding them weekly with a feed high in potash (comfrey liquid is ideal).**

Many gardeners pinch out old fashioned indoor varieties, removing the growing tips when they reach the top of their supports. This encourages side shoots and stops the plants growing too tall, so the plants are encouraged to flower and not produce more foliage. Outdoor varieties can usually be left to do their thing and scramble up their supports, and all modern varieties are best left alone.

TIP

Place jam jars over outdoor-sown seeds to offer them protection from the cold and remove them as soon as the plants get too big. You're sure to see jam jars all over your allotment site!

Considering varieties

Outdoor or ridge varieties are usually stumpier than indoor types and covered in little spines. Lots of varieties are available but here are some of the best:

- **Boothby's Blonde:** An unusual variety buts easy to grow and produces abundant white fruits that can be eaten straight off the plant when they're small. They can reach 20 centimetres in length at which point they're best cooked or pickled.
- **Burpless Tasty Green F1:** This one does exactly what it says on the tin – it doesn't make you burp. It's more like an indoor type and produces long and relatively smooth fruits, with a few spines. It's easy to grow and prolific.
- **F1 Prima Top:** An award-winning variety that can be grown outdoors and in the greenhouse. It's disease-resistant and easy to grow.
- **Marketmoore:** This is a very popular variety that produces multiple 25 centimetre long, dark green fruits.
- **Sunsweet:** This is an odd variety in that it produces round, lemon-coloured fruits that are extremely tasty and can be eaten as you do an apple. This is a greenhouse variety.

Greenhouse cucumbers are best grown as F1 hybrids, so you don't have to remove all the male flowers. Unless you're a heritage purist, choose from the selection below:

- **Carmen F1:** Probably the best all-rounder there is. It's easy to grow, crops heavily and produces the best fruits around! Has excellent disease resistance so is ideal for organic growers.
- **Euphya:** An all-female variety that produces lots of long, tasty, smooth cucumbers.
- **Passandra F1:** A variety that crops after 12 weeks and is covered in mini tasty fruits around 12 centimetres long. It's also disease-resistant, making it a good option for the organic grower.
- **Tiffany F1:** Great in the unheated or heated greenhouse, Tiffany F1 is vigorous and mildew-resistant. It produces an abundance of long, thin, slightly ridged fruits.
- **Valentin:** An easy-to-grow greenhouse variety that's great for beginners and produces 'shop-bought' smooth cucumbers.

Harvesting and storage

Cucumbers can be picked at any stage of their development but are best picked when mature. If left on the plant for too long they start to turn yellow – they're still edible but need coring and skinning to be eaten. To harvest, simply cut them off as required. They don't store well so eat them as soon as you can after picking.

Growing Fine Produce

Allotments are great places to grow all the basic fruit and veg for the plate but they're also ideal for growing those vegetables that are expensive or just a little bit special. To me, these next three vegetables are home-grown produce at its absolute best, with one – asparagus – being, in my humble opinion, the finest vegetable on the planet. The following veg are not necessarily hard to grow, they just need some time invested in them and a bit of know-how. Asparagus is quite easy to grow and has a very short harvesting period that's the highlight of spring. Celery, which many find hard to grow, is a challenge but fresh off the allotment is one of the tastiest vegetables around. Okra is a beautiful plant also known as *ladies' fingers*; a real challenge for most gardeners, it can be really rewarding. It seems odd to me that okra aren't seen more often, because they're so nice looking and they even look good in the borders at home. If you have success with okra you'll certainly be held in high esteem all over your allotment!

Asparagus

Asparagus is the king of all vegetables, slender, elegant and tasty and the highlight for all seasonal food lovers, gardeners and chefs. The spears taste sublime and epitomise the best of British produce, for the short six weeks that they're in season. You see road signs everywhere with farms, smallholdings and shops selling this wonderful vegetable. Introduced briefly to the pan, this vegetable can be complemented with rich sauces or just drizzled with butter, making it the perfect starter or accompaniment to any meal – my mouth is watering at the mere thought of it, so I'll get right on with how to grow it!

Asparagus is a long-term crop as it takes several years from planting to full production, but once established it will crop for years to come. Asparagus is expensive to buy, so growing your own makes perfect sense. The only problem is that asparagus takes up a lot of room and is a permanent fixture, which is why growers want such a premium for their produce. Rightly so!

Getting started with asparagus

Asparagus likes mild moist summers and cold winters. It's dormant for at least half the year, so is ideally suited to our climate. Severe frost damages the plants, so many gardeners cover the asparagus beds with straw over winter. In terms of soil it likes light, well drained loam, but it can be grown in both sandy soils and clay. In sandy soil you need to add loads of manure, and on heavy clay you need to grow your asparagus with added sand and muck to stop it becoming waterlogged.

The entire growing area must be free of perennial weeds, so it's worth waiting a year and seriously going to town on preparation, covering the area with fabric to suppress all the weeds. This is because the roots of asparagus are far reaching (up to 1.5 metres long), and you can never be rid of these weeds if they become entwined with the roots. Dig the entire area the autumn before and go through it with a fine-tooth comb, removing all the weeds, their roots and any evidence you can find of them. The soil should have a pH of 6.5 (see Chapter 6 on how to work out your soil's pH level) and add plenty of well rotted manure a good time before planting. Because asparagus is a perennial,the ground should be thoroughly prepared as your plants are going to live there for a good number of years.

Asparagus can be grown from seed but it isn't really worth the effort. Traditionally, asparagus is grown from one-year-old crowns (tuberous roots that look like mass of roots all joining at a central point) that are planted in spring and harvested repeatedly year after year. If you want to grow it from seed it's not hard but results can be variable. To plant your asparagus, follow these steps:

1. **Plant out the crowns in early spring in prepared trenches. Dig a trench 15–20 centimetres deep and 30 centimetres wide with a fine layer of sieved soil in the bottom. Make the bottom of the trench convex in profile (i.e. with a slight ridge running along the middle), as this helps the roots slope downwards.**
2. **Lay the crowns 40–60 centimetres apart, carefully spreading out the roots in a star shape. Then gently backfill with fine, sieved soil to cover the crowns.**

Asparagus needs a lot of care and attention. You need to carry out the following jobs throughout the growing year.

1. **As the crowns grow fill the trenches to the top always leaving the 8 centimetres of the tips exposed.**
2. **Stop harvesting in the middle of June and allow the plants to grow freely so they build up food reserves in their roots for next year.**

3. **Cut the plants down to ground level in the autumn when they turn yellow. Alternatively, you can leave the plants to die back and rot down where the goodness returns to the soil as they rot.**
4. **The following year, when the spears start to show above ground, spread a 5centimetre mound of compost over them as they grow, earthing them up so the tips are always exposed as before. The spears need some general fertiliser spread around them in early spring just before they show.**

You have to plant quite a few to be able to feed a family of four, so buy at least 20–30 plants and plant them in rows at least 30 centimetres apart.

Considering varieties

Asparagus plants are either male or female – the male plants are considered to be far more productive than the female ones. If you want really high yields go for an all-male modern F1 hybrid. The female plants waste energy producing seeds late in the season, which diverts their efforts away from building up the heavy crowns that the male plants are producing during this time.

- **Ariane F1.** This early, male variety is quickly gaining fans in allotments. It produces a good crop of tasty, tight-tipped spears.
- **Gijnlim F1.** This is a productive variety that out crops all others by up to 25 per cent, producing early spears from mid-April to June, when you stop cropping.
- **Jersey Knight F1.** A great all-male hybrid, vigorous and producing lovely purple-tipped spears.
- **Stewart's Purple.** Another new variety, but this one produces sweet, purple spears that are considered even tastier than the green ones. If gently steamed they retain their colour but if you boil them they lose it.
- **Thielim F1.** A great new hybrid variety that produces a really heavy crop of long, tasty spears.

Harvesting and storage

In the first year after planting, only harvest a few spears from your asparagus bed. This is to allow plants to become well established and build up strength for the future. Spears can be harvested in spring in their third year when they reach 15 centimetres tall and should be cut at an angle, 2–5 centimetres underground. An asparagus knife with a curved tip to the blade is the ideal tool for the job. You can harvest them as soon as the spears are large enough, until mid-summer's day when you should cease the harvest to allow the plants to grow up and build up strength for next year's crop.

Celery

Celery has long been considered a difficult and time-consuming crop to grow. Older varieties need to be planted in trenches and slowly earthed up to blanch (whiten) the stems, but you can now get self-blanching varieties that are much easier to grow and require far less care and attention. The self-blanching types aren't quite as tender and tasty but for the amount of time they save are well worth considering.

Getting started with celery

Celery relies on a rich organic soil that's permanently moist. It originates from plants that had their feet permanently in moist soils next to streams and rivers, so it suffers if you allow it to dry out. It's therefore essential that you add plenty of organic matter to the soil to aid water retention. Celery also likes a slightly acid soil so don't add lime to your celery bed.

To sow your celery, follow these steps:

1. **Sow seeds in trays or pots in January or February and keep them at about 16 °C to germinate in a propagator, or cover themwith a sheet of glass near a window sill.**

   This may seem rather early, but celery needs a good long growing season to perform well. Do not cover the seed with compost, as light is needed for germination: instead cover with perlite or vermiculite, or cover the containers with polythene.

2. **Prick out the seedlings when they have two true leaves (not seed leaves) and move them into seed modules, or space them 4 centimetres apart in trays.**
3. **Keep the seedlings moist at all times. This is best done with a fine spray, or by placing the trays in another tray with a few centimetres of water in the bottom, so the seedlings can take up the water when they need it.**

   If you let them dry out you'll pay the price later on when they're planted out because they'll be more likely to suddenly bolt (flower prematurely).

4. **Plant out seedlings in spring when the risk of frost has passed.**

   Frost damages young celery plants but mature plants actually taste better after being hit by a light frost in late autumn into winter. Having said that, heavy frosts damage the plants, so be prepared to cover them with a cloche tunnel (see Chapter 3 for more on these) if you want them to last through winter.

5. **Plant self-blanching celery in blocks 25centimetres apart in all directions in prepared soil. Celery is usually planted in this way so that the foliage above helps to naturally blanch the stems below. Also this helps suppress weeds, which celery hates.**

Trench celery

Trench celery is sown and grown following the same directionss as with self-blanching celery. The difference comes when you plant the seedlings out on your plot. Trench celery needs to be planted in special trenches following the steps below.

1. **Plant trench celery in trenches prepared with plenty of manure the previous autumn. The trenches should be 15 centimetres deep and 30 centimetres wide, and you need to plant the seedlings in the bottom about 40 centimetres apart.**

   This trench not only means you can earth up your celery as it grows but also is the ideal way to keep it well watered – you can literally flood the trench, which keeps them happy.

2. **Blanch your trench celery**. In late summer when the plants are fully grown, tidy any dead or yellowing leaves from the plant from the top and sides. Tie up the celery gently at the tops with some string, and earth up the trenches, leaving the top leaves exposed.

   Keep doing this over the next couple of weeks. The higher you can get the mounds the more tender and longer the white stems will be. As an alternative, you can wrap the entire plant around the stem with some newspaper or anything else that keeps the light out. Again, leave just the tops of the foliage exposed. This turns the stems a pale greeny-white and protects them until harvesting. The only problem with this method is that is gives the slugs somewhere to hide, so if slugs are a problem, earth up instead.

Considering varieties

Here are some self-blanching varieties that are easy to grow and require little maintenance:

- **Galaxy (Lathom self blanching):** This is a prolific celery that produces stringless, tasty stems.
- **Tango F1:** A lovely pale green celery with smooth stems, it copes well in hot weather.
- **Victoria F1:** A good one to try if you've had a hard time growing other varieties. It's very tasty and really crisp.

The trenching types below are ideal for those who want more of a challenge (the extra effort is worth your while because they usually taste much better):

- **Giant Pascal.** A beauty that grows big and tastes good too.
- **Giant Red.** Avery well known variety with a red tinge to the stems and widely regarded as the easiest type to grow.
- **Hopkins Fenlander.** This is a traditional celery that's been an allotment favourite for years.

Harvesting and storage

Trench celery is best harvested during winter. Simply lift whole plants as required, removing the outer leaves to tidy them up a bit and giving the stems a good wash. I think celery tastes better after a frost and my granddad would always wait until one hit before harvesting – he was never wrong! Self-blanching celery can be harvested from autumn into winter, harvested in the same way.

Okra

Okra is a tropical plant related, surprisingly, to cotton and hibiscus. It has very similar flowers to both. Okra produces delicate pods that are a delicacy often used in Indian cooking. The pods can be eaten whilst young or they can be left to mature with the 'peas' inside being edible too. They have a slimy texture which may sound nasty but this quality means that okra is often used as an aid to thicken sauces and chutneys. The whole plant is actually beautiful, and it always surprises me that gardeners don't use them as ornamentals more often then they do. They bear the most gorgeous pale yellow or red flowers and can grow quite large, so two or three are plenty to feed the family.

Getting started with okra

Okra needs to be grown under glass or in polytunnels for best results, but can also work planted outdoors. As a guide, if you get a decent crop of outdoor tomatoes that ripen well then you should be able to grow okra.

Okra needs similar conditions to tomatoes and peppers, and can be grown directly in the soil, in growbags in the greenhouse, or even in pots as long as you keep them well watered. If grown in the ground they like a free-draining soil. The soil should be rich in organic matter, but not manure – use compost from your heap instead (see Chapter 6 on making your own compost). Okra plants must get plenty of warmth and direct sunlight, so site them carefully. The plants can grow big, so unless you get a dwarf variety give them plenty of space – some reach 2 metres tall. To plant your okra, follow these steps:

1. **Sow seeds indoors in biodegradable pots or trays in early spring, and place in a propagator at around 20 °C in good light.**

   Okra plants can be sown outdoors when the soil is warm (warming can be speeded up by placing a cloche over the soil).

2. **If sown in trays *prick out* the seedlings when they have four leaves. Gently lift the seedlings using a widger, and replant them in 8 centimetre pots to continue growing.**

   You may find your plants seem to stop growing all of a sudden, but they are actually concentrating on producing roots, and will shoot with some vigour soon afterwards! Plants should be kept at a minimum night time temperature of 15.5 °C for optimum growth.

3. **Harden the plants off (put them outside during the day to acclimatise) when they're 15 centimetres tall, and then plant them out to their final position.**

   In all but the warmest parts of the country this positon is usually in the greenhouse or a polytunnel. It isn't usually warm enough outside until spring weather has truly arrived, so don't rush it!

4. **Water and feed. During dry spells, water thoroughly once a week to improve yields.**

   Feed weekly with a high potash fertilizer once the first flowers have formed.

Considering varieties

You can grow a couple of different types of okra: slow-maturing varieties and the fast-maturing ones that are more suited to our climate, but varieties can be hard to track down. The slow maturers are the most readily available types, with the quicker growers worth looking out for.

- **Red Burgundy:** This one looks great with its red stems and lovely red pods.
- **Clemson Spineless:** An easy-to-row variety that produces neat green pods on a fast maturing plant, probably the most popular variety around.
- **Hill Country Heirloom Red:** This one is a rare variety and a truly beautiful plant with red stems and red-tinged pods.
- **Pure Luck F1:** Ideal for the British climate because it matures early, Pure Luck is fast-maturing so well worth a try.

Harvesting and storage

You can harvest okra about two months after sowing – its pods are best picked when they're young. You need to pick them every couple of days so that the plant keeps on producing more pods. You'll probably get more than you can cope with, so give some to friends or freeze the excess for later use.

Part IV

Extending Your Allotment Repertoire

'So this is why you've not brought me any fresh vegetables home all year!'

In this part . . .

Allotment gardening isn't just about bringing home piles of perfect potatoes or loads of leafy lettuces. As I show in this part, you can spread your wings into a whole range of juicy fruit and gorgeous flowers, too.

This part covers all the techniques you need to grow all the fruit you could possibly want, from apple trees to whitecurrants. I describe the basic regulations on allotment fruit trees, the varieties available and everything you need to do to get the best yields you possibly can.

I also run the rule over growing flowers on your allotment, whether you want them to add beauty to your home or zest to your salads.

Chapter 17

Growing Fruitful Fruit

In This Chapter

- Making the most of a small space
- Growing apples and pears
- Enjoying berries and currants
- Experimenting with the exotic

An allotment should be as productive as possible, and along with your vegetables and herbs you should also think about growing fruit. Some fruits are fast-growing and give you results in one season, whereas others need time to become established before you can reap the benefits. The main thing about your allotment fruit garden is that the trees and shrubs need to be compact and trained in a way that doesn't take up too much space. They also need to fit in with your allotment's rules and regulations.

Planting Fruit Trees

Fruit trees are slow-growing investments that take a good few years to become established before they become productive, so you must be prepared to wait before they become worthwhile. On the plus side, when they've become established they're productive every year for as long as you have your plot, so are well worth including. Fruit trees are often ignored by allotment holders due to the amount of space they can take up, but you can buy specially prepared trees grafted onto a *rootstock* (the bottom 10 centimetres or so of the trunk and its roots) that restricts the size of the tree, making it ideal for a smaller space. You can also train fruit trees as cordons, espaliers and stepovers (all of which I discuss in the 'Training trees' section below), which are ideal for even the smallest plots. You can also grow many fruit trees in pots, saving even more space.

Figuring out fruit families

Many fruits are members of the *Rosaceae* family, which includes apples, pears, cherries, peaches, plums, quinces, raspberries, blackberries and strawberries. All of these are fruits are ideal for growing in a temperate climate. They all bear pretty flowers, which attract the insects that pollinate them, and are all relatives of the most beautiful member of this family, the rose.

The members of the *Grossulariaceae* family include the important *Ribes* genus that boasts such fantastic fruits as the currants and the highly underrated gooseberries.

The *Moraceae* family includes some tropical fruits such as figs, but also one of my favourites from far northern mountain reaches – the blueberry. This family also includes the all-important grape and the Mediterranean favourite, the olive.

Many allotments have very strict rules as to what fruit trees you can plant on your plot. The basic rule is that you can't plant anything that can cause nuisance to another plot holder, and on some sites you need written permission before planting any tree or shrub that takes longer than 12 months to mature. Now this 12-month rule is a little excessive, but it's there to stop people planting great big apple trees that shade adjacent plots and cause issues with your neighbours. Many sites allow you to grow small fruit trees as long as they don't overshadow other plots and as a general rule these shouldn't exceed 2.5 metres in height.

Training trees

You can train trees, and thus restrict their growth, in one of three ways: as *espaliers*, *cordons* and *stepovers*. If you're a novice gardener I suggest buying ready-trained trees so that all you need to do is plant them and help them on their way. Training trees from young plants is for the slightly more experienced gardener, but cordons are fairly easy to train. Espaliers and stepovers are much more difficult. If you do want to have a go yourself though, you have a far more varied selection of trees to choose from.

Cordons

Cordons are fruit trees in which growth is restricted to just one main stem. Cordons are probably the best way to train fruit trees on the allotment because you can train them in rows of single stems. The trees are usually grown at a 45-degree angle to the ground so they can grow taller without gaining too much height. This also encourages the sap to move slowly up the tree, helping to produce more flowers and therefore fruit. Trees for cordons are usually bought as one-year-olds called *maidens*. To train your trees in a cordon, follow these steps:

1. **Insert a post at either end of a row and attach three horizontal wires to them at 60, 120 and 180 centimetres off the ground**. In a 2-metre run you can place three or four trees. If you're using a longer run you may need additional posts in the middle as extra support.
2. **Place three bamboo canes equally spaced at roughly a 45-degree angle tied into the horizontal wires, then plant your maiden at the base of each cane.**

   It's important to plant the cordon with the join where it's grafted onto the rootstock with the bump (*scion*) facing upwards otherwise you run the risk of it breaking later on. The bump is usually easy to find and looks like a knuckle so plant it knuckle side up. Remove the growing tip of each tree right at the top to encourage lateral growth.
3. **Secure the plant to the bamboo cane and take off the growing tip to encourage side shoots.**

   Be sure to check the tie every month or so to ensure that it's not damaging the stems.
4. **Take out roughly a third of the new growth at the tip of each tree every year for the next three of four years until the plants reach the top of the wire.**

   Doing this encourages new lateral growth instead of the plant growing taller. The plants crop from the bottom up before the top reaches the top of the cane support.
5. **Cut all the side shoots back every August leaving three or four leaves on the main stem.**

   If one of these primary side shoots has a side shoot then cut that back to one leaf from the primary side shoot. When the tree has reached the end of the cane (about 2.4 metres tall), from then on all you need do is prune in August by removing side shoots back to four leaves on the main stem. Figure 17-1 shows finished cordons.

Figure 17-1: Finished cordons.

Espaliers

Espaliers are a way of training trees, particularly apple and pear trees, onto a flat plane so they take up less space and are more visually appealing. The most usual form of espalier consists of an upright central stem with between three and five horizontal branches. They're also useful for training more tender fruits against sunny walls. The walls warm quickly, allowing growers to grow more tender fruits that in an open position would suffer. Figure 17-2 shows an espalier. Fruit trees can also be trained against walls in fan shapes (see Figure 17-3).

Figure 17-2: Fruit tree trained as an espalier.

Figure 17-3: Fruit tree trained as a fan.

Stepovers

Stepovers are specially trained fruit trees (usually apples and pears) that resemble short espaliers with only one horizontal set of branches. Stepovers are ideal for edging herb gardens or for the main sections on the plot or even the fruit garden. They produce quite heavy crops for such small plants but being so close to the ground are easy targets for slugs, snail and birds who can swiftly ruin your crops. You can buy stepover trees or train them yourself but for instant results you're far better off buying them ready trained and saving three or four years in training them.

Buying fruit trees

The usual ways to buy fruit trees is to buy *standards* (tall, standard shaped trees with a bare stem of about 1.8 metres topped with branches) or *half standards* (with bare stems 1.2–1.5 metres tall). To be perfectly honest these are not ideally suited to an allotment site because they grow too big. You can buy trees grafted onto dwarf rootstocks but generally they're still too large for an allotment. By attaching the tree to a smaller root stock enables growers to determine how large a tree will become. When buying fruit trees you'll find that you can often choose which rootstock they come supplied with. Figure 17-4 shows the different sizes and shapes of fruit trees.

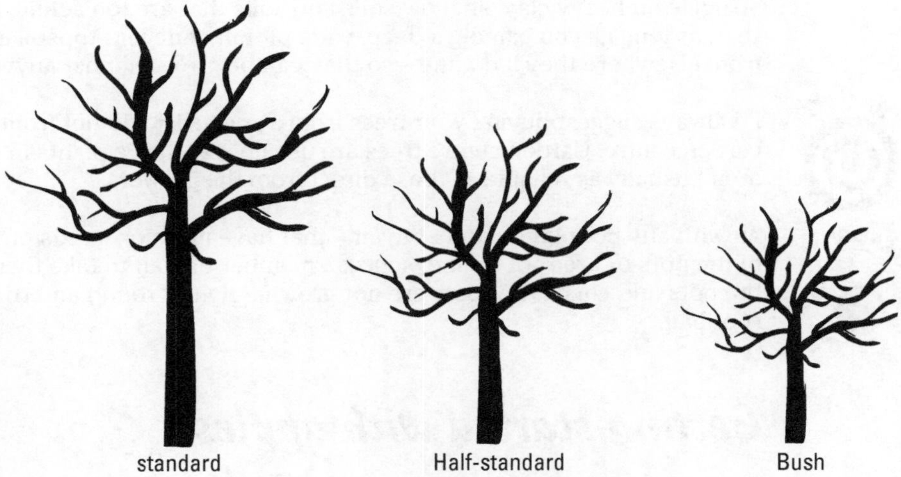

Figure 17-4: Different sizes of fruit trees.

Apple rootstocks have a varied history and some are hundreds if not thousands of years old, simply having been perfected by modern growers. Most will go on to grow into apple trees but they are often slow to produce fruit, which can be of inferior quality. What we are looking for, though, is not the quality of the fruit but the characteristic of the *rootstock* which when grafted onto an other superior tree combines the qualities of both. These rootstocks usually have a code so we can identify what characteristics the plant has, and this is usually a letter and some numbers such M26, M9 and MM106.

For example, a tree on an M27 rootstock (which is considered the least vigorous) doesn't usually grow over 1.8 metres tall but an MM106 rootstock reaches over 3 metres. On an allotment you're restricted as to how tall a tree you can grow, so the only one that's really suited to an allotment is the M27 rootstock. M27s are problematic due to the fact that they have very small root balls, and require heavy staking, fertile soil and a lot of care and watering. But some say that they're no more labour intensive than other crops on the allotment, so are worth using. Many other allotmenteers do use M9 (which reaches 1.8– 3 metres) and M26 (2.5–3.6 metres) and both can be trained well as cordons.

Growing Apples

Apples are simply the best fruit to grow in the UK; they're perfectly suited to our climate, they love the warm (well, warmish) summer days and the cooler summer nights and they're tough, hardy plants that like a period of dormancy that comes with winter. Apples are suited to most soil types but struggle on heavy clay, shallow soils and soils that are too acidic. Having said that, as long as you can dig a deep, wide pit full of decent topsoil and muck from elsewhere they'll do fine – so they can be grown almost anywhere.

TIP

I'd always suggest buying your trees from a specialist and not from your local garden centre. Garden centre trees are usually expensive plants in pots that aren't usually as reliable as those direct from the growers.

WARNING!

As with any pot plants, don't buy any that have moss or weeds on the surface of the pots or are root bound, so ask a member of staff to take them out of the pots and check the roots are not growing tightly round and round the root ball.

Getting started with apples

To plant your apple tree, follow these steps:

1. **Clear and cultivate the soil well before planting the tree. Dig a pit 1 metre square and 50–60 centimetres deep, adding loads of organic matter mixed in with the soil as you replace it. This step is vital.**
2. **Let the soil rest for a couple of weeks if you can spare the time. If not, then only partially fill the hole leaving it about 30–40 centimetres shy of the top.**

3. **Put the root ball of the tree into a large bucket of water for at least an hour before planting. Alternatively, if your tree is in a pot, give it a really good soak an hour or so before planting. This allows the plant to take up plenty of water right up into the top of the plant, which gives it a boost that sees it through the stress of moving house.**

4. **Place the tree in the centre of the pit ensuring that you plant it at the same level it was at in the pot, or for bare-rooted plants, make sure that the nursery mark on the stem is the same when planted. The nursery mark is often found on the trunk and is the ring left by the soil where it was originally planted. Place a stick on the soil surface over the hole like a bridge and line up the *nursery mark* on the trunk so it is the same level as the surrounding soil.**

5. **Shovel some soil around the tree to hold it upright and then hammer a tree stake into the ground at 45 degrees to the tree so that you can tie the tree to it one third of the height of the tree above ground level. Tie the tree to the stake using an appropriate rubber tree tie. You can hammer in the tree stake after you have planted the tree, but doing so before ensures that you don't damage the roots.**

6. **Replace the soil around the roots and the stake giving the roots the odd shake to ensure that the soil is well distributed around them, and then fill the hole. Firm down the soil with your heel and water it well.**

7. **Apply a deep mulch around the tree and keep it topped up at all times. It'll soon disappear and be taken into the ground by earthworms so keep it well stocked. Also be sure to place some form of protection around the base to keep hungry rabbits from nibbling away the lower bark. You can buy simple coils of plastic that you place around the trunk, which work well.**

When staking trees do so on the side of the prevailing wind so that the tree is blown away from the stake. By attaching a single stake at one third of the height of the tree you're keeping the root ball safe from movement but are also allowing the top to move. This movement helps the trunk thicken , thus increasing the strength of the tree.

Considering varieties

Literally hundreds of different varieties of apple are available to try but the main thing to remember on the allotment is that the size of the tree needs to be easily manageable. This is where it gets a bit complicated, because apple trees need to be pollinated by pollen from two or more other apple varieties to produce a fruit. There are a few exceptions, such as Golden Delicious, which is self-fertile, but this is why you always see apple trees planted together or at least near other types to aid pollination. To be honest on an allotment you haven't got the space to plant an orchard but you may well have room to plant three or four stepover apples or a row of cordons. Just make sure that they're self-fertile varieties or groups of suitable varieties that all flower at the same time. This is where the expertise of specialist growers comes in as they can suggest suitable trees for your plot in the sizes and varieties that work together in terms of pollination. You can also buy trees that have 2 or more different apples grafted onto the same rootstock: These are called *family trees*, and produce different varieties of apple on one tree. Family trees do require lots of care but can be good fun.

Growers have placed a simple system of letters or numbers to help you group trees that pollinate each other. They're either in groups A–D or 1–4, so if you buy three trees all from group 3, they'll all work together by pollinating each other. These groups help identify when the trees flower, thus ensuring that they'll all be viable for pollination at the same time. These groups can be slightly flexible, so you can plant a couple of trees from group 3 and one from group 4 and they'll cross over and pollinate each other. Self-fertile trees will pollinate themselves to a certain extent but they produce more fruit if planted with another tree that flowers at the same time.

Just to confuse things even more, meet the *triploids*, trees that don't produce any fertile pollen and therefore need to be planted with two other non-triploid pollinating varieties to produce any fruit. This may sound a total bore but triploids include some good varieties, such as the Bramleys and the lovely Blenheim Orange, so they can be worth the extra effort.

Here are the tastiest dessert apples you can grow and the groups each one belongs to:

- **Blenheim Orange:** A triploid variety that produces abundant large apples good for eating and cooking. It grows quite large unless you can get one on a dwarfing rootstock. (It's also sold as a cooking apple.) Group C.
- **Braeburn Helena:** Braeburns are amongst the most popular apples around but are usually difficult. However this variety is much easier for the average gardener to grow. Braeburns usually do much better in warmer areas – this is still true of Helena but it does well in the UK's warmer spots. Group C.
- **Cox (self-fertile):** Cox has to be the classic English apple variety that we all adore – crisp and sweet, yet sharp. Cox's apples are quite hard to grow but the self-fertile variety is more disease-resistant and much easier. Group C.
- **Discovery:** Offering no real problems for the grower, Discovery is an early cropping desert apple that's easy to look after and tasty. Group B.
- **Egremont Russet:** This popular russet apple has a rather tough skin (Russets have rough, brownish, thick skins) but is a real treat on the

inside – tasty, sweet and yet not overly juicy with a lovely texture. Group B.

- **Fiesta:** This is an easy-to- grow variety similar to the Cox's apples and stores really well. It has a delicate floral flavour and is often grown commercially because of its long shelf life. Group B.
- **Gravenstein:** Is a delicious triploid desert apple that is not that popular because it is susceptible to attack from many diseases. But saying that it is also one of the tastiest apples you will ever find, so worth a go if you like a challenge. Group A
- **Greensleeves:** This apple makes excellent eating and is so easy to grow. It has good disease-resistance and is partially self-fertile. Group B.
- **Katja (also sold as Katy):** A well known variety developed in Sweden, Katja is good for cooler parts of the country. It produces attractive red-flushed green apples that have a sharp taste that's simply delicious. It's also good for juicing and making cider. Group B.
- **Spartan:** One of my favourites because it has a slightly wine-like flavour – simply delicious. It's a late cropper so is picked in early October and best eaten straight from the tree. Group D.

Some good cooking apples include:

- **Bountiful:** Because of its disease-resistance Bountiful is ideal for organic gardeners. It's a good cooking apple that 's available on all the root-stocks from the small patio M27s to the larger MM106. Group B.
- **Howgate Wonder:** The largest of the 'cookers', it produces loads of fruit per tree. It's great for exhibition apples and goes really fluffy when cooked. Group D.
- **James Grieve:** An excellent cooking apple that when picked mellows into a great eating apple as well. It holds its shape well and it's great sharpness is ideal with a cheese course. Group B.
- **Jumbo:** A triploid variety that can't be used as a pollinator but it's well worth growing for its strong, healthy growth. It produces lovely red-flushed apples that hold their colour well during cooking. Group C.

Harvesting and storage

You can find a variety of apple trees that are ready to harvest at different times of the year – if you have a few varieties that mature at different times you'll be well covered with a decent supply. When they're ripe they snap off easily in your hand so cup them in your palm and lift and they should just come away. Most are ready to eat straight away but early varieties are best picked before they ripen and stored for up to a month to allow the sweetness and flavours to develop. Store these in trays (which you can buy online or in many garden centres) in a cool, dark place for best keeping. You can keep apples for a few weeks in the fridge or even slice and dry them to add to cereals and cakes, but most are best simply plucked and eaten as required –or why not try making some cider?

Apples for storage a best wiped with a dry cloth and checked for any signs of damage or disease, ideally wrapped in newspaper or at least not touching each other and stored in trays in a cool dark place. Check them often, and discard any you find with signs of rot (these are great for the birds to feed on)

Growing Pears

Like apples, pears are an English classic that you can easily grow on your plot if you select carefully to ensure that the trees are trained to be small and come on a dwarfing rootstock. They can be trained in exactly the same way as apple trees (see the 'Training trees' section earlier in this chapter). Pears are a little harder to grow than apples because they tend to flower slightly earlier and can be damaged by a late frost. Pears are best trained as cordons or along a sunny wall as espaliers (or cordons) because they love to be exposed to plenty of sun light to sweeten up those fruits. If you do have a sunny wall on your plot they act as heat traps offering shelter for your fruit, they will ripen quicker and be sweeter tasting.

Pears are usually grafted on to rootstocks in the same way as apples to control their growth but they're categorised in a different way. There are three main groups of pear rootstocks:

- **Quince A** . This is the standard rootstock used for strong growth and trees that can be trained into any shape or size. This rootstock is good for cordon training on poor soils.
- **Quince BA29** . The strongest rootstock, it's used to grow plants that are not so vigorous to give them added strength.
- **Quince C** . This dwarfing rootstock is used to grow trees that reach 3 metres in height but are good for training in cordons and espaliers or for use as hedges. It's the best rootstock for training on the allotment.

Getting started with pears

Pears prefer a sunny position exposed to as much warm sun as possible. This makes them ideal for training in rows as cordons or against a trellis network as fan trained or candelabra-shaped espaliers. By keeping the framework flat you expose as much of it as possible to the sun, which helps the fruits to ripen and sweeten. They're trained and planted in the same way as apple trees so check out the details in the section 'Training trees' earlier in this chapter. Pears are grouped as to when they pollinate – just like apples – so they need to be grown with suitable pollination partners.

Considering varieties

Take pear pollination groups (either 1–4 or A–D) into account when choosing your varieties. Hundreds of varieties are available out there, so your selection depends on personal taste, what size area you can dedicate to them, and when they pollinate.

TIP

To train your trees as cordons, always buy pear and apple trees as one- or two-year-old plants because they're easier to train well.

Here are some of the best pears you can buy and the groups each one belongs to:

- **Beth.** Is a popular heavy cropping variety that is easy to grow. Firm flesh and sweet flavour. Group 3
- **Beurre Bedford.** Produces very large juicy red tinged fleshy pears that are lovely and sweet. Group 4.
- **Concord.** A relatively new variety that's great for smaller gardens being compact and a heavy cropper. It produces lovely sweet, green fruits that are full of juice. Group 3.
- **Conference:** By far the most popular pear variety available and for good reason, it's easy to grow and crops well having abundant juicy, sweet pears. Group 2.
- **Doyenne de Comice:** Comice pears are second only to Conference pears in the taste race. They're best picked to ripen off the tree and they then become lovely and sweet. They do best in a really warm area so train them nice and flat against a sunny wall or as cordons facing the sun. Comice is good pear for low areas where frost gathers (frost pockets) because it flowers later than most. Group 2
- **Onward:** Is an English dessert pear that has lovely crisp sweet flesh. Ready for picking in September and October. Group 2.
- **Williams Bon Chrétien:** Is one of the most popular of all pears and cannot be missed from the list! Not the heaviest cropper but produces delicious white fleshed fruit that is divine. Group 2.

Harvesting and storage

Pears need to be ripe to be good to eat. The problem with many supermarket pears is that they're unripe and never really ripen well after being picked. Pears suddenly just ripen with no warning and their shelf life is quite short. The best thing about growing your own is the fact that you can pick them at their prime, so just keep an eye on them and eat them as soon as they're ready. Some varieties ripen on the tree and others are best picked unripe to ripen off the plant; this simply depends on the variety you choose so take this into account when ordering your trees. Pears that ripen on the tree don't last as long when picked as those that are picked to ripen.

Growing Berries

The berries are the most important fruiting group for allotment growers but they can also be the most problematic: not only do we love to eat them, but so do the birds. Many of the berries I'm going to introduce you to in this section are perfect for allotments, small compact plants that fit easily within the confines of your small plot. It's only worth buying these fruiting plants as ready grown plants, not seeds, because those grown from seed are often unreliable, and even the ready grown plants need a good few years preparation and care in which to start producing good crops.

WARNING!

As soon as your berries (all types) start to appear you need to protect them from hungry birds who'll soon strip them. Lay fruit netting over the plants like a tent to keep them out.

Blackberries

Blackberries are good for allotment growing as long as they are trained on a support, such as trellis panels or a post-and-wire framework. It's also vital to keep them well pruned to prevent them from becoming too established. Blackberries are heavy croppers, and produce fruit even in their first year. By the second they'll be heavy and delicious.

TIP

Thornless varieties are available that are ideal for use in areas where people may be passing, so no one gets scratched or cut.

Getting started with blackberries

Blackberries grow absolutely anywhere, as you can tell if you drive around any part of the country and just look around. They grow on wasteland, woodland edges, and roadsides. As with most plants though, they produce much better fruits if grown in improved soil.

To grow your blackberries, follow these steps:

1. **Create support for your plants. Drive two sturdy 2.5-metre poles spaced 2 metres or more apart deep into the ground. Then run some lengths of wire horizontally between the posts, set at intervals of 30 centimetres above the ground from 30 centimetres high to 180 centimetres, with a final strand 2 metres above the ground. You then train the stems along these wires.**
2. **Dig a hole in the centre of the frame twice the size of the root ball in a spot in full sun. Mix the soil with some compost. Place the plant in the hole and backfill so that the plant is at the same level it was in the pot or if it's a root-ball-variety plant, at the same level it was in the ground. You can easily see this by the nursery mark around the main stem. Blackberries need plenty of space; I'd only ever plant one or two on the allotment, or you'll have too much work on your hands. Place them a minimum of 2 metres apart but check the instructions on the plant label for more information.**
3. **Tie in the stems as they grow. You get loads of long, sprawling stems that need to be tied in to the wires at regular intervals they should be trained horizontally along the wires. This will encourage flowers and more fruit. You'll find that they soon reach the ends of the wires where you can simply cut them off to keep the plant in check. Blackberries fruit on wood from the previous year, so as soon as they've fruited and been harvested you should cut them back to the ground.**
4. **Lay a deep mulch around the base of the plant and keep it well watered and weed-free. Reapply the mulch every spring to help feed the plant and apply an annual feed high in potash to encourage fruiting.**

WARNING!

Blackberry plants self-root really easily and soon spread if you don't tie in the stems. If any stem touches the ground it soon sets root and if this keeps on happening you end up with a knotted mess that's next to impossible to handle.

Considering varieties

Try to find a compact variety that can be trained easily. Many people claim that you can't beat the flavour of the wild berries you find all over the countryside, but I disagree; there are some excellent varieties that produce lovely fat fruits far superior to the comparatively tiny fruits found in the wild. Consider these:

- **Chester:** A variety that produces loads of fruit on thornless canes, it has a long cropping period and tastes wonderful.
- **Helen:** This very early cropper has no spines and gives plenty of large fruits that taste great.

- **Karaka Black:** You get enormous sweet berries with terrific taste from this variety and it's good for training on wires to keep it in check.
- **Loch Tay:** A new variety that's ideal for the allotment because it's so compact – it needs only 1 metre between plants – and produces loads of very juicy fruits.

WARNING! You may find that the fruits don't ripen well and ripen unevenly. Unfortunately this is caused by mites and the only remedy is to cut the whole plant down and burn the cuttings. The plant soon grows back the following year but won't fruit again until the year after.

Harvesting and storage

You can start to pick the fruits from late July onwards – it's simply a case of picking them off as required. Any extra can be frozen or turned into jams and jellies.

Gooseberries

Gooseberries are like Marmite: you either love 'em or hate 'em! Personally I wouldn't be without them. Many varieties are rather acidic but you can also find ones that are super sweet and that can be eaten straight from the bush without the need to add ridiculous amounts of sugar. Gooseberries will grow on any reasonable soil apart from waterlogged ground, although avoid light dry soils which can make plants liable to mildew. They're extremely tough plants and are ideal for those who struggle to grow other types of fruit due to being on exposed sites. They're usually grown as single bushes on clear single stems and can also be trained as cordons (see the 'Training trees' section earlier in this chapter for more on these), or up a trellis on a fence or wall, but the easiest thing to do is let them grow as nature intended, as a single bush. Varieties of gooseberry range widely from small, fruiting sweet ones to large, red dessert gooseberries ideal for stewing. I'd grow two or three different varieties to extend the season and below I give you a few options.

Hailing the hybrids

You can also buy all sorts of hybrid berries that are, in general, a cross between blackberries and raspberries. These include Boysenberries, Marionberries, Tayberries and Veitchberries. They all are grown in the same way as blackberries, and most are very vigorous plants. Growers have developed new varieties of thornless varieties which make harvesting much safer, but a word of warning: You will need to train many of them otherwise they will easily reach 5 or 6 metres in spread. They are all harvested, eaten and stored in the same way as blackberries, so if you want to try an alternative give one of these a go!

Getting started with gooseberries

Gooseberries are best planted in the autumn in a sunny spot in good, improved, organically rich soil. Prepare the ground well by forking it over, incorporating plenty of well-rotted manure or compost, and removing all the weeds. To plant your gooseberries, follow these steps:

1. **Dig a hole in prepared ground a little larger than the root ball.**
2. **Plant the bush to the same depth as it is in the pot, or, if bare-rooted, spread the roots in the hole and backfill, gently shaking the plant slightly to ensure that the roots are well covered. Ensure that the plant is planted to the same depth as it would have been at the nursery. Heel the plant in and water well.**
3. **Prune dead or broken branches back to a bud and remove any weak stems.**
4. **Lay a thick mulch around the base of the plant, using bark chip or compost. This helps to retain water and feed the plant.**

Autumn planted bushes rarely need watering unless the winter is unusually dry. During dry spells the following spring keep the gooseberry well watered to encourage the roots to grow deeply. Don't water it too lightly: Give it a good soak so the roots are encouraged to venture deeply into the soil.

Gooseberry bushes are best pruned in winter to shorten the longest stems, keeping your plant nice and neat. Also, remove any diseased or crossing stems that can rub on each other and damage the plants.

By pruning you also keep the centre of the bush nice and open making picking easier and the plant less susceptible to American mildew and sawfly infestations (see Chapter 7). Prune out any shoots that are growing into the centre of the plant, and cut back the long outer growth by a third to a half. Also remove the tips of shorter stems, as this helps encourage more flowers Then give the plant a good feed using a potash-rich feed.

Gooseberries should be watered well especially during the time when fruits are growing. If they suffer drought during this time the crop will be smaller as well as the fruits.

Considering varieties

Of the many different varieties available you just need to make sure that you get them from a good supplier and know exactly what type you've bought, so it suits the plot and your needs.

Ideally, buy bushes that are two years old and come ready pruned, saving you time and effort. You simply plant them and off they go, producing lots of fruit in the second year you plant them after some in the first. Try these:

- **Captivator.** This thornless variety produces loads of sweet purple fruits ready to harvest in late May. It's extremely hardy.
- **Hinnomaki Yellow.** A really unusual variety that produces yellowish green fruits with a unique, almost apricot, note to their flavour. They're excellent used in tarts and pies.
- **Invicta.** A heavy-cropping plant that produces lovely green fruits, which retain their shape when cooked.
- **Pax.** A red-fruiting type that's thornless making the fruit nice and easy to pick. It forms a nice open shrub that air can circulate around easily, so is pretty mildew resistant.

Harvesting and storage

Gooseberries are ready to pick from late May onwards at which time it's best to remove roughly half the crop. This early crop can be cooked and sweetened with sugar for use in pies and other recipes. By doing this the plant then concentrates its efforts on the remaining fruits and provides a longer season for picking. They'll be ready a few weeks later and will be really sweet and not as acidic. Gooseberries don't store well unless cooked and then frozen where they'll keep for months.

Blueberries and bilberries

The blueberry has all of a sudden become a king of fruits. Blueberries are considered a 'super-food' by nutritionists who hail their health giving antioxidant content and high levels of vitamin C. Apart from that they taste great, and are quite easy to grow as long as you can provide the correct conditions.

In Sweden and other northerly countries you also get bilberries, and I grew up scouring the forest floor in Sweden picking thousands of these super-sweet bilberries that to me taste even better – they're both from the same family but shouldn't be confused.

The blueberries you find in garden centres are shrubs that can reach well over 1.5 metres high but they do need acid, moist soil on which to thrive, whereas bilberries are much smaller and harder to grow, and don't produce as large a crop. If you can find them, though, they are well worth a go. Bilberries and blueberries are quite different in flavour and colour: blueberries are green on the inside whereas bilberries are purple and when you eat bilberries they dye your tongue purple as a result. Bilberries have a much stronger flavour but aren't as sweet, so they're often cooked with added sugar.

Getting started with blueberries

Most gardeners grow their blueberries in pots because they have very specific needs. Blueberries like quite an acidic soil and soil that never dries out so they can be grown in soil on the plot as long as it has sufficient acid levels and you can ensure that the roots stay nice and moist. They benefit in the ground by the addition of copious amounts of well-rotted manure to preserve moisture and like lots of leaf mould added to help increase acid levels especially if it contains well rotted down pine needles (which take ages to rot and can be collected from any pine trees you might have at home). Moss peat is the ideal growing medium for blueberries as it's acidic and acts like a sponge, retaining loads of water. You shouldn't really use peat, because it comes from a non-renewable source but I leave that one down to you (I don't use it!).

You can make soil more acid by adding sulphur chips, potash, or sulphate of ammonia to soils. Just be sure to read the instructions well on the packets so you get the dosing right. This kind of treatment is only ever temporary though, and isn't a permanent fix. To plant your blueberries, follow these steps:

1. **Plant in open ground, in acid soil and in full sun or part shade, leaving at least 1 metre between plants. If you're growing plants in pots, use an ericaceous compost mixed with some lime-free loam, mixed 50/50. Choose a pot large enough to take the root ball comfortably with an inch or so extra around the plant, then increase the pot size yearly until the plant is in a 50-centimetre pot, where it can stay.**
2. **Keep well watered at all times. Use rainwater if you can because tap water (especially hard water) is full of calcium, which is alkaline and neutralises the acid soil.**

Considering varieties

Lots of different varieties are available, and if you plant two varieties pollination will be far improved; try these blueberries:

- **Bluecrop.** A mid-season fruiting type that's well known and widely grown, producing lots of lovely fruits and with a great autumn colour.
- **Coville .** One of the latest-cropping types, it has large fruits that have the bonus of lasting well on the bush.
- **Earliblue.** An early fruiting variety that carries small, sweet berries and has a good autumn colour.

TIP

Grow one early, one mid-season and one late-cropping bush to extend your blueberry season.

Harvesting and storage

No special instructions are necessary as to how to pick your blueberries – simply pick them as soon as they're ripe and scoff them with glee! They don't store well after picking, but if you can't eat them all they're fine for freezing.

Strawberries

Strawberries have to be the archetypal flavour of the British summer. They're fairly easy to grow and are simply the tastiest treats from the plot. Many of the fruits you buy in supermarkets are sourced from abroad, and lack the exquisite flavour of good British strawberries. They're ideal plants for beginners and children to grow because they're quick-cropping and with a little care are very productive.

Strawberries are available both as ready grown plants or grown from seed, but more often than not gardeners skip the whole seed-sowing malarkey and simply plant ready grown plants from the nursery.

Getting started with strawerries

You can get strawberry plants in many places almost all year round including from your local DIY store, and even in supermarkets. The varieties in these places are usually limited, though, so you're far better ordering plants from a specialist nursery where the choice is greater and the quality more reliable. Most nurseries sell bare-rooted plants in little bundles, that you plant straight away. Sometimes they sell the plants on *runners*, the *adventitious* (long reaching) stems that naturally grow on strawberries with young plants attached to them. Strawberry plants can be productive for six or seven years but are best replaced every three years because after that point they become less productive and often diseased. Dig them up and plant a new batch in a new area of the allotment.

Strawberries grow in most soils as long as it's not heavy clay or too wet. The ideal is a well-manured, free-draining soil in full sun. In addition, add some fish blood and bone a week or two prior to planting out to get them going.

To plant your strawberries, follow these steps:

1. **Plant in rows 35 with centimetres between plants and 75 centimetres between rows. This allows you to walk down the rows and maintain and harvest them easily.**

   Don't plant them too deeply, because they'll struggle, so plant them with the crown (point where all the stems meet) at soil level. When they come bare-rooted make a small hole and spread the roots out in all directions and then backfill gently and firm down slightly.

2. **Water them very regularly and keep them weed-free at all times.**

3. **Protect them from slugs by using pellets, crushed eggs shells or some sharp grit around the base of the plants.**

4. **Remove the flowers of plants planted in the early spring so that the plants' energy is diverted into foliage and root growth, and not wasted on producing fruits.**

   This may sound drastic but in the long run you'll have better plants. This also applies to those planted late in the season – in September or October – on which fruits haven't had time to develop before the first frosts. The exceptions to this rule are plants bought on runners that are meant to grow quickly for a quick crop; spring-planted ones can be left to do their thing.

5. **Protect fruits from birds. As soon as the fruits start to develop, lay some fruit netting over the entire crop – ideally over some kind of frame support – so even persistent blackbirds cannot peck the netting and reach the fruits.**

   Strawberries may well have the lovely bright red colour and seeds on the outside that makes them so attractive to us but this attracts the birds as well who then happily devour your crop.

6. **Lay some soft barley straw (which you can get from most garden centres), or guinea pig hay bedding under the plants when the fruits develop.**

   This acts as a mulch to suppress the weeds and also protects the fruits from touching the ground, where they're likely to rot. If you cannot get barley straw don't worry – it is softer than other types, but they will do.

TIP

You can bring strawberries on early in March by placing a cloche or cloche tunnel (see Chapter 3) over the early plant varieties. This can bring the fruits on a couple of weeks earlier than usual.

Strawberry plants produce runners as soon as you start picking the fruit, and you need to remove these as soon as they appear, otherwise the fruits won't grow so large and the plants' energy is diverted into producing foliage on the new plants on the runners. If you're nearing the time to replace the whole strawberry bed, then allow some to develop and you can use these new plants in the new bed.

To propagate these new plants insert a small pot filled with compost into the ground near the mother plant and peg the runner into the top of the pot where a new plant is forming. Within a month you can simply chop the runner and you'll have a new, perfectly potted plant ready for the new bed. But if you see signs of an virus this is best avoided, or the new plants too will be infected.

Considering Varieties

There are three main types of strawberry available. The main ones for allotment growing are classified as *summer strawberries*, the second is a group called *perpetual strawberries* and the final group is *day neutral strawberries*.

Summer fruiting are the standard choice for the allotment, and there are early-, mid- and late-fruiting varieties. You get large fruited ones and others with small fruits, some are super sweet and others proper old fashioned English strawberries. Here are a few of my favourites.

- **Alice:** One of the best midseason varieties, and ideal for organic gardeners. It combines good disease resistance with super-sweet juicy red fruits.
- **Cambridge Favourite:** A traditional favourite grown on many pick your own farms. We used to grow this in my Granddads garden and the my Grandma would make the best jam out of them. Mid season with great flavour.
- **Christine**: One of the earliest to come to fruit and offers sweet uniformed red fruits. If grown under cover in a polytunnels will crop as early as mid-May.
- **Darlisette:** If you like them sweet this is the variety for you, an early fruiting variety that always goes down well!
- **Florence** is a late variety that shows great disease resistance and produces vigorous high yielding plants.
- **Marshmello** is one of the sweetest I have tried and produces lovely mid season crops.
- **Pegasus** offers good disease resistance and good full sweet crops. Great for organic gardeners. Mid season.
- **Rhapsody** produces perfectly formed glossy red fruit in heavy yields, long medium to large fruits that offer good disease resistance.

Perpetual strawberries produce fewer flowers and less fruit, but over a much longer period than summer fruiting types. You can remove the first flush of flowers to encourage the plant to crop later. These plants can run out of energy if the first crop is not stopped in this way, but will fruit into autumn if well managed.

- **Albion**: A vigorous variety that has good disease resistance and sweet, large fruits with that proper strawberry aroma.
- **Aromel:** An old variety that has an old school flavour, is susceptible to disease and is not the heaviest cropper . . . but is worth growing for the taste!

- **Mara des bois**: Exclusive to one grower, but still easy to get hold of, this variety grows great, sweet fruit that offers excellent disease resistance and a full flavour. Has a hint of the alpine strawberry taste which I love, and which reminds me of the wild strawberries we used to pick in Sweden when I was young.

Day neutral strawberries are only really worth growing if you want strawberries during early winter or early spring. They lack the flavour and size of summer strawberries, but do crop for a long time – which is why they are the type most supermarkets sell (and unfortunately not for the flavour). They will need to be grown in the green house so are usually grown in individually in 15cm's pots or in groups or 6 or more grow-bags.

- **Flamenco:** A pretty new variety that offers really heavy crops of sweet fruits and is great for organic gardeners due to its disease resistance.
- **Albion:** Number one for organic growers because of its disease resistant qualities. Long conical red fruits.

You can also have a go at growing alpine strawberries, which have intense flavour, although they are less juicy. They are usually grown from seed. Give these two a go:

- **Alexandria** is a nice variety that produces sweet little fruits on a really pretty little plant.
- **Baron Solemacher** is an readily available and popular variety that offers tiny sweet strawberries.

Harvesting and storage

Check your strawberry plants every two days when they're in fruit, and remove all ripe fruits as soon as they're ready. Any fruit that rots is liable to become diseased and this can quickly spread to the other fruits and plants.

Strawberries are ideal for jam, jellies, cordial and freezing.

After you've harvested the plants and they've finished for the year, cut all the foliage off and rake up the leaves and straw and they soon start to shoot again with new growth for next year.

Raspberries

Raspberries are a popular fruit to grow on the allotment, partly because they taste so good but mainly because they cost a small fortune in the shops. As a result they can be a truly money-saving crop. They're so easily damaged that nine times out of ten most of the fruit you buy is damaged and only suitable for pulping in sauces and jams.

Raspberries are quite easy to grow and very productive, so are ideal allotment crops. Also, they establish quickly so you don't have to wait ages for a decent crop.

Getting started with raspberries

Raspberries are sold during autumn and winter as packs of *bare rooted* canes (with bare roots not in a pot), which can be ordered from specialist fruit nurseries or bought from garden centres. Only buy named varieties from a trusted supplier. They grow best in soil that's slightly acidic, and won't be happy in alkaline soils, so you may need to adjust the pH levels using the appropriate methods (see Chapter 6 on analysing and balancing your soil). Add a good load of well rotted manure or compost to the soil two weeks before planting, remove all the weeds, and dig over the area well. These plants like a sunny spot. Summer raspberries can be grown satisfactorily in semi-shade but autumn varieties need lots of sun to ripen.

To plant your raspberries, follow these steps:

1. **Hammer in some 2.5-metre pointed stakes at 3-metre intervals and then attach three rows of 3 millimetre galvanised wire at 75, 105 and 165 centimetres from the ground.**
2. **Plant your canes at exactly the same depth as the nursery mark on the stem, which should be between 5 and 8 centimetres deep. Any deeper and the plant won't shoot or thrive at all. Dig a channel 30 centimetres wide and 5–8 centimetres deep and space the plants 40 centimetres apart. Spread the roots evenly in the hole, backfill and firm down gently.**
3. **Cut the stems down to 30 centimetres above ground level, ensuring that the cut is just above a bud, and then water well.**
4. **Let the plants grow to 15 centimetres above of the tops of the wires and tie them in as they grow.**

After the first year cut down to the ground any stems that have fruited in autumn leaving between six and eight new canes for fruiting the following year.

Raspberries are hungry feeders, so after planting and each spring lay a good mulch of well rotten manure or compost around the base of the plants.

Considering varieties

Raspberries come in summer- or autumn-fruiting varieties. The summer varieties are ready to harvest in July and August and the autumn ones in late summer right up until the last frosts. Try these summer varieties:

- **Cascade delight**: A mid-season variety that produces really sweet fruits in heavy crops. Not too spiny for easy picking.
- **Glen Ample:** A mid season variety that is spineless and a heavy cropper. Likes shelter and warmth to do well though.
- **Glen Fyne:** My favourite summer season variety for flavour, it produces heavy crops over a long season.
- **Glen Moy:** This is probably the best early variety for heavy crops and flavour, and, being easy to manage, is ideal for the allotment.
- **Malling Admiral:** Easy to grow and very popular, offer some resistance to aphids and virus (See chapter 7) and produces a great, hearty, sweet crop.
- **Octavia:** Produces really late crops that are heavy and sweet.
- **Tadmor:** Crops later than most and produces a lots of lovely fruit; crops for up to six weeks.

Autumn varieties are gaining popularity because they produce fruit on side-shoots (from the main shoots) sent up the same year. At the end of the season all you do is cut them to just above the ground after you have picked all the fruit in autumn.

- **All Gold**: A freak variety from a seedling found growing amongst a crop of Autumn bliss. Produces yellow fruit that have an even better flavour than its parent plant.
- **Autumn Bliss:** A really sturdy variety that will not usually need to be tied to a support. Heavy cropper in August and September
- **Polka:** Dead easy to grow and produces tasty berries for a long period. Has won awards for its flavour in county shows.
- **Tulameen:** Produces lovely really large berries that are delicious, rady from late July and not too thorny.

Harvesting and storage

Raspberries ripen over a good few weeks, and you need to check every day to pick the sweet fruits. Simply squeeze them gently between your fingers and pull, leaving the plug in the middle on the plant.

If you have an abundant crop, raspberries are perfect for jam. You can also freeze them to enjoy all year round.

Growing Currants

Blackcurrants, whitecurrants and redcurrants are fantastic fruits that are full of antioxidants and a whole range of vitamins, but strangely many people have never eaten them fresh from the bush and only ever as jams and jellies or in juices. They're easy plants to grow, and are very productive and hardy – when I was little at our family home in Sweden, we had a row of currants that were subject to temperatures of –18 degrees centigrade or colder. Blackcurrants and redcurrants are the two main types; they require the same conditions but are pruned differently. Whitecurrants are treated in the same way as red.

Blackcurrants

Currants like a fertile clay loam soil but grow in any well improved soil full of organic matter. They're shallow-rooted plants but benefit from a deeply dug, well drained soil. Incorporate a load of manure or compost before planting, clear all the weeds and they'll do fine.

Blackcurrants can be bought as pot-grown plants from garden centres or during autumn and winter as bare-rooted plants from specialist nurseries, and planted straight away. Blackcurrants are easy to propagate from cuttings so you only ever need to buy the plants once and you can have a lifetime supply.

Getting started with blackcurrants

When you get your new plants, check the roots for any damage and cut off any very long or damaged roots and if they're dry soak them in a bucket for a few hours to get them nice and moist. They're planted in the same way as gooseberries (see the relevant section earlier in this chapter) with 1.2 metres between plants. Ensure that you plant them at the same level as they were in the nursery by looking for the nursery mark on the stem.

Pruning

The main thing to consider with blackcurrants is the pruning, which needs to be done annually in early winter to remove old wood that's already fruited in order to encourage and make room for new stems that will fruit in future. Prune newly-planted bushes down to just above the crown to encourage a flourish of new stems, leaving two buds on each stubby stem (see Figure 17-5). You won't get any fruit for the first year, but by pruning like this you're creating a plant that's easier to look after and train well. Blackcurrants only fruit on the previous year's wood, so after the second year you need to cut out at the base the old wood that's fruited, leaving the new stems to fruit the next year. This is an ongoing process year after year. You can easily tell the old wood because it still has the little stalks left behind on it after picking the fruits.

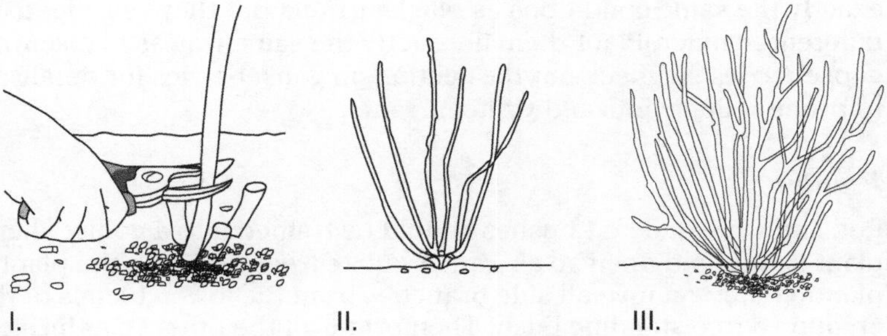

Figure 17-5: Pruning a blackcurrant bush.

Considering varieties

Here are some of my favourite blackcurrants to try.

- **Baldwin**: A really old fashioned mid-season variety that in my mind still tastes amongst the best.
- **Ben Lomond:** Another compact variety that is ideal for the allotment, producing a good heavy crop.
- **Ben Sarek**: A neat, compact shrub that is ideal if you are short of space (it reaches 90 centimetres). Really hardy, and produces a great crop every year.
- **Big Ben:** Produces a bumper early crop of currants that are twice the size of normal berries. Late cropping and mildew resistant (see chapter 7)
- **Wellington:** A really hardy variety that produces heavy, shiny crops.

Harvesting and storage

Blackcurrants can be picked over a long period any time from when they become ripe. To make sure that they prune things properly many gardeners snip the whole fruiting stem off at the base and then pick the berries off afterwards; this is a great way to prune and harvest at the same time. Alternatively you can just pick them as required and then prune the bush in the winter. Blackcurrants, of course, are ideal for making jams and jellies, juicing and even freezing.

Redcurrants and whitecurrants

Redcurrants and whitecurrants are delicious additions to summer puddings adding colour and a sharp bite. They make an attractive garnish and can be made into jellies, juices and cordials. Redcurrants and whitecurrants like exactly the same conditions as blackcurrants but they're pruned in a slightly different manner. Plant them in exactly the same way as blackcurrants and gooseberries so check out the section on gooseberries for details. Here's how to prune redcurrants and whitecurrants.

Pruning

Red and white currant bushes should be trained into a goblet shape so the plant is nice and open so air can circulate freely through the plant. After planting they remove all side branches from the lower 10cm's of the plant creating a free standing bush. Then prune all the other to a third of their initial length, making sure you cut just above a bud that faces away from the centre of the plant.

Redcurrants and whitecurrants fruit on two- or three-year-old wood so after planting you do no other pruning for the first year (unless removing damaged or diseased wood). After this, in winter remove any 3-year-old wood that has previously fruited (this old wood is usually darker in colour than the rest of the plant). Prune close to the main stem near a bud which will grow and replace it. You can then prune back all side shooting stems back to one or two buds, to encourage new healthy flowering spurs on which fruit will develop.

In subsequent years, prune all new shoots that come from the main framework to one bud from a main lateral stem, and remove any unproductive stems down to the nearest productive bud.

In a nutshell, you can cut out any wood older than 3 years old where it joins the main plant. Doing this every year keeps the plant healthy and open in its shape, allowing air to circulate and reducing the risk of disease.

Considering varieties

Some good redcurrants include:

- **Junifer.** This is the earliest variety and bears fruit from July onwards. It can fruit on new and one-year-old wood so you can get crops quite quickly.
- **Rovada.** This variety is the latest cropper and produces up to 2.7 kilos (6 pounds) of tasty red fruits per plant.

Amongst the best of the whitecurrants are:

- **Blanca.** Blanca crops late and produces heavy crops of white, pearl-like fruits in August.
- **White Pearl.** Carrying honey-coloured white fruits, White Pearl are excellent made into jellies and deserts.

Harvesting and storage

Harvest and store redcurrants and whitecurrants in the same way as blackcurrants. All three contain vitamins B1 and C, and are rich in iron, phosphorus, potassium, fibre, copper and manganese – tasty and good for you too.

Growing Greenhouse Exotics

All sorts of exotic fruits that don't thrive outside on the plot can be grown in the greenhouse. Many of these crops aren't hardy enough to grow well in the British climate, but some can be grown under glass. Grapes, for example, can be grown outside fairly easily in the south of England but won't ripen well in cooler parts of the country. Lemons, oranges, limes, kiwis, passion fruits and melons can all be grown under glass or in polytunnels.

Kiwi fruits

Kiwis can be grown quite well outdoors in the UK as long as you can offer them a sunny wall or trellis to grow on. Our climate is fairly similar to that in New Zealand, where these fruits thrive, so it's well worth you having a stab at it. They're best trained as espaliers (see the 'Training trees' section earlier in this chapter for more on these). Most female varieties are only pollinated by males, so if you use these you will have to plant two varieties to get a crop. In an allotment setting, don't bother: Just get a self fertile variety.

Getting started with kiwis

Kiwis like a very rich soil full of organic matter. Train them flat against a wire network in the greenhouse, or grow them up a trellis and wires outside, tying them in as they grow. They are really vigorous plants that need regular trimming back or they will swamp their given space. To plant your kiwis either in the greenhouse or outside, follow these steps:

1. **Plant the kiwi in improved organic-rich soil in full sun in the middle of its supporting trellis or in the greenhouse in a30-centimetre pot for the 1st year (transfer to a 60-centimetre pot the next year).**

2. **Water well, mulch with composted bark (or similar), and keep weed-free.**
3. **Tie in new shoots to develop an espalier shape over the support, tying in side shoots along vertical wires.**
4. **Reduce these fruiting shoots after fruiting in winter to two buds passed where the last fruit was.**
5. **Continue pruning each fruiting shoot as in the last step until they plant fills the space.**
6. **Keep the plant pruned to within the space given.**

In the green house you will need to hand-pollinate the flowers by rubbing the centre of a male flower using a small paintbrush, then rubbing the brush on the centre of a female flower. In the garden this will help, but the bees should do the job.

Considering varieties

In past times all kiwi plants were either male or female and you had to have one male plant for every six females to get a crop....fine for commercial growers but for the home grower impossible so don't bother. Nowadays you can get hermaphrodite plants that bear both male and female flowers – these are much better for those of us with restricted space.

Harvesting and storage

Harvesting your kiwis is easy – just pick them when needed. Kiwis are a great low-calorie food, high in fibre, vitamin C and potassium. Try kiwi ice cream as a way of preserving excess fruit.

Melons

Melons are becoming more and more popular as a home-grown fruit, and you can expect good results if you can provide the right conditions in the greenhouse. Don't try and grow them outside – you may well get lucky but they're far more suited to the warmer conditions inside the greenhouse. They're fairly easy to grow, but the trick lies in getting the fruits to pollinate at the right time and in selecting the best four fruits to develop into large melons.

Getting started with melons

Melons are a challenge to grow and the best starting point is getting good seeds. Don't use ones you have collected from shop bought melons, as these will have been grown in much warmer countries and the seeds will more than likely grow but not produce decent fruit. Always buy seeds from a UK-based supplier to be sure. Melons need lots of organic matter, regular watering and for great results if you can provide a constant temperature of 18 °C or more.

To sow your melons, follow these steps:

1. **Sow two seeds directly into a 8-centimetre pot and place in a propagator at 20–25 degrees centigrade to germinate in late April to May.** If both germinate, remove the weaker plant. They soon shoot and as soon as they have two true leaves are ready to be transplanted into growbags or organic-rich soil in the greenhouse.
2. **Draw up little mounds of soil about 10cm's high and plant the seedlings deep into the mound about 5cm;s deeper than the were in the pots.** This stops them getting waterlogged and rotting.
3. **Place a fan trellis behind the plant to grow it up, and also tie some strings from the trellis up into the roof of the greenhouse.** The vines can grow up and along this if they get that big.
4. **Remove the growing tip on the main stem when the plant has four leaves growing.** Doing so encourages the plant to grow four shoots, each of which will produce a single melon if you are really lucky!
5. **Keep the plants well watered and reliably moist but not too damp otherwise the fruits split this applies throughout their entire growing period.**

Once the flowers have formed, use a paintbrush to brush the male flowers and then the female ones, transferring the pollen between them. This fertilises the plant to enable it produce fruits. The female plants can be identified by the swollen mini-melons behind the flowers. Do this a few times over several days to ensure pollination. To look after you developing melons carry out the following steps:

1. **Once the melons have formed and are the size of cricket balls suspend them using string nets from the ceiling like little hammocks so they don't snap off the plant.**
2. **Thin out fruits if necessary. Only allow 4-5 fruits per plant to develop.**
3. **Feed weekly as the fruits form using a liquid tomato feed to encourage sweet, healthy fruits.**

TIP

During the summer, place a large bucket of water in the greenhouse. The water will evaporate and create a nice humid environment for your melons to grow in.

Considering varieties

The three following varieties are definitely worth trying:

- **Castella (Amber Nectar).** This variety is claimed to do well outdoors but I'm not convinced – but it may be worth a go in warmer parts of the UK. It produces large, 1.3-kilo (3 pound) melons that are really sweet.
- **Edonis F1.** A fast-to-flower-and-mature variety that's well suited to growing in the UK, producing lovely melons with pale orange, sweet flesh.
- **Galia F1.** This is a vigorous variety that produces fine melons quite quickly. It's easy to grow and usually very successful.

Harvesting and storage

You can tell easily that melons are ready to harvest by the sweet smell they give off. Melons are unsuitable for freezing, so you'll just have to share them with your allotment friends. To get the perfect melon, wait for the stem that holds it onto the plant to start to crack – a sure sign that the melon is ready to drop. Pick the melon, chill it for a couple of hours and eat straight away. If you meet with success, then I tip my hat to you: You will experience a taste that you can never get from shop-bought melons, which are harvested before they ripen properly so they can travel without going bad.

Chapter 18

Nurturing Flowers on an Allotment

In This Chapter

- Creating colourful cuttings
- Cultivating flowers to eat
- Selecting super seed heads

Some plot holders consider growing flowers a waste of space; I disagree. Allotments would be far less attractive spaces without flowers, and the beneficial insects they attract can help your fruit and vegetables to thrive. Also, to many the allotment is a way to save money. If you figure that a decent bunch of flowers from a good florist sets you back anywhere from a tenner to fifty pounds or more, growing flowers is a great way to have your house fully stocked with cut flowers from spring right through until autumn, for the price of a few packets of seeds. Flowers are not always just ornamental: Some are also edible, and can be grown to decorate salads and make main courses and desserts a real event.

Growing Beautiful Flowers for Cutting

Picking flowers for the house is one of life's simple pleasures. My little girl loves bringing flowers in to her mum. Growing flowers on your allotment for cutting means your garden at home remains intact. You can choose from all sorts of fantastic blooms, but if you go for cut-and-come-again varieties you have a constant supply. Not only are these types of plant really productive but they won't leave a gaping hole in your flowerbeds. In general, allotmenteers want to dedicate most of their plots to food production, so cut-and-come-again flowers offer the best use of a limited space. Some keep flowering for four months or more.

Sweet peas

Sweet peas are all-time favourite annuals and very easy to grow. They come in a range of colours, ranging from white to pink to mauve, with flowers that are usually scented and – you're sure to find one to please everyone.

As members of the pea family, sweet peas have the really distinctive pea-type flowers. They are climbing flowers with twining tendrils that they use to attach themselves to wires, trellises or other plants. You can grow them to provide temporary screens, which can be useful if you plan to grow crops that need shelter from the midday sun, such as some types of lettuce. Sweet peas can reach up to 2 metres in height, and keep flowering over a long period. If you pick them regularly, this delays the plant setting seed and prolongs the flowering period.

Unlike most peas the seeds and foliage of sweet peas are poisonous, so they are definitely for the vase and not the plate.

Sweet peas like a sunny aspect with well-drained soil and benefit considerably from a good load of compost worked in before planting. They're best grown up canes with horizontal wires attached every 20 centimetres, so put in a cane every 20 centimetres to create a row and then wire them together. Sweet peas are traditionally sown in special tall pots or *root trainers* (similar to seed cells but they open like a book so you can remove the plants without disturbing the roots). Do this indoors or in the greenhouse from autumn through to February so they are ready to plant out in April. Alternatively, plant them *in situ* as soon as the soil is warm in the spring. Seeds sown *in situ* are best sown in April and May, but you may have less success than with indoor-sown plants.

To sow your sweet peas, follow these steps:

1. **Soak the seeds on blotting paper until they sprout. Throw away any that don't swell and shoot, because they won't grow.**
2. **Sow the shooting seeds gently, 1 centimetre deep in root trainers.** Root trainers are great for plants that don't like to be transplanted. Alternatively, you can grow them in toilet roll inner tubes or rolled up newspaper, but these rot quickly and need to be planted as soon as possible (toilet roll tube and all) into their final home. As a result this method is only good for spring-sown seeds.
3. **For cordon-grown plants (see the nearby sidebar), very carefully pinch out the growing tip when three leaves have been produced.** The tip might otherwise develop into a long main stem that usually won't produce loads of flowers. Pinching out encourages side shoots to grow, and these are more vigorous.
4. **Plant out in well-prepared ground at the base of a pole for support, or in pots or by a trellis ready for them to race up.**

Cordon training for top quality flowers

Sweet peas can be left to find their way up the supports, but if you're willing to spend some time and effort training them you reap the rewards with show-quality flowers. Choose one main stem and pinch out the others, leaving one strong main stem. You then train this up the support, removing all the side shoots. It's advisable to remove the tendrils as well because these tend to twine with neighbouring plants, making training difficult, but you need to tie the plant onto the supports gently.

Dahlias

Dahlias have been a garden favourite forever, with well over 50,000 varieties out there to choose from in every conceivable colour – apart from the seemingly impossible blue. Dahlias have recently experienced a surge in popularity and are deemed pretty cool again, popping up in gardens at Chelsea and flower shows all over. You can find a dahlia for every style of garden, they make great cut flowers, they repeat flower over a long period and they look marvellous. Dahlias range from 30 centimetres all the way up to giants 2.5 metres tall, and the flowers range from the sizeof a golf ball right up to 30-centimetre diameter dinner plates.

The history of dahlias is long and complex but basically they're from South America and Mexico and are *tuberous* (grown from an underground tuber) perennials. Dahlias are grouped according to their flower type, of which there are ten, and I could write a whole book on them alone (many people have). I suggest you look closely at what your stockist offers and then chose the ones you like the look of.

Getting started with dahlias

Dahlias are usually grown from tubers that you can buy in garden centres or from specialists who have a far greater range if you want something that little bit more unusual. Some can also be grown from seed. Dwarf varieties can be grown from seed, or from cuttings and division, and can be a lot of fun. You may well be surprised with a totally new variety and unusual colours (good luck identifying a new one if you do: there are hundreds).

Dahlias like well drained soil with a pH of around 7 (see Chapter 6 on analysing and balancing your soil). They like a heavily manured soil and a good dose of bone meal, so in the autumn dig in some muck and, after a few weeks, spread and rake in some bone meal and leave it over winter ready for planting next year. This kind of treatment is exactly what you do for all sorts of vegetables, so you can do it as part of your autumn tidy up and preparation for next year.

Dormant tubers can be planted around six weeks before the last frost, and as soon as the soil is warm enough they'll start to shoot and grow. The foliage should form well after the final frost, which will strike the plant down instantly. If you see a shoot appear above ground and then are faced with an imminent frost, cover it with a cloche (see Chapter 3 for more on these).

Pot-grown plants and those grown from cuttings grown in the greenhouse or under cover can be planted out when all risk of frost has passed. This is something not to rush, so do make sure that winter has well and truly turned its back before planting out.

Because dahlias are all very different in size, the best thing is to read the instructions that come with the plant to work out planting distances. On average, plants that reach between 1.2 and 1.5 metres in height need about 70 centimetres between them; those that reach between 75 centimetres and 1.1 metres need 55 centimetres and the smaller dwarf ones need about 40–45 centimetres between them. All plants need some kind of support, especially if you're growing them for display; the delicate stems break easily in gusts of wind.

TIP

To support tall varieties, insert a stake in the planting hole when you plant the tuber, then backfill. As the plant grows, tie it in gently. For smaller varieties, insert three canes around the plant and wrap some green twine around the canes to create simple support.

About two months after planting, apply a high-nitrogen, slow-release fertiliser. Professional growers apply all sorts of potash, super-phosphates and other fancy feeds during different parts of the development, but if you just apply some general fertiliser you get more than adequate results.

If you want to collect the seeds from dahlias you need to leave some flowers intact in the plant and wait for the seed heads to be produced. After flowering, the plant produces green seed pods, which you can pick when they turn yellow or brown. Cut the seed stems off, leaving about 15 centimetres of stem, and hang them in bunches in a dark place with a paper bag over the pods. You can then store the seeds for sowing next year. To extract the seeds simply pop the pods open onto a sheet of newspaper and blow the small bits away, leaving the seeds on the paper.

Lifting and storage

Dahlias are tender and won't survive any frost. This applies to the tubers as well. You may be able to leave them in the ground in warmer areas of the country as long as you can offer them protection with a thick mulch, but generally they need to be lifted each year and stored.

When the foliage has turned black from the frost in autumn, trim it all back to about 15 centimetres. Then lift the tubers, brush the soil off and trim any small roots. Wash the tubers and allow them to dry for a couple of days. Some gardeners then treat the tubers with a dusting of fungicide powder – you can get the right ones in garden centres. Hang the tubers upside down so they can dry, but don't allow them to get too hard. Then place them in a crate and cover them with vermiculite (you can get this at the garden centre) or some other dry material. You should check them every now and then over winter and cut off and discard any bits that turn mouldy. You can use these as planting tubers in the spring.

Sweet Williams

Sweet Williams are a long-standing garden favourite. They're easy to grow, sweetly scented and brightly coloured. Although they're short-lived *perennials* (coming up every year) they are generally treated as *biennials* (grown from seed one year, flowering the next and then dying). The flowers come in various shades of pink, purple, white, red and all the colours in-between. They're brilliant additions to the allotment because they encourage bees onto your plot to work their magic. Sweet Williams like loamy, slightly alkaline soil and a position in full sun, but tolerate partial shade as well.

Sweet Williams can easily be grown from seed direct on the plot, and should be sown as soon as the last frosts have long gone. They can be *propagated* (creating more plants) from seed and cuttings, which you sow in late spring or early summer to flower the following year. Alternatively, buy ready grown *plugs* (very small containers holding an individual plant in soil that you simply pop out and transplant), which are usually pretty cheap. These will flower the following spring. Personally I'd buy them as ready grown plugs. For about a tenner – you can expect between 50 and 70 individual plants, and this saves you all the bother of sowing them. All you need to do is plant them out each year and you'll have plenty of fragrant flowers on your plot. Sweet Williams often reseed themselves if they're left to set seed, but you may end up with the parent variety appearing if you planted hybrid varieties.

Sweet Williams can be helped on their way by applying a balanced fertiliser before sowing or planting out, and then again every six weeks or so to keep them healthy. To sow your Sweet Williams, follow these steps:

1. **Sow seeds direct in the soil in July, 6 centimetres apart and cover with a sprinkling of fine soil. They germinate in a week or so.**
2. **Thin plants to about 10–15 centimetres apart and keep them well watered and moist at all times. Young plants suffer from drought, so make sure that you don't let them get thirsty during dry spells.**

These plants flower the following year. *Deadhead* them (remove the dead flower heads) to encourage new flowers. Leave some flowering heads to produce seeds to self-seed for the following year. Cut back older plants 50 per cent to encourage a new lease of life and a second flush of flowers.

Zinnias

Zinnias are mostly grown as annuals from seed and they come in a huge variety of colours: Pink, purple, yellow, orange and green. They're quite easy to grow and are usually sown *in situ* because they don't like much root disturbance. Alternatively you can grown them early indoors for later transplanting. Zinnias are often confused with dahlias because the flowers look similar on some varieties. They're becoming increasingly popular again because of the exceptional range of colours they come in, and the ease with which they can be grown from seed.

Zinnias like a position in full sun in a rich, loamy, well drained soil and some shelter from cold winds. Prepare the soil well before planting or sowing by raking to a fine tilth, and apply a balanced fertiliser to the soil a week before planting or sowing.

To sow your zinnias, follow these steps:

1. **Sow seeds indoors *in succession* (every other week or so to get flowers over a long period)) between March and May. Sow seeds in seed modules or in individual pots, cover them with a sprinkling of fine compost and water gently, or sow directly in the soil when the soil has warmed in spring and the risk of frost has passed. Sow seeds in shallow 3-millimetre drills covered with finely raked soil. Drills should be 30 centimetres apart. Water with a fine rose.**
2. **Place indoor sown seeds into a propagator by a sunny window at a constant temperature of around 20–25 degrees centigrade and they'll germinate between one and three weeks.**
3. **When indoor-sown plants reach a size ready for handling, harden them off for a week or so to get them acclimatised to the outdoors.**
4. **Plant out at 23–30-centimetre spacings or thin those sown in situ to the same. (Always check the package for correct sowing and planting distances.)**

Then they're easy! Just keep them well watered and moist and pick them as required.

Cleome

Cleome, or spider flowers, are visually striking and will certainly receive the odd glance of admiration from other plot holders. Cleome originate from sub-tropical and tropical regions all over the world and the commonly cultivated ones are half-hardy or frost-tender annuals. They're a little difficult to grow from seed, because they need fluctuating temperatures to germinate well. The flowers are most impressive, with an almost spiky appearance and lots of 'spider legs' jutting out from them. They come in pinks, whites, purples, and mauves and have distinctive *palmate* (like an open hand) foliage as well. They can grow quite tall – up to 1.8 metres.

Cleome like a fertile, free-draining soil. They grow best in sandy soils but also grow in improved soil on the allotment, as long as it's free-draining and not soggy and heavy. They're best raised under glass and need careful temperature control to germinate well.

To sow your cleome, follow these steps:

1. **Sow seeds in large seed modules in good, well-drained seed compost from mid-January to mid-March. Just cover the seeds with a sprinkling of compost and moisten with a fine rose.**
2. **Place in a propagator in a light place with plenty of sunlight. Now this is the important bit: daytime temperatures should be around 24– 28 °C and at night-time temperatures should be allowed to fall to around 20 °C. This may sound a bit of a range, but the fluctuation in temperature is needed for the seeds to germinate. If you have a sunny window sill or conservatory you may well get some success in a non-heated propagator because the seeds get warm in the day and cool at night, having the same effect.**
3. **When large enough to handle, transplant the seedlings into small pots and then harden off when all risk of frost has passed.**
4. **Plant out when the frosts have long gone and are no longer a risk. Space plants 20 centimetres apart in a sunny spot and be sure to keep them well watered during dry spells.**

Feed every four to six weeks with a balanced general fertiliser for the best flowers, and deadhead regularly.

Growing Edible Flowers

Flowers are grown to beautify a garden or to adorn your home with gorgeous blooms, but they can also be grown to add a real statement of seasonal colour to the dinner plate. The simple act of adding a few edible flowers to a boring green salad turns the otherwise green and dull into something far more exotic and pleasing to the eye. Half the pleasure of eating food is in the way it looks, so if it looks good it (usually) tastes good! Not only are flowers used to decorate, they can also be used to add flavour to dishes and can be used as a food colouring.

Whenever you're using flowers for culinary purposes it's important to ensure that they're bug free. Pollinators and other insects can often be found hiding inside the flowers so be sure to clean them well. A small, soft paintbrush is ideal for dusting any unwanted bugs out of flowers. Another easy method is to pick the flowers, place them in a container of water, then put them in a shed or garage where the insects will leave the flowers and head to the window in search of light.

You can find loads of edible flowers to try, but here are a few suggestions.

Nasturtiums

Nasturtiums for me conjure up vivid memories of childhood: down the allotment garden with my granddad, nasturtiums planted in large blocks along the paths, like a sea of bright orange flowers held above green scrambling foliage and covered in caterpillars. They're cool-season plants that seem to add an exotic flair to the garden.

Nasturtiums are a great addition to an organic garden because they're effective in keeping pests away from other plants such as peas and beans. Even better, the caterpillars of the Cabbage White butterfly like to feast on the nasturtium foliage instead of your cabbages.

The leaves are a great alternative to other peppery leaves, such as rocket and mizuna, adding a brilliant 'zing' to salads; they're also really nice finely chopped and added to cheese spreads and mayonnaise. You can eat the flowers in salads or serve with a dollop of mayonnaise inside the flower as a canapé. You can use the seeds in salads and even pickle them and use them in much the same way as capers.

Nasturtiums are amongst the easiest plants to grow, as they'll grow almost anywhere and in poor soils they still produce wonderful flowers – but for really lush foliage add lots of compost. They do require lots of sunshine and should never be allowed to dry out.

Some nasturtiums can become invasive and quickly fill a dedicated space; others are great in pots that contain their growth. They come in a few different varieties: some are climbers, some are busy and others are trailing and therefore ideal for hanging baskets and troughs.

In late spring sow seeds in rows 2 centimetres deep and 20– 30 centimetres apart and watered in lightly. They shoot and grow with very little attention required.

Lavender

Lavender is one of the most useful plants around and, as a garden designer myself, I see it used in almost every classical, modernist and cottage garden ever designed. But it's also useful as a kitchen herb – it's related to mint. The flowers are very good when added to sugar, a combination that's often used as flavouring for deserts. The leaves can be used as an alternative to rosemary in nearly all dishes, and is especially good in herb breads. One of the best uses I have come across is to use the stiff lower stems as skewers for kebabs. This is particularly good for fruit kebabs (be sure to soak the stems in water for a good few hours first). Lavender is also a traditional ingredient in Herbes de Provence.

Lavender is a very useful plant on the allotment as it's one of the best attracters of beneficial pollinators you can find. Bees swarm to it and honey growers often sell lavender honey at a premium because of its superior flavour.

Lavender is best bought as a ready grown plant and planted in a sunny spot on the allotment. You can grow it from seed, but be patient: seeds can take up to three months to germinate after an initial period of up to six weeks kept in the fridge. I'd always buy ready grown plants in order to save time and effort.

Lavender likes a free-draining soil and is no good planted in heavy clay where it simply won't thrive. It can be grown in heavy soil that's been improved with plenty of organic matter over a number of years. Grow it on mounds so that the roots don't sit in waterlogged soil.

Ideally plant lavender in April or May, and then trim it back so that the plants can concentrate their efforts on growing healthy root systems and bushy growth. Lavender can also grow well in pots, but these need to be large because lavender has a deep root system. Also use a compost that's soil-based and free-draining.

Prune lavender once a year when the flowers have died in the autumn or in the spring before the new growth starts. Trim the dead flowers off and lightly trim the foliage back by 2–3 centimetres to maintain a compact, bushy shape.

Lavender is traditionally used as an edge-of-path plant, so why not adopt a little bit of flair on your plot ? Paths edged with a compact variety look attractive. Also, you can edge the herb area on your plot with a neat lavender hedge. Allotments may well be used mainly for crop production, but they can look great too!

Alliums

The *allium* family of plants is vast and includes the obviously edible onion and garlic. Actually, you can eat all parts of every member of this family, and the flowers are often used in salads and as decoration for all sorts of dishes. The seeds can be used as a potent addition to recipes. Be slightly wary of allium flowers, because they can be rather powerful, but some offer a pleasant, mild, oniony flavour.

The most obvious flowering alliums are chives, which are dead easy to grow and not only provide the hollow stems so often used in cooking but also the bulb, which can be eaten like a small mild onion. The flowers are lovely tossed in a salad. You can also eat garlic flowers, and even Ramsons, the wild garlic that you can smell from hundreds of metres away in its natural woodland habitat.

Most alliums are available as bulbs, so don't bother growing them from seed unless you've collected some and want to try for a bit of fun. Alliums like a free-draining soil that doesn't really need to be to rich, as long as it's not waterlogged. Waterlogged soil can cause rot. Plant the bulbs in the autumn to flower the following spring.

Most alliums reproduce bulbs underground, and these can be lifted and divided every couple of years to replenish and expand stocks. You'll soon find that you have loads of bulbs – I often take lots home and use them as ornamentals in the garden, or donate some to friends and family. Many also do well in pots for seasonal displays on the patio.

TIP

Alliums don't repeat flower readily, so if you pick all the flowers, that's your lot. Leave some flowers on the plant and let them set seed. You can sow the seeds indoors in late winter to plant out in spring, or just keep the dry flower heads for flower displays. Many will self-seed rapidly across the garden as well, so if you want to stop this don't let them set seed.

Growing Flowers for Drying and Seed Heads

Many flowers can be grown in the allotment with flowers and seed heads that are ideal for drying and using in displays or in pot-pourri. Garden designers use these flowers to add interest in the autumn and winter to planting schemes they are ideal for cutting too. Hundreds of flowers can be artificially dried using silica gel, but many dry easily simply by air drying. These to me are the most useful, unless you want to set up a flower-drying cottage industry!

Poppies

Poppies are very short-lived flowers that grace the garden or plot for what seems such a brief moment, but the seed heads that follow last for months or even years, especially if you dry them. The many different types of poppy range from the great big Opium poppy and oriental poppies to really colourful varieties ideal for cutting, such as the Iceland poppy. They're all easy to grow from seed and are generally species that thrive on poor, recently disturbed soils.

Do poppies really induce sleep?

Most poppies do contain certain levels of opium, which is well known as the source of medicinal drugs such as morphine and codeine. Of course illegal drugs such as heroin also come from processed opium derived from opium poppies. The old Wizard of Oz scene when Dorothy falls asleep in a field of poppies would be very unlikely to happen – the opiate that comes from poppies is actually the secreted sap from the flower heads as they're cut, so unless you absorb lots through you skin by running naked through a poppy field full of sliced seed heads this is pretty unlikely! In the film it was more of a suggestion of the opium poppies' potential. Poppy seeds themselves don't contain any significant source of narcotic but can in fact be contaminated by the sap while inside the seed pods and therefore carry some narcotic level.

Getting started with poppies

Poppies are easily grown from seed sown in the ground, directly on your plot. Between March and May, sow the seeds in shallow drills 30 centimetres apart, in soil raked to a fine tilth. Thin the seedlings to 30 centimetres apart as soon as they're large enough to handle. Alternatively, sow in pots indoors in September and October and overwinter in a cool greenhouse or cold frame ready to plant out in spring, 30 centimetres apart.

Harvesting

Poppy flowers can be cut and used in flower arrangements but they generally don't last too long. You can make them last longer by dipping the cut ends in boiling water for ten minutes, or by holding the end over a candle to seal the end and stop the milky sap escaping. If you're drying seed heads, let the flowers fade and the petals fall off. You can then leave them on the plant to dry and cut off when they turn brown. These seed heads are very effective used in dried flower displays, or sprayed gold and silver for a funky centrepiece.

Poppy seeds can be collected as soon as the seed heads are dried out. When the seed heads turn brown simply split the seed heads in a brown paper bag and collect the hundreds of seeds that pop out. You can then use these seeds the following year.

WARNING! Not all poppy seeds are edible so don't use them for culinary purposes. The only one that produces edible seeds is the Opium poppy. Many other poppies are poisonous so heed this warning well!

Physalis

Physalis alkekengiis is a herbaceous perennial grown for its brilliant, long-lasting seed heads or fruits that can be used for decorations, wreaths, and flower displays during the autumn and winter months. Often called *Chinese lanterns* because the papery orange covering of the fruits looks just like a lantern, these plants are grown as ornamentals in gardens. They are also called Cape gooseberries.

Physalis can become really invasive with their searching underground roots, but they only reach between 40 and 60 centimetres in height. *Physalis peruviana* is a similar but much larger species, reaching up to 1.8 metres and is grown for its edible fruits encased in similar 'lanterns'. These small yellow fruits are quite tasty and you can use them in salads, desserts, dipped in chocolate or made into preserves.

Physalis can be grown as a perennial in southern parts of the country and mine keeps coming back year upon year. But you may find in cooler parts of the country that it should be grow as an annual or in pots taken in during the winter.

WARNING!

The unripe fruit of any Physalis variety is poisonous so don't eat them until they're fully ripe.

I would suggest growing one of the cape gooseberry types that produce edible fruits rather than the more ornamental Chinese lantern. Both look quite similar but at least the cape gooseberry tastes good too!

Getting started with physalis

Physalis is part of the *Solanaceae* family along with potatoes, tomatoes and the infamous deadly nightshade. It's said that if you can grow tomatoes then you can easily succeed with physalis. I think they in fact are much easier to grow, as even with some neglect they seem to thrive. On highly fertile soils they seem to produce too much vegetative growth (leaves) at the expense of the ripening fruit. They like free-draining soil and in fact thrive on sandy soils. It isn't worth sowing from seed unless you want loads of plants because one is usually enough, so get your plants ready grown from a nursery garden or a mail order company which specialises in them.

You can of course sow them inside in spring. To do so sow seeds in 8-centimetre pots and keep them in a propagator at around 18–21 °C until they show. Then keep them on a light window sill until late summer and plant them out in their final position. Some plants reach 2 metres in height, so need support as soon as they're about 30 centimetres tall.

Harvesting and storage

When picking fruits from cape gooseberries, ensure that they're fully ripened or they won't taste good and are slightly poisonous. They mature in early to mid-autumn and the seed heads turn a gorgeous bright orange colour. For drying, cut off the stems and hang upside down to dry in the shed for a week or so. They store for months ready for decorative displays. The orange lanterns sometimes disintegrate, but this doesn't matter because they leave behind a fascinating-looking skeleton 'cage' around the orange berry: This looks cool too!

Sedums

Sedums are great allotment plants because many of them are magnets to bees. Hundreds of varieties are around, all of which are *succulents* (plants with specially adapted fleshy leaves to store water). They can be planted and pretty much ignored while they do their thing. In terms of choosing varieties to suit your allotment needs I'd always keep to the more common garden varieties such as *Sedum spectabile* and its *cultivars* (named varieties), and *Sedum telephium* and its cultivars. *Sedum spectabile* is commonly known as the ice plant and is an autumn-flowering plant that livens up late summer and autumn gardens, adding a splash of colour to your fading plot. Sedums are extremely easy to grow, and are best bought as three- or five-litre plants from your local nursery. Most sedums like a sunny spot and free-draining soil and are easy to look after.

Getting started with sedums

You'll be hard pushed to find *Sedum spectabile* and *Sedum telephium* seeds anywhere, and as many varieties are hard to grow from seed you're best simply buying ready-grown plants. Once you've planted and established your plants, they're easy to propagate from cuttings or you can split clumps to make new plants.

To propagate your sedums, follow these steps:

1. **In early spring, just before they shoot into growth, dig up your sedum 5 centimetres all around the root ball and carefully lift it out the ground.**
2. **Place the root on the ground on its side and using a sharp spade slice it right through the middle. If the root is large enough you can then place the two halves flat on the ground and slice them in half leaving you with four quarters. Make sure that each section has some decent roots and at least two or three new shoots on it.**
3. **Replant the sections direct into the ground or you can pot them up in good compost to grow on or give to friends. Water them well.**

Sedums are brilliant plants for the allotment due to the fact that they're magnets to the bees and other useful pollinators. *Sedum spectabile* is often covered in bees during the late summer so I'd always have a few on my plot!

Harvesting and storage

To collect the seed heads, let them dry full on the plant. Cut them off at the base and use them in flower arrangements. You can also use the flowering stems in arrangements where they'll last for ages before fading.

Hops

Hops (*Humulus lupulus*) are useful plants to grow for winter arrangements but they grow very large and take up lots of space. I suggest growing them to cover your shed so as not to cast too much shade over your plot. Hops are climbing plants that scramble for 6 metres or more, but you can hack them back to keep them in check. They have vivid green foliage (although the Aurea variety has greenish-yellow foliage) and during the summer they carry spikes of straw-coloured, cone-like flowers that smell amazing .

Getting started with hops

Hops can be grown fairly easily from seed, but you're better off buying a ready grown plant and planting it directly onto your plot. They like a well drained, fairly rich soil in full sun or semi-shade and they're no problem to look after. Simply plant your hop plant and off it goes. Hops are perennial plants, so cut them right back to the ground in late autumn and they will come back the following spring.

Plants are either male or female, and the ones you buy in the garden centre are female plants. The name *hops* refers to female flowers. In commercial farms where they're grown for brewing, only female plants are used, because if the flowers become pollinated, they're no good for brewing.

Harvesting and storage

Hops make attractive foliage decorations for inside the home, and the aroma is a relaxing anti-stress remedy. The aroma comes from some pungent essential oils contained within the flower that are slowly released into the air. Dried hop garlands are a traditional decoration in old beamed houses where they're pinned to the beams or over doors and fireplaces. On a recent Internet search I found that a 45-centimetre garland from one supplier costs £15! So if they're your thing, grow them: Don't waste money buying them!

TIP

Dried hops are brilliant for aiding restful sleep. Place a good handful of the dried flowers in a cloth bag under your pillow and the aroma will send you off in no time.

Sea hollies

Sea hollies (*Eryngium*) are amongst the best flowers for decoration and drying you can grow. They have striking, thistle-like, bluish-purple flowers held above a brilliant silvery green foliage. Sea hollies are often used in flower arranging, and when dried look good in winter arrangements. The roots also used to be candied and eaten as sweets in times past, and were even used as an aphrodisiac, so they have many uses.

Getting started with sea hollies

Sea hollies are best bought as established plants and then planted on your plot. I'd buy at least two or three to give you plenty of flowers for cutting in the summer, and dry flower heads for autumn and winter. They like a free-draining soil and are best in coastal locations where they thrive in stony soils, but you can grow them happily on the allotment as long as the soil is not heavy clay and has been improved with plenty of grit. Some varieties do like moist conditions, but for the most part the ones you find in garden centres are the types that like it dry!

Harvesting and storage

Sea hollies flower in the summer and are best picked before the flowers are fully open. They last for ages. They can also be picked and dried for winter displays.

Part V
Getting the Most Out of Your Allotment

'Small garden, giant vegetables, just doesn't work, Ernest!'

In this part . . .

Taking on an allotment changes your life. For a start, you're suddenly part of a whole new community with a wealth of new friendships to make and knowledge to share. In this part I show you how to make the most of your new gang and how to give something back as well.

I also talk you through the ticklish subject of introducing children to the allotment. Showing kids that growing crops on their own patch of land can be absorbing and good for them and brings huge rewards. And talking of huge rewards, no book on allotment gardening would be complete without a discussion of what you need to do to grow your own prize veg – so I've included a chapter about that, too.

Chapter 19

Involving Children on the Allotment

In This Chapter

- Encouraging your children outside
- Picking easy, fast-growing crops for your children to try
- Creating projects to involve your children
- Promoting a healthy diet

Children and gardening is a subject very close to my heart. Children love gardening. I've worked in schools all over the country and also held talks at the Chelsea Flower Show and Gardeners' World Live exhibitions, and no more captive an audience exists than a group of children. For a child, there's something almost magical about planting a seed and watching it grow into something good to eat. When I was little, I couldn't wait to rush round to my grandfather's garden to see how well (or how badly) my plants were doing. When it came to harvest time I actually wanted to eat what I'd grown, not necessarily because I liked it, but because the vegetables were mine, from seeds that I'd sown. Gardening teaches children so many lessons they can't learn on a computer or in a classroom, such as how to take responsibility for nurturing their plants, and how to respect their own patch of land. They come to appreciate that hard work can reap fantastic rewards, and get to understand exactly where their food comes from.

This chapter gives you ideas for getting your children out and about and excited about your allotment (really, it's not hard!).

Reaping the Benefits of Gardening

I think that most parents have an image in their minds of their kids and how they'd like them to spend their time. We love the idea of them toiling away, getting fit and healthy, helping grow their own food in the safety of the allotment. Well, you know what? This can actually happen! I'm not claiming that an allotment is a cure all and can solve all youth's problems. But for children an allotment can be a great place to assert some kind of ownership and pride that they may never have had before. I feel it's essential to give your children a small patch of land that they can call their own and grow whatever they want on it (with your influence of course). This area will give them the sense of duty that's needed to grow their own. It doesn't have to be a huge area and they can stick to really easy-to-grow crops, but with your help it can be great fun for both of you. You don't have to do it thisway, of course, and it can be just as much fun simply getting them to help you on the plot but it definitely worked for me as a child.

Gardening helps your children understand nature and science, and how life cycles work. They also gain the most important benefit of all – spending time with you!

Keeping fit and healthy

Keeping an allotment is hard graft and involves a lot of mud! My kids actually enjoy digging and getting covered in dirt in the garden and it keeps them in the fresh air in safety.

Outdoor pursuits tend to be orientated around school or sports clubs, and the opportunities to get outside are more limited. I'm now going to mention the dreaded games consoles. Let's be real, the allotment isn't going to be a more attractive option to most kids than sitting in the warmth of your house playing 'Ninja Space Mice from Hell' or whatever, but if you get them interested at a fairly young age the seed will have been sown and the desire will always be there.

By far the most important fact about children growing their own food in a garden is the fact that they're far more likely to eat healthily – by being aware of where the food is from and having the pride of growing it they'll more than likely want to eat the stuff.

Digging, weeding, lifting, breathing fresh air, pushing a wheelbarrow, raking and so on are all physically demanding and help keep you and your kids in good shape.

Making magical memories

I always feel emotional when I write about my childhood in my grandfather's vegetable garden, not because it makes me sad but because of the lifelong memories it created for me and what it taught me about the important role that gardening played in his life and the positive effect it had on his family and friends. People who grow their own seem to exude something comforting and their sense of wellbeing and calm has a positive influence on children. I also talk from experience as I have three children and they love spending time in the vegetable garden. They spend hours with their grandfather on his plot forging exactly the same memories I have from my childhood; they experience the same excitement I did from simple tasks such as picking a pumpkin that they've grown ready to ripen and carve for Hallowe'en. I don't want to get all poetic on you but seeing history repeat itself and my own children knowing the same joys I did is truly wonderful.

Being outside and caring for a patch of land also improves your children's mental and social wellbeing. If they're involved in community garden projects, for example, this can help their team-building and confidence skills both of which have a great positive psychological effect on their overall wellbeing.

A really important lesson they also learn on your plot is to respect their surroundings. If they have to care for a patch of land in what's almost a public space, they'll surely learn to respect other green areas where they meet their friends. If you can let your children design their own area of your allotment they can also learn creative skills and, hopefully, a mutual admiration of public spaces and areas in the future.

Recognising where food comes from

I can say with some pride that my kids generally know the origin of their food. They can recognise most vegetables; they can even tell you where and how they grow. More importantly, by being exposed to fresh veg all the time, they like all of them. I'm sure that most children who hate their greens hate them because they weren't exposed to them from the word go or they were over cooked and mushy . Admittedly when I was young I went through phases of hating anything green but it didn't last and I'd always eat stuff that came from 'my patch'.

Parents all want to provide the best they can for their kids and by eating freshly grown veg you know exactly what is going into their bodies. I know that there are no nasty chemicals on the food I serve up to my children, and

I know that they are eating fresh veg as nature intended – full of nutrients and goodness. Many vegetables start to lose their nutritional content as soon as they're picked, but in the time it takes to walk down to the plot, pick some produce and get home again, you can give them the freshest veg around.

Growing Easy Vegetables and Flowers

Many vegetables are easy to grow, and as children can be pretty impatient the best veg to start with are the ones that grow fast. Thankfully, loads of veg are out there for them to try, most of which include the easiest to grow. Many can be grown in pots if you just want to start your children off gently, or you can simply involve them in what you're doing already and give them a few plants in your beds to call their own. Many cut-and-come again salad leaves are easy to grow along with radishes, pumpkins, and super-fast crops like snow peas. They can also grow sunflowers, strawberries, and their own cherry tomatoes.

Quick and easy leaves

Lots of really easy and quick salad plants can be grown by children on the allotment, and the best thing about many of these plants is the speed at which they grow. Some cut-and-come-again lettuces are ready to harvest within eight weeks or less. Most lettuces can be sown straight onto your plot and covered with a cloche (see Chapter 3 for more on these) and off they go but if you want an early harvest for the kids let them grow lettuce indoors in biodegradable pots so they can be planted out with little root disturbance. You can use cardboard egg boxes as cells, which can be great fun for kids. They can plant out the egg box cells and all direct onto the plot when the seedlings are ready. Try fast-growing salad leaves or just buy a cut-and-come-again blended seed mix, and they can be picking their own salad in as little as 40 days.

For more information on growing lettuces see Chapter 14.

Always choose fast-growing lettuce varieties for children so that they can see the result of their labour as soon as possible. Try these:

- **Lattuga Verde A Foglia Riccia:** These can be sown thinly in rows and sown 13 millimetres deep. You don't need to thin this variety and it grows quickly, offering a cut-and-come-again crop that's really easy to grow. It can be harvested in as little as 20 days.

- **Valamine:** This really popular fast-growing variety is one that everyone can grow with ease. It produces crisp, almost romaine-type leaves that have no bitterness and are great for summer crunch. They're fast-growing and easy to germinate direct in the ground from April to mid-May and then from August onwards.

Super-fast radishes

Radishes are ideal crops for children to grow because they're easy, very fast, not too fussy about soil, and don't need lots of space. I remember growing radishes as a child, and they have often been the starting point for many young gardeners. They can be sown direct in the soil from spring onwards and can be grown in between slower-growing crops such as carrots, or used as a marker to show where other plants are soon to sprout. They're mostly eaten raw but you can use winter radishes in stir fries and other cooked dishes. The most popular types to grow are summer radishes, which have a spicy taste that many children don't like, but they can be cooked and disguised amongst other veggies.

For more information on growing radishes see Chapter 10.

Radishes are usually ready to harvest anywhere from three to six weeks after sowing (for summer ones) and ten to twelve weeks (for winter varieties). Just pull them up as you need them. They're always best harvested as required for freshness but the long, white Japanese types should be lifted in the autumn: Others can be left in the ground until required.

TIP

Sow seeds at regular intervals to keep the supply constant and try several different varieties. This is a great way of showing your kids all about how even simple plants can come in all shapes, colours and sizes.

Chapter 10 has a section on radishes and provides a selection of varieties for you to try.

Perfect pumpkins

Pumpkins have to be the ultimate vegetable for children to grow on the plot; they're quite easy to grow from seed and the end result is so satisfying, and sometimes enormous, that the children will be hooked for life. The only drawback with pumpkins is the amount of time they take to mature: Some take over 100 days, and that's a long time for a small child to wait.

My eldest is five years old and she's grown pumpkins for the past two years. When we go and harvest one so we can place it in our conservatory to ripen, the excitement on her face is plain for all to see. In fact she struggles with the fact that on Halloween she has to cut it open and gouge its insides out to carve it – she likes to keep it whole and just look at it!

You can grow a single pumpkin plant in an area one metre square. For more detailed information on growing pumpkins and varieties to try, see Chapters 13 and 21.

Towering sunflowers

Another great plant for your children to grow on the allotment is the sunflower. No other flower grows quite so tall and no other flower makes people smile quite like it. Sunflowers can reach heady heights – the tallest one to date reached over 7.6 metres high and the largest ever sunflower head measured 82 centimetres across. When we were little, my three brothers and I used to see who could grow the tallest sunflower (I think it had something to do with the TV show 'Blue Peter'!) and it was always dead exciting waiting to see whose would win! The best thing about sunflowers is that they're so easy to grow and require very little attention. They also seem to be a natural part of the allotment landscape.

Getting started with sunflowers

Sunflowers like a fairly rich soil and thrive in the good soil on your plot. Always be a bit conscious of other plot holders when siting your sunflowers so as to ensure that you don't cast too much of a shadow on their plots. They like a position in full sun and do require regular watering during dry spells , otherwise they wither.

To sow your sunflowers, follow these steps:

1. **Sow three seeds in 8-centimetre pots in from March to May, water well and cover with clear plastic bags or some cling film with a few holes punched in it. Place them by a sunny window to germinate.**
2. **When the seedlings appear, remove the covering and then remove the weaker two, leaving the strongest to grow.**
3. **When the seedlings are large enough and have a good root system, plant them into their final position on your plot and watch them go! But do watch out for slugs, who love young sunflowers. Offer protection in some form, such as sharp grit or eggshells placed on the ground around the base of the plant.**

4. **If you want a really tall one, feed with a balanced liquid fertiliser weekly when it reaches 60 centimetres or more. When the flower heads appear, change to a weak tomato feed, watering only the base of the plant.**

   Tall plants may need staking and tying in to support their enormous stature, but dwarf varieties will be okay on their own.

Alternatively, you can sow straight onto your plot. Sow 5 centimetres deep in good soil, from April onwards, and water regularly. Indoor-sown plants should be hardened off to acclimatise them to the outside.

If you're growing a few for cutting, plant them closer together than you usually would – say 20 centimetres apart – so you can cram them into an area. Cut the blooms, leaving a long stem, and place them in a bucket of water for a few hours. Re-cut the stems under water to avoid creating an 'airlock' before putting them in a vase.

Varieties to consider include the following:

- **Big smile.** Is an extra dwarf variety that only reaches 30 -35cm'c tall. Has bright golden yellow flowers.
- **Pastiche.** Multi stemmed variety with red, and rust coloured flowers, reaches about 1.5meters tall.
- **Ruby sunset.** Produces velvet red flowers on 1.5 meter stems
- **Russian Giant.** If you wanna be a record breaker this is the one for you. It will easily reach 2.5 metres tall and more often than not 3 metres.

Cheerful cherry tomatoes

Every year we plant copious amounts of cherry tomatoes and the kids each look after a plant. They're easy to grow and look after, and the amount of fruit from each one is sometimes overwhelming. Ideally, plant them in pots for the kids to look after at home, but you can just as easily have a few plants in their section of the plot where they'll thrive.

The easiest way for kids to grow cherry toms is simply to buy ready grown little plants and then get them to plant them out. Many varieties are available from seed or as baby plants, and some are even suitable for hanging baskets, such as a famous variety called Tumbler. Chapter 13 has all the information you need about growing tomatoes.

The beauty of these cherry toms is the fact that they require very little attention and are the easiest tomatoes to grow, making them ideal for children. They're usually really small and sweet making them a firm favourite for fussy eaters. They also look really cool, and the plants are literally smothered in little red, sweet gems that can be picked and popped straight into the mouth. The other bonus is because these plants are so productive the children can always pick some and bring them to grandma and granddad's house, which will make them both as proud as punch! The tomatoes mature quite quickly and I bet you that the kids devour them as treats every time they visit their patch.

Go to Chapter 13 for details of a range of cherry tomatoes to grow with your children.

Organising Projects for Wee Ones

The allotment is a perfect place for learning and keeping your children busy so why not set them projects to do while you're busy tending you precious crops? Something always needs doing, whether it's weeding, digging, spreading mulches or even watering crops. If you set them specific tasks they can be creative and learn at the same time.

If they get bored – digging isn't really that much fun and weeding can be disastrous for your young seedlings – you can spice things up a bit. My grandfather buried bags of sweets in the garden so we'd have to dig it over to find them – a good plan, but only for so long. Give your children tasks to do that are fun and they won't get bored so quickly.

Building sweet pea pyramids

A sweet pea pyramid is a really easy thing for a child to produce and can be lots of fun, in fact you can do it with runner beans and climbing beans as well. Sweet peas are wonderful as cut flowers, the heady aroma is so enticing that even little ones appreciate them and they're also a great plant to grow for a bunch of flowers for mum or grandma.

If you intend cultivating sweet peas or beans, show your children how to create a pyramid to grow them up, as shown in Figure 19-1. Follow these steps:

1. **Push between four and six 1.8 metre canes in a circle with a 1 metre diameter, and tie in the tops with some wire (you may need to do this because the canes are so tall).**
2. **Tie some wire around all the canes at 30– 40-centimetre intervals up the structure.**
3. **At the base of each cane plant one seedling so that it can grow up the support.**

You can read more about how to sow and grow sweet peas in Chapter 18.

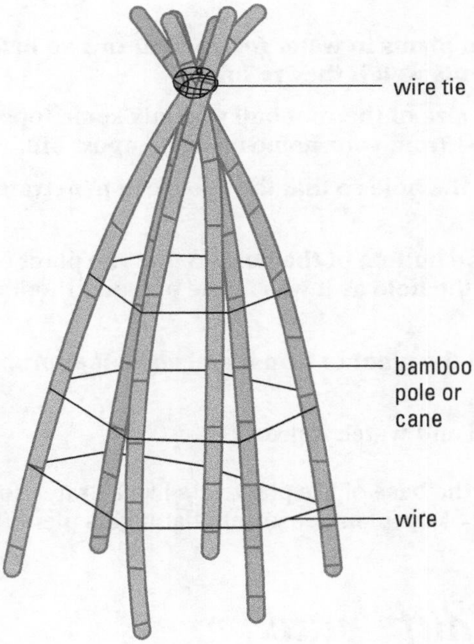

Figure 19-1: A bean or sweet pea pyramid, suitable for children to build.

Planting trees, shrubs and seedlings

It's amazing how many children have never planted anything in their lives. I held a lesson at my son's nursery and I was surprised that five kids in a group of ten had never planted anything before. Children will love the simple act of planting a row of seedlings on the plot. If you don't want to risk your own crops grow a few extra seedlings for them to plant in their own patch.

Fruit trees and shrubs are easy to plant, and if you prepare everything in advance they can learn how to plant them and what techniques to use for ultimate success. I've planted hundreds of gardens on TV makeover shows, and involved the contributors' children. They can't wait to get involved. It's fundamentally satisfying to dig a hole and plant something that will grow, live and eventually produce lovely food for them to eat.

If you get your child to plant a tree or shrub on your plot the likelihood is that it will grow up as your child does, and for them it will be a permanent reminder of their child hood as they get older. It's a great feeling looking at a plant five, ten or even twenty years later knowing that you planted it, especially if you were little when you did so.

1. **Soak the bare-rooted plants in water for an hour or two before planting, or water the plants well if they're in pots.**
2. **Dig a hole twice the size of the root ball and mix some topsoil with a good load of compost from your home-made compost bin.**
3. **Loosen the edges of the hole so that the roots can penetrate the surrounding soil easily.**
4. **Place some soil in the bottom of the hole so that the plant can sit at the same level in the hole as it was in the pot, and then backfill around the roots.**
5. **Heel the soil around the plant to firm it and stake it appropriately if it's a tree.**
6. **Water the plant well and watch it grow!**

It helps if the soil around the base of the plant acts like a crater so that rainwater collects at the base of the plant, ensuring that it gets plenty of water.

Creating a wildlife patch

Allotments and gardens are ideal places for wildlife to thrive, and if you can encourage it onto your patch you'll be helping nature control all the little creatures that can attack your plants. Allotments are, of course, important for growing food, but they can also be havens for wildlife that would otherwise struggle on intensively farmed areas in the surrounding countryside. First, by adopting organic methods and not using any chemicals you can take the first step to preserving the delicate balance of life on your plot. But you and your children can do a number of other things to encourage even more wildlife:

- **Build a pond.** Ponds are fantastic for attracting wildlife. Frogs soon move in and they eat a lot of the slugs that would otherwise be happily munching your crops. Birds drink from the pond and they in turn happily snack on insects that attack your plants. A pond is a drinking hole for other creatures too– hedgehogs, for example, which also feast on your resident slug population. Check your allotment rules and regulations for any restrictions on building ponds.
- **Make a compost heap.** Compost heaps are a must on your allotment, and apart from providing the 'good stuff' that feeds the soil on your allotment, they can act as a great hiding place for all sorts of creatures. Worms quickly move in and start working their magic, munching down the rotting food to make superb compost. Beetles, slow worms and even hedgehogs really appreciate the warm, cosy hiding place the heap offers.
- **Buy or make a ladybird house.** Ladybird houses are an excellent way to encourage these helpful little beetles onto your plot. Good garden centres sell them for around twenty pounds, and I assure you that, because ladybirds eat so many aphids, over the long run they'll save you more money than anything you'd have spent on pesticides! You can even buy ladybird larvae to pop inside the ladybird house and make sure that the population thrives. Many ladybird houses have little windows in the sides so that you can watch them develop and keep an eye on them, offering a great learning opportunity for your kids.
- **Get a ladybird breeding kit.** You can buy these from many places online and they're fascinating projects for children that also benefit the plot. These kits consist of all the bits you need to care for the ladybird larvae, such as the food and the storage chamber in which you can watch them develop, over a 30-day period, from larvae into adult ladybirds – great fun and good for the environment.
- **Get a lacewing chamber.** You can make or buy lacewing chambers to provide a home for this other great allotment friend. Lacewings feast upon aphids, but many lacewings don't survive the winter because they can't find appropriate lodgings, so their population diminishes. By providing a home to these garden friends you'll almost instantly notice a reduction in aphids.
- **Make or buy a wildlife house.** You can easily make a little house for wildlife to hide in during the winter or you can buy frog houses and hedgehog houses, both of which encourage them onto your patch where they may well breed, and will certainly feed.

- **Get a bee house.** By this I don't mean a hive for honey bees but a bee house. A few different types are available, some for bumble bees and others for non-swarming solitary bees. The ones for solitary bees have a series of holes drilled into the face into which the bees crawl to lay its eggs before sealing up the hole. Over the next few years the bees and their offspring will return to lay more eggs, and the population in your patch increases. Bumble bee nests provide a cosy home for the queen bee to make a home and get on with the job of laying her eggs: soon you'll have a population to be proud of. Also, many of these houses have clear windows so that you can watch your bees safely, which is just the job for kids.
- **Create a wild patch.** If you can afford the space, dedicate one corner of your plot to wild flowers and nettles. Nettles are a breeding ground for all sorts of beneficial insects and butterflies and wild flowers are a haven for pollinators. Do make sure to cut the nettles back before they set seed, or you wont be popular with your neighbours.
- **Get a wildlife watching kit.** Many different kits are on the market, enabling your children to note and record all the wildlife they can find on the plot, from insects to birds to amphibians – it's great fun becoming a wildlife watcher! Often your local environmental clubs run schemes where they send you a wildlife kit and you fill in what you see and when. You then send back this data to them and they use it to track, conserve and record nature's patterns. The RSPB (Royal Society for the Protection of Birds) also run an annual scheme that asks people to record their local wildlife sightings. This data gives a useful picture of what's happening to our environment.

Preparing fresh food

This may sound an obvious thing to say but after all that hard work on the allotment the most satisfying part of the whole process is the eating. You'll find that if your kids have been on the journey with you, they're just as keen to get in the kitchen and get cooking as you are. Shelling peas and broad beans, washing carrots, and simply preparing what they and you have grown is a great lesson in cooking healthy, fresh food. Of course depending on how old your little ones are, they can slice, chop and peel what they've grown. My little boy is only three and he helps me in the kitchen every day. He loves it, and (using a plastic knife) happily slices soft vegetables like courgettes and celery and willingly has a go at trying to slice tomatoes (well, he squashes them). The sense of pride he gets from helping dad and then serving up to his mum and sisters what we've grown, prepared or cooked is great to see. I'm sure that because he's had a hand in growing and preparing the food, he's eating things that he'd have otherwise turned his nose up at.

This is a terrific way of introducing children to all the varied vegetables and fruits that you've grown and the different flavours and ways of preparing food. Not only do they learn about fruit and veg but also gain culinary skills, from using a knife properly to recognising vegetables and other ingredients and how they taste. By exposing them to the kitchen and fresh produce at a young age, you arm them with an arsenal of knowledge that'll stay with them for life. To this day I still remember preparing beetroots, shelling peas, pickling onions and chopping carrots with my grandparents' skills – memories that have stayed with me forever.

Chapter 20

Hobnobbing with Allotment Society

In This Chapter

- Gaining knowledge from a mentor
- Observing the unspoken rules
- Enjoying your new social life

This may well sound like a really silly title for a chapter, but an etiquette definitely applies to holding an allotment and being the new kid on the block can be pretty daunting. Fortunately, the type of person that wants to till the soil to produce food is usually down-to-earth, approachable and generally really helpful. Becoming a vegetable gardener is quite therapeutic; you find a new sense of calm and a feeling of being at one with your plot. The sooner you can get your feet under the allotment table the better, so speak to as many people as possible and make a beeline for the gardeners whose plots look tip-top. Complimenting someone on her produce is a sure-fire way to gain a new friend to show you the ropes.

Allotment holders despise a messy plot, especially one covered in weeds. Those weeds aren't just your problem but affect all the plots near you, so if you want to make a good impression, get weeding as soon as you can! Many people have to wait years to get their hands on a precious allotment, so leave it untouched at your peril, nothing is more frustrating than someone who has a plot and doesn't make the best use of it.

Finding an Allotment Mentor

Some people have it easy. I was brought up on gardening, with both my grandfather and father being avid vegetable growers. Even today, I regularly tap into my dad's infinite pool of knowledge – and sometimes he taps into mine! I make this point because allotment gardening isn't something you suddenly become good at. It takes time, knowledge and determination, and the best way to learn is to be shown how. You need to find someone on your site who's willing to pass on her knowledge to you; you'll achieve far better results from your plot with that person's help. This book provides you with the basic knowledge you need to get started on your plot, but every site is unique, every area has different soil and weather conditions, and many other variables need to be considered that only someone with local knowledge fully understands. Even if you can't find someone to directly help you along the way, you can still wander around the allotment to see what others are planting, and use this information as your guide.

Nationwide, groups offer mentors to allotment holders and they can be really useful, especially when it comes to the running and setting up of allotment groups and new sites. One example is the Allotments Regeneration Initiative (they have a website at `www.farmgarden.org.uk/ari/`), who help out with new allotment sites and community projects. They're more useful for allotment regeneration projects and advice on creating new allotments, but all the same are a good group to be aware of.

Many local allotment clubs and groups offer allotment mentors to encourage and educate new plot holders. Check out local clubs and the Internet for information.

Following Allotment Etiquette

Every allotment has set rules and regulations that you must adhere to or face eviction (see Chapter 3 for more on these). Each allotment has an unspoken law that develops over the years, a kind of etiquette that should be followed. On an allotment near me, for example, the gardeners adopt organic techniques. If a few plot holders do use chemicals, the possibility of cross-contamination makes everyone else's adherence pointless. Here are some unofficial rules that I've come across:

- **Keep your plot tidy.** The official rules regarding tidiness on the plot are only enforced in extreme cases. But you won't make any friends if your plot is disorganised and unruly. A messy plot is a magnet for pests and diseases that spread and cause problems for other plot holders. Be as tidy as possible.
- **Deal with weeds.** Weedy sites are a pain for neighbouring plots and if yours is a weed-ridden mess you'll be excluded from the allotment posse and dubbed a heathen yob with no respect for others. Sounds harsh, but

weeds spread and all you're doing by not weeding is creating work for other people. Weeds spread via both underground roots and seeds, and these seeds are spread by the wind and through animal droppings, so by not weeding you'll really get on the wrong side of people.

- **Respect other people's space.** This applies to both their personal and physical space. First, not everyone wants to chat; some people have allotments to escape nagging partners, some simply relish the peace and quiet. Don't be too surprised if the person next door never speaks to you even if you're digging right next to each other. Many people are simply shy or insular and go into a kind of hypnotic trance when they're on their plots. Second, never walk onto someone else's plot unless they invite you to. Never take short cuts across other plots to get to yours, it's so annoying when you notice some seedlings have been damaged by inconsiderate people taking a short cut.
- **Tackle diseases.** Always deal with any disease attacks as swiftly as possible, because disease quickly spreads to other plots. Dispose of any infected plant material off site or burn it to limit the spread. Also, if you find any diseases on your plot, tell your neighbours so they can set up defences and be on their guard.
- **Don't borrow tools without permission.** People generally take very good care of their tools so treat other people's as you'd like your own to be treated. Nothing's more annoying than being stuck into a particular job, reaching for the necessary tool and discovering it's not there.
- **Keep paths clear.** Always make sure that other plot holders can get past yours, even if they're pushing a wheelbarrow,.
- **Help your neighbours.** This rule's a biggie! Allotments are all about community and helping each other out. If your neighbour is off on holiday, offer to water her crops, and she'll do the same for you. Share tips, cuttings, seeds, ideas, produce, whisky, tea, cakes and so on and you'll soon be in the gang! You reap what you sow (no pun intended!).

Learning From Others' Hits and Misses

This sounds really selfish but learn from your neighbours' mistakes. Gardeners are more than happy to pass on stories and tales of success and failure – well, especially success! But some hold onto their growing tips as if they're covered by the Official Secrets Act. The best place to find stories of what went wrong and what went right is to look around your site, and ask people how they managed to do so well, or so badly! Also get online and look at some blogs, they're full of discussions from real allotmenteers who are struggling with the same problems you'll encounter, and you're sure to learn something from their mistakes. The website `www.allotment.org.uk` has links to all sorts of blogs and advice pages and is packed full of useful info.

Gardening is also rife with old wives' tales and lore, and to me this is a fascinating part of gardening. Many of the tips you get from the old boys are based on years of experience and real-life gardening. Many seemingly insane tips are have real horticultural and scientific grounding even if those using such techniques have no idea what's actually happening. My favourite items of allotment folklore include:

- Put some rhubarb leaves in the planting hole when putting in your brassicas to help prevent clubroot.
- Use banana peel as a fertiliser. It's full of phosphorous, potassium, magnesium, iron and zinc and is brilliant for all sorts of plants. Simply add the peels to your compost heap or chuck the peel onto the plot around plants that will appreciate the boost. Put a banana peel in the planting holes of tomatoes, peppers, aubergines, and all fruiting and flowering plants.
- Make a tonic with horseradish leaves as a clubroot deterrent. It can also be used as a pesticide.
- Use a horsetail brew to prevent fungal attacks on strawberries and tomatoes, and help prevent *damping off* (a fungal disease that causes seedlings to turn limp and mouldy) in seedlings. Dig up the whole plant and mix with boiling water at 25 grams of horsetail to a litre of water, and leave for a day or two.
- Spray a mixture of milk and water – about 7 per cent milk – onto brassicas to help keep the dreaded Cabbage White butterfly at bay.
- Use bicarbonate of soda, mixed at the rate of 2 grams to a litre of water, to combat grey mould.
- Use Epsom Salts mixed with water as a spray to help strengthen weak stems on any plant.
- Pour used coffee grounds around leaf crops to give them a nitrogen boost, and to keep slugs at bay.
- Plant vegetables during a full moon. Some argue that the moon affects the movement of water in the soil up into the plants and helps to bulk up the roots and foliage of vegetables – well if the moon can move oceans I guess you can't discount it!

Always wear protective gloves when handling any potions and home-made tonics. Test them on a small area of the plant first to rule out any negative effects and don't store these potions because they quickly turn.

Getting Involved in Clubs and Societies

Nearly all allotments have groups and societies who promote your rights and help allotment holders organise get-togethers. In addition, all sorts of nationwide clubs exist with newsletters, magazines and tips and advice available to their members. Consider joining one of these:

- **The National Vegetable Society (`www.nvsuk.org.uk`):** A charity dedicated to promoting and improving the culture, study and cultivation of vegetables. It offers advice to professional and novice growers alike.
- **The National Society of Allotment and Leisure Gardeners (`www.sslag.org.uk`):** The national representative body for the allotment movement in the UK. This group works to preserve, promote and protect allotments all over the country.
- **The National Allotment Gardens Trust (`www.nagtrust.org`):** A group that promotes the recreational and environmental benefits of allotment gardening. It promotes health, food production and education.
- **The Allotments Regeneration Initiative (`www.farmgarden.org.uk`):** A body that help groups and individuals involved in campaigning for allotment sites and also those wishing to regenerate existing allotments.
- **Allot more Allotments (`www.allotmoreallotments.org.uk`:** A group resource for those wishing to start up campaign groups pushing for more allotment spaces. It offers advice and helps you set up your campaigns.

Most sites also have an allotment society. It offers plot holders advice and help with problems, and sometimes collects the rent and oversees the site. Many societies work closely with the local councils, the society being a representative voice for you as a plot holder. It's advisable to become a member of your local allotment society, and annual membership really won't break the bank. For example, my local allotment society costs £2.50 per year! Allotment societies offer a range of benefits to their members, including tool loan schemes for rotavators, strimmers and so on. Many have discount deals with seeds suppliers, and other suppliers offering garden sundries.

Allotment societies usually organise social events on and around their allotments, and often trips to visit other gardens and related places. The local allotment sites near where I live all have open days and regular events throughout the summer, when they throw their gates open to the public, with barbecues, plant sales, seed swaps and fun and games for children. The societies work hard, raising awareness of the importance of allotments, the health benefits, and generally promoting green issues and sustainability.

Many allotments hold competitions between plot holders or between other sites where giant veg, floral displays and the best produce are usual themes. This can become serious competition but is generally just for fun, and is often a great way of getting children involved. (See Chapter 19 for more on kids and allotments.)

Socialising on Your Allotment

Socialising on your allotment depends a lot on you and what you want from the whole experience. Not everybody wants to instantly strike up friendships and exchange numbers, but you'll find a community of like-minded people who all share a passion. It's amazing how, if you get a bunch of gardeners together, they quickly start talking shop. You get all sorts of people up the allotment from serious veg growers to busy city workers who like to escape. With frequent get-togethers and barbecues using home-grown produce, it's down to you to get stuck in.

Looking out for each other

Allotments are hard work, and the new techniques and plants can involve a steep learning curve. It all takes a great investment of time, but the rewards make it all worthwhile, with new friendships, great produce and a new way of life. The great thing about allotments is the sense of comradeship. You all suffer similar problems and triumphs on the plot and your neighbours all have experience of the new problems you're encountering.

Most allotmenteers are really keen to spread the word and help motivate you never to give up and to keep your spirits up. It can be horribly depressing when you've spent the best part of half a year (sometimes longer) nurturing a plant from seed simply for it to fail from drought, disease or nibbles by pests. This is where looking out for each other comes in. If you notice something about your neighbours' crops that looks alarming tell them as soon as you can. If you have their contact details, even better. Sometimes with plants if you catch the problem before it sets in, you can reverse it in time. So after you've met and befriended your neighbours, it's good practice to exchange numbers so you can inform each other of anything potentially harmful that you notice. This could be disease, drought or even vandalism.

Offering holiday cover

Providing holiday cover for each other is an unwritten rule on allotments. Always offer to help out your neighbours if they're going away and they'll surely return the favour. I'd get established first, though, and make sure that you fully understand the principles of good watering practice – it would be a nightmare to get it wrong on someone else's plot! (See Chapter 7 for more on watering.)

Chapter 21

Entering the World of Giants

In This Chapter

- Preparing the perfect plot
- Breeding bumper beauties
- Joining the world of competition

Growing giant vegetables and show-quality fruit is a worldwide obsession. The English and Americans are particularly mad for giant veg. For some, it's an infectious, obsessive world of skulduggery, secrets and one-upmanship. Fortunately, you can also just grow giant vegetables for fun, and children particularly enjoy it. However, be warned that once you've honed your skills, you'll inevitably feel the pull of entering your prize giants into local competitions. Gardeners who take growing huge vegetables seriously really do see it as a sport – a sport for anyone with a small patch of land, not for the elite or wealthy.

The king of all giants is the pumpkin but it does take up stupid amounts of space for each plant, but you can grow all sorts of other large veggies – such as leeks, carrots, onions, courgettes – that are better suited to small plots.

Creating Perfect Growing Conditions

The secret to growing giant vegetables is all in the soil, these giants are freaks of nature, given conditions to grow in that never occur naturally. You need to provide copious amounts of feed and water to allow them to reach the colossal sizes that can be achieved. There are specific techniques used to grow specific vegetables to enormous proportions and we will look at these in more detail in this chapter but the first place to start when grow any of these giants is to look at your soil and make it just right for these monsters!

Preparing ideal soil

When growing giant vegetables one must ensure that the soil is really well prepared and absolutely full of organic matter, homemade compost is ideal and also a good dose of really well rotted farmyard manure will add vital nutrients, help with water retention and also add those all important micro-organisms that help break down the soil. Ideally you should prepare the ground the autumn before sowing in spring by digging in copious amounts of well rotted farm yard manure into the soil and leaving it over winter to break the soil down into a lovely fine crumb. Before planting I tend to incorporate a good 4 inches of home made compost into the top layer a couple of weeks before sowing or planting out and spread a balanced granular feed as well.

The fertilisers you choose whilst growing your giants will need to target the specific needs of each type of vegetable. For example if you want to grow giant leafy vegetables like cabbages, you will need to give them fertiliser high in nitrogen that will promote leafy growth. Whereas if you are growing giant tomatoes or pumpkins you will need a feed high in potassium and phosphorus. These are best added weekly in liquid form on top of the already improved soil. Many growers have their own concoctions of special compost teas which to be honest are often the most effective 'plant tonics' around and we will look at these later in this chapter and if you are an organic gardener these are the best option for you.

I am a little daunted writing a section on how to grow giant vegetables because there are so many different ways of growing them. Someone always has an alternative method that they see as being better so I am going to cover just the basics and you can experiment to find your own methods.

Watering your way to success

Watering your giants needs to be a well planned affair. Any vegetable hates sporadic watering, and this applies even more so to large ones. Any check in growth can cause the skins to split, or simply slows down the growth, so the end product is not as large. The best method of watering these veggies is with some form of drip feed or computer irrigation system, so long as you have access to a constant supply of mains water or can install a large water holding tank on your plot. This is by no means essential, but if you are really serious about growing large veg, it will ensure that they never go without water, and that conditions remain constant in the soil. The soil will never become too dry and many of these computer driven systems have a sensor that will automatically stop watering if it has rained to compensate.

I know that this all sounds very grand, but these computerised systems are easy to install and can be bought for as little as £50. They really do help maintain the perfect conditions for your giant vegetables.

Choosing the right seeds

When growing giant vegetables it is vital to choose the right seeds. Growers have selected varieties that are proven to grow giants, and these are the best ones to buy to get started. Open pollinated varieties are usually the best option, because you can collect the seeds from the largest examples and keep them for next year. In theory, these seeds will grow to be the same size as, or bigger than, their parents next year. By only collecting seeds from the biggest examples you are selecting the strongest strains, which will continue your success. Seeds from giants can go for astounding amounts of money. For example, seeds from world record breaking pumpkins have been sold for between £300–£500 each! You don't need to spend that much. Simply buy seeds from specialist suppliers and keep the seeds from your best plants each year.

Growing Giant Vegetables

Cabbages, carrots, leeks, marrows and pumpkins are all stars of the vegetable competition circuit. You too can create impressive crops to dazzle your allotment friends. The following sections cover these giant staples and everything you need to know for success.

Colossal cabbages

Cabbages are second only to pumpkins as the holy grail of giant vegetable growers. They can grow massive, and you may well need to hoist them into a wheel barrow to be able to move them. The largest ever cabbage grown weighed in at a colossal 57 kilograms, so get your brassica bed ready to take on the cabbage challenge.

Cabbages like lots of nitrogen while they are growing, and as with all giants their growing conditions need to be perfect. Feedand water constantly so as not to check or slow their growth. Giant cabbages can put on around 1.5 kilograms a day in growth, which shows how much they will take from the soil.

To sow your giant cabbages, follow these steps:

1. **Prepare seed trays by filling the tray with compost right to the top and then tapping the tray twice on the counter to settle the compost. Run a straight stick over the top to level it, and press down the surface with a flat bit of board about the same size as the tray to get a nice level surface.**
2. **Half fill a larger tray with water and place the compost tray into it. The compost tray will absorb the water from the tray below without disturbing your carefully levelled compost tray. If you were to water the tray from above the compost would become pitted and rough again.**
3. **Place the seeds on the soil surface at the right sowing distances stated on the packet. Through a sieve sprinkle compost over the seeds to the appropriate depth.**
4. **Spray the surface lightly with a fine spray and place in a warm bright place to germinate.**
5. **Transplant seedlings when they develop 2 true leaves into small pots and place them in a greenhouse or by a window ensuring a constant temperature above 10 °C.**
6. **Harden off seedlings in a cold frame and then outside for a couple of weeks before planting out.**
7. **Plant out in a prepared bed full of organic matter spacing plants at least 1metre apart with rows at least the same. Cabbages will only grow as big as the space they are provided with, so it is pointless only giving them 30 centimetres space.**

Giant cabbages must be watered and fed weekly to ensure they are kept growing with no checks to growth. Feed them with a nitrogen-rich feed during the initial growing stages and keep them well watered during dry spells. Most giant cabbages, unlike many other giants, are pretty tasty, so you get the best of both worlds.

TIP

Cabbages are liable to be greatly affected by club root (see Chapter 7 for more on this nasty), so ideally plant them in ground free from the disease. You can grow giant cabbages in infected ground, but they will not do as well and will prolong the number of years the land stays infected. Put a small amount of lime in with the compost when transplanting seedlings and move them into a 8-centimetre and then 13 centimetre pots before planting out, so they can develop a decent root system. Add lime to the soil on your plot to bring the pH to around 7.5 or even up to 8.5 (see Chapter 6 on how to work out your pH level) because club root prefers acid soils with lower pH. When planting, dig a large hole around 30 centimetres wide and deep, and sprinkle some lime around the hole. Then plant the cabbages in the hole using homemade compost and discard the emptied out soil.

Monster carrots

Carrots that are grown for size are usually grown to be long rather than fat and large. Carrots need deeply-dug, loose soil that is free from stones to grow well in, so the roots can venture deep down with no obstruction. Some people grow their competition carrots in barrels or even in long drain pipes to encourage really long roots and others simply grow them in situ in their plots after first ensuring deep preparation of the soil.

Growers grow their large carrots in many ways, but the two methods that seem most popular are to grow them in oil drums or direct in the ground. When preparing the ground it is important not to use fresh manure; ideally sow seeds on ground that has been manured the previous year, or the roots will probably fork. Grow carrots in barrels using the following steps:

1. **Fill your barrel with sand, and make six holes in the sand with a metal bar. Fill each hole with a mix of 1 part sand, 1 part compost and 2 parts really finely sieved soil and leave to rest for a week or so.**
2. **Sow six seeds per barrel and thin to the strongest one when they are growing well this ensures that you get success with one main plant.**
3. **Water your plants deeply to encourage the roots to grow down deep into the soil.**

Use the following steps when planting directly on your plot:

1. **Ram a long crow bar into the ground, at least 60 centimetres down, and wiggle it about to make a 12 centimetre round hole. Fill the hole with a 50/50 mix of sand and compost. Repeat for as many carrots as you want to grow.**
2. **Sow your seeds directly into the holes on your plot when the soil has reached about 10 °C in spring. Sow four seeds per hole and thin to the strongest one when they are growing well.**

Apart from some food and water every now and then, your carrots will need little attention during the growing season. If you overfeed them they'll develop into short fat carrots, but it is usually the long carrots that are the winners at the end of the day!

Because these carrots are grown in pretty loose soil they should be fairly easy to pull out when they have reached their optimum size. Remove the soil from around the top of the root as far as you can and then straddle the root and give it a sharp tug, pulling it straight out.

You can also grow your carrots in drain pipes filled with a sand and soil mix; this is a tried and tested method that works really well. I would get 9 or more 5ft lengths of soil pipe from a DIY store and build a frame to hold them all upright. Fill them with the same sand/soil mixture described earlier in this section and let them settle for a week or so. Then simply sow 5 seeds in each, removing all but the weakest as soon as they have reached a good size to handle. During their growing season start by watering from the top and then in the second half of the season water from the bottom to encourage the roots down to find the water. This can be done by gently lifting the pipes and immersing them in buckets containing a small amount water that will rise up the pipes by capillary action. To harvest, you can simply pull them gently out as before.

Long leeks

Leeks are also often grown for competition and can reach some fairly impressive sizes. The largest one recorded weighed in at 8.3 kilograms and had a diameter of nearly 60 centimetres!

Leeks like a sunny spot with free draining soil to do well, and are pretty easy to grow. Even without any special treatment they can reach giant sizes. The world record leek was supposedly simply a freak that had no extra care to reach its mammoth proportions.

Leeks like lots of sunshine and free draining soil which has been well manured in the previous autumn. Sow in early spring either indoors in trays pots and troughs or in situ in drills 6 centimetres apart. They should be thinned to 20 centimetres apart or (for giants) a little more, say 30 centimetres apart, by summer to give them plenty of space. You can use the thinnings as baby leeks. (For more details on sowing and growing leeks, see Chapter 13.)

To grow extra-long leeks, follow these steps:

1. **Sow seeds indoors in late February or early March to give them a head start.**
2. **Transplant the seedlings outside 10-15 weeks after sowing to get the best results.**

3. **Make sure to harden them off gently so as not shock them. Ideally do so over a 2 week period slowly getting them used to outside conditions.**
4. **Plant them out after the last frost. Leeks are really frost hardy, but when they are young this could check growth and hinder their development.**
5. **As the plants grow, earth them up right up to the green top leaves which will encourage them to grow tall, and blanch the stems.**
6. **Give them a balanced top dressing high in nitrogen after transplanting to give them an initial boost. Dried blood and bone works well.**
7. **Keep them well watered in the initial stages of growth until they become established. Be careful not to overwater, because they hate being too damp and are likely to rot and get fungal infections. Water weekly as opposed to daily.**
8. **Cut off any long foliage that drapes on the soil as this is likely to rot, and the rot could spread up into the plant.**

Place collars around your plants to protect the stems from the soil and keep them clean and grit free whilst you're blanching them (see Chapter 13 on how to blanch your leeks). Many growers do this even if they're not growing their veg to competition standard as a great way to produce perfect leeks, and the ideal material is a roll of damp proofing from a DIY store. It can be easily cut and bent around your leeks. Collars are placed around the base of the leek and are slowly increased in size as the leek fattens. Be careful to ensure that the collar is never too big, or it simply becomes a great hiding place for slugs and other critters that could damage your plants.

Mammoth marrows

I always remember going to my Great Granddads house in Tollesbury in Essex as a child and in his side garden being faced with mammoth marrows and praying that we were not ready to be picked for Sunday lunch. Nowadays I can't think of anything better than a slowly roast marrow stuffed with tomatoes, peppers and marjoram – how one's tastes change! Marrows are really easy to grow and with a bit of extra feed and water they can grow to king-size proportions pretty easily. To grow the real monsters you require lots of space and copious amounts of manure. In fact they are very closely related to the pumpkins and squashes (see Chapter 13) and need exactly the same conditions.

Choose a site that is sheltered in full sun and to prepare the plot for your marrows you will need to dig in copious amounts of really well rotted farmyard manure in the autumn so that the winter frosts can break down the soil. To sow your giant marrows, follow these steps:

1. **Seeds can be sown indoors in early April into May in 3 inch pots (3 per pot) about one inch deep in a propagator around 20°C or in warm place until they start to show. Remove all but the strongest seedling once they are large enough to handle. Or sow outdoors 2.5 centimetres deep in mid-May.**
2. **Protect the new foliage from direct sunlight, because this can scorch the delicate foliage.**
3. **Plant monster marrows in the middle of a 2.5 – 5 meter space. But if you just want to grow some decent biggies to show your friends leave 1 meter spacing.**
4. **Once the first fruit develops, feed with potash fertiliser and remove all but the strongest fruit, leaving only one on the main vine. The main vine should be about 4.5 meters long by this time**
5. **Cut back all lateral growth to about 1.5 meters, some growers bury these side stems to promote new roots and therefore better growth on the main stem.**

Feed twice a week with a high-potash fertiliser and keep the plants well watered but not waterlogged. Do not get water on the foliage because just like pumpkins this can scorch the leaves and damage the plant. When the skins have turned hard, measure the marrow over a few days to make sure it is as large as it is going to get and then cut it off. Marrows grow very fast and mature quickly, so you'll soon find another marrow growing elsewhere on the plant and you can get a good few giants off one plant.

The world record so far is 65 kilograms (but is constantly changing!) so get that plot ready and full of good muck, and see if you can get yourself into the *Guinness Book of World Records*.

Prime pumpkins

Now it is my great pleasure to introduce you to the unrivalled King of the land of giants . . . the pumpkin. No other vegetable gets so much hype, gains so much attention or can reach such gargantuan sizes as the humble Jack o' Lantern. The vines can grow at 90 centimetres every day, and sprawl over vast areas. When talking record breaking veggies, a single pumpkin vine may need 70 square metres of open ground in order to establish a root system large enough to support each giant fruit.

Growers often bury the lateral shoots in the same way as with giant marrows. These shoots will then set root all over the area. The plant then becomes one giant feeding machine, drinking up to 270 litres of water each day: Amazing stuff. But if you imagine the current world record pumpkin weighed in at 781 kilograms, it is no surprise they need so much space and water.

I am not suggesting that anyone on an allotment will want to even consider taking on the world record but you can produce enormous fruits pretty easily and it is great fun having a go.

Pumpkins need a really organic-rich soil that is well drained, and a spot in direct sunlight to thrive. Add loads of well rotted muck or homemade compost to the soil before planting in early spring, or ideally add it in the previous autumn to allow it to improve the soil. Add a good couple of inches all over the soil and dig it in really well, digging deeply. Before planting out also apply an all round fertiliser such as fish blood and bone and rake it into the surface. To grow your mighty pumpkins, follow these steps:

1. **Sow the seeds indoors in late April, sowing three seeds in an 8-centimetre pot in good potting compost 2.5 centimetres deep.**
2. **Place the pot in a propagator between 20 °C and 28 °C and water lightly, they should shoot within a week or so and once two true leaves are showing remove the two weaker plants to allow the strongest to thrive.**
3. **Harden the seedling off as soon as you can, when the risk of frost has passed. It can be planted out as soon as the two true leaves develop but just make sure that there's no chance of frost.**
4. **Transplant the seedling into its permanent position, leaving as much space around it as you can afford. Make a mound in the middle of the plot and place the seedling at the top of the mound. Ideally the plant should have a space 20ft x 20ft in which to grow.**
5. **Place a cloche over the seedling to protect it from slugs and other pests.**
6. **Feed the plant in the early stages with a feed high in phosphorus to promote root growth. Bone meal is ideal.**
7. **Change to a fertiliser high in potassium, such as potash, when the fruits start to develop. Doing so will encourage fruit growth.**
8. **Allow 3 pumpkins to develop removing all the others check every other day for any new ones. Let these grow for a while until one becomes your favourite and look the healthiest.**

9. **Remove all but one fruit. By removing all but one fruit the plant will put all its effort into giving you one massive fruit as opposed to many smaller ones.**
10. **Once it reaches its boundary – and the vine can reach up to 15 metres long – prune the vine tips to keep it in line!**
11. **As the pumpkin grows it puts pressure on the stems around it so you will need to cut the roots away from the vines within a few feet of the main pumpkin. Otherwise as the fruit grows it could bend and split the main stems that supply the fruit with food and water from the rest of the plant.**
12. **Pumpkins need about an inch of water a week to grow well so if the weather is dry, water and feed weekly with a weak soluble fertiliser (weak tomato feed works well!)**
13. **Protect the fruit from direct sunlight using a sheet. Direct sunlight will harden the skin and eventually stop the fruit from growing, or cause it to split.**
14. **Keep the area free from weeds and watch out for pests!**

Your pumpkin will be mature in around 80 days and if you are lucky you will have produced a monster worthy of the village show. When they are ready simply cut it off at the stem and roll it onto a large strong blanket, get some friends to help and lift it onto a trailer ready for transportation. If you have managed to grow a prize specimen you may well need to get a digger in to lift it onto your transporter ready to take to the show.

Mentioning Some Other Monsters

You can apply the techniques necessary to growing giants to all types of vegetable. At shows around the world there are competitions for everything from giant radishes to the longest parsnip, the heaviest tomato to the longest runner bean if you provide enough nutrients, water and the right training you can get most plants to produce freakishly large veggies. Here are some others for you to try:

- **Runner beans:** There are two varieties that I would suggest for show quality enormous beans, the first is called Enorma and the beans can reach well over 50 centimetres long, and the second is Stenner, a reselection from Enorma bred by the famous bean grower Brython Stenner.
- **Tomatoes:** You can grow enormous tomatoes fairly easily as long as you choose the right varieties, remove all but a few fruits and care for them

well. The only problem you might find is that the season may be too short for them to ripen fully outside so they are best grown in the greenhouse or in polytunnels. Try Giant Delicious, Giant Belgium or Big Zac.

- **Cucumbers:** These can be grown freakishly large. In fact the largest measured 1.2 metres in length and was grown by chance by a total amateur. In the UK, competition cucumbers are best grown under glass but you may find you get a freaky long one even outdoors. Choose a long variety such as Armenian, which can grow pretty long, and remove all but the best three or four fruits.
- **Onions:** Many village shows hold the largest onion competitions and they are highly prized as a show vegetable. The standard show onion of choice is the 'Kelsae' onion which has been around since the 1950s and has the word record of 15lbs 15.5 ounces to its name. Sown indoors in December and January growing giant onions is no mean feat and it takes dedication, careful planning and a keen eye but if you are a serious grower it is well worth exploring more!

Honing Your Techniques

Growing giant veggies is an art, honed and developed over many years. Most competition winning gardeners have been gardening for a long timeand have developed their own techniques, which will stay with them to their death beds. However, many now realise that by passing on their knowledge competitions become more exciting and the produce gets better and better. Size isn't always all that matters, and there is just as much importance placed on the 'perfect' carrot as there is on the longest.

As a beginner it is well worth wandering around your allotment site and talking to growers who seem to have the green fingered touch when it comes to growing monsters. Then it is always worth getting seeds that have a proven record when it comes to growing giants. Finally, remember: It is all about the soil, so as long as you can ensure the soil they live in is the best it can be, you are sure to do well.

Letting you in on my top-secret tricks

There are literally hundreds of tricks and techniques gardeners use to gain the all important best in show rosette, or simply outdo their neighbours. Here are a few tips to get you on your way:

- **Use compost tea:** Compost tea is about as good a plant tonic as you will ever find. See the section on it in Chapter 7.
- **Buy heirloom or non-hybrid (open pollinated) seeds:** Also make sure to keep the seeds from the largest or finest crops to perfect the strain for next year. The more you do this, in theory the better the seeds will become.
- **Reduce the number of fruits on each plant:** By reducing the number of fruits on each plant you will be making the plant concentrate all its efforts on producing bigger and better fruits instead of many smaller ones. This applies to pumpkins, squashes, aubergines, tomatoes, cucumbers and anything that produces fruit. Ideally aim to have three fruits per plant if you want a good crop of largeish fruits. In the case of some vegetables like pumpkins, go for just one monster!
- **Eliminate competition:** I don't mean other gardeners! Keep on top of weeds and be ready to swoop to the defence of you precious crops if a disease or pest attacks.
- **Use organic fertilisers:** Organic feeds maintain the health of your soil and seeing the soil is the most important part of the allotment this can only do your plants good. Chemical fertilisers and pesticides should only be used as a last resort many pesticides are non selective and can decimate useful insects and micro-organisms in and around the soil.
- **Drip feed to succeed:** By using a drip feed irrigation system you will not over- or under-water your precious crops. Also, if the soil is well watered the moisture will reach far down into the soil, encouraging the roots to delve deep. This will give you far more healthy plants.

Breeding Selectively

Many winning growers now have their own websites where you can become a member and gain access to their seed banks. These are not usually cheap, but if you are serious about growing you will be able to your hands on some supreme quality seeds and access to a lot of knowledge as well. Many big seed suppliers now supply 'giant seeds' and these are usually from seeds that have been proven competition winners – in some cases even world record breakers. Most serious growers have been keeping their seed year upon year, developing their own strains from established varieties, and this is definitely the way forward. This can only be done using open pollinated varieties, because hybrids will not come true to seed.

Collecting seeds

You cannot collect and sow hybrid seeds and expect them to grow like the parent plant. You may well have some success and produce a productive plant, but it will be true to the grandparent plant. Secondly, many open pollinated plants cross breed easily so try and only plant one variety of each or you will surely end up with crossbred seeds. You may well be lucky and end up with a hybrid that is better than the parents, but this is pretty unlikely! This applies especially to sweetcorn, tomatoes, squashes and pretty much any flowering vegetable. You will always run the risk in an allotment site of cross pollination with other plants, especially with plants that are insect pollinated, so try to plant things away from neighbouring plots that contain similar plants. You also need to remember that many vegetables are biennial (most root crops, carrots and cabbages), so you may wish to leave some in the ground so you can collect the seeds the following year.

Place all the seeds you collect in envelopes and label them clearly, including when they were collected, what variety they are and when the original plant was sown (it is always nice to know the exact history of your plants!). Store them in an airtight container ready for planting next year. By collecting seeds in this way year upon year, you will be, in effect, selectively breeding plants that are perfectly suited to your plot only. These seeds will have been specially created by you to be uniquely adapted to your allotment's conditions.

Harvesting seeds

Seeds from pulpy vegetables such as pumpkins and tomatoes should be scraped out of fully-ripe fruits. Only select the largest, most healthy, best looking examples and scoop them. For squashes and pumpkins you can simply clean them up and lay them out on a tray to dry in a well ventilated place, but for tomatoes the business is a little more complex.

Tomato seeds will only germinate if they have fermented for a while, and this usually happens inside the rotting fruits. You can speed the process up to collect seed by following these steps:

1. **Scoop out the seeds from the best-looking fruits and place them in a glass jar.**
2. **Pour in an inch or so of water.**
3. **Cover the jar around the top with some cheese cloth or kitchen roll (this helps keep the smell in).**

4. **Leave the jar in a warm bright spot for a couple of days.**
5. **When you see a film of mould appear over the surface of the pulp and bubbles coming up through the liquid, this is the fermentation process. Remove the mould and rinsethe seeds in a sieve to get them clean.**
6. **Put the seeds on a dish and let them dry naturally, making sure they don't stick together.**

For other vegetables that produce seed heads, simply collect the seeds from the pods or heads when they are mature by shaking them into a paper bag. You can then lay them out onto a sheet of paper and blow them gently to remove the dusty bits of debris leaving the seeds for storage.

Entering Competitions

Growing for competition is great fun and very competitive, so only choose the best produce you can possibly select from your plot. You will not be looked down on for having a go, so my advice is to dive straight in and get involved: You can only get better!

Growing for competition is fun, but it is also deadly serious. People exhibit their veg and they are examined by growers and industry professionals who are perfectionists. Only the cream of the crop will get a look in.

Joining the elite

If you become really hooked on growing for competitions you will be faced with some really stiff competition, especially as a new recruit. But you will also find that you will be welcomed with open arms into the elite world of vegetable growing. This is a world where the elders of the tribe demand respect because of their superior knowledge, and with prize money often at stake, competition is fierce.

The world of competition is very strictly judged, with levels of perfection set really high. Plenty of local competitions take place, and national competitions where produce is judged as severely as at any show garden at the Chelsea Flower Show.

I think many people see such events as laughable, but to me these traditions must be kept alive in order that the skills survive. Vegetable growing will always be a popular pastime, because it is something the average bod can get into at very little cost. With only a small plot of land, some seeds and a little know-how, you can become a highly regarded figure in thecompetition world.

The only way to keep face and show what you are made of is by producing some great produce. Judges will be following a strict range of criteria for each category, and the vegetables will have to be presented in the manner required by the competition. For example some will require your runner beans are exhibited in a fan of 5 beans placed on a black 40 cm × 30 cm cloth, whereas others might require them laid straight on a white cloth, so before you enter any competition ensure that you read the guidelines in detail.

I should make it clear that size in most competitions is not of any real importance unless you are entering a specific giant vegetable competition. In most village shows and especially shows run by the Royal Horticultural Society, size should be put to the back of your mind and you should be thinking quality first. It is true that a large, perfect onion will always beat a smaller, perfect one, but you should concentrate on quality to do well. There is a saying 'If you cant eat it, don't show it' and this is particularly true in all events that are not about size!

Finding out where to exhibit

Finding where to exhibit your veg should be fairly straightforward, and your allotment society will be able to point you in the right direction. You could always search the internet for local parish shows and events where you can enter your vegetables, and also the RHS run local and national horticultural shows that are the pinnacle of excellence.

Part VI
The Part of Tens

'That's the one drawback with growing coconuts.'

In this part . . .

In this part I offer you two chapters containing bite-sized chunks of advice. In the first, I spell out ten of the basic mistakes that novice allotmenteers make and what to do to stay clear of them. In the second I give you ten top tips to help you revitalise an allotment that's gone stale.

Chapter 22

Ten Common Mistakes to Avoid

In This Chapter

- Failing to deal with problems immediately
- Planting in incompatible combinations
- Thinning out inadequately

You'll soon become in tune with the signs that something isn't quite right on your allotment, or that something requires your attention before a problem emerges. Learning the signs to look for and the things to avoid is an important part of becoming an allotmenteer. You also need to be prepared and know how to give things the best shot year after year, so here are ten ways to steer clear of trouble pave your way to allotment heaven.

Buying Inferior Seeds and Plants

It's often tempting to rush out and buy the first plants and seeds you can get your hands on so that you can plant up and get things going ASAP. But you really need to make sure that all the seeds and plants you purchase are the best quality, from the best varieties for your needs, and in the best possible health, or you just end up disappointed. You may be tempted to take the kind offer of plants from other plot holders, but you should always do so with extreme caution as you never know if the plants are carrying pests and diseases. This advice applies especially to the brassicas, because clubroot spreads really easily. You should be all right exchanging seedlings grown in pots from seed, but always be sure to look at them carefully and check them for any signs of attack before planting them on your plot.

Always buy seeds from a reputable supplier and store the seeds in an airtight, dry, sealed container. Be sure to use them before their sow-by date, which should be clearly printed on the sachet. You often see old packets of seeds for sale in car boot sales,and as long as they're not too far out of date you'll get some success, but in general the older the seeds the less likely they are to germinate.

You often find that the big companies don't have as many unusual plants and seeds on offer, so for these, go to specialist plant nurseries. The Internet really comes into its own here.

Ignoring Problems Until It's Too Late

Ignoring problems on your allotment is foolish, as problems won't go away by themselves. Allotments are unnatural in every way. As a gardener you're playing with nature, trying to control it and curtailing Mother Nature's bid to overtake a plot and turn it back to the wild. Having a plot, you also have the responsibility for managing and controlling all those things that want to attack it and ruin all your hard work.

Pests and diseases need to be hit hard and quickly, otherwise they linger and take control. If you ignore a problem it gets a stranglehold and becomes a persistent problem that won't go away. Also, ignoring problems from pest and disease means that they spread from your plot to neighbouring ones.

Sometimes a problem such as soil infertility can develop over a number of years and the only way to fix that is to add more organic matter. At first the plants simply don't grow well, as over the years they've sucked all the goodness out of the soil. One year my dad's crops suddenly started to suffer and look as if they were struggling. The simple explanation was that there wasn't enough muck in the soil – so we didn't ignore the problem, we fixed it by digging in two tonnes of well rotted manure that will have sorted the problem out for next year.

The key to success is to be rapid in your response to any problem you may detect on the allotment – those who dilly-dally must pay the price!

Planting Combinations that Don't Work

Some planting combinations simply don't work in *any* allotment garden and should be avoided. These combinations of plants cross-pollinate, creating new plants that lack vigour or taste nasty. Certain combinations are wrong simply because the soil doesn't match their requirements. If you follow a crop rotation calendar (see Chapter 7) and group the plants accordingly you shouldn't have any troubles.

The most obvious plant combination that doesn't work on the allotment is dill and fennel. These two plants are very closely related and cross-pollination causes the seeds to become a hybrid mix of the two parents. The flavour of any plants grown from those seeds will be ruined. Also, don't plant fennel near coriander because they hinder each other's growth. In fact avoid planting any plants within the *Umbelliferae* family together if you plan to collect seeds for sowing next year because they tend to cross-pollinate; these include dill, fennel, carrots and coriander.

Sweetcorn should be planted in blocks using only one variety, because if you have more than one they cross-pollinate and you may end up with smaller cobs or no cobs at all.

Cucumbers shouldn't be planted near strong-smelling herbs as these herbs contaminate the flavour of delicate vegetables such as cucumbers.

Other examples occur where plants in the garden just don't like the same conditions. These include planting potatoes in the brassica plot. Avoid this combination, as brassicas like limed soil, which causes scab on your spuds.

Planting Root Crops in Manure-Rich Soil

Most crops like a manure-rich soil in which to grow, loving the moisture-retentive qualities and thriving on the nutrient-rich environment they sit in. But most *root* crops actually don't like too rich a soil as this causes them to produce small roots that are likely to split and become deformed. This is no big problem when it comes to the flavour of the vegetables – they just look a bit odd and are fiddly to prepare for eating.

Everything depends on how fresh the manure you use is. If it's really well rotted then you should be okay manuring a few weeks before planting out your root veg, but if it's not that well rotted you should grow other veg on the plot and then use that patch for root crops the following year. Most root veg do better in light soils that are free-draining. If the manure is too fresh it can make the soil too rich and moist, which won't agree with your root crops at all. Chapter 6 has the low-down on soil types.

Spreading Clubroot

Clubroot disease is a real problem for the brassica family, and once established is an ongoing issue that persists in the soil for 15 years or more, even if you leave the area plant-free for that length of time. Clubroot causes the roots of plants to become deformed and to develop rot, which causes the foliage to turn yellow and affects the plants' growth. Clubroot is easily transferred from plot to plot and can be spread by transplanting contaminated plants. Even crop rotation can't stop this once it has become established.

However, you can still grow brassicas pretty well on a plot that's infected with clubroot if you follow these tips:

- Plant your brassicas in pockets of imported soil and they often survive without infection.
- Introduce lime to reduce the acidity of the soil which helps limit attacks. Additionally, dipping the roots of plants in flowers of sulphur can help plants survive attack.
- Plant clubroot-resistant varieties such as cabbage 'Kilaton' or cauliflower 'Clapton'.
- Discourage weeds in the brassica family such as shepherd's purse, charlock and wild radish.
- Grow transplants for longer than you usually would before planting them out on your plot. If you can grow your seedlings so they fill 8-centimetre pots before planting out, they'll have bigger root systems than normal, and these are more likely be able to sustain the plants through an attack.

Planting Out Too Early

Planting things out too early is a common problem that many gardeners have experienced at some point in their lives. The arrival of spring gives gardeners an urge to rush out and get things planted so that the gardening year can start – this is a mistake. Many a good plant has been struck down by a surprise late frost, so planting too early is such a waste of time and money if you're too impatient. If you do find yourself facing a frost and you have planted stuff out too early, have some cloche tunnels at the ready and appropriate forms of protection that can possibly save the day (see Chapter 3 for means of protecting your plants).

The most useful indicator as to when it should be safe to plant things in spring is to research when the last frost in your area is most likely. Some websites tell you when this is: Try `www.gardenaction.co.uk`, for example. But there's no better way of finding out than learning from experience. Look, too, at what other plot holders are doing and nine times out of ten if you follow their lead things will be all right.

Always check seed packets and plant instructions for when seeds should be sown or be planted out and remember that plants need hardening off before you can take them from the nice warm greenhouse and plant them outside in the cold. So take time to introduce the plants to the outside.

Underestimating Climate Zones

Climate zones have a massive impact on when and what you can plant in the garden – the difference in climate between the far north and the far south is dramatic. Not only are temperatures markedly different, but the arrival of spring and the change from autumn into winter differ too.

Climate also impacts greatly on what plants are suitable for growing in your plot. A saying that gardeners' use goes, 'Right plant, right place', which basically means you have to select plants not only to suit your soil and space restrictions, but also the climate you garden in. It's great fun pushing the boundaries and seeing if you can grow unlikely plants on your plot, and you may have some success with these, but you're always best choosing crops that are going to be easy to look after and ultimately thrive in your given climate.

It's well worth working out how long a growing season you have in your area, from the last frost of the season to the first in autumn. With this knowledge you can work out which crops fit within these parameters.

You can extend the growing season by purchasing protection for your plants (see Chapter 3), but apart from that, you can't do much more.

Getting Watering Wrong

It's vital to have a water source on your plot because you often have times during periods of drought when the plants rely on you for a drink. This is especially important during certain periods of plants' development such as when they're young and setting their roots, or during periods when fruits or flower buds are forming.

The first sign that your plants are suffering is all in their appearance: they start to droop and wilt. If this happens, jump into action and get out the watering can. Other signs that there may be a problem include fruits failing to develop well and cracking, rough surfaces on fruits (especially tomatoes).

The best approach to take during dry spells is to water those plants that need water the most: Young plants, seedlings, leafy salad crops, beans, tomatoes and cucumbers should all be priorities.

Pay particular attention to plants inside the greenhouse and under cloches and polytunnels, because they rely solely on you for their water. Don't forget them or they'll shrivel up and die.

Allowing Your Plants to Bolt

Many vegetables are prone to bolting, which is when they send up a flowering shoot that then sets seed. The main function of all vegetables is to reproduce, and we, as gardeners, are getting in the way of their primary goal and eating them before they get a chance. Many external factors can cause a plant to bolt and gardeners need to control them to prevent plants setting seed. As soon as a plant sets seed it quickly deteriorates in flavour and more often than not becomes useless as food. Common causes of bolting include:

- **Water stress.** If a plant becomes stressed by a lack of water, it's programmed to reproduce to maintain the survival of its genes. This means throwing up a flower spike that then sets seed.
- **More daylight.** Many plants, spinach for example, bolt if the daylight hours become longer than the hours of darkness. A number of cool-season crops are the same, meaning they can only be grown during the spring and late summer when daylight hours are shorter.
- **Heat and cold.** Many plants also bolt if temperatures become too high or too low for them. You can avoid this by successional planting, ensuring that you have a range of plants growing that have been through different conditions at different times of their development.

The best way to avoid bolting is to try and provide the most stable conditions possible on the plot and by planting suitable crops at the right time of year. For example, many lettuces bolt in the summer simply because it's too warm, so only grow them during times either side of the height of summer.

Failing to Thin Out

For several reasons it's common practice to sow seeds in trays or outside in rows closer than is eventually needed. First, if you were to sow the seeds at the right spacings to start with, you'd end up with gaps where some of the seeds had failed to germinate. Second, from the seedlings that have germinated you can to select the ones most likely to succeed.

Thinning out is the process of removing the extra plants and eating, discarding or even replanting them elsewhere. When seedlings have germinated you should check the packet for the correct distance required between plants.

Seedlings that are too crammed together compete for light, water and nutrients, so they all struggle to survive well and this may well cause them to bolt. By thinning out seedlings you're giving them the space they need to grow to an appropriate size for transplanting or to grow in permanent homes.

Chapter 23

Ten Ways to Revive a Flagging Allotment

In This Chapter

- Saving your struggling plot
- Tidying up your plot
- Re-discovering good habits

When you start looking after an allotment, it will always need your attention to some degree. It's all too easy at times to lose track and allow the plot to slip into disrepair, and if this happens you need to know how to regain control. Allotments are productive sites and they need to be recharged constantly, so that all the nutrients and goodness that your plants suck out of the soil is replaced. Regular maintenance helps you keep on top of it all, so here are ten great ways to give your plot the kiss of life.

Doing Double Digging

Soil is everything and after years of cultivating, soil can lose its structure and may need invigorating to get it back in tip-top condition. Double digging is the process of digging the soil in two layers: first place the top, spade's depth of soil to the side and then dig organic matter into the second, deeper layer, effectively two spades deep. This is like a deep-conditioning treatment that adds the all-important organic matter into the lower tier of the soil profile. This improves the soil structure; the soil texture introduces much-needed nutrients and also greatly increases the water-retaining capabilities of your soil, all of which benefit the plants on your plot.

You usually only double-dig when you adopt or start a new plot, but it can be used to revive a flagging plot on which plants have started to struggle after years of cultivation. Carry it out in the autumn, so the winter frosts can get to work on the soil and help break down the large clods into a manageable fine tilth ready for planting in spring. It's hard work, but well worth it. For more on double digging check out Chapter 6.

Having a Jolly Good Tidy

This may sound like a really obvious thing to say but all too often you see plots that are neglected, have fallen into disrepair and could do with an end-of-season spruce up. The ideal time to do this is between autumn and spring when the plot is at its quietest and most of the beds are empty.

Staining the shed is a great job for spring or dry days in the autumn, just make sure that you do it on a dry day or your efforts will be thwarted. Also repair any fences, trellis panels or supports that you have on your plot. Check polytunnels and greenhouses and repair if required and check the shed roof for any holes and repair the felt if necessary.

Clean all your pots, trays, and tools using a suitable anti-fungal and anti-bacterial soap – this is a vital part of controlling the spread of disease on the allotment.

Clean the inside and outside of the greenhouse using a suitable disinfectant to kill off bugs and diseases that it may be harbouring inside (this should be done in spring and again in the autumn).

As plots become vacant during the winter, a good idea is to spread a generous layer of organic matter over the soil to rot down over the winter months. Dig it into the top layer of soil, leaving the large clods of soil on the surface. As the winter frosts get into the little cracks, these clods expand and help break up the soil into smaller, more manageable lumps. Earthworms will get to work on the added organic matter, taking it deep into the soil and improving the aeration, nutrient content, water retention and general health of the soil. Also by adding organic matter you darken the soil, thus enabling it to absorb the spring warmth quicker, which means you should be able to plant and sow your crops earlier in the spring.

As autumn comes it is a good time to build a leaf cage and collect all the fallen leaves from deciduous trees that you can get your hands on. Don't collect them from the roadside because these are contaminated with pollutants. Collect them from your garden and the surrounding areas if you can and add them to the leaf cage. They then slowly rot down, giving you a lovely, fine, leaf mould soil-improver.

Finally you need to protect your plants from winter weather, so if you have perennials, lay a thick mulch over them to protect the plants from inclement weather. You may need to check ties and stakes around trees and shrubs. Heel-in any plants that have been rocked by the wind to make sure that there's no gap around the base of the main stem; water can get in these gaps and freeze causing problems for the plants. Protect any winter crops such as Brussels sprouts and broccoli and stake them to prevent them rocking in the wind.

Starting Again

Sometimes it may be worth clearing the whole plot and starting again. This sounds pretty drastic but if things fall into a bad way and your plants are suffering because of disease, pests and poor soil it's really worth clearing the plot and starting again. This is, of course, a last resort but I've seen plots that were looking shocking and where the owners have had a proper clear out and the following year the plots looked different places.

If you decide to do this you may be able to save some of the permanent plants by removing them and replanting or simply by clearing around them.

The ideal is to rest an area every four years, although this isn't always possible with the limited space available on the plot, but it may be a way of improving areas of the plot over a number of years without having to rest the entire plot at once (see Chapter 7 for more on rotation).

Investing in New Plants

Nothing is better for a failing plot than to invest in new plants. After years of hard graft many plants get tired and need replacing or at least propagating and replanting. Raspberries, for example, have a productive life of around ten years after which they need replacing. Having been in the same spot for so long they're also likely to be riddled with diseases and pests that have made a home in the soil around these plants, so replacing your raspberries in a new position is vital. The longer a plant is in one place the more established the pests associated with that plant become.

Re-establishing Paths, Edges and Beds

One of the most satisfying jobs on the allotment is re-establishing all the hard edges and beds. It's always best to use timber edges or, if you can be bothered, some kind of hard edging like brick to retain the vegetable beds and create paths through the plot. Timber rots after a number of years, and these rotten edges may need replacing or treating with a suitable stain to prolong their lives.

Laying out paths as a hard surfaces is a good idea, so that during wet periods you can get around the plot without getting claggy boots. Make sure that these surfaces are clean and weed-free. Not only are hard surfaces more practical but they look good as well, and that can be really satisfying. Hard paths allow easier access around the plot for wheelbarrows, making life much easier.

If you have any grass paths use a half-moon edger or a sharp spade to re-establish the edges, but cut vertically to create nice straight lines along your beds.

Planting Green Manure

As they grow, plants suck a lot of life out of the ground and gardeners often sow what's called a 'green manure' between crops. Green manure is sown on bare land, grows quickly and can then be dug into the ground to put back nutrients and add organic matter. You do this at any time of year but it is best done in the late summer. Rye and mustards add vital nutrients or for added nitrogen sow fine beans, alfalfa or clover. Plants for green manure should be dug in when they're young and soft, and before they flower, otherwise they may have a detrimental effect on the soil. If they're too mature they take much longer to rot down, removing nitrogen from the soil.

Green manures should be grown quickly and then dug into the top 15 centimetres of the soil, and incorporated well. Many companies sell all sorts of green manures and the packets of seeds are really cheap and easy to sow.

You need to be aware that some green manures are in the brassica family so should not be planted before or after the brassicas otherwise you could be building up the effects of clubroot that affects all members of the family.

Sowing Some Nitrogen Fixers

Nitrogen isn't the easiest thing to come by in terms of soil improving but it can be introduced by growing what we call nitrogen-fixing plants in the soil. All plants in the legume family have special bacteria on its roots that take nitrogen from the air and convert it into a form that can be absorbed by the roots of plants. Clover and alfalfa green manures are both nitrogen fixers that can be grown as quick, green manures (see previous section) in the spring or late summer and dug into the soil where it rots down, adding other vital nutrients. Any member of the legume family can be grown on a plot that needs a vital nitrogen fix and its special bacteria on the roots then work their magic. The ultimate nitrogen fixer is a bolt of lightning, which can in a flash fix nitrogen in the soil. The lightning breaks down the nitrogen molecules combining the atoms with oxygen, creating nitrogen oxide. This dissolves in rain and these nitrates fall to the earth in the rain – so if you can create a thunderstorm over your plot you can also help fix nitrogen in the soil – probably best to grow some clover!

Checking the Soil's pH Level

Most types of vegetable like neutral to slightly acidic soil (or alkaline in the case of brassicas) to grow well and you should keep tabs on the Ph levels on your plot at least every two years (Chapter 6 shows you how to do this). As you cultivate land you add lots of organic matter. As this rots down it produces hydrogen, which slowly increases the acidity of the soil and this is what you need to keep in check. Also, as you water land it leaches out certain nutrients and compounds that has the effect of increasing the acidity of soil and if this gets too bad the land then becomes sour. The perfect Ph is somewhere between 6.3 and 6.8 and at this level the bacteria in the soil are most active in speeding up the rate of decomposition and therefore the 'sweetness' of the soil.

Soil pH can be increased by adding certain chemical or organic compounds to the soil to correct levels. Liming is the standard way to make a soil more alkaline, with agricultural lime containing calcium carbonate that doesn't necessarily neutralise the acid but replaces the lost calcium that's washed out by rain and watering. Hydrated lime is the fastest method of increasing soil Ph because it's partially soluble in water, meaning it acts faster in reducing the acidity of your soil. Lime is often added to brassica beds to help them on their way. The effects of adding lime are fairly long lasting.

WARNING! You should never add lime and fertiliser at the same time: this has an almost effervescent effect and releases gasses that are harmful to the soil basically releasing all the nitrogen from the soluble form in the soil back into a gas that is lost into the atmosphere. You can decrease soil Ph by adding sulphur or aluminium sulphate. The latter is the quickest way of doing so and works as soon as it's dissolved on the soil. The downside is that it's only short-lived and it is really easy to overdo it and make the soil too acidic. The best way of decreasing the Ph is by adding sulphur. It can take a few months to work but has a longer-lasting effect. The sulphur coverts into sulphuric acid when in contact with the bacteria in the soil.

Considering Companion Planting

Companion planting is a holistic approach to gardening consisting of looking at groups of plants that if grown together help each other grow successfully. This works in a number of ways with certain groups of plants helping each other in terms of protection from the sun or wind, providing nutrients in the soil (such as the legumes) and also attracting beneficial insects to the plot. Some plants also act as a lure to encourage allotment enemies away from certain plants as a decoy. For example, if you plant hostas on your plot they attract slugs away from your crops because slugs prefer the leaves of hostas to almost anything else.

Here are some examples of companion-plant combinations:

- **Nasturtiums and Cabbages:** Nasturtiums attract the caterpillars of cabbage white butterflies, which then choose to munch the nasturtiums instead of your precious cabbages.
- **Leeks and Carrots:** If planted together these two plants benefit each other: leeks help repel carrot fly and carrots keep the leek moth and onion fly at bay.
- **French Marigolds:** These are a great companion plant for the whole allotment, but especially for tomatoes. They attract hoverflies who love to feast on aphids but also the marigolds' strong scent repels aphids.
- **The Three Sisters:** This is a classic combination traditionally used in the USA where corn, beans and squash are grown together, each helping the other out. The corn acts as a support for the beans, the beans help the other plants by fixing nitrogen in the soil and the squash crawls over the ground reducing the need for weeding.

Rotating Your Plants

Rotation is a really important part of having a healthy allotment. Plants from the same family, grown on the same patch year after year, are far more likely to harbour pests and diseases associated with those plants. These pests can get their feet under the table and be next to impossible to get rid of. Crop rotation also takes into account the nutritional needs of plants within the rotation calendar. For example, potatoes are hungry feeders whereas many root crops are not, so they should be planted on a different areas of the plot to meet both their needs.

Index

• A •

• C •

• D •

• E •

• F •

• G •

• J •

• K •

• L •

• M •

• N •

• O •

• P •

FOR DUMMIES®

Making Everything Easier!™

UK editions

BUSINESS

978-0-470-51806-9

978-0-470-74381-2

978-0-470-71382-2

FINANCE

978-0-470-99280-7

978-0-470-71432-4

978-0-470-69515-9

HOBBIES

978-0-470-69960-7

978-0-470-74535-9

978-0-470-75857-1

British Sign Language For Dummies
978-0-470-69477-0

Business NLP For Dummies
978-0-470-69757-3

Competitive Strategy For Dummies
978-0-470-77930-9

Cricket For Dummies
978-0-470-03454-5

CVs For Dummies, 2nd Edition
978-0-470-74491-8

Digital Marketing For Dummies
978-0-470-05793-3

Divorce For Dummies, 2nd Edition
978-0-470-74128-3

eBay.co.uk Business All-in-One For Dummies
978-0-470-72125-4

Emotional Freedom Technique For Dummies
978-0-470-75876-2

English Grammar For Dummies
978-0-470-05752-0

Flirting For Dummies
978-0-470-74259-4

Golf For Dummies
978-0-470-01811-8

Green Living For Dummies
978-0-470-06038-4

Hypnotherapy For Dummies
978-0-470-01930-6

IBS For Dummies
978-0-470-51737-6

Lean Six Sigma For Dummies
978-0-470-75626-3

Available wherever books are sold. For more information or to order direct go to www.wiley.com or call +44 (0) 1243 843291

8041_p1